GLOBAL MONETARY AND ECONOMIC CONVERGENCE

Global Monetary and Economic Convergence

On the occasion of the fiftieth anniversary of the Marshall Plan

Edited by
GUSZTÁV BÁGER
MIKLÓS SZABÓ-PELSŐCZI
Foreword by
ROBERT RAYMOND

LONDON AND NEW YORK

First published 1998 by Ashgate Publishing

Reissued 2018 by Routledge
2 Park Square, Milton Park, Abingdon, Oxon, OX14 4RN
711 Third Avenue, New York, NY 10017, USA

Routledge is an imprint of the Taylor & Francis Group, an informa business

Copyright © Robert Triffin-Szirák Foundation 1998

All rights reserved. No part of this book may be reprinted or reproduced or utilised in any form or by any electronic, mechanical, or other means, now known or hereafter invented, including photocopying and recording, or in any information storage or retrieval system, without permission in writing from the publishers.

Notice:
Product or corporate names may be trademarks or registered trademarks, and are used only for identification and explanation without intent to infringe.

Publisher's Note
The publisher has gone to great lengths to ensure the quality of this reprint but points out that some imperfections in the original copies may be apparent.

Disclaimer
The publisher has made every effort to trace copyright holders and welcomes correspondence from those they have been unable to contact.

A Library of Congress record exists under LC control number: 98045775

This volume contains contributions presented at the Seventh Conference of the Robert Triffin-Szirak Foundation in conjunction with Société Universitaire Européenne de Recherches Financières (SUERF) held on May 15-17, 1997 in Budapest.

ISBN 13: 978-1-138-31548-8 (hbk)
ISBN 13: 978-1-138-31550-1 (pbk)
ISBN 13: 978-0-429-45628-2 (ebk)

Contents

Foreword by Robert Raymond   ix
Editors' Preface   xi

Part I: European Convergence   1

1 The Fiftieth Anniversary of the Marshall Plan: A Significant Date for the European Union
Hans Beck   3

2 Humanly Acceptable Answers
Michel Carlier   7

3 Hungary's Macroeconomic Stabilization and Recognition of its Focal Position in East Central Europe
László Akar   10

4 Hungary's Recent Monetary and Macroeconomic Trends
György Surányi   14

5 The Marshall Plan and its Relevance Today
Bernard Snoy   18

6 Back to Fundamentals: Why a Monetary Union for Europe?
Alexandre Lamfalussy   35

7 European Monetary Union: Progress and Outlook
Robert Raymond   42

8 The Euro on Schedule: Analysis of its European and International Implications
Michael Sakbani   48

9 Does EMU Need to Converge on the US Model?
Daniel Gros and Erik Jones   75

10 Economic Relations of the EU and the Rest of Europe in View of the EMU
Olga Butorina   89

Part II: Theoretical Issues of Global Convergence — 97

11 Hayek and Triffin: Fragments on Divergence and Convergence in Policy Thinking
Nicolas Krul — 99

12 Globalization, Governance, and Transition – Managing Some of It
Jozef M. van Brabant — 121

13 From the Marshall Plan to New Balances
Gusztáv Báger and Miklós Szabó-Pelsőczi — 147

14 The Euro: Hopeful Sign of a New Long Wave Growth
Paul L. Mandy — 166

Part III: East-West Convergences — 187

15 Investment and Growth in the Transition Process
Nicholas Stern and Hans Peter Lankes — 189

16 Monetary Governance in Selected Transition Economies – What Has Been Achieved?
Maciej Krzak and Aurel Schubert — 207

17 Has the European Union the Right Strategy for Central and Eastern Europe?
Marie-Paule Donsimoni — 247

18 Seven Years of Financial Market Reform in Central Europe
Gerhard Fink and Peter Haiss — 254

19 Disinflation, Fiscal Positions, and Seigniorage – A Comparative Analysis of the EU Countries and Some Remarks on Economies in Transition
Peter Brandner and Eduard Hochreiter — 293

20 The Integration of Russia into the World Monetary System:
   Macroeconomic Consequences and Problems
   Dmitry Smyslov   332

21 Closing the Development Gap between Hungary and the
   European Union
   János Hoós   344

22 The Banking System in Slovakia – Actual Problems
   Otto Sobek   352

23 The 'Principal-Agent' Conflict in the Period of Post-communist
   Transformation in Central and Eastern Europe
   Márton Tardos   360

24 Financing Social Projects in Support of Convergence
   Martin Murtfeld   364

25 The Hungarian Banking System and the Development of
   Capital Markets
   Katalin Botos   374

Part IV: Global Convergences   411

26 Agenda for a New Monetary Reform
   Otto Hieronymi   413

27 Privatization and Corporate Governance: Some Lessons from the
   Experience of Transitional Economies
   Tito Boeri and Giancarlo Perasso   430

28 Narrow Banks in Today's Financial World: US and International
   Perspectives
   Dimitri B. Papadimitriou   445

29 Corporate Governance amid Global Monetary and Economic Convergence
   – Their Appearance and Development in Japan
   Yoshiaki Toda

  467

Contents

30 Globalization of the World Economy and the Lack of Regulation
of the Globalized World
Márton Tardos   473

31 How the World Has Changed Since 1980
Robert Solomon   478

Notes on Participants   487

Foreword

Robert Raymond

The 1997 Conference organized by the Robert Triffin-Szirák Foundation in Budapest not only built on the conclusion of previous similar events, especially on how to bring some order to exchange rate behaviour around the world, but also referred explicitly to the Marshall Plan, on the occasion of its fiftieth anniversary.

The Conference was combined with the 1997 Colloquium of SUERF (the Société Universitaire Européenne de Recherche Financière). SUERF's aim is to bring together academics and practitioners to discuss monetary and financial issues. The topic selected by SUERF for its 1997 Colloquium was corporate governance.

One might have feared that the choice of two such very different subjects, to be discussed in parallel within specialized committees but also in common at plenary sessions, would be a disaster. On the contrary: as the organizers or the two partner associations had hoped, it gave participants an opportunity to focus on some of the well-known instances of dialectic reasoning, or trade-offs, which are such a nightmare for decision-makers, obliging them to take positions in spite of their hesitations.

Among these conflicts one could mention the need to deregulate trade and capital movements to support growth and the disturbances triggered by exchange rate overshooting; the wish to rebuild an international monetary system and the difficulties of stabilizing exchange rates through intervention; the need to increase the disciplinary effects of competition and the difficulty of maintaining welfare in countries with an ageing population and a mature economy.

Some hope may be drawn from the experience of parts of the world where governments have become aware of the need to combine deregulation and sound macroeconomic policies leading to converging fundamentals. Liberalization tends to replace the former discretionary governmental decisions, either by means of regulation or through the nationalization of large companies, with decentralized and microeconomic decisions guided by corporate governance theories. The role of the state is then to create a level playing-field and to impose standards of business ethics and transparency. It is also to maintain a relatively balanced and sustainable fiscal stance. At the same time, central banks have to keep the inflation rate low and relatively stable over time to increase certainty.

It is, however, difficult to solve regional problems by recourse to these principles alone. Two examples were discussed in Budapest in 1997, both of which are relevant. The lessons learned from the Marshall Plan are that an inflow of capital into weak areas can be extremely fruitful provided that the allocation of resources is relevant and that sound corporate governance applies to the firms in charge of running the investment. Many recent examples show that the presence of the first ingredient (in the form of private or public transfers) without the second leads to financial disaster.

Another example of regional arrangements is the project of the European Monetary Union. Where various national economies are integrated in practice, it makes sense to apply to them a single and common set of macroeconomic policies, including a single monetary policy for the use of a single currency.

Incidentally, it was recognized that the Marshall Plan did encourage European integration, leading to the various further steps we have experienced in the fifty years since the Plan's inception. Both projects tend to increase the orderly functioning of market forces.

Should the globalization of economic activity go hand in hand with such principles, there is some hope that an international monetary order can one day work and help to build a better world.

Events such as the 1997 Conference of the Robert Triffin – Szirák Foundation are useful contributions to progress in this direction.

Editors' Preface

It gives us great pleasure to present this volume to the public, containing the papers of the Seventh Conference of the Robert Triffin-Szirák Foundation (RTSF) held on May 15-17, 1997 in Budapest.

Since the publication of the previous volume,* much had happened in the world in general, and in particular with respect to Hungary. The 1997 Annual Meeting of the EBRD classified Hungary as a high transition country, together with the Czech Republic and Poland. There are still key sectors of our economy in need of institutional support and long-term funding. Therefore, we still look for further capital inflows from international financial institutions including the EBRD, as well as from private investors.

During the Spring of 1997, the European Investment Bank held its Board Meeting in Budapest, – for the first time in a transition country. Our co-operation with this great institution has been always smooth and fruitful and we trust that it will continue to be so in the future.

The First Szirák Conference was held in 1986, in a period of glasnost and perestroika, when most people still have refrained from taking a view of the future. However, with great tact, courtesy and respect for the views of everybody in our surroundings, the participants were able to formulate their anticipations of the future without giving up an iota of their scientific integrity or without hurting the sensibilities of their partners in debate. It is this spirit of free-flowing ideas that has characterised our subsequent conferences. By now, it has become our trade-mark, not by chance, but by a deliberate effort to seek the truth in all matters closely touching on the human condition. Economics and finance obviously belong to these.

The historic role of financial institutions had undergone several changes during the past century according to the mode of economic thinking that happened to be in vogue at any particular time. From the gold standard to internationally managed fiduciary currencies under the Bretton Woods Agreement (1944); from fixed rates (1946) to general floating (1973); from the establishment of the gold-dollar anchor (1944) to its abolition (1971); and

---

* Fifty Years After Bretton Woods – The New Challenge of East-West Partnership for Economic Progress, Avebury, 1996.

to the commanding role currently enjoyed by off-shore markets as lenders-of-last-resort: the road travelled was breathtaking. The future can be full of surprises. For better or worse, we have to make it up as we go along on an essentially uncharted territory. It is one of the purposes of this conference to stake out at least an approximate course of action which might lead to success.

The past century was an age of ideologies based on dogmatic interpretations of economic and nationalistic values. Nothing could be worse than thoughtlessly applied 19th and 20th century dogmas to the problems created by 21st century technologies. If ever sound common sense pragmatism is needed, it is now. Human wants for decent living conditions, security and encouraging prospects for the future are given data within reasonable limits. Our technology should be able to satisfy these. It is up to us economists, to provide an institutional framework which would establish new balances between rational expectations for both production and consumption, for democracy and free enterprise. The constant search for these balances will assure societal coherence which is the alpha and omega of all good corporate and global governance.

With the wisdom of the last decades one can state unequivocally that the finding of such equilibria must be the result of good thinking and good action. Very few would doubt the basic propositions of a democratic free market economy. However, in reality those principles alone are insufficient to achieve optimal results. We must conceptualize, verbalize and put into action desiderata concerning optimal corporate governance. These depend as much on legal actions as on individual decisions. This is why we choose corporate and global governance as the subject of our conference especially on the 50th anniversary of a major public and private project, the Marshall Plan, which established and helped establishing desirable balances for private and public initiatives.

In spite of its many merits the global monetary system which has entered into force after August 15th 1971 is still not providing the degree of stability the global economy requires. It is the purpose of the Robert Triffin-Szirák Foundation to contribute as much as possible to the building of a safer global monetary system for the future.

In closing, we would like to express our thanks to Mr. Árpád Göncz, President of the Republic of Hungary for his support as High Patron of the Conference; to Professor A.J. Abraham, Chairman of the Société Universitaire Européenne de Recherches Financière (SUERF), for his indefatigable co-operation in jointly organizing this conference with the

Editors' Preface

Robert Triffin-Szirák Foundation; and to the European Union for its PHARE sponsorship of the conference.

Finally, we would like to say our most sincere thanks to our other sponsors; to our associates in preparing the conference and in editing this book, first of all to Ms Mária Boglári; to Chief Editorial Associate Mr Péter Sarkadi, and to Technical Editor Mrs Erzsébet Deme; to our Secretary Mrs Andrea Ánosi-Kárpáti; as well as to Ashgate Publishing Limited, and its Editor, Mrs Sarah Markham.

July 1998

Gusztáv Báger					Miklós Szabó-Pelsőczi

Part I

European Convergence

1 The Fiftieth Anniversary of the Marshall Plan: A Significant Date for the European Union*

Hans Beck

Today it is the fiftieth anniversary of Marshall Aid, a significant date for the European Union. There are many milestones along the road to the Union but Marshall Aid is often seen as one of the starting points. This was Aid given to the countries of Europe in *an undifferentiated* manner, by which I mean it was not confined only to the Allied victors. The principles behind Marshall Aid were the opposite to those behind the Versailles Treaties and the Trianon Treaty. Marshall Aid was about learning a lesson from the war through reconciliation, rather than sealing the divisions the war had made. Thus fifty years ago the reconstruction of Europe began, reconstruction that is still ongoing. This conference in Budapest brings together the two main concerns of the Union today: monetary union and enlargement.

In the world of increasing globalization many countries try to respond to the challenge of competitive pressures by increasing integration – and therefore convergence. This is true for the countries of Eastern Europe where the economic transition to a fully-fledged market economy is tied in with the desire for EU membership. But it is also true for the EU itself, which aims at increasing its global competitiveness by the introduction of a single currency. This will have a substantial impact on all segments and players of the markets. The impact and the required adjustment efforts will vary depending on the size, structure and openness of the sectors, but no firm, no sector, no member state can avoid the challenge of the single currency. The countries of Central and Eastern Europe are also effected, not because they will be expected to join EMU immediately – like other member states, they should

---

* Opening address, May 15, 1997.

join only when ready to do so – but rather because they will be expected to accept the political objectives of EMU.

What are these political objectives? Like the European Union itself, EMU is also in the first instance not only an economic but also a political enterprise. It has been a recurring ambition of the European Union since the late 1960s. However, a variety of political and economic obstacles barred the way until the signing of the Maastricht Treaty, in February 1992. At various times, insufficient political commitment, divisions over economic priorities, lack of economic convergence and developments in international currency markets outside the Union's control have all played their part in frustrating progress towards EMU. But the Union's long commitment to a single currency cannot be doubted.

It was clear that the full benefits of the internal market would be difficult to achieve with the relatively high transaction costs involved in converting between currencies and with the uncertainties created by unstable exchange rates. In addition, many economists and central bankers took the view that national monetary autonomy was inconsistent with the Community's objectives of free trade, free capital movements and fixed exchange rates. Today, when trade between member states accounts for more than 60 per cent of their total trade, the attainment of the common market and the liberalization of capital movements call for a logical and essential complement: the single currency.

As regards the benefits of EMU, let me just mention a few key words. The most obvious one is the decrease of transaction costs. Secondly, the common currency will eliminate day-to-day intra-EU exchange rate volatility and also the risk of long-term real exchange rate misalignments which is a serious problem in the Union. Thirdly, the introduction of the single currency will increase the sustainability of the bonds of the EMU countries, as a consequence of the elimination of exchange risk. Last but not least, Monetary Union should also promote and maintain price stability in the member countries.

The timetable will go ahead as planned. Member states across the Union are making huge efforts to cut their budget deficits and to control interest rates and inflation. These policies are necessary in their own right. There is no doubt that the EMU timetable is helping to maintain the pace of economic reform. Without this incentive, there would be strong political pressures on member states to relax their efforts. The effects would be felt in greater exchange rate instability, higher interest rates and less favourable conditions for inward investment. Growth and employment prospects would suffer.

Due to the continuous improvement of macroeconomic indicators, the Commission hopes that by 1 January 1999, most of the 15 member countries will qualify for EMU membership.

The creation of a strong currency area is also in the interest of the Eastern European countries seeking EU membership. Firstly, because in most of these countries trade with the EU represents more than 60 per cent of their total trade. Secondly, in terms of foreign capital inflows the EU is the main investor in this region. Thirdly, membership of the EU demands a functioning market economy and the candidate's ability to cope with competitive pressures and market forces within the Union. It presupposes the candidate's ability to take on obligations of membership including adherence to the aims of political, economic, and monetary union.

Those measures necessary for integration into the Single Market include liberalization of capital markets, establishment of the necessary institutions for a smooth functioning of the financial markets, as well as harmonization of taxation, of competition policies, of consumer and environmental protection, and further liberalization of markets of goods and services. The principal responsibility for implementing recommendations lies with the associated countries themselves. The sooner their laws, conformity tests, standard institutes and judicial procedures are adapted to those in the Union, the sooner their businesses will feel the benefits of the Single Market and the easier and quicker the accession negotiations will be.

In conclusion, let me stress that the political determination of Europe's leaders for monetary union is unflinching. Opinion polls show majority support for the euro. In France, support for the euro is 66 per cent. A recent poll in Germany showed a 50-50 split for and against. The main message from our polls is not opposition to the euro. The problem is that people do not feel they have enough information: 80 per cent want more.

The need to keep citizens well-informed is vital. In Europe, we have from our past, two examples of currency change. In France, at the beginning of the 1960s, a 'new franc' was introduced without much attempt at explanation. The result is that forty years on, many in France continue to calculate in the old francs.

In Britain, on the contrary: 18,500 public forums were organized between 1967 and 1971 in order to explain decimalization of the pound sterling. And the project was a huge success. The message from this is clear.

This conference can be seen as part of the informing process - it has brought together many people from different professions in Western and Eastern Europe to discuss important issues of finance. As such, it is part of the informing and questioning spirit which we would like to encourage in the period prior to the monetary union. I am sure that the papers emerging from this conference will add greatly to our understanding of all the issues.

I began this speech by mentioning monetary union and enlargement. Let me just return briefly to enlargement before closing. If enlargement is to succeed, it must be accompanied by considerable deepening of the Union. Deepening and widening are not mutually exclusive terms, as many believe. This is a crucial point as the current agenda for deepening is rather extensive; besides the introduction of the common currency, it includes reform of the union's institutions and of the budget. In addition, there are the decisions to be taken concerning the Structural Funds and CAP reform. Nonetheless, the history of previous enlargements shows that widening was always accompanied by deepening. The first wave of enlargement (involving the UK, Ireland, and Denmark) was followed by the introduction of Community policies in new areas such as environmental policies and technology, the setting up of the European Council and direct elections to the European Parliament. The second enlargement with Greece, Spain, and Portugal led to the further development of the Structural Funds and the adaptation of the Single European Act. It is thus clear from the historical evidence that enlargement can actually speed up the process of integration, cohesion, and of convergence in the Union and in this way contribute to the prosperity of nations.

2 Humanly Acceptable Answers*

Michel Carlier

If I am taking the floor today before this audience, it is out of my friendship with Mr Miklós Szabó-Pelsőczi, Chairman Emeritus of the Foundation, who has been kind enough to invite me to address the opening session of this colloquium.

My presence can also be attributed to the fact that Professor Robert Triffin, talented and brilliant as he was, while filling eminent posts abroad like the Frederic Beinecke Professorship at Yale University in the United States, was of Belgian origin, a country he was born in and to which he came back in 1979 to finish his days in 1993.

The memory of this scholar and exceptional man of action is still alive in my country, namely at the Louvain-la-Neuve University, where a lot of outstanding economists claim proudly to take their inspiration from Robert Triffin's masterly and unforgettable teaching.

They draw inspiration from his works as well. Let me remind you that Robert Triffin was one of the great architects of monetary systems which had the mission, after World War II, 'to put people back to work'. Triffin played an important role in setting up the International Monetary Fund – he was one of its first senior executives from 1946 – in creating the European Payments Union and was the principal architect of the Special Drawing Rights.

Years have gone by, people did not change, the debates dividing them are still going on, many economic and social questions, among others, have not been resolved.

This is normal: nothing is final in human activities.

We still remember the fundamental debate between the advocates of Professor Triffin's theses and those of Milton Friedman and the Chicago School of economists. The discussion is obviously not over. It seems to me that both of these outstanding scholars have been right, each in turn.

One of them had a 'globalizing' and humanist vision of the economy, the other inclined rather to favour a rigorous, mathematical and monetarist

---

* Opening address, May 15, 1997.

conception of the economic system. Economic theories are as they are: they create 'movements' and fashions. They come and go and contribute to 'progress' which, by definition, would or should never stop.

We are living through an exciting and disquieting period now, at the end of this century. Exciting, I think, mainly for the growing generations and, in this region of the world, experimenting in an original manner with the peaceful transition from an authoritarian system and a failing, in fact, sterile economy, to a democratic regime supposed to create new wealth.

Disquieting at the same time, because no substantial and humanly acceptable answers have been given as yet to the major problems of our times – to poverty, unemployment, the egocentrism of nations and of individuals and to all kinds of inequalities.

There are enough paradoxes. For instance: capital circulating all over the world, and the economic power getting concentrated in the hands of some 200 multinational companies; an overabundance of labour force mainly in the most underprivileged regions of our planet; a large number of workers qualified in all fields all over five continents, and finally, the existence of the most productive and advanced technologies, available for all those who want to 'transform' our globe.

However, the problems I have mentioned before have not been resolved and nothing points to their solution in the foreseeable future. But should we lose hope and just leave it at that? Surely not.

We have travelled a long way in 50 years. In fact at the end of World War II which, among others, destroyed and ruined the old continent, the appeal made by Robert Schuman on 9th May 1950 launched the idea of starting to construct or reconstruct Europe through the European Coal and Steel Community (CECA). You are familiar with the steps which followed: the Rome Treaty on 25 March 1957 and the successive broadenings in 1973, 1976, 1983, and 1994.

Central and Eastern Europe has also made a long way since the crucial and historical year of 1989, a year which marked the collective memory of mankind by the emergence and victory of the century's Great Peaceful Revolution which has made it possible for tens of millions of human beings to find again their identity and take their destiny in hand again as free men.

Exciting times, as I said, but full of challenges. And the challenges facing our continent are not easy to be taken up.

The people of Central and Eastern Europe will have to accept the burden of heavy sacrifices which have been imposed on them by the radical systemic changes of distributing and creating wealth.

The people of the present European Union will have to understand in particular that the upcoming broadening of the Union will crown a long-term undertaking, which, if successful, will have its place in the history books and will tell to future generations about the history of our times. We will get there, I am sure, providing, that we all have the courage and the will and a vision inspired by generosity and solidarity.

At a time when poverty and sufferings spread in a world which calls out for help, a great role is to be played, in my mind, by all those who think that it is time to 'put the church in the centre of the village' and remember that genuine growth must go hand in hand with social progress.

To conclude, let me say very simply that personally I am deeply convinced that we should put man back to the heart of the debate and to the centre of our great European project.

3 Hungary's Macroeconomic Stabilization and Recognition of its Focal Position in East Central Europe*

László Akar

Hungary is at present in a period of EU pre-accession adjustment. This adjustment is going to be demanding not on a scale comparable with the drastic phase of transition from a non-market-based system to a market economy – a phase which costs most countries of the region massive losses of employment and of the national product – but still one which will test the society's ability to adapt. Hungary is planning to become an equal member of the European institutions. We are fully aware that in order to achieve this goal, our economy should further increase its competitiveness, comply with safety and environmental rules, modernize its social services, and that we should remove remaining protective cushions.

A closer look at significant changes in Hungary's economic situation shows remarkable progress. Economic stabilization, started in 1995, successfully continued during the last year. The deficit of the current balance of payments dropped over a two year period from 9.4 per cent of GDP to 3.5 per cent. The deficit of public finances declined from 8.2 per cent to 3.3 per cent. The net external debt of Hungary decreased in two years by USD 4.5 to 14.3 billion. There is a persistent influx of foreign direct investment of a substantial volume.

The international perception of Hungary has improved substantially. Hungary joined the OECD in May 1996. A number of international rating agencies have upgraded their assessment of Hungary. Both Standard &

---

* Opening address, May 15, 1997 in Budapest.

Poor's and Moody's have raised their rating for Hungary's external debt to an investment grade.

Equilibrium came about primarily by the contraction of domestic absorption and, within that, the reduction of household and public consumption by about 10 per cent over the two year period in question. The most important factors of the above reduction of domestic consumption was a total of 17 per cent reduction of real wages.

As a consequence, the restriction of domestic demand has decelerated the rate of GDP growth, from 1.5 per cent in 1995 to 0.5-1 per cent in 1996, and has slowed down fixed investment. The volume of investments diminished over the past two years by 4 per cent a year.

Fortunately since the last third of 1996 an increase was observed both in industrial output and in fixed investment. Productivity has been increasing by 2-3 per cent per annum. Competitiveness has improved. The volume of exports in 1996 exceeded by 25 per cent that of 1994.

Besides successful macroeconomic stabilization, we have taken important initial steps in the reform of the public finance system. From 1997, this activity will be performed in a more concrete manner, focusing on the reforms of the pension and of the health care systems. The results achieved in the process of economic stabilization listed below provide a sufficient basis for this.

- The Hungarian State Treasury has been functioning since 1 January, 1996;
- the Public Procurements Act has been enacted;
- the so-called 'net financing scheme' was introduced in local governments;
- an Act on Higher Education, and legal regulations on taxation have been amended;
- the process of laying down the conceptual foundations of the transformation of the health care system is in progress; and
- most importantly the government has approved the draft legislation on the reform of the pension scheme, including composite financing.

Following the results achieved so far in the process of the transformation into a market economy and the success of the past two years' economic policy aimed at achieving economic stability, the economy is operating now in an environment in which the requirements of sustainable growth have been established and the leeway of economic policy has somewhat expanded.

- No further large steps are needed towards improvement of the equilibrium, although it is essential to preserve and further develop the results achieved so far.
- Inflation must be reduced to the maximum extent permitted by economic conditions. The fundamental factors of the stubbornly high inflation, a result of fast restructuring and dramatic disequilibria, for the most part, have disappeared by now. Inflation could be realistically expected to decline to 18 per cent in 1997, 13 per cent in 1998 and to approximately 10 per cent by 1999. Monetary and fiscal policies combined will cause the gradual diminishing of inflation, will preserve the competitiveness of exports and improve the relative position of import substitution.
- Economic growth which had been temporally halted by the austerity measures has recovered by the end of 1996. It is realistically expected to reach 2.0-2.5 per cent in 1997. Through a gradual acceleration, it may increase to 4-5 per cent by the turn of the millennium. The major driving force of growth shall be a recovery of fixed investment, besides the growth of exports. The improvement of competitiveness and economic performance, initially 1-2 per cent, later 3 per cent expansion of real wages and consumption, will also permit a modest improvement of living standards. The unchanging and then the gradually increasing level of employment will slowly reduce unemployment.
- This projected economic growth path will establish feasible, balanced and competitive conditions which can be financed. At the same time, it will be a scenario of growth converging to the Maastricht criteria.
- It will make possible for a long-term programme of more than a decade the gradual catching up with more advanced countries.
- It will be instrumental in reducing the consolidated debt of the budget to about 60 per cent of the GDP by the turn of the century.
- It will reduce the rate of inflation to one digit by the turn of the century. Approximately 3 per cent inflation could be achieved around 2005.

One of the major objectives of the Modernization Programme of the Hungarian government is to use the opportunities resulting from the geographic location of the country and from its traditional roles as a bridge between East and West, and as a regional centre. In the current phase of the change of the economic system and macroeconomic stabilization, conditions are now adequate for Budapest to become one of the major commercial and financial centres of the region.

In accordance with the indications of foreign investors, Hungary is considered to be the most stable country in the region. Our macroeconomic indices reflect serious stabilization results and the results of the current budget reform are also promising. In this region, the financial system of our country is the most developed one. In general, services are also relatively developed, although the process of catching up in transport infrastructure is slower than desired because of high expenses.

Hungarian banks have a good chance to develop into regional headquarters. Banking products sold here are basically different from Western products but products of other countries of the region are similar to those of Hungary. Consequently, the financial products and technology developed in Hungary may be exported.

As a result of bank privatization, influx of foreign investments and the bank reforms since the mid-80s, Hungary has a competitive advantage compared to the banks of the neighbouring countries. During the last ten years, a new bankers' generation developed and the number of bank employees increased from 15,000 to 80,000. Our bankers can compete with experts of Western countries, but human resources need to be further developed, otherwise the infrastructural advantages might be lost.

The development of a financial centre in Budapest will represent a meeting point. Therefore, it is not enough to look to the west only. It is at least of the same importance to convince players from Eastern and Central Europe and attract them to Budapest. We need to keep personal relations with banking experts of the neighbouring countries and they should be allowed to develop their skills in Hungary.

Development of these international relationships might be among the most important results of this conference.

4 Hungary's Recent Monetary and Macroeconomic Trends*

György Surányi

About two years ago, we launched a new monetary policy, as part of a comprehensive macroeconomic stabilization package. This policy's aim was to establish macroeconomic equilibrium, external and internal financial stability and to pave the way towards sustainable and fast macroeconomic growth. One of the goals of the programme was to bring down inflation which during the course of the 1990s fluctuated 20 to 35 per cent annually. The double-digit inflation is still with us. Therefore, it merits thinking about its causes.

During the course of the nineties, the Hungarian economy had gone through major structural adjustments, both in the financial and in the real spheres of economic life. When examining the details of these developments I have to refer to macro- and microeconomic demand and supply shocks which Hungary went through. In light of the degree and the extent of these shocks, it is not surprising that the rate of inflation accelerated to a double-digit level, somewhat similarly to that of the major Western economies in the 1970s under the impact of two energy price shocks. We have experienced a deceleration of inflation between mid-1992 and early 1994. Unfortunately, this disinflationary process was coupled with a serious deteriorization of both fiscal and external balances, similarly to earlier periods when the growth of the economy had taken place in stop-and-go cycles. During the course of these stop-and-go cycles, there was a clear-cut trade-off between external and fiscal balances, on the one hand and inflation, on the other hand.

The stabilization package of March 1995 corrected the major external and internal balances prevailing in the Hungarian economy in the 1993-94 period, while the implementation of the accompanying structural reforms have created an environment where the disinflationary process – after the temporary 1995 peak in the rate of inflation caused by the adjustment measures – could

---

* Opening address, May 15, 1997.

be continued without a deterioration of external balances. The main elements of the programme have been a substantial adjustment of the fiscal position supported by a 9 per cent devaluation of the currency and the introduction of a preannounced crawling peg exchange rate system, and the adoption of an incomes policy restraining wage increases. These policies have been designed to slow domestic absorption, while bringing about a shift of resources in favour of the enterprise sector. At this point, I would like to refer to the fact that behind the surface of the fiscal balances, there are provisions in the fiscal system including the pension and health care systems which have to be considered when the fiscal position is assessed. I wish to stress the importance of financial discipline, too. In many of the transition countries, interenterprise credit for payment arrears in the banking and the business sector is a common phenomenon. This deficiency makes monetary policy and any anti-inflationary policy ineffective. We addressed the bulk of those problems at the beginning of 1992, at a price of a substantial short-term fiscal burden. As a result, financial discipline and corporate governance have been substantially improved, thus creating preconditions for the stability of the whole macroeconomic environment and for the efficiency of the monetary policy.

There is another crucial element of stabilization policy: the exchange rate policy. It is always debated and questioned whether we could have run a more ambitious anti-inflationary policy by using the exchange rate regime as nominal anchor. Now we have opted for a regime, where monetary and exchange rate policies put in place a coherent macro framework with a predictable exchange rate policy: preannounced crawling peg, with a gradually decreasing rate of the crawl, in line with the deceleration of inflation. Fiscal and income policies acted in a concerted manner with monetary and exchange rate policies. Under this policy framework, the main device applicable by monetary policy to contain inflation is the gradual reduction of the pre-annouunced devaluation rate of the currency. While applying this device, the Hungarian authorities have carefully considered also the potential adverse affects of a too rapid reduction of external competitiveness of Hungarian producers.

In the present period, the focus of monetary policy is on the gradual reduction of inflation. Though the still high rate of inflation has substantial costs in terms of distorting savings and investment decisions, past experience in Hungary and recent developments in other transition economies indicate that faster disinflation cannot necessarily prove to be sustainable. If, for example, the exchange rate policy is overburdened with the task of containing inflation, external balances could deteriorate to such an extent that compels an exchange rate policy correction with sharp devaluation of the domestic currency and subsequent welfare losses. Monetary policy in Hungary seeks to reduce the present high inflation rate gradually by 3-5 percentage point a year in the period up to 2000. Today the market seems to be confident that the authorities will be able to keep inflation under control, and will adhere to its schedule.

In sum, monetary policy and exchange rate policy in particular, have been key stabilization devices with respect to strengthening competitiveness and to supporting sustained export-led growth. Interest rate policy, encouraging savings, serves the dual goal of sustained disinflation and restoring external equilibrium.

At the same time, I would like to emphasize our commitment to meeting the EU convergence criteria. Convergence, however, is not a spontaneous process, especially not for countries where structural asymmetries with the EU region are still large. At this stage of the accession period, the Hungarian integration strategy rests on the interlinked objectives of maintaining sound macroeconomic policies combined with a concentration upon real convergence toward developed market economies.

As the applicant countries are in the process of transition and of catching-up, the strict appliaction of the standards of nominal convergence as set by the Maastricht criteria for several reasons is not adequate to evaluate their economic performance. First, the catching-up process inevitably implies a closing income gap vis-a-vis developed countries which will obviously be reflected by the real appreciation of their currencies in the longer run. However, real appreciation is not compatible with the simultaneous fulfilment of the inflation and the (nominal) exchange rate stability criteria. Real appreciation results either from a similar inflation pattern combined with nominal appreciation, or from a (nominally) stable or depreciating exchange rate combined with higher inflation. Second, the deepness of structural changes taking place during the transition period itself justifies higher inflation for a certain period of time, as the need for relative price/wage adjustments is substantially larger than in mature market economies.

In the area of real convergence, efforts should concentrate on strengthening Hungary's competitive position, both at economy-wide and at sectoral level. The most important areas where substantial progress have already been made include comprehensive enterprise and banking sector reforms, the stimulation of inward direct investment (both through the sale of state-owned assets and via greenfield investment), privatization of major sectors of the economy (including the financial sector, telecommunications and large part of the energy sector), trade and financial liberalization and establishment of current account convertibility. The ongoing liberalization and structural reforms have to be continued and completed in fields like the complete liberalization of cross-border services and capital movements, transformation of the welfare systems (including the introduction of a fully funded pillar in the pension system and a comprehensive reform of the health system), increasing the flexibility of labour markets, and in many other sectors. The implementation of these measures will pose additional challenges for macroeconomic policies, as the Hungarian economy will be exposed to an even greater extent to swings in international financial flows, due to these reforms and liberalization measures.

5 The Marshall Plan and its Relevance Today*

Bernard Snoy

It is a great honour for me to speak today in this historic building of the Hungarian Parliament and to address a conference organized simultaneously by the Société Universitaire Européenne de Recherches Financières (SUERF) and the Robert Triffin-Szirák Foundation. My association with SUERF started in the 1970s and I always found its activities very stimulating. My links with the Robert Triffin-Szirák Foundation are more recent but solidly based on my admiration for and my friendship with Miklós Szabó-Pelsőczi, who has dedicated the Foundation to the promotion of the intellectual heritage of my fellow countryman, the great economist Robert Triffin.

The speech that US Secretary of State General George C. Marshall pronounced on 5 June 1947 at Harvard University is not only one of the great texts of world political history; it also marked a turning point in the history of the twentieth century: it was a turning point for the economic recovery of Western Europe and, more importantly, it helped set in motion the process of European integration; it was a turning point for America, away from the temptation of renewed isolationism and towards a permanent Atlantic partnership with Europe.

We have to remember the economic, social, and political situation in Europe at that time: the unprecedented scale of human and material destruction caused by the war, the pauperization and the hunger, which afflicted large segments of the population, the general shortage not only of food but also of fuel and power, raw materials and machinery, the inflation which plagued most European countries, although in varying degrees, and the high external debt accumulated by the European allies towards the USA. There was a widespread feeling of despair and 'it seemed that happiness and hope were incompatible with intelligence or sensibility'.[1] It is true that the situation

---

* Keynote address, delivered on May 15, 1997.

was not made better by the continuation of wartime controls over production and prices of major goods, the overvaluation of European currencies vis-a-vis the dollar, and the strict limits to trade within the narrow confines of a network of bilateral agreements.

On the political side, the cold war had begun in 1946, and great anxiety was generated by Soviet avidity in Central and Eastern Europe while the United Kingdom had to inform the US that it could no longer afford to provide aid to the Greek government beleaguered by communist insurgents. In the winter of 1946-47, the communists, with Soviet support, using a combination of political agitation, intimidation and outright violence, had taken over in Poland, Bulgaria, Romania, and Hungary (where the communist ministers of interior and defence started a series of arrests of political opponents without even informing Prime Minister Ferenc Nagy, who was soon forced to resign). The fear that Greece would soon meet the same fate prompted President Truman in an address he made to the US Congress on 12 March 1947, to commit publicly the US to the cause of supporting 'free peoples who are resisting attempted subjugation by armed minorities or by outside pressures'. The so-called Truman Doctrine was the first step away from the danger of isolationism and towards a decisive American involvement in the recovery of Europe.

It was in this spring of 1947 that the fundamental motivations and principles of what was to become the Marshall Plan took shape. The motivations combined generosity and self-interest. Since the war, the US had become more deeply involved in international commerce: in 1946 its total exports of goods and services were nearly four times the prewar average so that the capacity of Europe to absorb these exports was becoming a significant determinant for growth or recession in the US. With that, came the realization that a poverty-stricken Western Europe would become a breeding-ground for communism and a tempting new prey for Stalin. In this respect, the Truman Doctrine and the Marshall Plan, as Truman himself put it, were 'two halves of the same walnut'. The two basic principles of the plan, as they emerged at that time, were both apparently simple. The first was that the European recipient nations the US were willing to help, which included both former allies and enemies as well as the neutrals, had to be dealt with 'en bloc' as a collective entity; the second that Europeans themselves should take the initiative and be encouraged to stand on their own feet. They would be asked to behave as a unit and take together, with American help, the measures needed to ensure the recovery of Europe as a whole. In the circumstances, both notions seemed natural; but in fact they were very novel. Together they were the negation of the maxim 'divide and conquer' that previous world powers had taken as their watchword; together they contained in embryo the twin concepts of European unity and equal transatlantic partnership. In this way, almost without realizing it, a handful of officials[2] in Washington helped to make possible a gradual revolution in international affairs.[3]

An invitation to the Harvard Commencement Exercises for 5 June 1947 provided General Marshall with an appropriate opportunity to launch an important appeal.

What Europeans faced, Marshall told his Harvard audience, was nothing less than

> *the dislocation of the entire fabric of European economy: the modern system of division of labor upon which the exchange for products is based is in danger of breaking down.*

He continued:

> *The truth of the matter is that Europe's requirements for the next three or four years of foreign food and other essential products — principally from America — are so much greater than her present ability to pay that she must have substantial additional help or face economic, social, and political deterioration of a very grave character.*
> *The remedy lies in breaking the vicious circle and restoring the confidence of the European people in the economic future of their own countries and of Europe as a whole. The manufacturer and the farmer throughout wide areas must be able and willing to exchange their product for currencies the continuing value of which is not open to question.*
> *It is logical that the United States should do whatever it is able to do to assist in the return of normal economic health in the world, without which there can be no political stability and no assured peace. Our policy is directed not against any country or doctrine but against hunger, poverty, desperation and chaos. Its purpose should be the revival of a working economy in which free institutions can exist. Such assistance, I am convinced, must not be on a piecemeal basis as various crises develop. Any assistance that this Government may render in the future should provide a cure rather than a mere palliative. Any government that is willing to assist in the task of recovery will find full cooperation, I am sure, on the part of the United States Government. Any*

government which manoeuvres to block the recovery of other countries cannot expect help from us. Furthermore, governments, political parties, or groups which seek to perpetuate human misery in order to profit therefrom politically or otherwise will encounter the opposition of the United States.

It is already evident that, before the United States Government can proceed much further in its efforts to alleviate the situation and help start the European world on its way to recovery, there must be some agreement among the countries of Europe as to the requirements of the situation and the part those countries themselves will take in order to give effect to whatever action might be undertaken by this Government. It would be neither fitting nor efficacious for this Government to undertake to draw up unilaterally a program designed to place Europe on its feet economically. This is the business of the Europeans. The initiative, I think, must come from Europe. The role of this country should consist of friendly aid in the drafting of a European program and of later support of such a program so far as it may be practical for us to do so. The program should be a joint one, agreed to by a number, if not all, European nations.

This last paragraph had been revised by General Marshall in the flight to Boston. It revealed one important change. Where the drafters of the speech had written *'Western Europe'*, Marshall's text read *'Europe'*, and it replaced *'several European nations'* with the more comprehensive *'a number, if not all'*. Marshall, in other words, was anxious to keep the offer open to Eastern Europe.

As we know, at the Paris initial tripartite conference (France, UK, Soviet Union) at the end of June 1947, the Soviets refused to be included in the Marshall Plan, which they denounced as 'foreign interference'. They precluded the nations of Central and Eastern Europe that were already under their control from joining. Czechoslovakia, which had initially accepted the invitation to the conference in Paris on 12 July 1947, convoked to decide on a common response to the American proposal, was obliged to cancel its participation. The July 1947 conference, which lead to the setting up in April 1948 of the Organisation for European Economic Co-operation (OEEC), started with only 16 European countries from Western and Southern Europe (Austria, Belgium, Denmark, France, Greece, Iceland, Ireland, Italy, Luxembourg, The Netherlands, Norway, Portugal, Sweden, Switzerland, Turkey, and the United

Kingdom), which were soon followed by the Federal Republic of Germany when it recovered its sovereignty.

The assessment of the economic impact of the Marshall Plan has at least two essential dimensions: the impact of the generous transfer of resources involved and the impact on trade liberalization and European integration.

In his memoirs,[4] Robert Marjolin, who was the first Secretary General of OEEC, assesses in the following way the transfer of resources under the Marshall Plan: 'Consisting essentially of grants, it attained amounts never known before or since. Over the forty-five months from April 1, 1948 to December 30, 1951, when aid under the European Recovery Programme officially came to an end, the European Co-operation Administration (ECA) allotted $12.4 billion to Europe.[5] This figure represented 1.2 per cent of US gross national product for the years 1948-51. On a year-to-year basis, ERP aid amounted to nearly 2 per cent of American GNP in 1948 declining to 0.5 per cent in 1951. Some idea of the magnitude of that aid effort may be gained by recalling that the seldom achieved target set later by the industrialized countries for official aid to the Third World was 0.7 per cent of GNP. With war debts expunged, reparations forgotten and reconstruction financed in large part by non-repayable US government aid, and not by private capital as in the twenties, the extraordinary difference between the two postwar periods starts to become clear.'

Robert Marjolin draws also attention to the economic impact of the occupation by the US army of a large part of Germany and to the direct influence the US exercised on the economic, financial and monetary policies followed by that country, creating the conditions for an 'economic miracle', which would play an essential role in the economic boom of the fifties and the sixties in Europe.

More broadly, Robert Triffin assesses in the following way the Marshall Plan in his seminal book:[6]

> *The real significance of US aid was, first of all, to permit a much faster recovery of restocking, reconstruction, and new investment, and thus a much faster recovery of production than would have been possible otherwise. It did not contribute so much to the re-equilibration of Europe's balance of payments as to the fact that this equilibrium could be reached at much higher levels of production, consumption, imports and exports, involving a much fuller use of the benefits of international trade.*

Secondly, American aid helped preserve during the worst of the postwar years a level of consumption, which, although considerably lower than before the war, succeeded in averting the threatening breakdown of Europe's economic, social, and political order. The large deficits, financed by foreign aid, reduced correspondingly the internal inflationary pressures bequeathed by the war and further augmented by the excess of investment over voluntary savings during the reconstruction period. They probably averted a total monetary collapse in a number of countries, and facilitated everywhere the restoration of the monetary system and the functioning of free economic institutions.

The elimination of the foreign deficits was not achieved through a curtailment of consumption, investment, and imports, but through the persistent growth of production and exports. In volume terms, production increased by $78 billion (or 57%) and exports by $16 billion (more than 160%) between 1947 and 1955.

Of course, at the level of individual countries, the economic impact of the American aid depended on the use made of that aid and on the soundness of economic policies. As pointed out in more recent research,[7] many countries that were unwilling to reform the state's dominating role to open up or to adjust overvalued currencies, fared less well in postwar growth. Those countries that moved most decisively to an international division of labour achieved quicker returns to convertibility, full employment, and growth. This explains why a comparison of the aid receipt of individual countries, as a percentage of their GNP, and their economic performance as measured by the growth of GNP and exports reveals no clear picture.

However, by far the most important contribution of the Marshall Plan was the impetus it gave to European integration. Somewhat paradoxically, it was in America that the idea of a united Europe was, if not born – one could show that it was born in many different places in Europe itself, notably in the writings of Richard de Coudenhove-Kalergi (who published in 1923 his 'Pan-Europa') and in conversations of European statesmen in exile in London during World War II – at least expressed the most forcefully in the years that immediately followed the war.

As Marjolin recalls in his *Memoirs*,[8] 'the Administration in Washington and especially Congress were entirely wedded to the cause of a unified Europe....' However, on the European side, the fact was that 'at national government level at any rate, the need for a Europe assembled around a common policy was much less clearly realised... than on the other side of the Atlantic.

By and large, Europe was thinking mainly about overcoming her immense material difficulties. She needed dollars; that was her primary and in many cases her only concern. It is certain, however, that during those years from 1947 to 1949, she could have gone much further in the direction desired by the Americans, had it not been for the stubborn resistance of the British to the idea of committing themselves irrevocably to the Continent. Originally, America's ambitions went very far, as far as the creation of a European federation. The Americans were motivated first and foremost by a desire to see Europe stand on her own feet economically and politically, to live without American aid and possibly even without the presence of the American army. They imagined, somewhat naively, a Western Europe that would be an extension, as it were, of the United States in the Old World, inspired by the same values, following the same policy as they, relieving them of a responsibility they had always felt to be very heavy, that of defending Europe against all external aggression. Very quickly they realised that a European federation was not within the realm of possibility, at least for the time being . The Administration in Washington then fell back on the idea of a customs union... This more modest idea of European integration in the form of a customs union might have become a reality as early as the beginning of the fifties, had the British not rejected it out of hand. It would take nearly ten years before the scheme was reborn among the Six and nearly twenty-five years before Britain found her place in it....'

'Having failed in their endeavour to unify Europe, first politically, then commercially, the Americans settled for a less ambitious objective: to develop commerce between European countries to the utmost, by liberalising trade and multilaterising payments.'

In this last endeavour, they were more successful. Obviously, liberalization of trade and multilateralization of payments were closely linked or, more accurately, trade liberalization depended on a multilateralization of payments. We all know the crucial role played in this connection by Robert Triffin. He was the intellectual architect of the European Payments Union (EPU), which was introduced in 1950 and restored the interconvertibility of European currencies. The creation of the EPU opened the way to the adoption by OEEC in the summer of 1950 of a code of trade liberalization, involving the progressive removal of quantitative restrictions in intra-European trade and observance of non-discrimination in that trade. The combination of the EPU and liberalization of intra-European trade represented a gigantic step towards the goal of a system of free trade and payments – current payments at least.

The Marshall Plan and its Relevance Today

Let me conclude on the assessment of the Marshall Plan by quoting once more Robert Marjolin:[9]

> *Not only were the Americans giving massive financial aid to their allies and ex-enemies, thus making possible or accelerating the economic recovery of the world's best developed region outside the US itself – one that could quite foreseeably end up as a formidable competitor for its benefactors – but they were even urging, sometimes to the point of hustling, the Europeans to unite and thus increase their economic and political strength... This apparently absurd disinterestedness would bear fruit. In the 1950s it became possible for Europe's payments to the rest of the world to be financed increasingly without recourse to American aid, until came the day in 1958 when general convertibility, this time including the dollar, was restored. Discriminatory measures in respect of trade with the US were phased out and a unified system entered into force governing the whole of international trade among the developed countries. The gamble the Americans had taken during the last years of the previous decade had paid off. History can boast few examples of such long term calculation involving immediate and certain sacrifices in return for distant and uncertain advantages.*

The question for us today is whether our generation, faced with the aftermath of the cold war in Central and Eastern Europe, in the very countries that had been excluded against their will from the Marshall Plan, has been, is, or will be capable of the same far-sightedness as that of the generation of great Americans lead by President Truman and George Marshall. It would be very presumptuous for me to propose an answer to this complex question. Only eight years have passed since the government of Mr Miklós Németh took, here in Hungary, the courageous step of dismantling the Iron Curtain and of allowing, at the end of August 1989, the East Germans, who so wished to leave to the West, which led two and a half months later to the fall of the Berlin Wall. Let me only outline a few thoughts, which could guide our discussions.

First, we have to compare the situation of the countries of Central and Eastern Europe as they emerged from communism to Western Europe at the end of World War II to assess similarities and differences in the challenges of reconstruction.

Second, we must evaluate the response of the international community, distinguishing between the two same dimensions as for the Marshall Plan: the magnitude and forms of resource transfers and the provision of a framework of integration into Europe and the global economy.

Third, taking stock of the progress accomplished since 1989, we must ask ourselves where and how current efforts would most need to be reinforced or complemented by new initiatives.

A number of parallels can be made between conditions in Central and Eastern Europe in 1989 and those of Western Europe after 1945: the capital stock was insufficient and obsolete; although there had been no new physical destruction, the environmental legacy of communism was dismal; underemployment was paired with the availability of skilled workers; prices were out of lines with economic reality; the monetary overhang and the looming public finance crisis were about to unleash huge inflationary pressures; savings were insufficient; a number of countries had high external debts and low foreign exchange reserves.

On the other hand, the world, into which the countries emerging from communism were and still are seeking to integrate themselves, has completely changed since 1947: this is a new global economy with higher standards of living, much more integrated and in the grip of a new technological revolution – the information and telecommunications revolution – breaking all the barriers of distance, and allowing the newcomers immediate access to technologies the generation of General Marshall could not have dreamed of. Another phenomenon is the fantastic development and globalization of capital markets with private capital flows dominating over official flows, as not seen since before World War I. In these new international capital markets, private entrepreneurs can seize opportunities with foreign direct or portfolio investments and the public sector plays a subsidiary role, increasingly through multilateral institutions.

Not only are external circumstances different but there is a fundamental difference between the challenge of reconstruction after World War II and the challenge of reconstruction after communism, which is embodied in the word 'transition': transition means the change from a command economy to an open, market-oriented economy; it concerns primarily the establishment of the legal, institutional and human bases of a market economy, a vastly underestimated task that goes well beyond its two most visible components, namely price and trade liberalization and privatization. It involves also a complete redefinition of the role of the state in the economy with fundamental reforms in taxation and social security, new competition rules, the establishment of effective regulatory frameworks in particular for banks and securities markets, and the enforcement of financial discipline and more generally of the rule of law through a revamped and independent judiciary. Without progress in transition and the new type of governance it leads to, there is a danger that private capital flows will not be forthcoming and that official assistance cannot be used efficiently.

How has the international community responded to help Central and Eastern Europe meet this huge challenge?

First of all, how much external financial support did Central and Eastern Europe receive? Without entering into a detailed statistical discussion, a few basic trends can be discerned:

- From 1989 to 1996, cumulative foreign direct investment (FDI) inflows to Central and Eastern Europe (including the Baltics) reached $30.7 billion, which is equivalent to $266 per capita, while in the Commonwealth of Independent States (CIS), flows were only $11.3 billion, i.e. $40 per capita.[10] These figures are not insignificant but, except for a few countries such as Hungary, the Czech Republic, Estonia, and Slovenia, they are modest compared to other parts of the world. For example, last year Singapore received roughly half as much FDI as the whole of Central and Eastern Europe and the CIS, although its population is no more than 3 million.
- On the official side, countries of Central and Eastern Europe, benefitted over the four most crucial years between January 1990 and December 1993 from assistance commitments totalling ECU 61 billion, with 62 per cent going to the four Visegrád countries. The European Union provided 42 per cent of total commitments, the US a much more modest 13 per cent (less than Germany alone and without its contribution channelled through the EU budget) and international financial institutions a respectable 26 per cent. The IMF and the World Bank were joined by a brand new multilateral institution, the European Bank for Reconstruction and Development (EBRD), dedicated specifically to assist the process of transition through an emphasis on the development of the private sector.[11] Of the ECU 61 billion commitments, ECU 18.3 billion only were in the form of grants and a significant part was in the form of debt restructuring, which did not involve a genuine net transfer.[12] According to the World Bank, these flows amounted to 2.7 per cent of the GNP of the recipient countries. One can of course argue that more should have been done, particularly in view of the transition recession these countries went through, and I know that there has been in

Hungary sometimes a disappointment that the response of the West was not more forceful. Nevertheless, it can be said that official flows, particularly those emanating from multilateral institutions, have significantly assisted the processes of economic stabilization, liberalization, and structural reforms in the countries concerned. Transition indicators, compiled by the EBRD, show that progress has been overall more rapid than could have been expected but that it was unequal among the various countries of the region. The important point is that it does not appear that the lack of adequate external financial support was the reason for the less satisfactory performance of some countries compared to others.

For the countries of the CIS, it is more difficult to reach a clear conclusion for several reasons: the first is the dominating part of debt relief in the overall packages of aid; the second is the considerable discrepancy between the size of aid packages announced by the G-7 and actual disbursements which was due primarily to the fact that the Russian authorities were, on several occasions, unable to implement the stabilization and structural reform policies necessary for the release of IMF and World Bank assistance. Nevertheless, the IMF estimates that total new official financing provided to Russia in the crucial 1992-93 years amounted, net of debt relief, to 4 per cent of the Russian GNP. A fundamental question of course, which could be the subject of another conference, is whether there could have been more decisive success in stabilization and reform in Russia if the commitment of official assistance had been much larger. I am afraid it will be difficult to settle this counterfactual question satisfactorily. What can be said, however, is that the IMF did modify its policies to address the specific needs of countries in transition. It was with the countries of the former Soviet Union in mind that the IMF introduced in 1993 the Systemic Transformation Facility, a sort of bridge facility permitting disbursements before more ambitious policies could be put in place – that would qualify for support by the IMF's larger and more conditional facilities.[13] What is regrettable is that the membership of the Fund has been unable so far to come to an agreement on the proposal of its Managing Director, Mr Michel Camdessus, for a special SDR allocation, which would particularly benefit countries which did not participate in previous SDR allocations, including most of the transition countries.[14]

More important than the flow of funds to countries emerging from communism has been the capacity to offer them a framework for their integration in the global economy and in particular in the European Union.

The IMF and the World Bank, which in the late 1940s had not been in a position to help significantly the recovery of Western Europe, have assumed over the last eight years, together with the European Commission, a role of leadership in the international efforts to assist the countries of transition in the design of their macroeconomic and structural policies so as to facilitate their integration in the world economy. In many cases, their technical assistance, particularly in institution building and training, might have had a more lasting importance than the size of their financial assistance. The transition countries have also amended their trade regimes with the objective of joining the World Trade Organisation.

However, the process of economic restructuring to achieve a successful integration in the global economy is far from an easy one and the countries of Central and Eastern Europe could probably not have sustained the determination they have shown towards democracy and a market economy if they did not have the prospect of associating themselves and ultimately joining the European Union. Here is the belated and unexpected prize for General Marshall, Jean Monnet, Robert Schuman and the other founding fathers of Europe. It is the very success of the European model they helped create, that not only led to the internal disintegration of the communist bloc, as nobody thought worthwhile to fight for it, but also provided an attractive and already advanced model of economic, social and political integration, to which the reborn countries of Central and Eastern Europe could anchor their aspirations for well-functioning democracies and market economies.

Although we have today in the European Union many Eurosceptics and an understandable disappointment at the current high rate of unemployment, I do not think that we realize sufficiently what the process of European integration, combined with NATO, has given us: not only an extraordinary prosperity but more importantly 50 years of peace, democracy, rule of law and a model of interdependence among European nations based on common institutions, which does not allow any nation to dominate but insures the participation of all in the decision-making process. The EU is indeed much more than a free trade area: it is an integrated single market with free movement of capital and labour, supported by institutions that make the single market work and provide the indispensable common regulatory framework. Moreover, the EU will become a monetary union with a single currency and its own central bank. Since its origins, the Union has had not only economic but also social and political objectives. It is developing new pillars in the areas of justice, immigration, foreign affairs, and security. All this is based on shared values, grounded in the splendid heritage of the European civilization, to which the nations of Central and Eastern Europe made irreplaceable contributions.

This leads me to the view that the closest equivalent I can find since the end of the cold war to the Harvard speech of General Marshall is the declaration made by the EU Heads of State and Government in Copenhagen at the end of their 21-22 June 1993 meeting when they said:

> *The European Council today agreed that the associated countries in Central and Eastern Europe that so desire shall become members of the European Union. Accession will take place as soon as an associated country is able to assume the obligations of membership by satisfying the economic and political conditions required.*
>
> *Membership requires that the candidate country has achieved stability of institutions guaranteeing democracy, the rule of law, human rights and respect for and protection of minorities, the existence of a functioning market economy as well as the capacity to cope with the competitive pressure and market forces within the Union. Membership presupposes the candidate's ability to take on the obligations of membership including adherence to the aims of political, economic, and monetary union.*
>
> *The Union's capacity to absorb new members, while maintaining the momentum of European integration, is also an important consideration in the general interest of both the Union and the candidate countries.*

In the same way, as the speech of General Marshall quoted above, also each word of this statement would need to be analysed. The most important perhaps relates to the adherence not only to the *acquis communautaire*, i.e. the whole set of rules and standards governing the single market, but more broadly to the ultimate political objectives of the Union. These broader non-economic objectives explain why throughout Central and Eastern Europe, joining the European Union is a genuine *projet mobilisateur*. Only last week I was reading in the *Financial Times* how determined Hungary was in introducing and strictly applying the EU rules of the game.[15]

What then remains to be done, what additional initiatives would be warranted? Our recommendations should start from the diagnosis that progress in transition has been very unequal among the various countries and remains subject to slippages and accidents. The tragic events in Albania are an illustration of how hard-won progress in transition can be lost with frightening speed. More generally progress has been much slower in the CIS countries than in Central and Eastern Europe. Some countries have not yet experienced a genuine resumption of growth. Although the basic characteristics of a market economy are now present, with individual economic agents holding the initiative and government actions being sanctioned by market forces, the type of market economy that is emerging is significantly distorted. An uncertain investment climate, deficiencies of taxation systems, crime and corruption have discouraged domestic and foreign investment. Capital flight is continuing at high levels. The social situation remains alarming and pressing environmental problems, particularly those related to nuclear safety, remain unresolved.

This is why a number of existing initiatives need to be reinforced and perhaps new initiatives launched:

- Governments in the countries concerned, the local and the international business community and the international financial institutions should join forces in promoting sound business standards and corporate practices; the market economy cannot deliver its positive effects for society as a whole and ultimately cannot be successful if it cannot rely on a minimum of trust and self-discipline. I am pleased that corporate governance has been taken as the central topic of this conference. Better corporate governance is a central requirement for larger capital inflows and a successful transition. It is an area in which the EBRD can legitimately aspire to play a leading role.
- Whereas elsewhere access to private capital flows or to existing international financial institutions eliminates the need for new concessional facilities, the remaining areas where I still see a strong case for a Marshall Plan II concern the social and environmental sectors, particularly in the CIS countries. These two sectors are also sectors entailing very important externalities. Stronger social support programmes are needed to alleviate poverty and make reforms politically acceptable and socially sustainable, particularly in the CIS countries, where social indicators point to a dramatic decline in standards of living of large segments of the population. Problems of course are not only the funding but the institutional capacity to deliver effective programmes in co-ordination with local administrations and non-governmental institutions. The World Bank would be

well-placed to take new initiatives in this area, relying also on the experience of the Social Development Fund of the Council of Europe.[16] The EBRD could also play a greater role through its projects in the areas of energy efficiency and municipal and environmental infrastructure, which can bring tangible benefits to large segments of the population. Second, urgent action is needed to reduce environmental pollution, to reform the energy sector and to promote nuclear safety. The nuclear safety account administered by the EBRD represents a good starting point but is insufficient to induce the closure of dangerous nuclear reactors. Action by the G-7 for the closure of Chernobyl does not take sufficiently into account the broader issues of energy efficiency, including energy conservation. Furthermore the Chernobyl reactors are only a few among the many more dangerous reactors in activity in the former CMEA countries. The EBRD would be well-placed to formulate new initiatives in this second area. Robert Triffin, who was always very sensitive to the social dimension of economic adjustment and to the nuclear danger, would, I believe, have supported these two recommendations.

- Last but not least, we should accelerate the preparation of the institutional and financial framework, allowing a successful enlargement of the EU towards the candidate countries of Central and Eastern Europe, as well as the capacity for the EU to engage Russia and the other CIS countries into a more meaningful partnership. This requires first and foremost satisfactory progress in the institutional reforms discussed in the framework of the Intergovernmental Conference due to be concluded in June in Amsterdam. It will also require significant reforms in the Common Agricultural Policy and in the existing Structural and Cohesion Funds. On the side of the candidate countries, preparation for accession is also a huge challenge. The strategies of assistance to these countries not only from PHARE and the European Investment Bank but also from the World Bank and from the EBRD should be more proactive, better co-ordinated and primarily geared to this essential endeavour of a successful reintegration into Europe, from which these countries have been so long and so painfully separated.

Let me conclude with the first verses of a superb poem to Europe by one of Hungary's greatest poets, Dezső Kosztolányi (1885-1936):

Europe, to you,
by you, praising you, I present my plea
from this century's blind botching,
and as others bury you, tolling through the night,
with a shrill dithyramb, with joy,
with good morning, I greet you.[17]

Notes and references

1. Richard Mayne, *The Recovery of Europe, From Devastation to Unity*, Weidenfeld and Nicolson, London, 1970, p. 37.
2. In addition to General Marshall himself, the US officials which played the most crucial role in the conception of the Marshall Plan were Under-Secretary of State Dean Acheson, Under-Secretary of State for Economic Affairs William Clayton and George Kennan, Head of the State Department's Policy Planning Staff.
3. Richard Mayne, op.cit. p. 97.
4. Robert Marjolin, *Architect of European Unity, Memoirs 1911-1986*, Weidenfeld and Nicolson, London, 1989, p. 231.
5. The $12.4 billion represented 2 per cent of the combined GNP of the 16 recipient countries during that period. Adjusted for inflation in 1991, this would be the equivalent of $65.4 billion. See Daniel Gros and Alfred Steinherr's *'Winds of Change', Economic Transition in Central and Eastern Europe*, Longman, London, 1995, p. 474.
6. Robert Triffin, *Europe and the Money Muddle, From Bilateralism to Near-convertibility, 1947-1956*, Yale University Press, New Haven, 1957, p. 45.
7. Daniel Gros and Alfred Steinherr, op.cit. p. 151.
8. Robert Marjolin, op. cit. p. 212.
9. Robert Marjolin, op. cit. pp. 217-218.
10. See EBRD, 1996 Annual Report, p. 13.
11. With only six years of existence, the EBRD has already been able to commit about ECU 9 billion in loans, equity participations and guarantees, including about ECU 5 billion in the countries of Central and Eastern Europe (including the Baltics).
12. IMF and G-24 figures compiled by Daniel Gros and Alfred Steinherr, op. cit. pp. 481-486.
13. Eduard Brau, 'External Financial Assistance: The Record and Issues', in Daniel A. Citrin and Ashok K. Lahiri, (eds.), *Policy Experiences and Issues in the Baltics, Russia, and Other Countries of the Former Soviet Union*, IMF occasional paper No. 133, Washington, December 1995, pp. 108-112.
14. An agreement was reached in Hong Kong in September 1997 on the occasion of the IMF Annual Meeting, providing for a one-time SDR equity allocation of SDR 21.4 billion, which would equalize all members' ratio of SDRs to quotas at 29.3 per cent. This will allow 38 IMF members that have never received an SDR allocation to participate in the SDR system and will augment their reserves.

15. Emma Tucker, 'Hungary plays the EU rules with steely determination', *Financial Times*, 7 May 1997, p. 2.
16. The Council of Europe Social Development Fund has presently 25 members, only four of which are countries in transition, namely, Bulgaria, Lithuania, Romania, and Slovenia. Four additional member states of the Council of Europe – Hungary, Croatia, Estonia, and the Former Yugoslav Republic of Macedonia – have recently submitted their official request to join the Social Development Fund.
17. 'Europe', poem translated by Alan Dixon, in *Today, An Anthology of Contemporary Hungarian Literature*, Budapest, Corvina, 1987.

6 Back to Fundamentals: Why a Monetary Union for Europe?*

Alexandre Lamfalussy

I have accepted with pleasure and gratitude the invitation to speak and I have a number of reasons for that. One of the reasons is that the topic, monetary union is close to my heart. Another reason for which I am very happy to be here is that I really appreciate the work that has been done by SUERF. As you know, I had the good fortune to be among the founders, and I am proud of SUERF's achievements. A third very good reason is that I have great admiration for Robert Triffin: he played an instrumental role in postwar progress in Europe. And finally, those of you perhaps who are not Hungarians (and that happens even to economists) do not fully realize what this place means to Hungarians. The Hungarian Academy, which was founded early in the last century, was part and parcel of that period's reform movement. Practically everything that has been achieved in Hungary since then owes a great deal to the generation of people who worked during that period of Hungarian history.

First I would like to talk about some of the fundamental issues raised by monetary union, and then to touch on a few other issues that are linked to the establishment of the European Central Bank.

Let me begin by reminding you that a monetary union exists *de facto* from the moment when exchange rates are irrevocably locked. In such a situation national currencies become perfect substitutes for each other. There can only be one monetary policy, and financial assets carrying the same credit risk will provide the same yield. The single currency adds three things: it makes the commitment to be irrevocably more credible; in the operation of a single market, it reduces conversion costs to nil (note, however, that the locking of exchange rates and their transformation into conversion rates by themselves considerably diminish these conversion costs); and, of course, for

---

* Presented as the *Marjolin Lecture* during the SUERF/RTSF Conference on May 15-17, 1997, in Budapest.

the ordinary citizen it represents the practical (and also emotional) content of a monetary union.

I would not want to question for a minute either the practical or the political importance of these three contributions of the single currency to a monetary union; but for the purposes of economic analysis we can, I believe, focus our attention on the consequences of the irrevocable locking of exchange rates. Indeed, it is this locking which eliminates foreign exchange risks from the cross-border dealings within the single market. We should draw a sharp distinction between two kinds of exchange risks: those linked to relatively short-term volatility in nominal exchange rates; and those related to long-term shifts in *real* exchange rates, which, if persistent and not justified by 'real' shocks, we have become accustomed to calling real exchange rate misalignments.

Short-term exchange rate volatility is surely a nuisance and is bound to have some discouraging impact on the cross-border exchange of goods and services. The size of this impact is very difficult to estimate. But market participants can insure themselves against such volatility by having recourse to a wide variety of hedging devices: forward operations, futures and options. Hedging, of course is not costless, and it is the elimination of these costs (which increase sharply with the expected volatility of exchange rates) which constitutes measurable advantages of monetary union. This may not be a very big advantage, but it *is* an advantage.

The main point I should like to make today is that monetary union would bring a much more significant advantage by eliminating real exchange rate misalignments. Monetary union would stabilize real exchange rates because the fixity of nominal exchange rates would be accompanied by an equalization of inflation rates: a single monetary policy in a single market means that major inflation differentials between 'regions' are simply not sustainable. Wage increases can, of course, differ – but only to the extent that they are warranted by differences in the rates of increase of productivity. Otherwise, the inflation-prone region would simply price itself out of the single market.

I have three reasons for saying that monetary union would bring significant advantages by stabilizing real exchange rates. The first reason is that real exchange rate misalignments have highly distorting effects on cross-border transactions and prevent the optimum allocation of resources. They lead misdirected investment, so aptly called in German 'Fehlinvestitionen'. Moreover, the experience of investment decisions which have turned out to be mistaken because of major shifts in relative competitive positions is bound to have an inhibiting effect on future investment decisions. In more general terms, real exchange rate instability introduces a high degree of uncertainty into business decisions, and we know that uncertainty is the worst enemy of expansion oriented investment. The second reason is that failure in investment decision introduces an element of uncertainty which has a debilitating effect on the overall climate of investments. The third reason is that no hedging techniques are available to insure yourselves against lasting long-term shifts in relative competitive positions. The inventiveness of financial engineering has no limits, but I would guess that hedging against these risks would be murderously costly. Very large corporations can diversify both their investments and their trade flows in a way which would allow them to offset – at least to some extent – the losses incurred in some countries through unexpected real exchange rate movements by gains made elsewhere. But such 'self-insurance' is not available to medium-sized firms – yet the involvement of these firms in cross-border transactions is increasing and, moreover, their contribution to employment is crucial.

Let me develop further this line of thought by referring more explicity to the situation currently prevailing in Europe. The single market is not a free trade area, not even simply a customs union. When fully implemented – and we are moving quite speedily in that direction – it will allow the totally free flow of goods, services, people and capital. The result is an unprecedented degree of integration of our economies for manufacturing industry, agriculture, transport and the more and more dominant service industries. It also carries with it generalized and tough competition for hitherto protected activities. This will surely be beneficial to consumers, but implies cost management and pricing policies where every cent counts. Even small shifts in relative competitive positions matter. This is a new environment and one which is totally different from the Europe in which our enterprise operated only ten, or even five years ago.

Another fact also stands out in recent European history, one that I very much welcome: I refer to the significant downward convergence in inflation rates. Average inflation for the EU as a whole was running at around 3 per cent in 1995 and 1996, but is now well below 2 per cent. This is significantly lower than anything we have registered since the 'golden 1960s'. Even more importantly, the dispersion around the average has narrowed considerably: the standard deviation now is about 1.3 per cent, to be sat against as much as 5 to 8 per cent during much of the 1970s and 1980s. Quite a few countries have for several years been running inflation rates of around or below 2 per cent. Inflation, of course, is never dead, only dormant. But I do believe that with the consistent pursuit of stability oriented monetary policies (which is now the explicit commitment of all central banks in the EMI Council and will be the primary objective of the European Central Bank) this situation can be consolidated.

In an European economy where inflation is well under control and inflation differentials are small and receding, changes in nominal exchange rates translate themselves into changes in real exchange rates. And in a closely integrated, highly competitive European economy even small but lasting changes in real exchange rates can have disturbing and perhaps diruptive consequences for the functioning of the single market. Most of you have in mind the experience of some of the very large shifts in nominal exchange rates which occurred within the EU between 1992 and 1995. These shifts hurt so much not only because they were large, but because the inflation differentials were already small enough to translate these nominal exchange rate changes into major and lasting shifts in relative competitive positions. The point I would like to stress is that in an ever more closely integrated and ever more competitive but less inflationary European economy even much smaller exchange rate misalignments are apt to cause a great deal of damage.

Now let me comment on three counterarguments which are likely to come to your mind. The first is derived from one of the traditional theories of economics: purchasing power parity (PPP). The theory of absolute PPP has more or less gone out of fashion, but its 'relative' variety is still very much alive. Movements in real exchange rates may happen, indeed are needed, so goes the argument, when such movements respond to changes in the real economy: for instance when you discover large oil or natural gas reserves in your country. But when, as a result of a convergence in monetary policies, inflation rates are identical, there will be no lasting departures from PPP. So why should we worry about them? Real exchange rate misalignments may well occur in the relatively short run (when, for instance, markets do not believe in the sustainability of monetary policy convergence), but they tend to disappear in the long run. I suspect that many professional economists who are sceptical about the need for a monetary union derive their scepticism, at least partly, from their deeply rooted belief that PPP holds in the long run. Well, I do not claim to possess an alternative theory which could provide a convincing explanation for the large and persistent real exchange rate misalignments which have occurred over the past twenty-five years, but I am sure that we *have* had, indeed still have, major departures from PPP. Think of the long cycles in the over- or undervaluation of the US dollar; of similar developments in the yen; or, more closer to us, of what happened with the pound sterling or with the lira. It is possible that in the end corrective forces will prevail; but periods of over- or undervaluation, even if they last 'just' three or four years, can do a lot of harm. Perhaps not that much to large, relatively closed economies like that of the United States, but surely to our wide-open European countries. The facts being what they are, I prefer to take *them* for granted rather than trust theories which are not confirmed by observation.

The second counterargument goes to the heart of the matter, and I take it very seriously. It deserves lengthy, nuanced, development, for which I have no time in this lecture. So I beg your understanding for appearing dogmatic, which is not my intention. This counterargument refers back to part of the PPP argument: in cases of asymmetrical 'real' shocks, member countries of EMU may well need changes in their real exchange rates – changes which a monetary union would not allow to happen. My answer to this counterargument can be briefly summed up as follows. First, while I do not deny that such a situation could arise, I regard this as improbable. German unification was such an event: it would have warranted the real appreciation of the Deutsche mark at that time. But I do not believe that a shock of this kind and size is likely to be repeated. Second, I believe that the past ten to fifteen years have witnessed a considerable convergence of the economic and social structures of the EU countries. Accordingly, our problems – those relating to unemployment, social security, pension systems, and so on – have also become quite similar, and their solution will therefore require a similar approach. Third, most or the 'real' shocks in the past created genuine exchange rate problems not so much because they were asymmetrical, but because the policy responses were sharply different. The oil shocks of the 1970s were a case in point. Our policy philosophies – both in monetary and fiscal policies – have since then undergone a thorough convergence process.

The third counterargument runs on different lines. It is likely to be raised by practitioners rather than by academic economists. Could we not try to keep intra-European real exchange rates under control otherwise than by implementing a monetary union? Can we not argue that those EU countries which remained members of the ERM have managed to limit exchange rate volatility and prevent major real exchange rate realignments from emerging with greater success than non-participating countries? My answer to both questions is yes, but a strongly qualified yes. I do believe that the 'ERM 2' which has now been agreed on, will be able to avoid the exchange rate overvaluations which led to the 1992-1993 crises and to the subsequent excessive exchange rate depreciations. We shall be able to achieve this if we draw the lessons from those experiences: central rates will have to be agreed jointly; exchange rate realignments will have to be undertaken preventively – and, to achieve this, 'depoliticized'; as a general rule, we shall have to keep relatively wide margins; and, last but not least, convergence policies will have to be agreed upon and strictly implemented. We shall also have to adjust the ERM to the new environment which will prevail after the beginning of the monetary union. The ECB should play a major role in the system, and the basically asymmetrical nature of the ERM should be acknowledged. So far so good. But I would still regard any such arrangement as only a second best – or, more precisely, a provisisional, transitory arrangement which cannot be regarded as a good and safe substitute for a monetary union. This is so, first, because an ERM agreement simply does not possess the same kind of institutional stability and 'irrevocability' as does a monetary union. And, second, because the likelihood that the 'outs' will pursue a consistent convergence policy (which is one of the major preconditions for success) is strongly enhanced by their prospect of joining monetary union. If there is no monetary union to join, the incentive for pursuing a consistent (and in the short run potentially costly) convergence policy can only be enlightened self-interest. And this, unfortunately, is a rare commodity.

May I now turn to some forward-looking issues? My remarks will touch upon the 'economic' component of the prospective Economic and Monetary Union and, more specifically, on the working relations between the European Central Bank and the European governments.

There is one key area in which effective co-operation between the ECB and the governments will be indispensable. This is, broadly speaking, the euroareas's exchange rate policy. The need for co-operation would arise, firstly, if and when the euroarea decided to enter into a global pegged-rate arrangement of the Bretton Woods type. The decision to enter into such an agreement will have to be taken by the European Council, but the Treaty clearly states that the Council should seek to reach a consensus with the ECB in order to ensure that an agreement of this type does not put at risk the stability oriented monetary policy of the ECB. In any event, Bretton Woods mark II is not around the corner. It is highly improbable that the ability to co-operate between the ECB and the governments will be put to the test in this specific area.

The more practical problem could arise if the euroarea were to participate in co-ordinated, large-scale, exchange market intervention of the kind we have seen a few times within the framework of a global floating rate system. Here again, 'the general orientation' of the euroareas's exchange rate policy will have to be defined by the European Council. There are, however, two 'buts'. Firstly, ministers can act only either on the recommendation of the

ECB, or on that of the Commission, after having heard the view of the ECB. Secondly, no such 'general orientation' can put at risk the basic mandate of the ECB to ensure domestic price stability. My own interpretation of this second 'but' is that the ECB cannot be forced to intervene in the exchange market at times, or for amounts, which would lead to excessive money creation.

Why do I believe in this interpretation? Because in the recent agreement on ERM 2 it is explicitly stated that the ECB will have the right to suspend exchange market intervention vis-a-vis a EU member country which does not participate in EMU if and when it believes that any such intervention would endanger price stability within the euroarea. If this right is granted to the ECB vis-a-vis another European country, it should clearly be granted in the case of intervention vis-a-vis the US dollar, when the amounts involved would quite obviously be a multiple of intra-ERM intervention.

Beyond the specific area of exchange rate policy the need for co-operation would arise, of course, for the determination of the policy mix. From the angle of monetary stability what is needed is that fiscal policy should be supportive of – rather than antagonistic to – the stability oriented monetary policy of the future ECB.

I realize that this condition could be met in the most satisfactory way if our countries had achieved a far higher degree of political integration than they have hitherto. I do not believe, however, that the absence of prior, far reaching, political integration constitute an insurmountable handicap as long as (a) only those countries lock their exchange rates on 1st January 1999 which have demonstrated their ability to submit themselves to the hard discipline of a monetary union, and (b) the stability pact is effectively implemented.

Perhaps even more importantly, I believe that the hard discipline of a stability oriented single monetary policy will gradually steer our governments towards the required degree of co-operation – just as it will alter the behaviour of labour market participants and the pricing policies of our enterprises. The freedom of choice of all of us will be substantially constrained – in particular, the freedom to pursue irresponsible policies at all levels. Not by decree, but by market forces operating within an environment of monetary stability.

7 European Monetary Union: Progress and Outlook

Robert Raymond

Progress towards Monetary Union began many years ago, and the route taken by the thinking on the subject has been marked by several famous reports (associated with the names Barre, Werner, and Delors, respectively). With the start of Stage Two on 1 January 1994, preparation for Monetary Union took on a more concrete form under the aegis of the European Monetary Institute (EMI), which was established in accordance with the Maastricht Treaty. With twenty months to go until the introduction of the single currency, it is worth taking stock of what has been accomplished to date and looking at what has yet to be achieved.

A. Preparation for Monetary Union

I. Projects already completed

Some projects with far-reaching practical implications have already been completed, establishing an infrastructure which will permit the smooth functioning of the single currency area.

1. This is the case for the timetable for the changeover to the single currency, which was drawn up in 1995 and endorsed by the Heads of State or Government in Madrid in December of the same year. It envisages a number of different phases in the process:

- spring 1998: a list of the countries participating in the Monetary Union will be drawn up once reliable data are available on the results of the budgets for 1997;

- 1 January 1999: the start of Stage Three;
- the euro will be brought swiftly into use on the capital markets;
- 1 January 2002 at the latest: euro banknotes and coins will be put into circulation, with the transitional period taking no more than six months;
- in the interim, the new currency – use of which will neither be compulsory nor prohibited – will exist alongside the old denominations.

2. In order to avoid this period of around three years from resembling a system of fixed exchange rates which would be at the mercy of speculators, the euro will have to be – by law – the sole currency of the euroarea from 1 January 1999. A *lex monetae*, or monetary law, has thus been prepared. Based on Article 235 of the Treaty, it will apply in all the Member States of the European Union. It provides that 'euro' will be the new name of the ecu, which it will replace on a one-for-one basis with full legal continuity from the first moment of 1999, without there being any need to renegotiate contracts. The same principle of continuity will apply to contracts which are denominated in the national currencies merged within the euro on the basis of the irrevocably fixed conversion rates which the Council of Ministers will adopt at the end of 1998.

This monetary law will apply within the jurisdictions of those EU Member States which remain outside the euroarea, as may be the case of the United Kingdom. It will be mirrored by regulation adopted in the states of New York and Illinois and will therefore be respected in the principal financial centres and will govern the performance of most international contracts.

Another text will regulate the technical aspects of the relationship between the euro and the former national denominations in the participating countries.

3. The preparation of the banknotes is proceeding according to schedule. Following a competition, the EMI Council selected a series of draft designs for the banknotes in December 1996. The draft design sketches are currently being finalized and the security features incorporated. Printing can begin in the participating countries only once the European Central Bank (ECB) has been legally established.

4. The central banks are actively preparing a payments system which will allow funds to be transferred irrevocably and in real time within the euroarea. The existing national systems all now support real-time gross settlement and

their interlinking is being prepared at the EMI. This network, which is known by the acronym TARGET, will provide the infrastructure necessary for the existence of a fully unified money market within the euroarea. Private settlement mechanisms may, of course, continue to exist alongside TARGET.

5. On 15 January of this year the EMI published a report describing the general framework of the monetary policy which will be conducted in Stage Three. A more detailed document is due in mid-September.

6. The version of the European Monetary System which will be in force from 1999 has been broadly defined. The EMI published a report on this matter which was annexed to the conclusions of the Dublin summit in December 1996. 'ERM II', as it is called, provides a framework for the co-ordination of exchange rate relations between the euro and the currencies of the EU Member States not participating in the euroarea from the outset. This successor arrangement places greater emphasis than in the past on improving macroeconomic convergence, which is the true basis of stable exchange rates. Wide fluctuation bands will exist, in the same way as they do today, and closer exchange rate links may be negotiated between the euro and participating non-euroarea currencies.

7. Finally, I must mention the agreement reached on the substance of the Stability and Growth Pact which will apply to the Member States participating in the euroarea, in order to ensure the co-ordination of their budgetary policies. An annual deficit which exceeds 3 per cent may trigger sanctions. This Pact will be flanked by measures to strengthen the monitoring of the convergence programmes in place in the countries not yet participating in the euroarea. The governors of the central banks have welcomed these initiatives, without themselves taking part in the technical work.

II. *What has yet to be done*

1. First of all the preparations of the financial intermediaries, economic agents and public authorities need to be guided and co-ordinated.

2. Agreement must be reached on the timetable of events during spring 1998, when the procedure provided for by the Treaty comes into effect for drawing up the list of participating countries (i.e. those which meet the convergence

criteria and do not invoke an 'opt-out' clause, if they have one) and for establishing the ECB, which will be the case once the members of its Executive Board have been definitively appointed.

The Economic and Finance Ministers mapped out the major stages of the process at the informal meeting of the ECOFIN Council in Noordwijk on 5 April 1997. They are expected to be as follows:

- second half of March: reports by the Commission and the EMI on the state of convergence will be published simultaneously;
- at the same time, the Commission will adopt recommendations concerning, on the one hand, the revised list of countries subject to the excessive deficit procedure and, on the other, the list of the countries eligible to enter the euroarea;
- a period of several weeks will be allowed for the European Parliament to be consulted and, in some cases, for national parliaments to be consulted also, although this is not a requirement of the Treaty;
- the ECOFIN Ministers will approve a recommendation relating to the list of participating countries, which will then immediately be followed by approval of the final list by the Heads of State or Government;
- the latter are expected to nominate the members of the Executive Board of the ECB as soon as possible thereafter, which assumes that a recommendation will be made by the ECOFIN Ministers and that the EMI Council and the European Parliament will be consulted.

It is important that the time taken by the procedure is kept to a minimum, both in order to avoid turbulence on the foreign exchange markets and to allow the ECB to finalize all its rules and procedures.

3. At the appointed time, the list of participating countries will be drawn up, the European Central Bank will be established and the irrevocable conversion rates between the currencies of the participating countries will be adopted.

B. After January 1999

I. Internally

1. At the beginning of 1999, the single central bank responsible for administering the euro will start operating.

It will be a central bank with a federal structure, made up of the ECB at the hub and the national central banks (NCBs).

The European System of Central Banks (ESCB) will be governed by the decision-making bodies of the ECB, namely:

- the Executive Board, which will be responsible for the day-to-day management of the ESCB's monetary operations and of he ECB;
- the Governing Council, comprising the governors of the NCBs and the members of the Executive Board of the ECB, will meet regularly and will have sole responsibility in all matters relating to the ESCB's monetary policy; the Executive Board of the ECB will implement its guidelines and decisions on a day-to-day basis;
- finally, the General Council, comprising the governors of all the central banks in the European Union – i.e. including those of the non-participating countries – and the President and Vice-President of the ECB, will supervise the co-ordination of the monetary and exchange rate policies between the euroarea and the other EU Member States.

2. This central bank will be independent, and its primary task will be to 'maintain price stability' – that is, to achieve and maintain a low rate of inflation.

Monetary policy will be determined centrally. The Governing Council will determine the operational or intermediate objectives and the instruments. Virtually all the operations will be decentralized, i.e. conducted by the NCBs.

3. From 1 January 1999 the euro will be the sole legal currency, although banknotes and coins denominated in the former national currencies will continue to be in circulation for a certain period of time. Euro banknotes and coins will be put into circulation on 1 January 2002 at the latest. In the interim, use of the euro will neither be compulsory nor prohibited. Contracts expressed in the former national currencies will be treated as if they are in

euro, with the equivalent value being determined by the irrevocable conversion rate. However, monetary policy will be defined in euro, accounts held by commercial banks with their NCB will be denominated in euro and public debt instruments will be issued in euro. It is therefore reasonable to assume that from an early date in 1999, the interbank money market, the foreign exchange market and, more generally, the capital markets will operate in euro rather than in national currencies.

II. Vis-a-vis non-EU countries

1. The exchange rates between the euro and the currencies of EU Member States not (yet) participating in the euroarea will, as in the past, be treated – in the terms of the Maastricht Treaty – as 'a matter of common interest'. Although they will be under no obligation to do so, most of the non-participating countries are expected to join ERM II, the successor arrangement to the current exchange rate mechanism, thereby ensuring the co-ordination of monetary and exchange rate policies.

2. Internationally, the euro is expected, in time, to play an important role as a settlement currency and to represent a sizeable share of investors' portfolios.

***

These are the already very precise indications which can be given today.

What remains now is, first, to urge those responsible in the EU Member States to make sure that the criteria laid down in the Treaty in order to ensure the proper selection of the countries initially participating in EMU are respected and thus to enable the European Union to operate satisfactorily during the critical 'running in' period. Second, the support of public opinion also needs to be obtained and this has clearly not yet been achieved in all EU Member States.

8 The Euro on Schedule: Analysis of its European and International Implications

Michael Sakbani[*]

I. Introduction

The decision of the European council of finance ministers (and central banks) in September 1997 to fix European parities next April at the same time as the selection of the first-wave participants in the EMU was a clever technical decision allowing the launch of the euro in January 1999 with a minimum risk of speculation against individual currencies in the run-up to it. Under the previous monetary unification agenda, financial markets would have been allowed eight months for speculation against individual currencies, with all the consequent results for public treasuries. This decision also manifests, once again, the Europeans' determination to go ahead with their monetary project, regardless of the doubts expressed in various quarters.

There is no longer a shred of doubt that the euro will be a reality as of January 1999 and will thus in three years' time replace the members' currencies as a medium of exchange.[1] As was noted in a previous paper, this will be a seminal monetary event, with fundamental consequences in a variety of domains:[2] the composition of official reserves, financial markets and institutions, European monetary policies, international trade, developing countries, and eventually the international monetary system.

The purpose of this paper is to offer a comprehensive survey of the implications of this event and an interactive consideration of the issues involved in the light of recent developments.

---

[*] Director of Economic Cooperation, UNCTAD.
The views expressed in this article are those of the author and do not necessarily represent those of UNCTAD.

II. Who will participate and on what interpretation of Maastricht?

All indications now point in the direction of broad EMU participation. Next April, it is almost certain that 11 countries will be judged to have fulfilled the Maastricht criteria, and these will include Spain, Portugal and Italy.[3] Thus, the political mix will match the economic selection, and the EMU will have an internal balance that will accommodate the political sensibility of the French without sacrificing the economic rigour of the Germans. By fortuitous developments, the three monetary criteria of inflation, interest rates and exchange rates have all been fulfilled by the members of the EMU. The fiscal criteria, i.e. a deficit not in excess of 3 per cent of GDP and a stock of public debt not in excess of 60 per cent, seem to have become the subject of a common understanding. The first is now fulfilled *stricto senso* by seven of the eleven, while France is going to reach 3.2 per cent in 1997 and 3.0 in 1998 if the rate forecast by its government for GDP growth in the 1997/98 fiscal year, i.e. 3 per cent, is attained. Germany will just hit 3 per cent in 1997, while Italy, which was at 4.5 per cent in 1996, is now projected to be around 3.5 per cent in mid-1997 and perhaps 3.0 or lower in 1998. Spain should be around 3.1 per cent and Portugal at about 3.4 per cent in mid-1997, both moving down below 3.0 per cent in 1998. In the second half of October 1997, the Commission will reveal its estimates for all members, and these will be the basis for the discussions of the Heads of State as to who will qualify. The substantial fiscal reforms and efforts of Italy in particular are being recognized and have improved the chances of its membership. It is hoped that Italy's reforms will continue in this direction.[4] In other words, the criterion is interpreted fulfilled if a downward tendency is demonstrated. The other fiscal criterion, i.e. debt not more than 60 per cent of GDP, is not faring as well arithmetically,[5] but once again the judgement with regard to the public debt trend seems to have carried the day.

With such conversion, in effect, the euro will be launched on strong grounds. Coupled with the Stability and Growth Pact, which will anchor the fiscal policies, there is every expectation that the conversion criteria will hold in April 1998 and thereafter.

Of the four remaining members of the EU, Greece does not qualify by a long way, but the other three do so and with relative ease, except, obviously, for the exchange and interest rates. But they are not likely to join the first wave. On the other hand, however, we are now hearing statements by UK decision-makers in particular indicating that their future membership in the EMU is rather likely and might come sooner than thought before. I do not believe that Mr Blair's government will sign on for January 1999, but he is likely to do so once the euro becomes a going concern, perhaps in a couple of years from January 1, 1999. The financial institutions of the City are wholly in favour of joining, but politically Mr Blair must prepare his public opinion for a favourable referendum on joining, as he promised. The British public has long been fed jingoistic and economically slanted views on the EMU, always emphasizing what might go wrong with it. Only time and reality will change the public attitude. And when Britain joins, Sweden and even Denmark might have second thoughts about joining.

III. Why will the euro be a strong currency

Naturally, the relative economic size of the EU at 11, hereinafter the EU-11, the scope of its financial markets, and its large share in world trade, are all important economic indicators. In terms of population, the EU-11 is eight per cent larger than the USA, and the EU-15 some 40 per cent larger. At prevailing exchange rates, the EU-11 is only eight per cent smaller than the US economy, but the EU-15, is ten per cent larger (see Table 1). In terms of financial markets, leaving aside the size of domestic debt, the EU-11 is more than twice the size of the U.S. and Japan in the ratio of stock capitalization to GDP (see Table 2). These statistics nonetheless merely indicate the potential strength of the euro rather than substantiate a statement about its strength. The real reason for the likely strength of the euro lies in the nature of the underlying political and economic decisions which europe has made and will continue to make, as well as the type of macroeconomic policies they entail. The Europeans want first of all to redress a substantial deterioration in their public finances. Most European countries have reached the point where public budgets have approached 50 per cent of GDP, and in the Scandinavian countries these budgets are considerably higher than that. In 1991, the ratio of public debt to GDP in the EU-11 was 56 per cent. By 1996, it had reached 73.2 per cent. There is now a widely held judgement that reducing the ratio of public finance to GDP is a condition for growth and increased employment. This school of thought cites the examples of the UK, the Netherlands, Ireland, Belgium, Denmark and Spain, where growth took off after public finance reductions. Given that public finances have been mostly in deficit, it follows that, for a current account almost in balance, the volume of internal savings is not enough to finance the investments necessary for high rates of growth to deal with the twin challenges of applying the new information technologies in their economies and mopping up the observed unemployment phenomena, associated with the technological revolution and globalization. Besides, a strong euro means lower interest rates, which in the first place reduce the burden of the public debt, secondly do not put upward pressure on the euro, and lastly reduce the cost of invesment. Increased invesment is judged indispensable for high growth, which in turn is essential for easing the revenue constraints on public budgets. For example, two extra points over the current EU-11 growth trend would, in five years, transform public finances and cut significantly into unemployment. If one were to apply Okun's law (using the trend rate of growth of the EU-11),[6] it becomes evident that the solution to European unemployment and public finances surely depends, inter alia, on generating growth rates in the range of three to five per cent per annum in the various countries, as much as on structural reforms in the labour markets.

Such growth needs to be financed from a combination of higher domestic savings and/or foreign saving inflows. As the private saving ratio in the EU-11, at 21 per cent, is respectable, only public sector savings and/or a substantial decline in governments' absorption of domestic savings can fill the normative gap. It is thus clear that to attract foreign savings, there is a need for a stable and credible euro, characteristics of a strong currency. Up till now, individual European countries (e.g. Ireland, Spain) have succeeded in attracting European and other savings through fiscal and social dumping. This will not be possible in the future. Hence, the need to reform public finances and revive European growth. There is also an undeniable interconnection between the abilities of governments to remove the structural problems of European labour markets and their capacity to extend social safety nets to affected labourers. In the literature, the social safety net itself is considered by some a cause of structural rigidity. But this is conjectural, for there is no clear-cut empirical evidence showing the extent to which social benefits slow the search for employment. It is highly plausible that they do so, but the other factors, e.g. the availability of new jobs, the proper technical preparation of workers for these jobs and other factors of labour market flexibility, are of greater importance in the overall impact than safety nets. Nonetheless, without strong public finances, it will not be possible to effect the necessary structural reforms called for in the European labour markets while maintaining social harmony; without safety nets, there would be a severe political backlash against both European integration and globalization. Thus, there are fundamental economic and political reasons for the EU to insist on forging a strong and credible euro.

IV. The demand for the euro

At the present level of uncertainty, it is best to assess future demand for the euro on the basis of its three monetary functions: use in transactions, i.e. as a medium of exchange; a store of value by local residents and foreigners; and a unit of account, which is implicit in and dependent upon the previous two. The methodology employed is to use current indicators and then add or subtract possible changes, rather than the more rigorous method of estimation by structural equations.

A. The demand for the euro as a medium of exchange

This demand depends on the probable size of the membership. In principle, one can have three scenarios, namely EU-7, EU-11 and EU-15. But, as it was argued in section II above, EU-11 seems to be the most realistic scenario for the first wave. In view of the recent British declarations and their possible repercussions on Sweden and Denmark, however, it might also be useful to use estimates for the EU-15 scenario.[7]

The demand for the euro as a domestic medium of exchange can reasonably be equated to total current domestic demand at the current EMU central ECU rate, as it is most probable that the current reference rates of the ECU will be adopted for the euro in April 1988. In addition, one can use the present ratios of European to world trade as indicative of the short-run demand for the euro in international trade. On the present evidence, the total percentage share of five European currencies used in international trade, namely the French franc, the Deutsche mark, the lira, the guilder and the pound sterling, is 32 per cent. This contrasts with 48 per cent for the US dollar and only 5 per cent for Japan's yen. To gauge the potential of the euro, we can consider the long-run tendency in terms of the so-called 'coefficient of internationalization', i.e. the ratio of the EU-11, EU-15 currencies in use in international trade to the respective shares of the EU-11 and EU-15 in international trade. At the present, the five above-mentioned currencies yield an average coefficient of internationalization of 1.1. In the future it is expected a decline in the use of the dollar and an increase in the use of the euro resulting in a coefficient of internationalization of 2.35.[8] This long-run tendency would mean a substantial increase in the use of the euro over present levels and a corresponding decline for the US dollar. The tendency of equal coefficients is one probable benchmark. As one extends the time horizon, the magnitude of these coefficients might have to be adjusted downward to allow for an increasing role for an Asian currency such as the Chinese yuan or the yen. In sum, in the medium to long run, one can conclude that the use of the euro in international trade will double in relation to the present levels of use of the five European currencies.[9] But this will happen only gradually, after the euro establishes a reliable track record, and only if the EU carries out its present plans to extend its trading space to Eastern Europe and the Mediterranean basin.

B. *The demand for the euro as a store of value*

1. **Official foreign exchange reserves**[10]

Initially, there should be an approximately 15 per cent reduction in European holdings of reserves as a result of reserve consolidation in relation to intra-European imports. Europe, it should be recalled, conducts two-thirds of its trade among its own members. Its trade represents 25 per cent of its GDP, which would, *pari pasu*, imply a 15 per cent reduction in reserve holdings. This corresponds to $25 billion. After this initial period, there should be a gradual substitution in international official reserves in favour of the euro at the expense mostly of the US dollar. A strong euro with an established track record and a significant financial market will be a logical asset of diversification for official holdings. During the recent IMF-World Bank annual meeting in Hong Kong, many Asian officials expressed not only a keen interest in the euro, but also the intention to shift some holdings to it in the future.[11] Again, a good long-run scenario would be to consider equality with US dollar holdings, thereby implying a reduction of such dollar holdings to 40 per cent (from the current 56 per cent) and a doubling for euro holdings from the 20 per cent levels of the five European currencies to a future holding of 40 per cent in euros[12] (see Tables 3 and 4).

2. The demand for euro financial assets by non-residents

This includes demand for bonds, for equity and for all other financial securities (see Table 5). BIS and OECD current statistics show already that holdings in three European currencies, i.e. the Deuthsche mark, the pound sterling and the French franc, constitute some 28 per cent of international bond holdings as compared to 33.5 per cent for dollar bonds and 13 per cent for yen bonds. Moreover, in terms of total holdings of equity, bank assets and debt securities, EU-11 currencies account for 31.7 per cent of the total, and EU-15 for 41 per cent of the total. This compares to 34.4 and 24.6 per cent for the US and Japan respectively.[13] These figures, however, understate the extent of Europe's importance, because there are other European currency denominated bonds. The importance of the London market stands out in all these statistics, but whether the UK joins early or later the London market will shadow the euro bond market evolution. The conclusion is that euro denominated assets will be important in all financial markets, building on a relatively strong European ex post facto position vis-a-vis the US dollar.

The introduction of the euro will confer on euro financial assets several advantages over the present situation. These would include a reduction in transaction costs, the elimination of foreign exchange risk, the disappearance of entry barriers as well as regulatory and fiscal differences, and a considerable deepening in security trading across all maturities and instruments. The present indications are that the European Central Bank will be using repurchase agreements as its main operating tool. If, in the future, it moves out to more active open market operations, it will, in the manner of the US Federal Reserve System contribute to the development of an active EU security market.

In terms of non-resident equity holdings, the European position is strong despite the relative smallness of European stock capitalization in comparison with the dollar and yen domestic markets. Once the euro becomes a going concern, financial institutional restructuring and deepening of capitalization, whose signs are already in evidence, will propel the euro to an increased share in non-resident equity holdings from the present 34.2 per cent share. The same can be said regarding other financial security non-resident holdings (see the discussion below). But it should always be emphasised that the foreign exchange market apart, European financial markets, and by implication non-resident security holdings, are going to grow at the rhythm set by the restructuring, development and deepening of European financial markets; as we argue below, Europe has some catching up to do in this area.

The foreign exchange market represents a case apart, since not all its transactions are autonomous. Here again, the London market, the biggest in the world, is very important for Europe and for the future role of the euro in foreign exchange transactions. At present, dollar transactions constitute some 80 per cent of total foreign exchange transactions, with European currencies being counterparts in 70 per cent of them. The euro will cut into this dollar dominance in time, as its roles in security markets, in trade, in official reserve transactions and in speculative contracts, are all going to increase.

Finally, in this connection, one should bring up the implicit connection between the future role of euro, and hence the demand for it, and the financial diversification process of Asia and Latin America. In these two regions, the US dollar has had (along with the yen in Asia) a dominant role by virtue of both historical trade patterns and financial positioning and the dearth of viable alternatives to it on a massive scale. The diversification of Asian financial holdings, and perhaps later on Latin American holdings, will therefore be a very important factor for the future of both the international position of the US dollar and that of the euro. Unless Asia diversifies into an indigenous key currency, the expected shift in its portfolios will likely be at the expense of the US dollar and in favour of the euro. But here again, one is talking about long-term parity and not dominance.

V. The impact of the euro on financial markets and banks

Under the integrated financial and monetary space of the EMU, the European banks and the other financial institutions, together with financial markets, will experience a new situation in which many of the old practices, protected niches and local advantages will disappear. It is best to summarize these changes under the following subheadings:

A. Rating and yields on governments' securities

The rules of the single currency and the Stability Pact are such that it is no longer possible for member governments to borrow automatically as and when they deem fit. Up till now, government and government guaranteed securities were automatically accorded A ratings, precisely because of this unfettered ability to borrow and raise revenues. Henceforth, all members' securities will have to be rated by the financial markets. Since all members will abide by the same rules and follow one monetary policy, there should also be one yield curve for government securities. However, in view of differences in the perception of risk of the various members, the yield to maturity would diverge by a small risk differential. The financial markets, finding in the relationship between Canada and its states a similar constellation, now believe that the differences will similarly range over a band covering 10 to 40 basis points.[14]

B. Forward interest contracts and derivatives

The tendency for European interest rates to collapse within a narrow band around the yield curve, and the fact that there will be one single central spot rate, imply that forward rates, for a given set of foreign interest rates, will also collapse from some 20 or more at present to four to five rates for various maturities. Any differences will be arbitraged out by market operators throughout the one European financial space. But if the currency-based forward contracts and their derivatives become fewer, the same is likely to be not true regarding interest rate swaps. In this segment, there will be a considerable increase in liquidity as various currencies become perfect substitutes for each other. This is likely to enhance the use of interest swaps in general and go beyond the banking sector. The market will also encourage the creation of option contracts on interest rate spreads from the central benchmark rates. In sum, one looks for an increase in interest derivatives. Finally, it is likely that generic contracts for bond futures, instead of national bond options, will develop for euro denominated bonds, as in the USA.

C. Merger of the clearing houses and financial institutions

The merger of clearing houses into a few large ones, just like observed bank mergers, will accelerate, eliminating those incapable of covering the entire new euro market. In the months of August and September 1997, when this paper was conceived, more than two dozen acquisitions and mergers were effected among various financial institutions. This institutional reshuffling and repositioning will not wait till the euro is in circulation, but will be taking place as of now in order to be operational before the end of 1998. Since the euro settlement system, clearance facilities, cross-border lending, currency trading, security trading and derivative transactions will all be denominated in euros as of 1 January 1999, financial institutions must position themselves and prepare their capabilities right away. The European financial structure will evolve towards a few large institutions operating in the entire eurozone and offering products across the board, as well as some smaller specialized banks and institutions occupying specific niches.

D. *Legal problems of overlapping*

During the transition to a single circulating currency (1999-2000), there will be a variety of legal problems for banks and other institutions regarding conversion, reserve calculation procedures, accounting procedures, etc. as well as other dual system problems.

E. *Changes in the financial markets*

1. The bond market

All local bond markets in the EU-11 will be transformed and eventually subsumed by one euro denominated bond market and this will have implications for local bond dealerships. The factors that have favoured the local dealerships in the official and corporate bond segments were their knowledge of local conditions, their ability, based on their local networking, to assess correctly the risks of borrowers, whom they usually know and have dealt with often, and the local currency denomination of the bonds, sometimes conferred legal monopoly privileges. The empirical evidence garnered by study after study of local bond trading has shown a very close relationship between currency denomination and lead-bank identity.[15] It should be no surprise to market operators that all these factors except customer relationships will disappear in the unified eurobond market. While this is true on the demand side, the supply side might become pan-euro even faster. Clearly, European companies will want to borrow and float securities taking advantage of the entire market. And the same considerations should apply to the secondary market. Hence, the advent of one euro denominated bond market will sweep away most of the old established patterns of bond dealerships and result in considerable strengthening of the EU-11 denominated bond position. It would not be unrealistic to look for a relative share of 40 per cent of total bond issues. And it will be interesting to watch how this is going to play out as concerns the London market. As a matter of fact, not only are the City operators already positioning themselves on the continent's markets, but they will, most probably, hasten the British decision to join the single currency system. If that happens, the EU-15 would probably account for close to the half of world bond issues.

2. The equity markets

The factors driving local bond dealerships are similar to those prevailing in the equity markets. Hence, there should be a strong push toward one equity market throughout the eurozone. Such a unified equity market is likely to build up one electronic on-screen trading system of operations and one EMU settlement system, thereby increasing efficiency, cutting costs, and intensifying information availability and communication. Here again, the supply side will push and hasten the arrival of a pan-euro blue-chip market. However, equity capitalization (as a percentage of GDP), at 44 per cent in EU-11, lags considerably behind both the US, at 73 per cent, and Japan, at 79 per cent.[16] Hence, the advent of the euro will most likely impart a new impetus in terms of deepening the new single European equity market and building up the institutional capacity of its operators. Consequently, there should be considerable reshuffling, repositioning, capacity-building and creation of new alliances among European investment banks, brokerage firms and stock exchanges. This would imply consolidation and mergers among many institutions and a hunt for talent from the London City if the UK looks less likely to join soon.

3. Fund management

The management and market positioning of funds and the orientation of their strategies, as well as the business of portfolio advisory services, will undergo significant changes as a result of the euro. The situation up till now has been highly fragmented in the EU-11 national markets and differs across the EU markets. For example, in France, some 68 per cent of the funds are invested in short-term money market funds, while in the UK equity funds largely dominate the market. Here again, the euro will affect the factors that have shaped fund management and business relationships. These factors include: (i) customers' preference for home currency; (ii) funds' local marketing and distribution networks; and (iii) their economies of scale. Obviously, customers' preference for local currency will disappear in the not-too-distant future. Funds will continue to have advantages in marketing and distribution networks, and the factor of economies of scale will, if anything, be even stronger in larger euro-based funds. It should be noted however that regarding scale economies, there is a dearth of clear-cut empirical evidence about this factor.

It would thus be reasonable to conclude that eurozone-wide fund management and index trading in this market will gradually replace the present fragmented and differentiated situation. But all of this requires the evolution of institutional investing, which is rather underdeveloped in the EU-11.

4. Eurobanking and across-the-border banking operations

The European banks, in particular those of the City (London), have, over the past 35 years, been the important centres for what has been called the eurocurrency markets, the biggest segment of which is the eurodollar market.[17] This market has been driven by differences in regulations among countries, by the zero reserve cost of euro transactions, by the ease and low cost of the eurocurrency clearing system, especially the City, and by the availability of so many currencies desired by borrowers. Intra-bank transactions have constituted more than two-thirds of the very large volume of these markets. After the introduction of the euro, many of these factors will be transformed. On the assumption that the UK will not enter the eurosystem in the first wave, the difference in regulations will in principle obtain between EU-11 banks and London banks on the one hand and non-European banks on the other. Continental European regulations have become quite liberal in recent years and in a sense have approached those in the London market. Besides, to the extent that London will be shadowing the euro regulations, courtesy of the BIS work and the single market act, this factor should continue to be important only in relation to non-European banks, e.g. offshore and maybe US banks. The current indications from the European Monetary Institute are that the eurozone will have hardly any important reserve requirements. Moreover, the eurozone banks will be joining the Trans-European Automated Real-time Gross-Settlement Express Transfer system (TARGET system), which will complement national settlement systems but be compulsory for all monetary policy payments. If the London banks are not allowed to use the TARGET system, the effect of these factors on balance will be such that there will be some retrenchment in the operations of the eurocurrency markets of the first-wave-country currencies and London as well as in the eurosterling operations in favour of off-shore markets. Since there is a strong correlation between the currency of eurolending and the nationality of the borrower, the implication is that lending in Euro will cut into the lending business of the eurocurrency markets. The correspondent bank relationships will keep the intra-bank circuit busy, but the operation of the TARGET system will gradually shift some operations to the continent. Of all the factors which affect the banking business, only the customer relationship and local expertise in credit risk assessment are likely to persist as before.

The tendency for consolidating all the wholesale business of banks in big pan-euro entities (interest rate derivatives, bond trading, spot rate derivatives) will affect non-specialized banks, in particular middle-size banks in small member countries, thereby promoting niche banking for smaller entities.

The importance of London as a dominant financial centre, using English in its operations, will not be much affected. However, the City banks will have to source and offer end-products in euros, which implies expansion in their continental operations. The City will not be in a position to offer competitive regulatory advantages over the Euro banks lest its connections to the continent and the TARGET be placed in jeopardy.

VI. The macroeconomic implications of the euro

The macroeconomic effects of the euro can be discussed in two contexts: that of the EMU countries and the EU and that of the rest of the world. The latter will be taken up in section VII below.

A. The type of macroeconomic policies of the EU-11

Regarding the macroeconomic impact on the EU countries, especially the participating ones, it is best to start from where these countries are at present. The participating countries all have low interest rates, low inflation rates (below 2.7 per cent), rather stable exchange rates, historically low budget deficits but high rates of unemployment, especially in the larger countries (France, Germany, Spain, Italy), and slow rates of GDP growth. The EU-11 countries have public finances which, for the most part, have public debt at 60-80 per cent of GDP but over 120 per cent for Belgium and Italy. Their domestic saving rates, at 21 per cent, are generally satisfactory, and their overall balance of payments at $0.8 billion, is almost in balance. This situation means that the most pressing economic policy issues are unemployment and low growth rates, the state of public finances, the health and financial credibility of the euro after it is launched and the course of European integration. Having surrendered monetary policy to the would-be European Central Bank (ECB) and tied their fiscal policies to the objectives of the 'Stability and Growth Pact' of Dublin, their hopes for higher growth rates and lower unemployment now reside in stronger investment performance of the business sector, increases in productivity and structural reforms in the European labour markets. The state of public finances will be ameliorated by the observance of the conversion criteria and its continuance after the launching of the euro (the Stability Pact). That means that the only instrument of policy to shore up the euro and keep inflation under control will be in the hands of the ECB. The question therefore is whether stronger business investment and gains in productivity are in the cards.

One cannot be sure of the answer to this critical question. The single market has not yet produced all its effects. Various estimates place the gains in GDP growth on account of the larger market, the lower transaction costs and the cumulative multiplier effects at anywhere between half and one and a half percentage point over the short to medium term. This implies a growth performance for the EU-11 in the range of 2.0-3.5 per cent, still not high enough to mop up unemployment at a socially acceptable speed. Beyond that, not much more can be said about investment and productivity gains except in terms of a determined effort to cut the fiscal charges on European enterprises, a proposition which would weaken further the state of public finances.

Labour market structural reforms are needed in the EU-11 but, as argued elsewhere in this paper, they need the continued existence of social safety nets to be politically and socially feasible. And the state of public finances in the EU-11, as well as observance of the Stability Pact, will make it difficult to maintain, let alone increase, state expenditures for these purposes. Thus, the hope is that the EU, with the euro, will spur investment and productivity gains well into the upper ranges of these estimates.

Turning now to the last of these policy questions, namely the health and credibility of the euro, the ECB has what this requires and is likely to pursue prudent monetary policies for some time to come.

B. *The type of monetary policy under the ECB*

All indications are now that the ECB will use monetary aggregate and direct inflation targeting. There is some evidence that there is an EU-11 stable monetary demand function,[18] a necessary condition for successful monetary targeting. But two factors might mitigate against the future stability of this function. The first is the degree to which international demand for the euro will balk in relation to domestic demand. If this turns out to be large, then it is likely to impart volatility to the money demand function and render monetary aggregates unstable and not useful for monetary policy. The second is the fact that it is after the introduction of the euro and the transformation of the EU-11 financial scene that one would expect a very high degree of financial innovation. If so, the ECB will find itself in the same position as the US Federal Reserve in the early 1980s, when quantitative targeting broke down because of the speed of financial innovation and the resultant instability of the money demand function. In other words, aggregate targeting might not be reliable for monetary policy if volatility and financial innovations become important. In the event, the ECB might have to concentrate on inflation stabilization, which would necessitate adjusting the euro exchange rate and interest rates to protect its inflation targets.

C. Shocks and macroeconomic stability

The consolidation of intra-European trade (two-thirds of Europe's trade) and the unification of currencies should enhance the synchronization of the business cycle in the EMU. Indeed, the empirical evidence gained during the EMS shows significant cyclical synchronization among the members. According to a study by UBS economic research, all the EU-11 members except Portugal, Ireland and Italy had very high cyclical synchronization with Germany. In the case of Spain, its slight desynchronization was compensated by low volatility.[19] Furthermore, compared to the period 1975-1981, that of 1982-1989, shows a decline in output volatility for all EU-11 countries except Ireland, Germany, Spain and the Netherlands.

This evidence bodes well for the EU-11 cyclical synchronization, thereby sparing it stabilization policy conflicts among member countries. However, the consolidation of the EU-11 trade (about two-thirds) and the unification of currencies and exchange rates, might produce two opposite effects: a strong transmission of macroeconomic shocks via trade and investment but a locked-in step of cyclical phasing. The literature of Optimal Currency Areas suggests that internal shocks would be adjusted out by labour and capital movement and Federal transfers. In the EU-11, labour mobility, despite the single market act, remains low and will continue to be hampered by linguistic and sociological differences. Capital mobility is by contrast very high. The policy question is whether the direction of capital movement would be towards the adversely affected members. Regarding fiscal transfers from the centre, the EU-11 has neither a Federal budget nor an effective Solidarity Fund. This is in sharp contrast to federated states such as the US and Canada.

Hence, there might be some problems on that score since the exchange rate will be no longer a policy instrument.

Concerning external shocks, the critical issue is whether they will be symmetrical or hit different countries differently. Asymmetrical shocks are what one would worry about. If they happen, then the ECB cannot do much about them, and no member country would have monetary instruments to cope with them. But, if as a result of the Stability Pact and revived EU-11 growth, a fiscal surplus develops, then there would be room for individual countries to cope with asymmetric external shocks, and naturally, internal ones as well.

D. EU members outside the EMU and the exchange rates

For EU members not in the EMU, the EMU II arrangement is supposed to apply. This is identical to the EMU I arrangement except for the wider margins allowed and its voluntary nature. In particular, if the UK or Sweden were to decide to join the eurozone early on after January 1999, then both the current exchange rates and interest rates in these countries must be considered in relation to the euro. The pound sterling is at a historically high exchange rate in relation to the EU-11 currencies, and interest rates are some two points higher than, say, in Germany of France. The critical question is the level of the pound that financial markets would judge sustainable in the long run. It would seem to this observer that the pound is now at too high a level to join the euro at an economically sustainable rate. This implies a good margin for decline of the prevailing interest rates in the UK before the latter joins.

Last spring, the French press was awash with debate regarding the future exchange rate of the euro in relation to the US dollar, as well as the French franc parity to the euro. Naturally, this debate relates primarily to the French trade position and Europe's future competitiveness vis-a-vis the USA and other countries. That France has been a trade-surplus country did not deter public figures from advocating lower exchange rates to shore up competitiveness. The real worry behind this is jobs and trade shares in the global economy. The ECB's primary occupation will be to defend a sustainable exchange rate compatible with very low inflation. On this score, it will primarily pay attention to the credibility of the euro. It is doubtful that it can engineer a 'desired exchange rate' vis-a-vis the US dollar or any other currency. Only by shifting the internal saving investment balance in the EU-11, by obtaining an improved fiscal balance, and by achieving a satisfactory relationship between the cyclical phase of the EU-11 and that of other countries can the euro exchange rate be affected in the long run. Naturally, the other possibility is increased European productivity, the answer for which is not a simple one.

VII. International implications of the euro

A. The euro as an alternative to the US dollar

Elements of this discussion have already been presented in Sections III-IV above. The international implication is that, for the first time, all portfolio holders and all traders will have a viable alternative to the US dollar. This is the result of several inherent attributes of the would-be currency of the EU-11: a large share in world trade; deep, diversified and open financial markets; and, thanks to the ECB, the Stability and Growth Pact, the Maastricht conversion criteria and the economic interests of the EU-11, a probably credible track for the euro. Naturally, substitution and conversion will take place not overnight, but gradually and pari pasu with the establishment of credibility of the euro and the monetary policies of the ECB. Fore developing countries and their firms and businesses who hold their reserves and assets mostly in US dollars, this will open up a large window of diversification.

B. The euro as another denominator and an international unit of account

Related to the financial and means-of-payment functions of the euro, its use as a unit of account and an international pegging currency will also inevitably expand at the expense of the US dollar. In this function, it will not eclipse the dollar but will tend to strike a semblance of balance with it, reflecting the international importance of the EU-11. It will not be surprising to see the euro used in the future in oil transactions, in commodity pricing and in international service contracts, domains where the dollar has kept for itself what the French call *une chasse gardée*.

One implication of this is its possible impact on developing countries' barter terms of trade. Because Europe is a very large trade partner of Africa, the Middle East and Eastern Europe and a large partner of Asia and Latin America, the euro will have a stabilizing influence on these countries barter terms of trade, i.e. the balance of export and import values.[20] Beyond these terms, the broader terms of trade effects will depend on how liberal the EU-11 will be on technology transfer, investment and developing country service. In the final analysis, the impact of the euro on developing countries is only a part of the EU effect on these countries. In this respect, it will be imperative to divide the developing countries into three subgroups: those with which the EU has had bilateral agreements, those which are covered under the Lomé system, and those for which the EU-11 is an important commercial and financial partner. One would have to compare the situation of these countries in relation to the EU-11 before January 1999 and after this date to arrive at meaningful conclusions. This, however, would take us far afield in this paper, and hence will not be attempted.

C. The international repercussions of the ECB and EU-11 macroeconomic policies

The macroeconomic policies of the EU-11 to some extent shape the external economic environment of other countries. If the policy judgements of the previous two sections turn out to be correct, then it is reasonable to say that the EU-11 and its ECB will be pursuing, as of January 1999, prudent, rather tight, fiscal and monetary policies that meet the strictures of the Stability and Growth Pact. If that is the case, two scenarios are possible: one is for the EU-11 to achieve the fiscal surplus aimed for in the Stability Pact without deterioration of domestic savings. In this event, the euro will, after initial volatility, stabilize and move on a slightly mounting curve allowing for a reduction in EU-11 interest rates and a reduction in uncertainty, with the combined effect of increasing EU-11 investment and growth. If, however, this favourable situation does not materialize, the opposite will take place for the euro, interest rates and investment and growth. The repercussions of these alternative scenarios on exports, imports and investment are straightforward.

Regarding the external value of the euro, initially there will be an excess supply of dollars in EU-11 official reserves as a result of EU-11 intra-trade internalization. This should put downward pressure on the dollar. But both the ECB attitude about allowing this to happen, i.e. allowing the euro to appreciate, and the likely wait-and-see attitude of many financial portfolio holders would mitigate against a short-term euro appreciation. The financial markets will inevitably test the ECB resolve initially. Thus, there should be initial volatility in the foreign exchange market. This, however, will not destabilize the EU-11, economies as the weight of their external sector will drop to the level of the US (11 per cent). Thereafter, if the ECB establishes its credibility, there will be reduced uncertainty. Because of this and on account of the EU-11's acquired unified international weight, international interest rates might go down.

The favourable scenario sketched above, and for that matter the unfavourable one, will depend on where the EU-11 and the US are in their respective cyclical phase. The US is now leading the EU-11 cyclically. If the US economy flattens out and Europe does not experience a sudden pick-up in growth, then one might expect lower interest rates and perhaps a slight initial appreciation of the dollar. This might be helpful to the ECB for establishing and initial favourable external rate against the dollar and other currencies. If, however, Europe picks up immediately and tight monetary policies ensue, then this initial phase might result in appreciation of the euro from the start.

For developing countries, the EU-11 attitude and economic performance regarding imports and investment are other aspects to consider. If the EU-11's fiscal tightening does not increase after January 1999 and their imports from developing countries do not suffer a trade substitution (especially from new members and Eastern Europe), then the euro's introduction should be positive for these countries. Regarding investment, all depends on the direction of net EU-11 capital flows: will Europe attract more international capital investment after January 1999 than it has done up till now, thereby reducing the attractiveness of developing countries for direct private investors, or will Europe be a source of international private direct investment for developing countries rather than a competition. The overall effect would depend on the balance of these two eventualities.

D. Implications for the international monetary system (IMS)

If the initial phase of the euro with its expected exchange rate volatility does not pass quickly, the US and other members of the IMS might find it necessary to call for co-operative arrangements to control such volatility. And this might open up the question of how to deal with the international dollar overhang through some orderly consolidation and substitution arrangement.

The introduction of the euro will in any event have two important IMS implications: one is that it will increase the importance of currency blocs in the IMS; Europe, the US and Japan will become three central poles for currency blocs. The second is that the attitude of the US towards the external value of the dollar will have to shift from 'benign neglect', to one of seriousness if developments do not favour US interests. Thus, the IMS key currencies, namely the dollar and the euro, will attract competitive attention from their policy-makers. There is, however, a school of thought that argues that the EU-11 will have the same 'benign neglect' attitude as the USA. This writer finds this view doubtful; the EU-11 and its ECB will have interest in the credibility of the euro, and the euro's financial displacement effects on the dollar will not permit the past 'benign neglect' attitude of the USA to continue into the future without doing serious damage to the international position of the US dollar; nothing less than forcing asset settlement upon the US is at stake.

Will the euro discourage the development of a reformed IMS based on the SDR? The question has two parts to it: the reform of the IMS itself and the future of the SDR. On the first question, on balance, it can be surmised that an IMS less dominated by one member is likely to be a system more accepting of reform and change. Whether the SDR is part of such a change is, however, an entirely different question. For the time being, it is difficult to see a role for the SDR except as a source of extra liquidity in the event that neither the US nor the EU wants to allow its own monetary expansion. Only if these two giants want to promote a role for the SDR, by will or necessity, will it get anywhere.

Finally, will the euro, and the European construction in general, shift the balance of decision-making in the IMF? In terms of economic policy and vision, the EU-11 will not have a different attitude and policy approach than what we have seen up till now. But as one big bloc, the EU's more unified voice in the IMF councils will mark a difference from the present dispersion, and perhaps lend muscle to its hitherto muted differences with the US.

Notes and references

1. Between January 1999 and 2002, several arrangements will be put in place: the European Central Bank (ECB) will start denominating its bonds in euros, and the euro will be used in all the operations of the ECB, including reserve management and open market operations. All wholesale operations will be channelled via the Trans-European Automated Real-time Gross-Settlement Express Transfer system (TARGET).
2. See M. Sakbani, *The Euro Debate: Evaluation of the Issues*, 1 May 1997, internal memorandum for the Secretary-General of UNCTAD; also M. Sakbani, *The Advent of the European Single Currency: Implications and Consequences*, 27 March 1997, internal memorandum to the Secretary-General of UNCTAD.
3. This group of 11 EMU members will be referred to throughout as the EU-11.

4. Italy's determination to meet the criterion of 3 per cent is a political decision by its governing leadership not necessarily shared by all the components of its left-centre coalition. It will be interesting to see if the main coalition partners can carry with them the more extreme ones, or Mr Prodi's government will have to resign.
5. Belgium and Italy have exceeded 120 per cent, and most of the other EU-11 are in a band between 60 and 80 per cent.
6. The formula is: $\Delta U = -5(r_y - 1.5)$, where ΔU is change in European (EU-11) unemployment and r_y is the EU average weighted annual growth rate of real income. The EU-11 rate of income trend is taken at 1.5 per cent. It should be added that Okun's law is a statistical relationship derived from US data. Even though the EU-11 trend rate was substituted in it, the other coefficient might not be exact for the EU-11. The reader should therefore take the quantitative estimates as approximate.
7. The inclusion or exclusion of Greece makes no appreciable difference to the data.
8. The absolute figures are derived by multiplying the coefficient by whatever annual trade flow estimates, given the velocity involved.
9. Calculating on the basis of the five European currencies should actually understate the potential use of the euro, as even with an EU-11, the EU currencies outside the EMU will to a large extent be shadowing the euro under the EMU II arrangement.
10. The demand for official reserves is, in part, a demand for a medium of exchange to pay, principally, for imports. But with the increased international liquidity of transnationals and the increasing dominance of the private sector in international transactions, this type of demand is decreasing. Official reserve holdings are increasingly managed as a state-owned financial portfolio of 'liquidity securities', much as commercial banks do with their short-term financial assets.
11. See, for example, the account in *Le Monde*, 15 September 1997, p. 4, on the discussions of M. Yves Thibault de Silguy, the monetary affairs Commissioner of the EU, with Asian officials.
12. Actually, if ECU holdings are added up to those in five European currencies, then it can be said that the percentage share of Europe would go up from the present 26.7 to 40, a more reasonable departure point and in line with total asset denominations.
13. The figures were calculated on the basis of BIS and other data reported in an IMF publication. See Prati & Schinasi, 'What Impact will EMU have on European Securities Markets?', *Finance & Development*, September 1997, p. 48.
14. See Detken & Manzini, 'Further Convergence of bond yields in the EMU', pp. 6-8, in *Swiss Bank Corporation, Economic & Financial Prospects*, April 1997.
15. See, for empirical evidence, Federal Reserve Bank of New York, *International Competitiveness of U.S. Financial Firms*, Staff Study, 1991; Feldman & Stephenson, 'Stay Small or Get Huge: Lessons from Security Trading', *Harvard Business Review*, May-June 1996, pp. 116-123. M. Fox, 'Aspects of Barriers to International Integrated Security Markets', *Journal of International Securities Markets*, Winter 1992.
16. However, within the EU, this ratio varies from 16 per cent in Austria to above 105 per cent in the UK.
17. A eurocurrency deposit is one made in other than the national currency of the bank involved.

18. See Carlo Monticelli and Luca Papi, *European Integration, Monetary Coordination and the Demand for Money*, Oxford, 1996.
19. See Nannette Hechler–Fayd Herbe, 'Is a large EMU unstable', *UBS International Finance*, October 1997, pp. 9-10.
20. This stabilization effect concerns mainly the foreign exchange volatility factor and differences in price and income elasticities among trading partners.

Table 1. Comparative indicators

Country	Population	CDP in billions of US$	Gr. of GDP per annum	Price inflation	Imp/GDP
USA	260	7.6 (00)	2.0	2.7	10.2 (18.3)[a]
Japan	125	4.6 (00)	1.7	0.8	6.0 (15)
EU-7	177	4.7 (00)	2.5	2.6	14.0 (30)
EU-11	287	6.8 (00)	1.9	3.5	11 (22.5)
EU-15	370	8.5 (00)	1.8	3.6	8.7 (17.5)

(a) Figures in brackets denote percentage of total trade.
Source: UNCTAD Handbook & OECD statistics.

Table 2. Financial indicators & capital markets

	Foreign exchange market				Stock exchange		
Country	Daily averages	Share of trans.	Domestic debt	Int. debt securities	Market capitalization	Ratio to GDP	Average daily trading
USA	$245b	16%	$113	$435b	$5,655b	72%	12.2
Japan	$161b	11%	$49	$204b	$3,545b	76%	3.6
EU-7	$212b	13.5%	$41	$754b	$1,528b	43%	n.a.
EU-11	$261b	16.6%	$62	$915b	$1,933b	35%	n.a.
EU-15	$778b	50%	$76	$1,417b	$3,526b	49%	n.a.

Source: OECD secretariat & publications.

Table 3. Official reserve holdings excluding gold (end of 1996)

Country	Holdings totals and $ shares
USA	$65b
Japan	$215b
EU-7	$136b[a] of which $ share 126b
EU-11	$213b of which $ share 142b
EU-15	$280b of which $ share 246b
Rest of the world	$763b of which $ share 418b

(a) Net of own currencies.
Source: UNCTAD Handbook, OECD publications.

Table 4. Changes in currency shares of foreign exchange holdings (1990-1995)

Currencies	1990 (%)	1995 (%)
US dollar	50.3	56.4
Japanese yen	8.2	7.1
Five European Currencies[a]	25.2	20.2
ECU	9.6	6.5
Other currencies	6.7	9.7
Memo item: share of five European Currencies + ECU	34.8	26.7

(a) D.M., French Franc, Pound £, Dutch G., Swiss F.
Source: Various issues of IMF annual reports.

Table 5. Actual non-resident portfolio holdings of financial assets in various currency denomination (end of 1996)

Asset	3 European currencies[a]	$	Yen	Other currencies[c]
Bonds	28%	33.5%	13%	25.5
Equity	34.2	32.5%	9%	23
All financial assets[b]	32%	39%	14%	15

(a) £, D.M., F. Franc.
(b) Shares in all financial assets are calculated from BIS data.
(c) These are residuals.
Source: OEDC publications.

9 Does EMU Need to Converge on the US Model?

Daniel Gros and Erik Jones

All signs indicate that Europe will form an economic and monetary union (EMU) on the 1st of January 1999. However, for many in Europe, the political determination to construct EMU does not resolve concerns about the political viability of a European monetary union. The reason for this is straightforward. As with other aspects of European integration, monetary union is unprecedented both as a process and as a collection of institutions. Because EMU does not resemble the economic arrangements within the member states or other industrial democracies, the concern is that EMU will not be able to reproduce the political stability apparent in existing monetary unions.

The difference between EMU and existing monetary unions most often singled out is the absence of common fiscal institutions to support a common monetary policy. The argument is that while monetary conditions (meaning interest and inflation rates) tend to be roughly the same across a monetary union, economic performance varies from place to place and sector to sector. The supportive role of common fiscal institutions, then, is twofold. On the one hand, such institutions redistribute income to groups who are (or perceive themselves to be) disadvantaged by the common monetary policy; and, on the other hand, fiscal institutions provide a mechanism for stabilizing regional or sectoral economic performance in response to region- or sector-specific shocks.

The point to note is that the supportive role of common fiscal institutions is also an indirect one: the fiscal institutions present in existing monetary unions were not designed to support a common monetary policy per se, and the beneficiaries of state redistribution are not targeted on the basis of their vulnerability to fluctuations in monetary variables. Nevertheless, common fiscal institutions effect a redistribution and stabilization in support of the monetary regime. Put another way, the assumption behind the argument for common fiscal institutions is that these redistribution and stabilization functions are necessary to ensure that all parts of the monetary union agree on (or are at least willing to accept) the direction of the common monetary policy.

If the redistribution and stabilization functions of common fiscal institutions are not available, so the argument runs, the direction of monetary policy will become a politically contentious issue under EMU. What we see now as a consensus in favour of constructing a monetary union will turn into dissension about what policy the monetary union should adopt – to borrow from the language of EMU, what constitutes 'price stability' as opposed to excessive inflation or unnecessary deflation. In the worst case, this tension will lead either to a dissolution of EMU; or to an oscillation in the direction of monetary policy depending upon which groups happen to be more powerful at any given point in time.

Concern for the absence of common fiscal institutions has a long pedigree, and relies on analysis of existing monetary unions for support. The obvious case in point in this context is the United States, if only because the US approximates the European Union in the size of its population and economy, and in terms of the diversity of its industrial output and its economic geography. Numerous studies estimate the extent to which US fiscal institutions redistribute and stabilize income across the United States. And, while the results of such studies are ambiguous in the detail, there appears to be broad agreement in the assumption that common fiscal institutions do play some role in holding the US monetary union together.

Thus, the question we ask is 'Does EMU need to converge on the US model?' In other words, does the European Union require a set of common fiscal institutions in order to unite and maintain political support behind a common monetary policy? This question holds particular importance in light of the 'stability pact' – an agreement among potential EMU participants to sanction fiscal impropriety as defined through the excessive deficits procedure of the Maastricht Treaty. The heads of state and government have not only rejected the creation of common fiscal institutions, they have also constrained the use of counter-cyclical fiscal policy at the level of member states. In their enthusiasm to ensure that fiscal politics does not interfere with the functioning of the common monetary policy, critics argue, the signatories of the stability pact seem to have overlooked the widespread belief that fiscal institutions function to ensure political support for EMU.

We argue that Europe does not need to converge on the US model because the functions of US fiscal institutions can be reproduced by the member state without lifting the constraints of the stability pact. Moreover, given the different economic and institutional structures of the member states, national fiscal policy should provide a better redistribution and stabilization of income performance for affected sectors or regions than a unionwide approach. This argument is divided into four parts. The first reviews the evidence for redistribution and stabilization in the United States. The second considers how many of these functions derive from fiscal institutions and how many from fiscal politics. The third examines the extent to which member states are free to undertake redistribution or stabilization through national fiscal institutions within the constraints imposed by the stability pact. Finally, the fourth considers which groups are likely to be (or to perceive themselves to be) disadvantaged under a common monetary policy, as well as how this concern can be best addressed.

Redistribution and stabilization in the US

Our analysis of the role of federal fiscal institutions in supporting the US monetary union builds upon the recent work by Bayoumi and Masson (1995). Bayoumi and Masson obtain estimates of the redistribution and stabilization afforded by the US federal fiscal system using regression analysis of state or regional per capita income relative to national per capita income before and after accounting for all federal fiscal flows – meaning government transfers to individuals, federal grants to state and local government, personal contributions to social insurance, and personal income taxation. The redistribution effect of the US federal fiscal system is captured through cross-section regression analysis of the ratio of regional-to-national levels of per capita income after all fiscal flows as a function of a similar ratio before all fiscal flows.

$$\frac{Y^a_i}{Y^a_n} = \alpha_i + \beta_i \left(\frac{Y^b_i}{Y^b_n}\right) + \varepsilon_i \tag{1}$$

In interpreting equation (1), Y is per capita income, the superscripts a and b represent 'after' and 'before' all federal fiscal flows, while the subscript i represents an individual region or state of the US and the subscript n represents the United States as a whole. The coefficient for estimation, b_i, signifies how closely the two ratios move together, and so the difference between unity and the estimated coefficient indicates the degree of redistribution. Finally, in this and all subsequent equations we use 'real' (price-deflated) rather than nominal measures of income per capita.

In order to capture the stabilization effect of the US federal fiscal system, Bayoumi and Masson rely on time-series regression analysis of *changes* in the ratio of regional or state per capita income to national per capita income both before and after all federal fiscal flows.

$$-\left(\frac{Y^a_i}{Y^a_n}\right)_t = \alpha_i + \beta_i \_\left(\frac{Y^b_i}{Y^b_n}\right)_t + \varepsilon_{it} \qquad (2)$$

This equation (2) is interpreted in much the same way as equation (1), however it relies on year-on-year changes in the relevant ratio's (rather than the ratio levels), each denoted with the subscript t. Moreover, Bayoumi and Masson constrain the estimated coefficient to be equal across all states or regions, while allowing the constant and error terms to vary from region to region or state to state.

Using data from the period 1969-1986, Bayoumi and Masson estimate that the redistribution effect of the federal fiscal system works to mitigate differences in the levels of per capita income across states or regions at a rate of about 22 cents per dollar. Meanwhile, the US federal fiscal system stabilizes regional per capita income changes at a somewhat higher rate of approximately 30 cents per dollar. These findings are summarized in Table 1.

Table 1. Federal fiscal redistribution and stabilization in the United States

Equation	β_i	R^2	D.W.	Sample period
Equation (1) - Redistribution	0.781 (0.028)	0.945	n.a.	1969-86
Equation (2) - Stabilization	0.698 (0.018)	0.69-0.96	1.55-2.81	1965-86

Note: data from equation (1) are averages over the time period while data from equation (2) are ranges across the different regions examined. Standard errors are in parentheses.
Source: Bayoumi and Masson (1995) pp. 260, 264.

These estimates suggest that the US federal fiscal system plays an important role in underwriting the US monetary union – one which compensates for more than one-fifth of all persistent per capita income differentials and almost one-third of all temporary and idiosyncratic per capita income fluctuations. And while it remains unclear how these effects work to strengthen political support for a common monetary policy across US regions, such findings tend to reinforce assertions that a European EMU may have to converge on the US model.

Nevertheless, Bayoumi and Masson do not fully agree with the 'convergent' interpretation of their findings. In a concluding section to their inquiry they suggest that the stabilization effect apparent in the United States could be reproduced by the European member states at the national level and without creating a unionwide fiscal system. As evidence for this assertion, they point to regression estimates of equation (2) made using data for changes in the ratio of per capita income in five European countries (Germany, France, the UK, Belgium, and the Netherlands) to the average for the five. For the time period 1972 to 1989, Bayoumi and Masson estimate that national fiscal systems in the five European countries effectively stabilized per capita income after all taxes and transfers at a rate of about 31 cents per dollar change relative to the average for the five. Table 2 provides a summary of their regression statistics.

Table 2. National stabilization in five European countries

Equation	β_i	R^2	D.W.	Sample period
Equation (2) - Stabilization	0.692 (0.114)	0.45-0.83	1.32-2.47	1972-89

Note: data are ranges across the five countries examined (Germany, France, the United Kingdom, the Netherlands, Belgium). Standard errors are in parentheses.
Source: Bayoumi and Masson (1995) p. 267.

On the basis of these findings, Bayoumi and Masson claim that common fiscal institutions are not required for a stabilization of relative performance in per capita income across countries because separate national fiscal policies generate the same apparent effect. This claim is curious, however, because the assumption behind the argument for common fiscal institutions is that the redistribution and stabilization effects of such institutions are unintentional and therefore determined by the *structure* of the institutions and the flows of funds from region to region or state to state. If it is relevant to test for stabilization in the absence of common fiscal institutions, then surely it is also relevant to consider whether any redistribution or stabilization actually takes place across regions, and not across individuals and groups within (as well as across) regions, and whether it is fiscal politics that generates the apparent redistribution and stabilization in the US case rather than fiscal institutions.

Individuals versus regions and institutions versus policy

The difficulty with applying the framework used by Bayoumi and Masson at the European level is twofold. To begin with, it is necessary to consider the extent to which the redistribution afforded by the US federal fiscal system is directed at geographic states or at individuals or groups of individuals within and across states: clearly a programme directed at individuals can be replicated at the national level, while a programme designed to redistribute income from one geographic region to another would require some sort of common fiscal institution. We addressed this question with regard to the United States in a previous paper (Gros, 1993) and with surprising results. By using cross-section regression analysis to examine the flow of federal grants-in-aid per capita as a function of state per capita income and the share of agriculture in state income (to which 28 per cent of all grants are directed), it is possible to show that the net effect of the grants-in-aid programme is to exacerbate per capita income differences across states. Clearly a grants-in-aid programme targeted at income differentials across states would not have such an effect. For example, a similar analysis of EU structural funds shows that these funds do work to mitigate income differences across regions and countries. We conclude from this analysis that the redistribution function of the US federal fiscal system is directed at individuals and groups of individuals rather than at geographic states or regions. Therefore, the redistribution function of the US federal fiscal system can be replicated by the European member states.

A second difficulty with applying Bayoumi and Masson's framework to the European level is to distinguish between the effects of common institutions and the effects of common fiscal policy in generating the apparent stabilization of state or regional per capita income in the United States. We achieve this separation by introducing a measure of year-on-year change in the difference between national per capita income before and after all federal fiscal flows as an explanatory variable in the time series regression analysis of equation (2). The difference between national per capita income before and after all federal fiscal flows represents the common fiscal policy, and so the change in this difference represents a change in the common fiscal policy. A point to note here is that we do not include government purchases of goods and services in this notion of fiscal policy. Rather we focus exclusively on the balance between taxes as transfers as they effect personal income. The gamma (g_i) coefficient in equation (3) represents the impact of an increase or decrease of the difference between national per capita income before and after all federal fiscal flows on the change in the ratio of regional or state per capita income to national per capita income after all federal fiscal flows.

(3)

$$_-(\frac{Y_i}{Y^a_n})_t = \alpha_i + \beta_{i\_}(\frac{Y_i}{Y^b_n})_t + \gamma_{i\_}(Y^b_n - Y^a_n)_t + \varepsilon_{it}$$

We estimated this equation twice – once using the regional data relied on by Bayoumi and Masson and adopting the convention of holding the b_i coefficient constant across regions, and once using state data and allowing the b_i coefficient to vary from state to state. The relevant results were comparable in both cases, however, because we are interested in the variability of apparent stabilization across states we report on the state-by-state statistics below. Through our regression analysis of equation (3) we discovered that fully 60 per cent of the apparent stabilization of changes in the ratio of state-to-national per capita income derives from changes in national fiscal policy and not from the automatic workings of the common fiscal institutions. Our regression statistics are reported in Table 3.

Table 3. Stabilization as a function of institutions and policy

Equation	β_i	g_i	R^2	D.W.
Equation 3 - stabilization	0.86	-0.72	0.64-0.98	1.38-3.27
	(0.07)	(0.17)		

Note: time period is 1970-1989; coefficient estimates and standard errors (in parentheses) are averages; R-squared and Durbin Watsin statistics are ranges; sample is fifty US states plus the District of Columbia.

These statistics indicate that the common fiscal institutions of the US federal fiscal system provide an automatic stabilization of state per capita income after all federal fiscal flows of only about 14 cents on the dollar. The rest of the stabilization reported by Bayoumi and Masson is accounted for by changes in the national fiscal policy, meaning changes in the difference between per capita income before and after taxes at the national level. This finding is consistent with the methodology used by Bayoumi and Masson, as well as with their general conclusions.[1] In effect, all we have done is to separate the automatic stabilization from the policy effect.

This depiction of national fiscal policy as the difference between national per capita income before and after all federal fiscal flows builds on conventional notions of the stabilizing effects of national fiscal policy across the business cycle. When economic activity slows in the country as a whole, per capita tax revenues decline and per capita transfers increase. And, when economic activity accelerates, per capita tax revenues increase while per capita transfers decline.

Yet, if national fiscal policy is the primary mechanism responsible for the stabilization of regional income performance, then it is relevant to ask whether tension exists between this fiscal stabilization of relative income performance and fiscal redistribution to offset permanent income differentials. The logic behind the question is straightforward: if the stabilization is successful, why are income differentials so persistent; alternatively, if transfers work continuously to offset persistent income differentials, how can they serve an appropriate stabilization function?

In a first attempt to answer these questions we analysed the coefficients for automatic (β_i) and policy-induced (g_i) stabilization through cross-section regression analysis by state against a sample of industrial and demographic indicators: the shares of state income derived from mining and farming, as well as the shares of state population comprised of persons under 15 years of age (young) or older than 65 years of age (elderly). The regression statistics are reported in Table 4.

Table 4. The role of industrial and demographic structures in fiscal stabilization

Explanatory variable	β_i	g_i
Constant	0.83 (0.258)	-3.06 (0.614)
Mining income	-0.013 (0.006)	0.042 (0.014)
Farm income	0.010 (0.005)*	0.028 (0.013)
Elderly	0.010 (0.007)*	0.045 (0.017)
Young	-0.011 (0.027)*	0.23 (0.066)
Adjusted R^2	0.26	0.37

Notes: *coefficients are not significant at the five-per cent threshold; income and demographic data are from the 1980 census, which is the chronological mid-point for our time-series; standard errors in parentheses.

These findings suggest that while the automatic (or institutional) component of fiscal stabilization is largely unrelated to industrial or demographic structures, the policy component is inversely related to these structural variables and to a significant degree. Groups receiving permanent transfers from the federal government, such as the mining and farming industries, the elderly and the young, display less apparent stabilization as a result of changes in the national fiscal policy. This finding is consistent with the interpretation that changes in the national fiscal policy result from the automatic stabilization of national per capita income across the business cycle. This finding is also consistent with the claim (made above) that federal fiscal transfers are directed at groups or individuals rather than at states or geographic regions.

These findings lead us to three conclusions about the redistribution and stabilization function of US federal fiscal institutions: to begin with, the redistribution function of common fiscal institutions are directed at individuals rather than at groups and therefore can be replicated at the member state level. Second, approximately 60 per cent of the apparent stabilization of regional or state per capita income in the United States derives from changes in national fiscal policy across the business cycle and therefore also can be replicated by the European member states. Third, the redistribution and stabilization effects of fiscal institutions and policy are independent from each other, and therefore it is unnecessary to insist on common institutions in order to arrive at common (or at least similar) effects.

The possibility for fiscal redistribution and stabilization under the stability pact

Our analysis so far presents a comforting scenario for proponents of EMU. Nevertheless, it fails to address the extent to which the recently signed 'stability pact' will prevent the member states from exercising the necessary redistribution or stabilization functions through national fiscal institutions.

This question is most easily addressed in terms of redistribution: member states are free to implement any fiscal transfers for which there are adequate fiscal resources across the business cycle. Put another way, redistribution is possible so long as the structural budget remains in balance. This is not an unrealistic constraint. Evidence from recent European experience indicates no correlation between the level of structural deficit in government accounts and the rate of real economic growth (Figure 1). Therefore, we find no evidence to suggest that member states are somehow obliged to provide transfers that they cannot afford.

Figure 1. Structural balance and economic growth

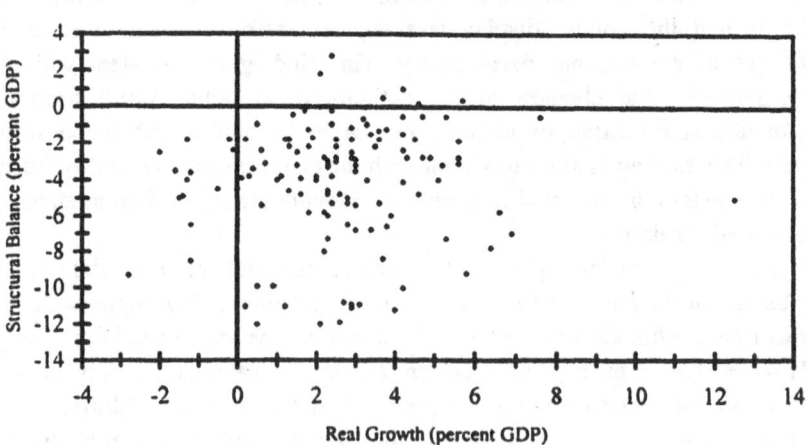

Source: European Commission.

In terms of stabilization, the question is whether the functioning of automatic fiscal stabilizers across the business cycle will breach the constraints of the stability pact. The answer to this question depends on two factors: the variability of income within the member states and the elasticity of member state budgets with respect to income. Even assuming the structural budget is in balance, it is possible to imagine either a wide variation in income resulting in a temporary deficit in excess of 3 per cent of GDP or a high elasticity of the budget with respect to income so that even a small variation in income performance results in an excessive deficit.

The authors of the stability pact have taken the first of these two possibilities into account. If a member state's income decreases by 0.75 per cent of the GDP then the government is no longer subject to *automatic* sanctions for an excessive deficit. Moreover, if a member state's income decreases by 2.0 per cent of the GDP, then the government is excluded from *any* sanctions for an excessive deficit. These concessions are meaningful in the sense that almost all member states have experienced a shortfall in income by 0.75 per cent of the GDP in the last thirty-five years, and five member states have experienced a shortfall in excess of 2.0 per cent during the same period.

The elasticity of government budgets to changes in income remain a concern. However, the OECD estimates that, on average, a one per cent decrease in the GDP relative to potential output results in only a 0.4 to 0.5 per cent-of-GDP deterioration in the fiscal balance of European member states. These estimates assume that only transfers for unemployment benefits are affected by changes in the business cycle, and that the predominant effect derives from the pro-cyclical movement of tax revenues. This assumption is consistent with our own findings in the US case, and the resultant elasticity estimates suggest there should be few problems providing adequate stabilization under the stability – provided that the structural budget is close to be balanced. Consider, for example, a country with a budget elasticity to income of 0.5 and a trend growth rate of 2.25 per cent. If growth were to decline suddenly to -0.75 per cent, the budget deficit would be expected to rise by only 1.5 per cent of GDP. A more radical decrease of growth to -2.0 per cent would push up the deficit by slightly more than 2 per cent of the GDP.

At this point, it is necessary to recall that the stabilization function of national fiscal policy is not equivalent to (and in our analysis does not derive from) the discretionary use of fiscal expenditures for countercyclical demand management. As in our analysis of the US case, we are interested solely in the stabilization resulting from changes in tax receipts and transfer disbursements as a result of changes in the business cycle. Therefore, objections that the simple arithmetic calculation just provided does not hold up to a cursory examination of past performance in Europe are misplaced. If past deficits have increased by more than we anticipate as the GDP growth declines, this does not imply that the OECD is somehow wrong in its estimate of the elasticity of the budget with respect to income. Rather it suggests that much of the variability evident in European fiscal performance derives from discretionary fiscal policy and not from fiscal stabilization per se. Evidence in support of this contention is provided through a time series regression analysis of changes in government deficits – aggregated at the EU level – as a function of changes in European GDP growth rates over the period from 1971 to 1996. The results of this analysis suggest that only about one-third of the variability in government deficits aggregated at the European level can be explained as a result of the variability in European growth rates. The other two-thirds of the variability should be explained as a result of changes in discretionary fiscal outlays.

$$-1.04 + 0.36\text{-GDP growth} \quad \text{Adj. } R^2 = 0.33$$
$$(0.28) \quad (0.10) \quad \text{D.W.} = 1.4$$

To summarize, the European member states can provide the redistribution and much of the stabilization apparent in the US case without creating common fiscal institutions and without violating the stability pact. Some fiscal adjustment is required to rein in structural budget deficits, however, that should not affect the stabilization or redistribution properties believed necessary to underwrite popular support for a common monetary policy.

Who cares?

Two issues remain unresolved. The first is how Europe will make up for the 14 per cent automatic stabilization provided by the common fiscal institutions in the US case. We do not have a strong answer to this concern. Nevertheless, the importance of such automatic cross-national fiscal stabilization should be regarded in light of the assumptions necessary for us to believe this is all somehow relevant to the future political stability for EMU. The initial assumption is that groups or regions that are or perceive themselves to be disadvantaged by the direction of the common monetary policy will either rebel against EMU or they will attempt to control the instruments for monetary policy-making. Such a reaction is considered most likely in the event that a particular group or region is subject to an economic shock not felt in the rest of the monetary union, or somehow adjusts less efficiently to common economic shocks.

The second concern is how best to respond to asymmetric performance within EMU. There is a substantial literature on whether idiosyncratic shocks occur in Europe either at all, or as often as in the United States. For our purposes, however, it is useful to consider the strongest case for asymmetry. According to writers such as Richez-Battesti (1996) the important point is not whether idiosyncratic shocks take place, but rather the fact that even common shocks will have different (and therefore idiosyncratic) effects across different national institutional frameworks.

Attempts to identify transnational support for or opposition to monetary integration provides substantial anecdotal support for the type of asymmetry suggested by Richez-Battesti. In general terms, Giovannini (1993), has noted the difficulty of finding consistent support for or opposition to EMU among any of a number of possible candidates across countries. Labour and capital, sheltered and exposed sectors, manufacturing and services do not line up in the same way on the question of monetary integration across different national contexts. Giovannini suggests that the reason for this variation is simply that 'the economic effects of a monetary regime depend on a number of institutional factors, which might differ significantly from country to country'. This argument is further substantiated through the comparative analysis of the EMU debates in Europe's nine smaller member states (Jones, Frieden, and Torres 1997).

Yet if the problem of asymmetry derives from different national institutional contexts, it is difficult to see how common fiscal institutions provide an adequate solution. Distributional considerations will vary from country to country, and so the first-best solution is to address these problems at the level of member states. Moreover, so long as national fiscal responses to national distributional problems are adequate, it is hard to see how significant opposition to EMU will take root.

The question of income stabilization remains problematic. Under our pessimistic assumptions, member states will perform idiosyncratically under EMU as a result of their differing institutional frameworks, and only part of that idiosyncracy will be absorbed through the income stabilization afforded by national fiscal policies. Nevertheless, this shortcoming should be compared with a meaningful alternative rather than being considered in the abstract. Where is organized opposition to European policy more likely? Is it under a common monetary policy given the redistribution and stabilization possible under national fiscal regimes? Or is opposition more likely under Europe-wide set of common fiscal institutions?

Given the argument that economic asymmetry among the member states derives from national institutional differences, we find it hard to believe that a common monetary policy will be more controversial than a set of common fiscal institutions. The opposite seems more likely to be the case. Any attempt to make EMU converge on the US model is more likely to arouse controversy and to politicize economic policy-making at the European level than it is to underwrite support for monetary union.

Note

1. Indeed, it is possible to derive equation (3) from equation (2) on the basis of uncontroversial assumptions about the data. See Gros and Jones (1994) Appendix 2.

References

Bayoumi, Tamim and Paul R. Masson, (1995). 'Fiscal Flows in the United States and Canada: Lessons for Monetary Union in Europe.' *European Economic Review* 39, pp. 253-74.
Giovannini, Alberto, (1993). 'Economic and Monetary Union: What Happened? Exploring the Political Dimension of Optimum Currency Areas,' in Guillermo De La Dehesa, et al., (eds.) *The Monetary Future of Europe*. London: Centre for Economic Policy Research, no page numbers.
Gros, Daniel, (1993). 'Comments by Daniel Gros on EMU and the Regions by De La Dehesa and Krugman,' in Guillermo De La Dehesa, et al., (eds.) *The Monetary Future of Europe*. London: Centre for Economic Policy Research, no page numbers.
Gros, Daniel, and Jones, Erik, (1994). 'Fiscal Stabilizers in the US Monetary Union.' *CEPS Working Document No. 83*. Brussels: Centre for European Policy Studies (January).
Jones, Erik, Jeffry Frieden, and Francisco Torres, (eds.) (1997). *Monetary Union and the Smaller Countries: The Challenge of Joining Europe's Monetary Club*. New York: St. Martin's Press (forthcoming).
Richez-Battesti, Nadine (1996). 'Union économique et monétaire et État-providence: la subsidiarité en question.' *Revue Études internationales* 27:1 (March) pp. 109-28.

10 Economic Relations of the EU and the Rest of Europe in View of the EMU

Olga Butorina

I. EMU and EU co-operation with the rest of Europe

A path to the third stage of the EMU discloses due to several reasons new facets in EU relations with the rest of Europe.

1. The extent to which the main economic goals of the EMU could be achieved (such as to encourage sustainable economic growth, to fight unemployment, to raise competitiveness and to strengthen Europe's position in the world) largely depends on further economic consolidation in Europe as a whole. On the one hand, wide co-operation with the rest of Europe may promote integration. On the other hand, the success of the single currency will greatly depend on how it will take root in the rest of Europe.
2. The CEECs and the CIS are important trading partners and emerging markets for the EU. They accounted for 11.2 per cent of EU total imports (ex-EU) and 11.4 per cent of exports in 1995.[1] Moreover, in recent years the volume of EU trade with these countries has been growing much faster than with the rest of the world. That is why it is in the European Union's interest that the switch to the single currency does not damage economic links with these regions and does not cut them off from the eurozone countries.
3. The advent of the single European currency opens new prospects for non-EU European countries as well. Thanks to a stable regional currency, they would be able to reduce losses in foreign trade due to exchange rate volatility and will benefit from using the same currency for transactions with a number of European countries. The

scope of revenues could be rather significant as the EU is the main trading partner for most East and Central European countries as well as for Russia. Non-EU European states are likely to welcome the single currency, as a two-currency world monetary system may be more stable than the present one. Relying not only on the US dollar, but also on the euro, might widen their possibilities for conducting more self-sustaining economic policies.

In other words, both parts of Europe, for their own reasons are interested in a positive outcome of the monetary union. Obviously, there are greater chances to achieve their goal, if they are acting together and developing a common strategy.

II. Problems arising in connection with EMU

Transition to the third stage of EMU poses a number of additional problems with regard to EU relations with the rest of Europe. Some are of a purely technical character while others require a new philosophy and fresh policy approaches. In any case, positive solutions are crucial for the future of the monetary union and the European integration process in general.

1. Legal issues

A significant part of the difficulties which could emerge in EU economic co-operation with third European countries is of a legal nature. The introduction of the euro will be the first attempt at putting into circulation a collective international currency. Though many countries have had experience at exchanging one type of banknote and coinage for another, there are no common rules and practices adopted by international law concerning a change from several currencies to one. The resolutions of the EU, although they *cannot* have an extraterritorial scope, will inevitably influence other countries not involved in the decision-making process.

For instance, the Council's 'Regulation on some provisions relating to the introduction of the euro' foresees that the contracts concluded in national currencies will be, after mid-2002, automatically denominated in euros. But the jurisdiction of the EU will not cover contracts with third countries (e.g.

the 'eurozone' members, and the time of execution is after 2002, there should be special clauses in the contracts regulating the above-mentioned situation. Article 4 of the Regulation determines the procedure of applying conversion rates (one euro expressed in terms of each of the national currencies of the member states with six significant figures), and Article 5 a method of rounding. These rules might not be be taken for granted by operators in third countries.

Similarly, the Council's 'Regulation on the introduction of the euro' is to introduce the *'no compulsion, no prohibition'* rule for the settlements inside the eurozone. It implies the right of a debtor to choose a currency of payment – national currency or the euro. Nevertheless, it does not seem clear how the EU and its counterparts from the rest of Europe would settle payments during the transition period (1999-2002). Will the debtors from the eurozone have a privilege to opt for a currency of payment if a creditor is located outside the EU and vice versa? Will, for instance, Russian financial institutions be obliged to accept payment in euros and feel free about using euros they have among their liabilities? This considered, it is highly desirable to arrange related questions at the international level reaching explicit agreements which would take into account the interests of the EU partners, including CEECs and CIS countries.

At present, 40 per cent of Russian external government debt is accounted for in German marks which is at the top of foreign currencies used. In March 1997, Russia for the first time issued a Eurobond, denominated not in US dollars as previously, but in German marks in an overall amount of 1.5 billion DM. Russia will have to repay the bulk of the credits after the year 2002, probably in euros. The related problems are to be the subject of future negotiations between the Russian Central Bank and the EMI, as a possible legal discountinuity could cause damage for both parties.

2. Organized markets

International organized markets present one more block of pending questions linked with the impact of EMU on the EU/Rest of Europe relations. One element of the coming changes i.e. currency derivatives - does not seem to cause serious problems. To most of the non-EU financial institutions they present a very modest portion of their incomes. Even now many major operators reduce the scope of such deals. This tendency is perceived as a natural path to the gradual disappearance of this market.

As far as securities are concerned, the market trend is expected to be quite the opposite. It is common knowledge that from 1999, government stocks are to be converted in the single currency. At the beginning of 1997, the EIB started to issue benchmark 'Euro-tributary bonds' on the terms, enabling to redenominate them in euros from 1999. The first two were a 1 billion 'tributary' Dutch guilder bond and the first euro 1 billion 7-year bond. One of the aims of this policy is to strengthen the market's liquidity from 1999.

Evidently, it would be advantageous if securities denominated in euros would be marketed not only in the EU but in the rest of Europe as well. At present, the situation does not look very reassuring. Investors in Central and East European countries and in the former Soviet republics are quite timid about European securities. According to experts' assessments, up to 95 per cent of foreign securities marketed in Russia are in US dollars.

The problem has two main roots. The first: doubts about liquidity. The lack of trust is provoked by fears that it might be difficult to sell large packages of euro-denominated securities at the same time. This obstacle could be overcome if the euro proves to be stable and if the stock markets dealing with the European currency would be strong. The second and major obstacle is much more difficult to surmount. It results from the current structure of companies' liabilities: the lion's share of these are in US dollars.

3. The euro as one of the foreign currencies

According to specialists, at least 8 of each 10 Russian foreign trade contracts are concluded in US currency. Nevertheless 40 per cent of the foreign trade value accounted in 1995 for Western Europe, 13 per cent for the CEEC, and 21 per cent for the CIS. On the whole, the weight of these regions was 74 per cent. Though this comparison is not entirely accurate, it says much for itself. Banking officials confirm that usually their clients posses US dollars and only 5-10 per cent of the operations are carried out in other mainly German and Dutch currencies.

This year (1997) the Russian government launched a number of measures aimed at forcing out dollars from internal circulation. One of them carried a deliberately low interest rate on dollar deposits in comparison with rouble deposits. Although these steps have been taken largely to facilitate the use of national currency, they might direct the interest of economic operators to European currencies. Regardless, there is more than enough room for European currencies and the euro to expand their circulation area in Russia in the future, along with other CIS countries. In the CEECs the chances (for the euro to squeeze out the dollar) are low – they already now rely more on the DM than on the USD – but still significant. As it has already been noted above, a success or a failure of the single European currency in non-EU European regions, will be one of the crucial factors determining the fate of the monetary union and the prospects for the euro to become a world reserve currency.

With regard to a potential role of the euro as a reserve currency, many representatives of financial circles in Russia consider it quite feasible. They think it will depend on three main conditions: the stability of the euro, interest rates for euro deposits, and the currency structure of companies' liabilities.

III. What can be done for the success of EMU?

It is often asked, what could be done to promote the use of the euro in non-EU Europe and to make it a stable European currency? Three major tasks are to be fulfilled.

1. It is necessary to settle controversial legal issues in EU relations with the rest of Europe. This will contribute to a smooth switch from national currencies to the euro in third countries. The overall scope of these juridical arrangements may be rather wide, including settlement practices, conversion rules, redenomination of securities, etc.
2. Deep economic co-operation between the two parts of Europe is an indispensable condition for the expansion of the euro. The most complicated side of the problem concerns the nature of the EU economic links with other European countries. In general, the co-operation develops not *inside* particular branches of the economy, but *between* them. In other words, it reflects inter-industrial and not intra-industrial trade. Thus its structure significantly differs from that between the EU members or between industrial countries in general.

The EU trade with Russia is one of the most illustrative examples. Russian exports consist mainly of raw materials and imports of manufactured goods. These discrepancies have negative effects on the demand for European currencies. World prices for many raw materials are quoted in US dollars. Therefore, Russian suppliers receive export revenues in US currency. Strictly speaking, such trade has very little in common with the division of labour. Due to the commodity structure, it is very vulnerable to external shocks and political changes. Obviously, one can hardly expect a crucial positive shift in the nearest future.

Nevertheless, progress in economic consolidation of both Europe, EU and non-EU, is possible. Common efforts in particular spheres of economic policy are quite real and could be mutually beneficial. For instance, it may turn productive if a future TARGET system could be somehow connected with similar real-time settlement systems outside the EU. Naturally, third European countries will not enjoy access to it on conditions similar to those of eurozone participants or even of 'pre-in' EU members. However, it does not mean that there is no other way for co-operation. Evidently, the financial institutions of both sides could find points of common interests and in future create something like corridors for real-time settlements for specific operations or areas (e.g., between major cities).

Once the euro gains a wide circulation all over the region, there may arise a question of regulating its market rate and the balance between supply and demand. Once the non-EU European countries rely on the European currency in economic policies and foreign trade, they will be highly interested in its stability. That is why they might be partly engaged in the ECB activities connected with interventions. It is that particular case where co-ordination of actions could be of great use for both sides.

Russia could have a specific role in this aspect purely due to its dimensions. If the euro is broadly spread in Russia, this country will significantly influence its market position. The EU might face serious difficulties if in a given year Russia would sharply increase demand for the European currency, while in the next year the euros would be returning home like carrier pigeons. An appropriate international mechanism could diminish possible negative consequences.

Before 2002, when euro banknotes and coins will be put into circulation, it would be useful to undertake common measures against forgery and counterfeiting. The non-EU European countries could conclude special agreements with the EU and participate in Europol activities. There already exists an experience of that kind, as a clause against money laundering has been included in the Partnership and Co-operation Agreement with Russia and similar agreements with many other European countries.

3. It is high time to develop a thoughtful strategy towards third European countries aiming at becoming potential users of the new currency. This strategy should be 'made to measure' and not a copy of similar strategies for the United States or Asia. At present, there is not enough knowledge about the EMU in most of the CEECs and the CIS. The general public is largely unaware of the program. However, without close co-ordination between the EU and its European partners any information campaign may have counterproductive effects.

Speaking about Russia, I can assume that there are few specialists who follow EMU developments in detail. Additionally, those who do, suffer from a constant lack of information. And for the EU specialists, it is difficult to understand Russian realities and to make a professional translation of documents concerning EMU into Russian. If adequate steps are not taken in proper time, it may trigger unfavourable market reactions, including attempts to get rid of European currencies.

IV. Conclusions

The construction of EMU opens favourable prospects for the European economy as a whole. It could provide substantial benefits for non-EU European countries and foster the process of European economic consolidation. The outcome of the monetary union notably depends on whether the euro could gain a wide circulation area all over Europe.

At the same time, a path to the single European currency requires additional efforts from both sides. In many cases, to be fruitful they need to be common. Once the monetary union is created, the measure of interdependence of the two parts of Europe will substantially increase.

The EMU, as any project of the same scope, may have extremely significant effects. It can become a mighty leverage for the European economy and integration. As any strong medicine if taken improperly, it can cause serious problems such as the segmentation of the region, outward resistance to the single currency and thus it could destabilize its own market position.

Note

1. 'Statistics in Focus'. *Eurostat: External trade.* Luxembourg, 1996, No. 7, pp. 2-4; Europe weekly selected statistics, Luxembourg, 1996, No. 977.

Part II

Theoretical Issues of Global Convergence

11 Hayek and Triffin: Fragments on Divergence and Convergence in Policy Thinking*

Nicolas Krul

The current debate on international and regional monetary management and the associated controversy as to the balance of market forces and policy increasingly crystallizes around the opposing visions of Hayek and Triffin, that is the pure market co-ordination principle advocated by the former and the pragmatic, policy-led search for compatibility proposed by the latter. Indeed, the outcome of the competition between these two central lines of thought on the organizing principles of the world system will, to a large extent, define the framework and, therefore, the economic, social, and political substance of international relations in the post-1989 world.

This crystallization is no mere accident. Hayek and Triffin participated in the collective effort which generated the new economics and its organizational characteristics after the upheavals, booms, busts, and inflations that marked the first half of the century. Both were typical products of the synthesis of the 1930s, which still constitutes the foundation of today's political economy. Furthermore, as Section 1 recalls, Vienna-born Hayek never ceased to argue whithin the fundamental methodological and theoretical assumptions of the Austrian school, which later formed Triffin when he came to study under Schumpeter, at Harvard, then working on his *Capitalism, Socialism and Democracy*.

Section 2 will be devoted to a brief description of what I see as Hayek's and Triffin's main contributions. This is a relatively straightforward exercise in the case of Triffin's policy oriented economics, even if it poses some critical questions of theoretical linkage arising out of his implicit

---

* In preparing this paper, the author has benefitted from discussions with Otto Hieronymi and Tad Rybczynski.

assumptions. In contrast, the shifts of emphasis in Hayek's epistemological and methodological approach raise substantial questions of consistency and purpose. In my view, however, Hayek's policy project can be legitimately be derived from the global failure to transform the concept of general equilibrium into a sufficient framework for dynamic economic analysis, and his subsequent effort to reformulate the methodological problems of studying economics, as from the seminal 1937 essay 'Economics and Knowledge'. Section 3 will endeavour to set and assess the respective contributions within the context of today's policy problems.

The assigned title of this paper obviously promises much more than can possibly by redeemed by its contents. What I intend to do here is to find some significant fragments of thought and apply them to selected portions of the vast material, in the hope that an interesting problem of divergence and convergence might be posed for discussion.

Section One. Formation

In Hayek's seven decades of scientific work, the understanding of economics was seen as a necessary step in the understanding of the wider problems of the political order and the organization of society. As such, his vision not only reflects Menger, Wieser and Mises, but also Max Weber and the particular kind of positivism of Ernst Mach and Moritz Schlick, which shaped the later Austrian epistemology. Triffin's inspiration at Louvain was similarly anchored in a multi-disciplinary training. But his initial foundation in economics was deepened and enlarged by Schumpeter's 'Social-Oekonomik', not only in terms of pure theory but also – and perhaps above all – by the Austrian's vision of economics as part of a continuous pluricausal evolution. Triffin, no doubt, was durably marked by the insights of '...the first of the great economists who carried his economic analysis of capitalism to its final optimistic conclusion, and then, disregarding the outcome of his economic thinking, pronounced doom on the system for a non-economic reason' (Heilbronner 1980, p. 314).

Hayek and Triffin, however, are also part of the immense creative spasm which – in the 1920s and 1930s – transformed economic theory from a conditional demonstration of a self-regulating, inherently self-optimizing, predictable and coherent system into a restless and disturbing account of how men try to cope with scarcity and uncertainty. From the beginning, Hayek was a main participant not only by virtue of his own contributions, but also in his ceaseless advocacy of novel ideas originating outside the Anglo-Saxon centres of high theory (his edition of the *Beitrage zur Geldtheory* introduced the innovative ideas of Myrdal and Holtrop in the international debate). Triffin's dissertation on 'General Equilibrium Theory and Monopolistic Competition' extended Sraffa's frontal attack on perfect competition and Joan Robinson's demonstration that value theory, in the sense of a simple, symmetrical body of universal principles, could not survive. Both Hayek and Triffin were deeply and permanently marked by the shift from a basically orderly and tranquil intellectual framework to the fruitful but disturbing, polemical cross-fertilizations of the 1930s.

Hayek, however, did not become the Hayek we know because of von Mises, the controversies of the 1930s, or external events; and neither did Triffin become the architect of European monetary integration we know today under the influence of Schumpeter, Chamberlin or Leontief. Deeper forces started to work, related to the state of economics itself as each of them perceived it, and new personal circumstances. The war played a role, especially for Triffin who came to be active in the practical world of the Federal Reserve. More important, however, was the failure on both sides to fuse general equilibrium and business cycle theory. Triffin, by invalidating one of Chamberlin's main assumptions – the concept of groups of firms – grasped the unrealistic nature of pure theory, or rather the existence of incommensurabilities, which set limits to theoretical ambitions. As he noted later, 'I left "the ivory tower" (...) and gladly forgot monopolistic competition and pure theory' (Triffin, 1981a, p. 242). Hayek, whose *Pure Theory of Capital* was still to come (in 1941), first hinted to his shift in 1937 (in *Economics and Knowledge*). The disenchantment, however, emerged more clearly in 1938 when he wrote: 'Whether there is scope for a separate theory of the trade cycle must for the time being remain at least doubtful' (Hayek 1938; in 'Discussion on the Trade Cycle', Royal Statistical Society, III).

Triffin's practical activity in Latin-America, and later in Europe, translated into two essential Triffinite principles, extended and deepened when he returned to academia. The first one was ethical, close to the original Keynesian and the Louvain Socratic-Thomistic tradition, i.e that choice has value only in an environment that offers and promotes 'choice-worthy' options. The second was instrumental, i.e. that economics is largely a matter of balancing competing claims of similar validity and mediating conflicts that can hardly ever be resolved by rational reconstruction. Together they generated the search for 'policy-oriented economics' and 'compatibility' because 'The problem in economics, as in politics, is to choose among the different alternative paths leading to (such) inevitable compatibility'. (Triffin 1981a, p. 251).

Did Hayek indeed become Hayek when he completed '...the first half of my career as an economist' with the *Pure Theory of Capital* (Hayek 1967, p. 253) and embarked on *The Road to Serfdom*? For many, this is the unquestionable turning point, since it was the latter work which became emblematic for the 'liberal' cause in Britain and the United States. Yet, the economic, ethical, and political ideas, which Hayek defended with so much consistency over the rest of his life have clearly an origin prior to the 1944 publication. Indeed, John Gray has argued that the key to Hayek's fundamental methodological and theoretical assumptions is to be found in *The Sensory Order: An Enquiry into the Foundations of Theoretical Psychology* drafted in the 1920s but only published in 1952. No doubt, Gray is right in pointing out that the Kantian rejection of the rationalist concept of reality, and hence the distinct Hayekian epistemological foundation, runs as a red line from *The Sensory Order* to *Economics and Knowledge* and beyond. There is equally little doubt, though, that the sulphurous controversies with Sraffa and Keynes, and the subsequent denaturation of Keynes' principles in the hands of his followers, compelled Hayek to sharpen the specific identity of his preanalytic cognative foundation and analytical effort.

The cross-fertilization produced by Hayek's 1930s struggle to clear the site and invent a new architecture is a complex story, and even in its most general formulation extremely diverse. On the one hand, the failure to meet the analytical and operational needs of the time called for a re-examination at three levels of thought: the real world of linkages, facts, and institutions; the abstract world of pure reasoning, able to exist on its own internal coherence; and in between, the changing nature of their relationship as a means of revealing and incorporating those vital new links which in themselves are the essence of theoretical innovation. On the other, the intrusion of expectations, and more broadly of the inherently disorderly dynamics of the modern credit and technology based economy, which have no solid basis in observed or deductive fact, eroded the moorings of Hayek's previous macroeconomics. As a radical scientist, he therefore felt compelled to extend and deepen his earlier meditations on the open-ended, indeterminate, evolutionary economic process, to link his methodology to an anchoring view of the world and his participation in the debate accross paradigms. *The Road to Serfdom* was the polemical – and provisional – reaction to the societal proposals of the 1930s. *Economics and Knowledge*, which identified the division of knowledge as 'the central problem of economics as a social science', and denied that the function performed by an expectations-driven market could be understood intellectually – and hence improved upon – provided Hayek with the epistomological foundation from which to develop his economic policy views.

Triffin's intellectual itinerary was sturdily immune to the disappointments which marked the early years of monetary integration, during which Jean Monnet, Robert Marjolin and Fritz Machlup deepened his understanding of modernity, and the concept of institutional accumulation which Monnet drew from Amiel's observation: 'Each man's experience starts again from the beginning. Only institutions grow wiser: they accumulate collective experience; and, owing to this experience and this wisdom, men subject to the same rules will not see their own nature changing, but their behaviour gradually transformed.' Marjolin's penetrating intelligence and negotiating experience contributed to Triffin's understanding of sectoral integration and the notion of '...a controlled system of free competition.' Machlup, and the *Bellagio Group*, offered a jousting ground for competing policy ideas and the strict definition of monetary problems once the Bretton Woods system started to decay. For a whole generation, *Europe and the Money Muddle* (1957), and *Gold and the Dollar Crisis: The Future of Convertibility* (1960) made explicit what had only been vaguely felt.

The challenge thrown down by neo-Keynesianism similarly forced Hayek to deepen his understanding of prices as 'signals' of the 'division of knowledge' and of 'a spontaneous order', intertwining economics with philosophy and political science. *Individualism and Economic Order*, *The Constitution of Liberty* and *Law, Legislation and Liberty* were the successive reactions to creeping collectivism, which Skidelsky later described saying in effect that: Keynes's disciples, the policy makers of the 1960s and the 1970 could not hold Keynes's original balance in mind. 'They actually did start to act as though they believed that the power of economists over economies was virtually unlimited. This is because they had inherited Keynes's machinery but without the philosophy which sets limits to the scope and effectiveness of that machinery. Their *hubris* was inevitably succeeded by Nemesis' (Skidelsky 1992, p. 409). It was the emergence of electoralist economics, the deepening monetary disorder, and the increasing indebtedness they caused, which made Hayek into the crusader and ideological entrepreneur of a restored scientific liberalism.

Section Two. Contributions

Interest in Hayek's theoretical work on the trade cycle and the role of money revived with the publications of the so-called 'new classical school' by Lucas, Barro, Sargent, and others. Laidler (1982, p. IX) even qualifies their body of doctrine as 'a modern version' of the Austrian approach – preferring the term 'neo-Austrian' to 'new classical' – and qualifying its protagonists as '...firmly in the intellectual tradition pioneered by Ludwig von Mises and Friedrich von Hayek'. Scheide (1986, p. 595), similarly observes that, although the new classical theory does not fully follow Austrian traditions, '...many of the differences appear to be small or are only semantic in character'. Arena (1994, p. 216), however, convincingly argues that 'Hayekian and modern exogenous business cycle theories belong to a common great tradition but, on many crucial points, their similarities are more apparent than real'.

We share that view. No doubt, Hayek was an important link in the fusion of scientific traditions. In 1967, Hicks recalled that: 'The obstacle which confronted one on his side was the Böhm-Bawerkian model; an analytical framework that had become familiar, even orthodox, in some continental countries, but was unfamiliar in England. "Prices and Production" was in English, but it was not English economics' (Hicks 1967, p. 204). The attempts at that translation filled the journals of the 1930s and certainly forced English economics to make the Wicksellian distinction between a money and a 'real exchange' economy (in his rejoinder to Hayek – November 1931 – Keynes conceded that his *Treatise* lacked '... any satisfactory theory of capital and interest' and promised to remedy this). With hindsight, however, the Hayekian contribution to the interwar business cycle and money debate seems to be one of synthesizing, perfecting and disseminating overall ideas, which by their outstanding quality provided for novel avenues and enriched the architecture of analysis, but at the same time, remained part of the arrestingly suggestive tapestry of the times rather than a separate case of innovation.

Likewise, little remains of Triffin's efforts to modernize the edifice of monopolistic competition. With Robinson and Hicks, he levelled the old building. But once that work of destruction completed and the theory of value reduced to a special case, his contribution became part of a collective renovation.

The postwar story is, of course, very different. By turning to social and political theory with the gains of economic insight previously accumulated, Hayek reconstructed a coherent vision of the nature and workings of the modern society. Admittedly, Hayek's reference points, the partisanship of his followers, and his association with such vocal 'new right' politicians as Mrs. Thatcher and President Reagan, blurred the picture – the more so as '..Friedrich Hayek has been cursed by sneerers who dismiss everything he has to say without giving it a hearing, and even more by admirers, who agree with it before they have studied it, and regard it mainly as a highbrow stick with which to beat the left' (Samuel Brittan 1983, p. 49). Even so, Hayek's vision of economics as part of the identity and meaning of Western civilization, his ideas on the nature and organization of its political economy, and his proposals for the mobilization of its instrumental values in the defence of individual freedom, represent a particular project to deal with modernity. In the same way, Triffin's heterodox formulation of the problem of economic governance – 'The enormous expansion of the objectives and techniques of state intervention in economic life seems to me incompatible with the restoration and maintenance of convertibility on the basis of uncoordinated national decisions and policies of several scores of independent sovereign states' (Triffin 1957, p. 303) – and the then isolated call for a supranational organization of world money and capital set a particular project for action and tacitly, the modernization of society. As such, and with collectivism part of history and hegemonism fading, Hayek and Triffin are the emblematic representatives of the two competing governance projects of today.

That competition, furthermore, is legitimized by the coexistence of 'scientific research programmes' of equal validity, in the sense that both contain a theoretically progressive strategy (i.e. the successive formulations of the respective programmes display an excess of empirical content compared to their predecessors), and both are clearly marked by an empiric progression, (i.e. the corroboration of that content by previously unanticipated developments). However, whereas Hayek's programme sees the irreducible *division* of knowledge as 'the really central problem of economics as a social science', Triffin's programmatic foundation identifies the inevitable pooling and *sharing* of knowledge as our main intellectual challenge.

And finally, the competition is sustained and dynamized by the explicit articulation of these epistemological options around conflicting organizing principles: the Hayekian vision of automaticity inherent in the absolute, self-regulating discipline of a universal, spontaneous price co-ordination system in which the essential driving force is individual choice; and the Triffinite principle of a negotiated adherence to collective rules and norms to ensure compatibility among the divergent national or regional interests and, at the national level, among the requirements these agreed co-ordination norms imply.

This view of Hayek's contribution implies, but also goes beyond the one contained in the Nobel Memorial Prize citation of the Royal Swedish Academy: 'The Academy is of the opinion that von Hayek's analysis of the functional efficiency of different economic systems is one of the most significant contributions to economic research in the broader sense.' In part, this reflects the shift of emphasis which then (1974) seemed far away, if not inconceivable, i.e. the discredit of neo-Keynesian policies and the collapse of collectivism (Even Gorbatchev now admits that: 'The crisis of the communist movement and its collapse were fundamentally unavoidable'; M. Gorbatchev, 1995). More importantly, however, the Academy's assessment sits – in my view – somewhat uneasily with the asserted open-endedness and essential unpredictability, the '...voyage of exploration into the unknown, an attempt to discover new ways of doing things better than they have been done before' (Hayek 1946, p. 101), which Hayek claims for the market process in his later writings ('The validity of the theory cannot be tested empirically' because '...if we do not know the facts we hope to discover by means of competition, we can never ascertain how effective it has been in discovering those facts that might be discovered' Hayek 1978, p. 180). As Buchanan and Vanberg convincingly argue: 'if the market is genuinely perceived as an open-ended, non-determined, evolutionary process, in which the essential driving force is human choice, any insinuation, however subtle, of a goal toward which the process can be predicted to move must be inherently misleading' (Buchanan and Vanberg 1991, p. 180).

As I see it, Hayek's project does not aim to represent the world but represents a particular view on how to cope with it within an explicit ideology seeking to promote a regime of economic liberty necessary to the order constitutive of it. As such, its contributions are twofold.

Thus, the subtle and complex analysis of how scarcity, uncertainty, institutions, and individual choice interact and lead to a dynamic process of discovery and change poses a series of fundamental questions about the relationships between preferences, prices and information, which can neither be assumed away nor solved by the current tools of price determination theory. Hayek thus focused scientific attention on problems which later formed the platform of the new institutional school, the efforts to set the theory of the firm within a framework which included information and co-ordination, and the development of the new financial theories of Sharpe and Rosenberg etc. In sum, by taking the idea of competition as a dynamic process beyond the co-ordinating role of the 'invisible economic hand', Hayek was one of those who changed the way economists look at reality.

At the same time, Hayek's foundationalist celebration of the positive side of decentralized decision-making provided for a particular politically-efficient intellectual agenda to deal with the legacy of discredited or repudiated doctrines and for a renovated perception of the role and limits of the political economy. Here, as elsewhere, Hayek opens up problems rather than solves them, and contrary to the claims of his more ardent followers, he does not supply us with easily recognizable economic criteria to distinguish between benign and malign intermediation. Nevertheless, the singular service of intellectually devising a way out of electoralist or corporatist economics is now an essential component of any policy agenda, as Triffin recognized it in 1981: 'I have learned only more recently [...] to appreciate fully the crucial grain of truth in the basic philosophy of a man whose advice was often repellent to me: Professor Hayek. While governmental interference in economic life might be useful, or even necessary, to redress blaring injustices, and promote higher levels of production and welfare, policy makers will often be motivated by their own electoral interests and those of powerful interest groups' (Triffin 1981, p. 254).

It is often forgotten, though, that Hayek's agenda had two components. The first, and in his eyes crucial one concerned the clarification of liberal thought itself. Hayek's opening address at the first Mont Pelerin Society in 1947, thus said: 'If the ideals which I believe unite us [...] are to have any chance of revival, a great intellectual task must be performed. This task involves both purging traditional liberal theory of certain accidental accretions [...] and also facing up to some real problems which an oversimplified liberalism has shirked or which have become apparent only since it has turned into a somewhat stationary and rigid creed' (Hayek 1992, vol. 4, p. 238). The second was initially directed against the fallacies of socialism and neo-Keynesianism (*The Road to Serfdom*), but gradually came to focus on the degeneration of the majoritarian democracy into an unprincipled auction system animated by rival interest groups. This line of thought was set out *in The Constitution of Liberty* (1960) and in *Law, Legislation and Liberty* (1979), which explicitly warns: 'Although I profoundly believe in the basic principles of democracy as the only effective method which we have yet discovered of making peaceful change possible, and am therefore much alarmed by the evident growing disillusionment about it as a desirable method of government, much assisted by the increasing abuse of the word to indicate supposed aims of government – I am becoming more and more convinced that we are moving towards an impasse from which political leaders will offer to extricate us by desperate means.' (Hayek 1979, p. 112).

Hayek's doctrinal agenda is still with us, or rather, now stands out as a main dilemma of economic modernity. For one, the unreflective individualist bias of contemporary Anglo-American market fundamentalists represents a precise case of an oversimplified creed of the type Hayek feared. For another, both the European difficulties in restructuring an economy which increasingly appears a mere contingent historical phenomenon, and the American problem of reconciling rapid and continuous market-driven change with the stability of US institutions, amply demonstrate the persistence of the analytical economic policy challenge.

Triffin's postwar disregard of abstract economics, and his reluctance to explicitly define his political philosophy, complicates the identification of his specific contributions. As said above, though, his implicit constructive rationalism – or conjectural realism – and explicit insistence on policy-led institution building to lead economic trends, position him at the opposite side of Hayek. The contrast is most vividly illustrated by Hayek's concept of competitively issued means of payment, i.e. the system of free banking and the dismantling of the central bank monopoly, as compared to Triffin's proposals for policy-led, rules-based monetary integration. But even if his Bagehot-like vision of a managed monetary system as a central 'balancing factor' is close to the original Keynes, Triffin also posed a challenge to the neo-Keynesian income/expenditure orthodoxy, and its narrow, technical concept of economics as 'hydraulics'.

In my view, Triffin is at the centre of two specific theoretical developments. On the one hand, his perception of the vital practical importance of what he called his 'Tableaux à la Quesnay' – in which national accounts are related to external accounts and domestic money flows, and the thus collected disparate national data are harmonized so as to allow the analysis of global liquidity and actual or potential international monetary disturbances – is not only a landmark in logical-quantitative economics, but also an explicit statement of a single, integrated, closed world money system. Triffin's global approach to the cash-balance variant of the quantity theory in stock as well as flow terms, and the direct integration of money in balance-of-payments analysis, became an important element in the emergence of the monetarist approach pioneered by Mundell (which also falls within the genealogy of Wicksell and the Dutch monetary school as developed by Koopmans, Holtrop, Polak, and Witteveen).

On the other hand, Triffin's analysis and proposals enlarged the scope of assignment problem solution and sharpened the perception of 'organizing principles'. The former materialized in the clearer and more communicable distinction between the goals-and-means and the causes-and-effects approaches by explicitly extending the Tinbergen-Meade framework to conceivable *and* available institutional arrangements. The latter was the result of his insistence to integrate the notion of 'hidden agendas' and concerns about geoeconomic and technological change, distributional equity, into the longer-run general equilibrium analysis of the world monetary organization.

Triffin's main contribution, however, lies in his tenacious, innovative pursuit of institutional ideas which are simple, self-consistent, and relevant to the times, and notably the idea that regional monetary co-operation and integration are complementary to feasible world monetary arrangements rather than a hostile – and counterproductive – alternative to universal collaboration. The first main initiative was his proposal for the creation of a European Clearing Union in 1947 (which met streneous opposition from the US Treasury and the Federal Reserve Board as well as with polite scepticism in the circle of professional economists). From 1957-58 Triffin started to work on European monetary integration within the Community and Jean Monnet's 'Action Committee', carefully selecting 'seminal' or 'germinal' steps liable to develop an internal momentum of their own toward the ultimate objective of European monetary and political union (Triffin 1978, p. 17), now the core of the European policy agenda.

Section Three. Looking ahead

Hayek and Triffin were political economists in the tradition of Smith, Mill, Marx, and Keynes, who rejected the innocence of history and society on which abstract economics prides itself. They were deeply concerned with what economics, philosophy and social theory had to teach us about how needs and aspirations change; how tradition and innovation interact and, more generally, how the production of knowledge influences real events and the opportunities in the realistically imaginable world.

Hayek's project, in that sense, is built on certain unavoidable, irreversible features, and yields a single outcome attained by the constant experimentation and competition that liberal institutions encourage. Even so, he shared Schumpeter's sceptical view on the immanent tendencies of the capitalist order: 'The evolution of ideas has its own laws and depends very largely upon developments which we cannot predict. I mean, I am trying to move opinion in a certain direction, but I would not dare to predict in what direction it will really move' (Hayek 1994). Triffin's constructivist rationalism is built on the Monnet inspired concept of positive institutional accumulation, sceptical of the production of theories and hypothesis yielding precise prescriptions, but certain of a positivist extension into previously unexploited fields of expansion.

Today's skirmishes largely obscure Triffin's optimistic vision. The short-term technicalities of the transition to EMU, and the fierce nationalistic and corporatist reactions to the Maastricht Treaty, have set a reductionist climate, which, although not alien to Triffin's experience, tends to distort the essence of his project. Hayek's ideas, on the other hand, suffer from the abusive assimilation with a particular Anglo-American practice propagated by the followers of Thatcher and Reagan, and from the simplistic interpretation of the link between Hayek's reasoning and the collapse of collectivism and neo-Keynesianism. The kind of free market fundamentalism now advocated in Hayek's name is, in reality, an ill-disguised restatement of hegemonic objectives and the conventional conservative discourse, a '...pursuit of a managerialist Cultural Revolution seeking to refashion the entire national life on the impoverished model of contract and market exchange' (John Gray 1995, p. 87).

It must be admitted, however, that Hayek and Triffin are partly to blame for the blossoming of the degenerative interpretations we observe today. The first pointed to an ideological ideal and to the narrow path to reach that single, universal project of life, but the ideal is seen as free from the politics of the day ('It is because, whether he wills it or not, the historian shapes the political ideals of the future, that he himself must be guided by the highest ideals and keep free from the political disputes of the day' Hayek 1992, p. 214), and guided by the spontaneous, exclusive discovery and co-ordination functions of the market. As notably Berlin and Buchanan have observed, this concept of an indeterminate evolution within a value-free context has little to say about positive fundamentals, or about the actual transition from today to tomorrow. In principle, Triffin's constructive rationalism, implicitly set within a realistic perception of liberal historicism, regards the form of contemporary capitalism, with a large public sector and universalist welfare programmes, as a legitimate, inevitable starting point and a necessary part of the future. Nonetheless, in his case also, the evolutionary nature of the compatibility principle allows for a range of outcomes, hence for a debate that constantly oscillates between ideological extremes and different interpretations of how to link existing conditions with the proposed matrix.

I attach little importance to the theoretical speculations or interested extrapolations which suggest a moral stalemate by virtue of either an extremist Hayekian evolution or a fatal convergence on bureaucratic centralism as a result of Triffin's ideas. But the very fact of their existence is revelatory of immanent tensions which are of importance if we engage in thinking about the prospects ahead. For one, Hayek's ideological closure implies an explicitly assumed straitjacket. As Gamble says: 'Hayek correctly diagnosed that the iron cage of modernity would frustrate the realization of socialism. But the greatest failure of his analysis stems from his refusal to accept that part of the iron cage consists of the structures of the modern state, especially its security, surveillance and welfare apparatuses. He encouraged a liberal utopianism suggesting the possibility of bringing the ideology and culture of modern society into harmony with its economics, built on a moral community of property owners. The political implications of attempting to realize this utopia, however, involve an assault upon the realities of modern life just as great as does the socialist utopianism he criticized' (A. Gamble 1996, p. 187). Triffin, for his part, inevitably participates in the ambiguities of 'modus vivendi' capitalism in which ideology is a mere veil for the conflicts between national interests, and between individual and collective agendas. By implicitly adhering to the economic theory of politics, which analyses the political balance as the end result of a competitive bidding process, Triffin inevitably became an objective ally of a kind of European mandate doctrine, or at least vulnerable to accusations in that sense.

Hayek's willing straitjacket is the source of many fruitful insights, and Triffin counted on the unwritten ethical norms of his project to set limits to the mandate doctrine. However, if we look beyond these contemporary skirmishes and *procés d'intention*, we encounter some fundamental problems of legitimacy and economic sustainability which are of more direct interest for the prospective configuration of the global political economy. Among these, cultural pluralism occupies a central position.

Cultural pluralism is not only a pervasive permanent feature of economic life which explains institutional diversity – 'Market institutions are stable when, and only when, they come embedded in cultural forms which constrain and inform them' (J. Gray 1995, p. 103) – it is also the root of a dynamic differentiation process caused by different reactions to structural change as associated with the operation of the free market or the implementation of integration projects. Hayek's philosophical anthropology, nevertheless, implicitly states that cultural diversity is inessential and a mere transitory phenomenon vis-a-vis the spontaneous, universal convergence on a market-determined modernity. And while, Triffin's project recognizes that the very existence of incommensurabilities among ultimate values requires a constant search for compatibilities, he nevertheless implicitly assumes that those incommensurabilities can be identified, benchmarked, and be made subject to rational solutions.

Quite clearly, however, we cannot but share Berlin's view that the very existence of value pluralism invalidates any project based on the ambitions of universalism and severely limits those which assume the possibility of a mediation among conflicts that can never be resolved (Berlin 1990).

For one, value pluralism is a recognized feature of the pervasive diversity which marks the economies of the 'West', separates the latter economies from those in Asia which were never associated with the moral culture of individualism, and an unmistakenly specific source of new patterns in the Islamic countries and perhaps in China and Russia. For another, it is increasingly emerging as a dynamic political phenomenon. Lately, the triumphalism of market fundamentalists has started to provoke reactions which led Huntington to warn against an image of an emerging universally Western world as '...misguided, arrogant, false and dangerous' (Huntington 1996). Before Huntington, however, Gellner showed how the mix of market-led Westernization, new technologies, and widening inequalities had produced a conjunction of traditional militancy and modern tools of action in the Islamic countries (Gellner 1994, Ch. 3), while Funabashi explained how expanding economic and media links favour the 'Asianization' of Asia. (Funabashi 1993).*

---

* Joan Robinson never ceased to stress the politics of national self-interest in the free trade doctrine, and her reference to an appendix to Marshalls 'Principles', in her 'Economic Philosopy' (Pelican. 1964, p. 64.) is an apt reminder in the present debate on the liberalization of financial services: 'While recognizing the leadership of Adam Smith, the German economists have been irritated more than any others by what they have regarded as the insular narrowness and self-confidence of the Ricardian School. In particular they presented the way in which the English advocates of Free Trade tacitly assumed that a proposition which had been established with regard to a manufacturing country, such as England was, could be carried over without modification to agricultural countries. The

A similar dynamic process has been triggered by the Maastricht Treaty and the plans to enlarge the European Union. Cultural diversity is one of the declared values of the Union, but the lack of a convincing programme to protect it from market-led obliteration has legitimized both direct defensive reactions and the intrusion of value pluralism in the debate on the Union's democratic balance.

It is because value pluralism is intractable by Hayek's fundamental discovery and co-ordination principles that his universalist project remains illusory and could be reduced to the self-serving, impoverished and impoverishing economism of market fundamentalists. And it is because it is intractable both to a rational reconstruction and an enduring reconciliation that Triffin's model is likely to turn into a necessary complement to the common market rather than the road to supranationality he envisaged, at least for the foreseeable future. Transformation is a slow process as Braudel noted when, in over 400 pages, he established the impersonal constraints that limited the power of Philip II before introducing him to the scene.

The second fundamental issue raised by both projects concerns the new risks they introduce in economic life. The first is the risk to sustained growth, in the sense that both the Hayek and the Triffin projects generate novel deflationary forces which undermine the legitimation drawn from the implicit argument that they 'will deliver the goods' (or rather from the unstated hypothesis that neither the free market nor closer integration need legitimation as long as they promise general prosperity). The second concerns the risks of market failure, market abuse, and critical policy erosion inherent in the workings of unregulated international finance under Hayek's model or Triffin's plans for Europe.

Market fundamentalism and integration have triggered a permanent revolution in markets, management techniques and production systems which stands in stark contrast with the assumption of a basically manageable and foreseeable world, which prevailed up to the 1980s. To be sure, even then we had lost the certainties of the 1950s and 1960s, but we were still able to reconcile contradictions and divergent ambitions in a more or less predictable

---

brilliant genious and national enthusiasm of List overtrough this presumption; and showed that the Ricardians had taken but little account of the indirect effects of Free Trade. No great harm might be done in neglecting them so far as England was concerned; because they were in the main beneficial and thus added to the strength of its direct effects. But he showed that in Germany, and still more in America, many of its indirect effects were evil; and he contended that these evils outweighed its direct benefits' (A. Marshall, *Principles*, p. 767).

way. However, globalization, successive waves of adjustment and 'creative destruction', rapid technological and institutional change, and a number of costly policy failures have started to pervade the world economy with a feeling of insecurity, undermining confidence and expectations, hence lowering both actual and potential growth. This debilitating brittleness, furthermore, is aggravated by the defensive macroeconomic management style which the asymmetric workings of the unfettered world financial system imposes on most economies. On the one hand, indeed, the nature of the competitive, expectations-based entrepreneurship which marks today's financial flows tends to validate individual deflationary policies. On the other, national expansionary policies are usually regarded with suspicion and tend to be invalidated by capital outflows driven by adverse exchange rate expectations and/or adverse interest rate anticipations. The net effect is a global bias to defensive monetary and fiscal management which further constrains potential growth.

Partisans of the free market consider the output losses thus occasioned as a mere temporary phenomenon, and in Europe the dark side of structural change is reasoned away as a typical case of 'creative destruction' and 'market completion'. Further arguments mobilize the US success in restarting and sustaining growth, or the fact that Europe has tested neither full integration nor full market liberalization. In actual fact, however, there is now accumulating evidence that the more free market capitalism prevails, the more destructive it becomes, with many of the gains highly concentrated and up-front, and most of the costs hidden in future collective accounts. Moreover, it seems increasingly unlikely that Washington will be able to sustain indefinitely the present balance between capital and labour, consensus and casualization, or dollar diplomacy and external liability accumulation. In sum, if actual and prospective losers continue to outnumber actual and prospective winners, today's cramped conventional political horizon may well start to undermine the growth legitimacy of both what is essential in Hayek's vision and what is the core of Triffin's project.

Equally menacing, for both projects, is the revolution which has transformed the balance between international financial intermediation and policy management. Neither could have possibly foreseen the technology and information jump which transformed an embryonic world financial community under powerful governance into a fully globalized, expectations-driven behemoth dominating domestic as well as international monetary management. Hayek, of course, welcomed what he saw as the beginning of a mutation which allowed market forces to arbitrate between domestic and foreign expectations, time preferences and asset-liability strategies, i.e to determine most if not all key money and capital prices in a dynamic momentum ultimately liable to denationalize money and to end central bank monopoly. Triffin, on the other hand, feared additional confusion and asymmetries as the mutation blurred territorial, analytic and instrumental correspondences and in doing so, fatally affected the assumptions drawn from history and the structural conditions of monetary integration.

There are three reasons why the neo-Hayekian evolution of international finance is likely to prove self-undermining in both general and Hayekian terms. First, its base, i.e. the collusive conjunction of a nationalistic dollar diplomacy, trading-driven finance – largely dominated by US firms – and an uncontrolled world liquidity creation, is patently unsustainable over time.

Its continued existence ultimately depends on a power constellation centred on a set of special conditions many of which are already in decline. Second, there is ample evidence that market failure and abuse are not an incidental by-product of market completion but inherent to the human praxis in an environment devoid of international regulation and marked by a deepening, maldistribution of information and the non-linearity of technical progress. On this particular point, market fundamentalists wrongly present the process of competition as a theory of optimum price determination, an error which Arrow saw as cumulative (1959, p. 41) and Hayek himself denounced (1978, p. 180). Third, the evolution is increasingly vulnerable to a political backlash. That danger was recently stressed by Soros, but it goes back to the one main question raised by Orwell in his review of *The Road to Serfdom*: 'He [Hayek] does not see, or will not admit that a return to free competition means for the great mass of people a tyranny probably worse, because more irresponsible than that of the state.' In sum, at some point of time, neo-Hayekian finance will either fall victim to a revolt against a vision which '...depends for its continued existence on a system of production and exchange that is fundamentally at odds with its deepest moral precepts' (Friedman 1989, p. 401), or come to resemble a self-destructive machine when, shaking and trembling, its motor runs ever faster.

Even before the financial revolution Triffin protested against interstate and private asymmetries, and he never thought that conforting the have-nots with the abstract beauty and prospective justice of the free market might be persuasive. The new developments, therefore, were met with proposals for a pragmatic narrowing of the institutional gaps and, more crucially, the establishment of the ECU '...as a reserve asset and parallel currency alternative to the inconvertible and disorderly fluctuating paper dollar of today' (Triffin BNL, 1987, p. 254). The latter proposal is important as it signalled an increasing focus on an autonomous European mix of discretionary policy and systemic rules within the new context of competing key-currencies, optional collective management and the emerging prudential supervision of the BIS. He was fully aware, however, that this further shift away from his hopes of consensual global reform and a collectively managed reserve system pointed to a sinuous and bumpy road.

On the one hand, indeed, Triffin's suggestions raised the hostility of a new range of vested interests, often able to mobilize nationalism, value-pluralism or corporatism as an effective veil. That is because the issues went well beyond mere traditional consistency problems and touched upon such crucial issues as the balance between governments and central banks, large and small member states, finance and real activities, ultimately also posing the question whether the construction of a coherent form of thought and action for the Union as a whole would imply a decoupling from American political, economic, and financial ambitions, or a mere resignation to a new hegemony. The Anglo-continental split on EMU, the debate on the degree of independence of the future European Central Bank, and the speculation on the 'hardness' of the euro, are in that respect typical illustrations of intra-European cleavages. On the other, the prospect of an enduring world non-system, volatile international finance, defensive policies and expectations, and a more divided Europe, heralded a substantial aggravation of the implementation problems. The form and contents of his 1987 essay, 'The IMS (International Monetary *System*...or *Scandal*?) and the EMS (European Monetary *System*)' (Triffin, BNL, 1987, stressed in the original), reflect both a renewed combativeness and a deepening of frustrations.

Most of these problems have not remotely been solved, and, in several respects, the gaps are widening. In fact, despite the dymamics of convergence now successfully active, there remains considerable disagreement about the balance between market forces and policy, the relative value and achievability of the US and continental models in terms of potential growth and the creation of choice-worthy options and, underlying it all, the very sustainability of the respective political programmes. Maastricht has set lines of institutional development which might prove 'germinal' in economic terms and ultimately, in political terms. For the moment, however, the overall European outlook is one of plural and provisional perspectives which lack the transcendental ground and rational constructivism which Triffin endeavoured to supply.

There is growing evidence that Hayekian tools useful in the struggle against the stagnant corporatism of the 1970s are not applicable to the radically different problems of the next century. The generalizations we owe to Hayek show how an acquisitions-driven, competition-constrained system continuously adapts its organization to the changing preferences of the market, and how such a self-ordering machinery can provide for a powerful drive toward economic expansion. But Hayek remains unable to stave off the moral questions which Smith already posed when he stated that the interest of those who live by profit is never exactly the same with that of the public (and that they '...have generally an interest to deceive and even to oppress the public and [...] accordingly have, upon many occasions, both deceived and oppressed it'). Neither does he deal with the problem of economic negative externalities, or is able to deflect the ultimate spectre of saturation which never ceased to haunt Smith, Keynes, and Schumpeter.

Likewise, Triffin's constructivist vision on the collective organization of modern industrial societies increasingly appears to reflect a historical contingency rather than the balance between personal and political freedom, economic and non-economic values, the short and the long-term, which the new generations view as constitutive of a new community. To protect the legitimation by growth from the strains and stresses of financial capitalism, the political, social, and economic forces of Europe are undeniably to be set in the institutional framework Triffin designed, if only as a new fulcrum to overcome national or nationalistic rigidities. But scepticism may yet turn into a wedge of disbelief unless EMU is perceived otherwise than an itinary ceaselessly generating new difficulties in the course of overcoming old ones. In other words, there is a dim and largely unspoken recognition that both the Hayek legacy and Triffin's precepts have to be completed.

That recognition, however, translates for the moment more into an opportunistic readiness to sacrifice the purity of the respective doctrines on the *modus vivendi* altar than into convincing efforts of renovation. Economists still struggle with the invalidation which Townshend drew from the theoretical debate of the 1930s, i.e., the direct causal influence of expectations on all prices means that: 'there is no position of equilibrium. The foundation of the (economic) theory has disappeared. The future is not merely unknown to the economic man; it is also undermined' (Townshend, 1937, p. 326). They supply political leadership with useful, sometimes brilliant fragments of a technical solution but remain unable to propose a system of unique, inevitable order that is both socially sustainable and economically efficient.

Politicians have found in Hayek a partial response to what Samuel Brittan calls a '...clear and present danger', i.e., the 'Political auctioneering, interest group pressure, and the combination of excessive expectations from collective action with excessive contempt for governmental and legal institutions, (which) are a threat not merely to some pure imaginary laissez-faire dream, but also to a functioning "mixed" or "corrected" market economy – and for that reason a threat to individual freedom and popular government' (Brittan 1983, p. 79).

They have benefited from Triffin's insights and fertile imagination for the development of a minimum of collective leadership at the international level and the re-invention of regionalism which now promises, at least in Europe, an efficient complement to the common market and some measure of protection against degenerative paradigms. But the subversive dynamism of the neo-Hayekian financial market, with its asymmetries, over- and undershoots, self-feeding aberrations and sheer indeterminacy, has unleashed new – hitherto unaddressed – threats to prosperity, stability, and equity. Defensive regionalism, on the other hand, fuels resistance and uncertainty as short-term costs are high, and its very functioning bodes ill for peaceful economic coexistence in a pluralistic but undermanaged world.

The prospect of inevitable change has generated a wide range of scenarios, from the resurgence of antimodernist political reactions and violent economic self-destruction to various forms of self-corrective adaptations and new partnerships to promote prosperity and stability. In a way, their very existence is comforting as, however diverse, all of them perceive the immanent tendencies of today as providing us with a general direction, which is still more or less foreseeable. In another, however, they all confirm a troubled, volatile transition, and nagging doubts about our capacity to successfully manage it.

In that perspective both Hayek and Triffin supply us with valuable complementary elements to imagine the new organizing principle that might secure a constructive linkage of diverse twenty-first century capitalisms (and I stress the plural). Hayek provides us the definition of liberty in economic terms, and many of the prerequisites we will have to respect if we want to travel on the path of stabilizing, self-optimizing change. Triffin teaches us the role of political governance that it is unreasonable to expect institutions and practices to survive unaltered, and that equity and pluralism are indispensable building blocks, not only for the relations among individuals, but also and foremost for those among different communities. Both, finally, showed us that progress is not so much a matter of rational choice as the recognition of the limits of rational choice. In sum, any realistic project for the future requires that we clean the site and examine the blueprints with the help of some essential Hayekian insights. But if we look for a genuinely novel, technically workable, and morally compelling reconstruction of a common life, it is from Triffin that we draw the main principles of a new architecture.

References

Arena, Richard, 'Hayek and Modern Business Cycle Theory', in *The Economics of F.A Hayek*, Edward Elgar, Aldershot, 1994.
Arrow, Kenneth, 'Towards a Theory of Price Adjustment', in *The Allocation of Economic Resources*, Stanford University Press, Stanford, 1959.
Berlin, Isaiah, *The Crooked Timber of Humanity*, John Murray, London, 1990.
Brittan, Samuel, *The Role and Limits of Government*, Wildwood House, Aldershot, 1983.
Buchanan, J.M. and Vanberg V., 'The Market as a Creative Process', in *Economics and Philosophy*, pp. 167-186, Oct. 1991.
Colonna, Marina (and H. Hagemann and O.F Hamouda) (ed.)., 'The Economics of F. A. Hayek', Vol.1, *Money and Business Cycles*, vol. 2, *Capitalism, Socialism and Knowledge*, Edward Elgar, Aldershot, 1994.
Friedman, Jeffrey, 'The New Consensus: The Fukuyama Thesis', *Critical Review*, 3-4, 1989, pp. 373-410.
Funabashi, Yoichi, 'The Asianization of Asia', *Foreign Affairs*, Nov/Dec 1993, pp. 75-85.
Gamble, Andrew, *Hayek: The Iron Cage of Liberty*, Polity Press, Cambridge, 1996.
Gellner, Ernest, *Conditions of Liberty: Civil Society and its Rivals*, Hamish Hamilton, London, 1994.
Gray, John, *Enlightenment's Wake: Politics and Culture at the Close of the Modern Age*, Routledge, London, 1995.
Hayek, F. Von, *Prices and Production*, Routledge, London, 1931.
——, *Beitrage zur Geldtheorie* (ed.), Springer, Wien, 1933.
——, 'Economics and Knowledge', *Economica*, 13/12/1937, pp. 33-54.
——, *The Pure Theory of Capital*, Macmillan, London, 1941.
——, *The Road to Serfdom*, Routledge, London, 1944.
——, *Individualism and Economic Order*, Routledge, London, 1948.
——, *The Sensory Order: An Inquiry into the Foundations of Theoretical Psychology*, Routledge, London, 1952.
——, *The Constitution of Liberty*, Routledge, London, 1960.
——, *Studies in Philosophy, Politics and Economics*, Routledge, London, 1967.
——, *Law, Legislation and Liberty: A New Statement of the Liberal Principles of Justice and Political Economy* (vol. 3), Routledge, London, 1973-1979.
——, *Hayek on Hayek* (S. Kresgeand L. Wenar, ed), Routledge, London, 1994.
Heilbronner, Robert L., *The Worldly Philosophers*, Simon and Schuster, New York, 1980.
Hicks, John, *Critical Essays in Monetary Theory*, Clarendon Press, Oxford, 1967.

Huntington, Samuel P., 'The West Unique, Not Universal', *Foreign Affairs*, Nov/Dec 1996, pp. 28-46.

Krul, Nicolas, 'La Neutralité de la Monnaie et l'Equilibre Monétaire dans l'Optique de l'Ecole Monétariste Néerlandaise', in *Revue Internationale d'Histoire de la Banque*, Droz, Geneve, 1970, pp. 1-35.

——, 'Teoria e Politica monetaria: Tappe di un ravvicinamento' *Il Risparmio*, XV, N°11, pp. 1929-1995.

Laidler, D., *Monetarist Perspectives*, Phillip Allan, Oxford, 1982.

Marjolin, Robert, *Le Travail d' une Vie*, Robert Laffont, Paris, 1986.

Monnet, Jean, *Memoirs*, Doubleday, New York, 1978.

Rueff, Jacques, *Le Péché Monetaire de 'Occident*, Plon, Paris, 1971.

Scheide, J., 'New Classical and Austrian Business Cycle Theory', in *Weltwirtschaftliches Archiv*, 1986/3.

Skidelsky, Robert, *John Maynard Keynes: The Economist as Saviour 1920-1937*, Macmillan, London, 1992.

Townshend, Hugh, 'Comment', *Economic Journal*, vol. XLVII, 1937, pp. 321-326.

Triffin, Robert, *Monopolistic Competition and General Equilibrium Theory*, Harvard University Press, Boston, 1940.

——, *Europe and the Money Muddle: From Bilaterism to Near Convertibility*, Yale University Press, New Haven, 1957.

——, *Statistics of Sources and Uses of Finance*, OEEC, Paris, 1960.

——, *Gold and the Dollar Crisis: the Future of Convertibility*, Yale University Press, New Haven, 1960.

——, 'Intégration économique européenne et politique monétaire', in *Revue d'Economie Politique*, Sirey, 1960.

——, 'The Evolution of the International Monetary System: Historical Appraisal and Future Perspectives', *Princeton Studies in International Finance*, No. 12.

——, *Rapport sur la Création d'un Fonds Européen de Réserves (1969)*, and *Vers l'Union Economique et Monétaire de la Communauté* (1970), Comité d 'action pour les Etats-Unis d' Europe, Paris.

——, 'The International Monetary Chaos: Causes and Cures', Proceedings: 'European Monetary System and International Monetary Reform', College d' Europe, Bruges 1981.

——, 'An Economist's Career: What? Why? How?', *Banca Nazionale Del Lavoro*, Rome, Sept. 1981.

——, 'The IMS (International Monetary System...or Scandal) and the EMS (European Monetary System)' idem, Sept. 1987.

Whitman, Marina v. N., *Reflections of Interdependence*, Univ. of Pittsburgh Press, Pittsburgh, 1979.

12 Globalization, Governance, and Transition – Managing Some of It

*Jozef M. van Brabant**

Nicolas Krul in his fine paper (1997) to the conference draws a learned, quite useful comparison between some of the main thoughts of Hayek and Triffin. In particular, he points out potential and desirable complementarities between the two approaches to 'governance,' though Hayek's doctrine hardly qualifies for that august label in my book! Both authors presumably hold broader philosophical precepts on policies and institutions apt to foster economic prosperity and sociopolitical stability, transparency, predictability, and some measure of equity in global economic relations. All this should be seen from within the context of the postwar, and especially the current, world economic system or, paraphrasing Triffin, non-system. I find Krul's focus on what was wrong and right with their respective approaches quite illuminating. I certainly do not want to till that ground once again.

Instead, I focus here on the implications of globalization[1] and of the debates around it for regional and global economic management, but with a deliberate penchant toward the plight of the transition economies. I first try to come to grips again (for an earlier attempt, see Brabant 1995b) with what Robert Triffin might have had to say about the present opportunities for managing the global economy as a counterpoint to Krul's erudite, more philosophical dissertation. Next, I grapple with a workable definition of globalization. Then I examine the core question that globalization should have raised, but has not; at least not sufficiently in my thinking about what could and should be done by way of response to the prevailing and emerging challenges. Thereafter, I look at the meaning of managing change, harking back to Schumpeter's notion of 'creative destruction,' but suitably deconstructed. The advantages of managing systemic pressures emanating from 'globaliza-

---

* Staff member of the Department for International Economic and Social Information and Policy Analysis of the United Nations Secretariat in New York. The views expressed here are the author's and do not necessarily reflect those of the UN Secretariat.

tion' I take up next. Then I inquire into the role of transition economies in the contemporary world economic order (or disorder) and whether close association of some with the European Union (EU), as the latter lumbers toward the conclusion of the ongoing Intergovernmental Conference (IGC), is a desirable objective, indeed a doable policy matter. In conclusion, I return to second-guessing what Triffin might have advocated and, health and energy permitting, how he would have mobilized himself in an attempt to persuade policy makers and the broader international community of what he deep down felt to be correct.

Section 1: Robert Triffin, pragmatism, and the 'new economic order'

As indicated, Krul views Hayek's approach to market-based solutions as a monistic theory. This is fine as far as theory is concerned. It can be quite misleading, however, when applied in actual economic policy, whatever the country and its circumstances. I shall not repeat Krul's instructive elaborations. For one thing, I am not particularly enamored by monistic, all-or-nothing, grand-design approaches to structuring a community. In addition, applying the theory to actual policy-making is fraught with treacherous pitfalls. Since Hayek advocates a peculiar form of organization in which the state and its various and associated governance organs for all practical purposes desert society, this cannot amount to useful policy-making under most real-life conditions. I agree here with Ralf Dahrendorf's characterization of Hayek as 'an all-or-nothing theorist, which is fine so far as the constitutional preconditions of politics are concerned, but dangerous, if not disastrous, in the world of real political conflicts' (Dahrendorf 1990, p. 34). The latter realm is necessarily the arena in which are played out 'competitive bidding' or 'political auctioneering,' as Krul sees the real world of policy-making. And it is thus within that realm that one must identify ways and means of improving matters over and above what spontaneous market order à la Hayek could possibly accomplish.

Although he does so with greater circumspection and circumlocution, Krul appears to ascribe a similarly monistic, perhaps even all-encompassing, script of a preferred manner of organizing policy-making also to Triffin's vision of global economic collaboration. That he states to be the 'negotiated adherence to collective rules and norms to ensure compatibility among the divergent national and regional interests and, at the national level, among the requirements these agreed coordination norms imply'. I find that view misleading in three respects. For one thing, it is far too static, as if Triffin envisaged the negotiation of a once-and-valid-for-all-times constitution on behaviour among states. I believe a much more dynamic view is in order here, one woven around the need to maintain regimes, to supplement them as history marches on, and indeed to revise them as lessons are drawn from experience, including failures. Krul has it right in the latter part of his paper but wrong earlier on. Second, I find it hard to accept that Triffin insisted on only one set of rules and norms as did Hayek, whose alternative is a passive system to be sure, but one complete in itself and necessarily intolerant of untidy realities. Realist that he was, Triffin certainly would not have ignored that coordination frequently occurs because of a shared culture (Legro 1997); that it is at times easier and wiser to recognize – what modern discourse on co-operation refers to as – subsidiarity or solving 'local' solutions by 'local' rather than 'global' means; and that some problems may generally be more amenable through alternative forms of organizational decision-making (Sah and Stiglitz 1985). Finally, the implications of ascribing such a self-contained, negotiated universalism in a world that is necessarily pervaded with value pluralism to Triffin I must reject: that he cherished a logically self-contained, coherent economic doctrine, as did Hayek, around universal management entailing necessarily another variant of 'totalitarianism' (Dahrendorf 1990, p. 36).

Unlike Hayek, however, who has always displayed a fatal tendency to hold up another immutable system, save the immanence of its self-projection, against that of socialism, I simply do not see Triffin advocating anything like a self-contained system; or for that matter insisting upon any proposal as being the unquestionably unique sole solution to the problems at hand. If that had been the case, Triffin would never have been a useful policy adviser in the best sense of that often misunderstood term (Cairncross 1985, Harberger 1993). Whatever his own deep convictions may have been, Triffin was the quintessential pragmatic designer of and adviser on economic policy. I do not wish to be misunderstood here: Triffin's pragmatic bent had nothing to do with impulsive experimentation. Instead, it was meant to be constructive realism, a tactic to move closer to rendering the more coherent solution feasible at the earliest opportunity.

Triffin's approach relies on two propositions. One postulates that there are gains to be had from complementing national policy-making through some arrangements by which nation states try to extend their respective national policies to a higher, multilateral (but not necessarily global, let alone supranational) level. This should in principle be entertained whenever the object of national economic policy has, directly or indirectly, complementary or conflictual intersections for other countries. I presume that economic remit could be easily extended to other domains of social intercourse among nations or 'communities.' But I am not aware that Triffin dealt with those issues. After all, he was and remained the quintessential academic economist with more than a pragmatic policy penchant.

Also, and this is my other proposition, the particular shape in which these deliberations among governments on selected issues take place should transcend the purely intergovernmental level. Triffin believed strongly in the appropriateness of having multilateral regimes and institutions endowed with a capacity to 'manage' those interdependencies better than what any one country in isolation might have been able to achieve, even under the strictest hegemony format. One might add that by referring the issues to 'professional' organs, rather than intergovernmental political or diplomatic deliberations, a step back could be set to work out, within specified limits, technical solutions. Naturally, some could be applied directly, whereas others would need the approval of the membership or be managed through representative governance.

That said, I find it hard to subscribe to the notion that Triffin saw such institutions, policies, and the underlying regimes as chiselled in granite in any possible meaningful sense of that term.[2] Two counterexamples may suffice. Triffin appears to have been ready to propose deviations from the institutional set-up when warranted by concrete circumstances in the hope of steering the deviant country or situation back to the mainstream for which the global regime in place could then be applied. The quintessential example is his involvement with the policies and institutions embraced in an effort to restore convertibility in Western Europe after World War II via the European Payments Union (EPU) – by definition a pragmatic subregime of a temporary nature. Its goal was not only the restoration of convertibility among the Western European countries; it was deemed to be a necessary prelude toward enabling that part of the world to play a constructive role in the context of the international monetary regime; indeed without it, the international monetary system could not, and did not, function. The other example that bears on the issue is his involvement, almost from the moment the international monetary regime could begin to function as originally designed, to reanchor the very foundation of that system away from a dollar-based fixed-parity system.

True, as these examples illustrate, in a sense Triffin shared a bit of Hayek's fatal conceit, namely the belief that man is able to shape the world around him according to his wishes; but I hasten to qualify this with: 'at least to some degree.' I do so too! Unlike Hayek, however, Triffin's approach to the issues at hand was and remained pragmatic. Rather than coming forth with all the answers, as does Hayek, Triffin was prepared to tackle the untidiness of the real world and of policy-making, and thus to learn and draw conclusions from failures as well as successes. That Hayek simply rejected 'state interventionism,' as he termed this approach once the basic framework was in place, would inevitably distort the spontaneously self-regulating market economy as a discovery process (Gray 1989). And I very much doubt that Triffin's conceit would have extended to the design of a 'system' purported to be the ideal variant from his days to eternity.

I submit that it is Triffin's enduring commitment to working for pragmatic but policy-relevant, and thus constructive, solutions apt to contribute toward resolving actual and potential conflicts in global economic, especially monetary, affairs that marks his legacy. His generous and unwavering commitment to innovating, formulating, fine-tuning, and promoting best-practice policy pragmatism in a world of sovereign states with, at best, lukewarm commitment to multilateral disciplines deserves our admiration and gratitude. And so he was almost constantly engaged in demarcating areas in which a narrow reading of national economic sovereignty might be infringed upon by recognizing the other's equally valid areas of national sovereignty.

As I explained on an earlier occasion (Brabant 1995b), I have often wondered how Robert Triffin would have reacted to the debates about the transitions in the eastern part of Europe what he would have proposed by way of easing the required structural transformations in the affected countries had these events transpired a bit earlier, and how he would have engaged himself in the grand debate, and indeed in the policy deliberations, to ensure that his agenda and rationale would at least be known and understood. I have also wondered how he would have positioned himself in the current debate on globalization. Krul has pointed out several areas in which Triffin might have had serious doubts about the wisdom of fostering the Anglo-American variants of completely free markets, notably in the case of speculative capital movements. But I am not aware that he advanced any concrete proposals on either set of daunting issues.

As explained earlier, with regard to the calamity in the eastern part of Europe, he would almost certainly have favoured a modernized version of the approach taken for Western Europe in the postwar period. He would have looked at the tumultuous mutations that have transpired in the eastern part of Europe since 1989 and the international community's timid, disorganized response, with incredulity. I am convinced he would have been appalled by the fact that the highly instructive lessons about multilateral economic cooperation learned the hard way after World War II have been so completely ignored (Weiss 1997). I suspect he would have wondered whether the tedious struggle for providing effective economic assistance to the Western European countries at the time, and indeed the forms it ultimately assumed, deserved to be fully forgotten. Realist that he was, he would not have suffused his bewilderment and reactions within the context of a pure textbook model. Instead, it is safe to conjecture that he would have projected them against the backdrop of historical experience and realistically prevailing policy options. He certainly would not have ignored the broader ramifications of the economic, political, and social revolutions in the transition economies.

I have similar inklings when it comes to perceptions and actions that he might have vigorously promoted in the context of the 'globalization debate,' and it is on this issue that I should like to expand here. Of course, it would be highly impertinent to pretend that I can second-guess with any degree of plausibility what Triffin might have formulated. Nevertheless, I feel on fairly solid ground that my thinking about how the globalization conundrum could be handled more effectively than it has so far in the international community would have 'pleased' Triffin in more than one respect. Inasmuch as globalization is taking place at a time that the transition economies are attempting to position themselves fully within the world economy, my hunches as to how Triffin would have 'dealt' with the turbulence in the eastern part of Europe can be combined with my second-guessing of the position on globalization he might have taken.

His starting point would probably have been the remarkable paradox that the global economic framework envisaged at Bretton Woods can now, after the momentous changes in the eastern part of Europe, at long last be reached. Doing so, however, would hardly be very relevant to the problems of the day, let alone the tasks ahead in managing the global economy. With liberalized markets and national governments unwilling or unable to manage their own national economic policies, and extremely reluctant to engage in any type of 'global' economic management, another solution would need to come to the fore. There is, of course, still a need for policy flexibility as debated at the Bretton Woods Conference, though that crucial marker of sensible policy was soon thereafter forgotten. Such flexibility might yet again be required to facilitate the accession to the globalizing economy on the part of categories of countries that for one or another set of special circumstances find it difficult to accomplish this feat. I am thinking here in particular of the catch-up hurdles the more advanced transition economies must confront, the modernization obstacles faced by many new and old developing countries, and indeed the adaptability problems that a large swath of so-called mature market economies need to overcome. Pragmatism in policy-making at the national, regional, and global levels might be required to enable those groups of countries to link themselves constructively into the global framework.

In all this, the art of the possible must be fully reflected. But that should not justify eschewing bolder approaches. For it is only by identifying the more ambitious, analytically coherent perspectives that the remit for exploring somewhat more timid policy-making can be traced. This applies as much to sovereign states participating in the global context as it does to the existing multilateral, regional as well as global, institutions and regimes. They too are in need of a much more forceful stance on their role in managing global economic affairs. By being rebuffed for solid reasons by their respective memberships, they will be able to locate the effective limits of their room for policy manoeuvre. Dialectically, that might in turn reinvigorate the debate in the international community and persuade leading actors therein that there are still palpable advantages to be reaped from doggedly pursuing a more comprehensive approach than simply muddling through at the national level.

As the evolution of the discussion about the international economic organizations (IEOs) since the breakdown of the Bretton Woods system in the early 1970s has underlined, there is probably little chance of replacing the existing organizations with new ones ostensibly better suited to the tasks at hand in managing economic interdependence going into the twenty-first century and beyond. The present difficulties around European integration, not only with the prospect of eastward expansion but even in steering the affairs of the committed member countries, have amply demonstrated how difficult *de novo* institutional innovation truly is. Acknowledging the art of the possible is one thing. Forgoing the opportunities for adjusting the constitutions of the supporting organizations, and indeed for innovating temporary derogations to meet a specific set of temporary policy challenges, is something else, something that I think Triffin would have relished in more than one respect. At the very least, it should be possible to suitably reinterpret existing mandates. In other words, accommodation for countries and economic models that fit incompletely into the existing regimes and their underlying multilateral institutions must be explored from within the organs in place, rather than from without. This could be accomplished by modifying standard adjustment programmes or by setting up special arrangements. But it is doubtful whether the organizations will wish to modify their 'proven' menus, or could readily do so for a select group of countries, on their own initiative. Their track record in a variety of developing countries is not particularly encouraging. Temporary derogations to ease adjustment problems need to be taken care of by other means, including special facilities.

Section 2: Globalization defined

'Globalization' has become a catchy moniker for many things. At the very least, it denotes a variety of phenomena (Akbar and Mueller 1997). Not only that, its justification is often contorted. When not too ill-defined, globalization's real importance, notably the reactions it should elicit on the part of various actors in the global economic framework, is rarely touched upon; it is at best handled with kid gloves rather than squarely faced. The current degree of globalization – say, the extent to which nations are intertwined through trade, services, finance, information, technology, and so on, a definition that I find too encompassing, as I argue below – is not nearly superior to what it was before World War I. What is fairly new is the scope of interactions within the global community, not just in economic affairs; the extent to which they have progressed; and indeed the speed with which they are being transmitted. The latter is not just a matter of technology, but also of lowered transaction costs all around, notably in communication, information, and transportation.

Many of the jeremiads about globalization simply miss the point, quite apart from the fact that they often disregard historical evidence. Global economic integration is with us to stay. It is, in fact, a much desired outcome of the sought-after postwar framework for international economic relations. This had two aspects. One was the institutional set-up for managing the 'global' economy erected during and after World War II. The other is how this framework was allowed to crystallize over time because of passivity, often inaction, on the part of major actors in the global economy. The latter situation may well be regrettable. Yet, it is not particularly fruitful to try and relive history all over again. Instead, I deem it more constructive to take the situation as given and instigate an honest search for ways and means of managing the changes that have been besetting the global framework by design or as a result of failure to maintain and update it. That is to say, the central message of globalization should be: because of the change in the speed and breadth of our near-oneness, even greater efforts are required to manage this transformation process, from the personal to the global levels. Note that this is not at all a mandate to promote all-around liberalization and privatization.[3]

Here I focus on what globalization entails for managing the world economy. But I do provide a small illustration of its implications for governing the European economy in two respects. One is the role of the Intergovernmental Conference (IGC) initiated in Turin, March 1996, as it inexorably draws to its closure. On the evidence at hand, this IGC is unlikely to achieve positive delivery on even the minimum agenda set out in early 1996.[4] That in itself has ominous implications, given the prospect of yet another, this time a rather contentious, enlargement. But many other aspects of governing the global or European economy could legitimately be explored.

There are undoubtedly meaningful alternative definitions of globalization that are not as all-encompassing, hence meaningless, as the one invoked earlier. In economic affairs the notion is as a rule invoked to capture the degree of cross-border economic interactions. In the literal sense, it implies that those interactions have now reached, or are nearing, their peak and that the probability for changes in 'technology' to occur and relocate that apex is not particularly strong (Bairoch and Kozul-Wright 1996). This view is much too static and ahistoric in any case. More useful is viewing globalization as a process of change, but not quite starting from the beginnings of economic interactions across state borders. As such, it is often confounded with concepts of openness, integration, and interdependence, which may reflect theoretical problems in linking trade in goods and non-factor services, capital movements, and foreign direct investment (FDI) in particular. Globalization should connote a fairly advanced degree of interdependence among the main economies in the global framework. It should also refer to the smoothness with which this process of rising interdependence advances over time. If it is dominated by forces that make for discontinuity and conflict, rather than being almost friction-free, market-driven adaptations, globalization should be of policy concern. I confine my comments to the latter, more restricted meaning.

Economic interactions include visible (such as trade in goods and in related services) and invisible (such as electronic financial services) transactions. Perhaps most important, globalization has been defined with respect to the rapid emergence (rather, *re*-emergence) of private capital flows (that is, all international financial flows that do not arise from official bilateral and multilateral agencies; in other words, loans extended from or guaranteed against public revenues – actual or expected). Note that such flows consist of three categories: commercial-bank lending, other portfolio investments (such as share purchases or bond holdings), and FDI driven principally by the search of transnational corporations (TNCs) for extending their presence, and expanding their market share, worldwide with a view to raising medium- to long-term profitability. These forces in particular have been leading to frictions in managing the global adjustment process.

True, the volume of trade, services, and financial flows has risen fast, say, over the past half century. Trade has continued to expand since postwar stabilization with the gradual opening up of national markets, lowering of tariffs and other trade-inhibiting instruments, and the re-establishment of full currency convertibility. All that, I submit, can be taken to be the realization of the outcomes desired when the architects of the postwar global economic order began to design their preferred path toward restoring national, regional, and global economic prosperity. The growth of services derives from the twinning with trade, certainly, but also from the gains in incomes recorded notably in developed countries, given the high income elasticity for leisure products; the finer division of labour in a broader range of products and services; and the risen technological capability to internationalize service delivery while lowering costs, owing chiefly to the revolutions in transportation, information, and electronics. The truly 'more recent' phenomenon is the presence of TNCs throughout the world in a widening range of economic operations, when countries permit more or less free capital flows and the TNCs adjudicate such new markets as promising sites for a reliable and attractive rate of return, at least in the medium to long term.

Allow me to repeat again a common sense observation: the increased interpenetration of national economies that some policy makers now lament has been a core item desired by the postwar economic framework. Indeed the latter's creed was 'liberalization.' Both domestic and foreign competitors in that reference framework should be enabled to vie for filling demand in a market with expanding horizons from a level playing field, a common platform from which largely privately owned firms design their microeconomic strategies driven by the quest for profit. To reach that stage, hindrances to 'fair' international competition were to have been reduced to a minimum. Quantitative restrictions were to have been abolished and replaced with *ad valorem* tariffs; tariff levels were to have been significantly cut and their span narrowed through multilateral trade negotiations; and market access was to have been facilitated by a return to current account convertibility and, in time, also capital account convertibility; but the architects of that framework had at best a murky vision of what TNCs, and financial flows more generally, could accomplish positively as well as negatively in terms of reaching the goals set for managing the global economy. Whether the latter is desirable in an unrestricted sense, and at what particular stage of economic maturity, poses incisive and intricate questions in their own right that I can touch on here at best tangentially. Suffice it simply to note that in major actors in the global economy full (that is, current and capital account) convertibility has recently been achieved. The core question is whether the relevant markets for current account and capital transactions can do their intended instrumental job. If they function not quite the way economic theory suggests, there is *potentially* room for policy intervention to ease various frictions.

It may come as a surprise to analysts ignorant or disdainful of economic history to discover the *déjà vu* element in the present degree of economic interpenetration in the world economy. The idea that global economic integration at this juncture in international economic affairs spells a 'new' stage in the dynamics of economic development throughout the world since the adoption of neoliberalism by major actors in the global economy and by the core IEOs (see Sachs and Warner 1995), is patently wrong, indeed a myth of sorts as cogently argued by Paul Bairoch and Richard Kozul-Wright (1996). Not at all a myth, however, is the origin of the current degree of economic interdependence: it is not the liberal agenda embraced by some global actors since the early 1980s, but the outcome of managed liberalization over a protracted period of time since the late 1940s. Not only that, the degree of economic interpenetration observed at the end of the 'long' century was anything but the result of a liberalized global economy with hands-off national economic policy-making (Bairoch and Kozul-Wright 1996). On its own merits, then, this evidence does not warrant pushing the neoliberal agenda even more forcefully, as is all too commonly recommended (Sachs and Warner 1995, 1996), notably by the multilateral financial institutions, without at least identifying at the same time areas of conflict and less than smooth adaptations in the global, regional, or national economies.

There is wide agreement about the fact that globalization has weakened the ability of the nation state to manage economic activity. Not only that, it has indeed changed the remit of actions by regional and global institutions and even the particular purpose of the regimes for which they act as custodian. It has also complicated the manner in which national policy makers can be found willing to defer managerial tasks to higher authority. Even so, neither the nation state nor the idea of management, possibly at a higher level than the individual state, has become irrelevant. In fact, continued prosperity, and the further extension thereof in time and across countries, depends crucially on enacting prospectively a suitably adaptable management style. Since the nature of globalization at this juncture differs qualitatively from that observed, say, about a century ago, the role of the state and of national and multilateral management may have to be updated to smooth discontinuities and avoid conflicts or to innovate ways and means of overcoming them. This may require deferring certain activities to 'market institutions' when they function reasonably well. But it also mandates the co-optation of issues that were not on the agenda, or under a different heading, when the framework for managing the world economy was first established and that the institutions in place have since not adequately dealt with.

Section 3: The core questions raised by globalization – managing change

The above characterization of the basic ingredients of international economic interdependence suggests that globalization refers to far more than simply the extent of cross-border economic exchanges. Once artificial obstacles to international economic interactions (such as tariffs and quantitative restrictions) are removed and 'natural' barriers are lowered by technological advances (such as communication, information, and transportation), growing interdependence becomes a 'natural' phenomenon. It is the logical collective outcome of the quest for raising profitability and productivity, and indeed average (material) welfare, by individual firms, mostly privately owned businesses. After all, if one subscribes to the notion of the profit-driven *homo economicus* as the paragon of economic comportment, one must rationalize this form of globalization as a salutary development (Krueger 1997).

Such a phenomenon does, however, lead to two classes of questions. One concerns the nature of globalizing linkages and how they are brought about, maintained, and expanded over time. On those grounds, the present globalization debate has several dimensions that diverge from the myth built up on the basis of measuring cross-border exchanges. The other real question revolves around the notion of management or governance. One can break it down into two component questions, limiting the inquiry to the economic dimensions of globalization: (1) has the current dynamics toward globalization eroded the ability of policy makers at the national (in sizable countries), regional (such as in the EU), and global level to manage economic affairs according to the spirit of their assigned mandates? and (2) has this erosion by now assumed such proportions that the degree of governance still available, if all capabilities at hand are properly exploited, has weakened the various institutions' responsibility over the direction of economic activity within their assigned space to such an extent that it falls well short of the desirable minimum to ensure basic features of the national, regional, or global order (such as smooth adaptation and adjustment on an equitable basis)? It is important to be clear about these desirable features at whatever level of aggregation. For if they have changed, possibly because of the stress placed on the relentless drive toward globalization, then there may be no need for tinkering with the lowered governance ability.

Change by definition engenders threats. These may take on various characteristics. But concerns in some group of countries, notably those erstwhile in the vanguard of ensuring global management, have been focusing chiefly on job security and income stability. These threats could conceivably be warded off through protectionist devices. In the short run, the country imposing those levies could undoubtedly benefit. However, as the disastrous results of policies adopted after World War I and later, including in many of the former communist and a swath of developing countries, have amply underlined, the longer-term outcome is invariably negative when the advantages for, in this case, the nation as a whole are *fully* factored into the equation. At the same time, these threats provide opportunities for seizing the moment and building thereupon. It is how best to move from the threatened state of affairs to one in which the proffered opportunities are exploited to best advantage, seen in a broad context for the 'society' being addressed and the goals pursued there, that merits attention. I assume that there is at least a non-empty set of tasks that the market, be it at the national, regional, or global level, is not delivering upon to the desired degree and in a complete format. Thus one could posit that economic actors, whether private or public, attach positive value to reliability, predictability, transparency, and openness – by definition public goods – of the global economic system; some are probably also valuing a measure of equity, not necessarily limited to income redistribution, in international economic development beyond what fair competition generates, and indeed may be capable of.

Once one agrees on this remit, the domain of 'dealing with' public goods opens up. At the national level, government can steer public goods via its powers of coercion and persuasion. This may also be the case at the regional level, although the EU's experience in recent years has not presented a compelling case for solving problems of regional public goods without appropriate regional governance. At the broader level of international economic interdependence, however, public goods need to be created and consumed for which there is no discernible appropriate government at this stage (Kindleberger 1986) and for which sheer intergovernmental synchronization falls short of the desirable minimum. One must therefore fall back upon the creation, maintenance, and enforcement of multilateral regimes for which the appropriate governance structure is to be streamlined through some form of organization in which governments participate but decisions are made largely consensually. Who should assure the production and distribution of these public goods? There are economic aspects to this conundrum; but also many others, including matters of foreign policy, security, health, and so on. In short, one can capture this ensemble under the label 'managing change.'

What does managing change mean? In this era of the minimalist state and liberalism, with unusual faith in the powers of the market (Krueger 1997) in spite of abundant evidence to the limits of market forces, even simply invoking the notion 'planning' elicits allergic reactions in a diverse lot of actors. It should not. Change in the sense defined can be so threatening and overwhelming that a transition phase, if feasible, becomes desirable to ensure an orderly progression from the old to the new. Its character may also assume dimensions that cannot be resolved at the level of decision-making for which capabilities are in place. The cited change in response to perceived or actual threats may materialize spontaneously, leading to recession, social discontent, or even rupture of the sociopolitical consensus for governance through elected or appointed government or chosen multilateral regimes. It may also be confronted in a positive manner by designing a purposeful strategy for moving steadily to the 'destruction' by design of the old while forging ahead expeditiously with 'creating' the new. Schumpeter's notion of 'creative destruction' as the motor driving dynamic economic expansion needs to be deconstructed into its manageable components.

Consider labour-market policies, such as in continental Europe. Double-digit levels of unemployment on average, with large swaths of those entering the labour force being unable to find employment and especially the unskilled in mid-career being relegated to chronic long-term unemployment, is scandalous and should not be tolerated. That it has for nearly a decade on average in the EU, and much longer in some member states, renders it even more puzzling. I cannot conceive of any explicit or implicit social consensus that would exclude reaching for high levels of utilization of resources, including employment. The issue has certainly not been addressed directly through imaginative policies aimed at both job creation and facilitating upward mobility. The failure of policy makers in a wide array of countries to support and oversee the changes required to tackle this blight on the European 'social model' must stem, in some manner, from the kind of 'distributive coalitions' and 'negotiated politics' that have tended to paralyse longer-term decisions in line with a vision of the direction into which society should move in the European parliamentary democracy. Managing change with longer-term implications than the length of the electoral cycle, even at the level of the nation state for which a credible government exists, has become a daunting assignment.

An example may illustrate this proposition. Labour-intensive economic activities in developed countries have been under threat via import competition and indeed the outward migration of capital simply because unit labour costs (that is, the total cost of labour per value unit of output) in, say, the EU exceed by a wide margin comparable magnitudes in many transition and developing countries. The reverse prevails in activities intensive in other factors (such as physical or human capital). That sets the stage for identifying comparative advantages. Existing advantages at one point in time mutate under impact of competition at home and abroad, shifts in relative factor costs, technological change, and so on. When the terms of trade move against activities, such as those intensive in the use of unskilled labour in developed countries, the response should not be protectionism. It may even be counterproductive to compress real unit labour costs by artificial means, such as by lowering real wages or social benefits unless there is a consensus on changing the 'social compact.' Rather, those resources should be encouraged to move to higher-productivity activities. That is usually only feasible when physical capacities are created and the affected individuals acquire new or higher-valued human capital possibly through organized retraining. To reach that platform, time and money are required. If nobody facilitates this adjustment process, chronic long-term unemployment results with generations of entrants to the labour force relegated to society's selvage. On the other hand, an orderly relocation of these workers, including early retirement when retraining is not feasible, can prevent the emergence of the personal, family, economic, social, and psychological costs of long-term unemployment and indeed smooth the process of adjustment from one economic activity to another.

One could take literally dozens of similar examples to illustrate that moving from the 'old' to the 'new' imposes 'transaction costs.' Managing those costs to advantage, essentially treating them as an investment into the acquisition of new, higher-productivity capabilities, is after all what economic policy should be all about: to infuse the remit assigned to policy makers with greater reliability, stability, predictability, and perhaps even a dose of equity in the arena within which otherwise economic agents, regardless of origin, can pursue their own interests. As noted, managing change cannot be confined to remits for which governance structures and capabilities are in place. There are spillovers of change from the nation state to the regional and global levels that cannot be managed, or are difficult to govern, from within the nation state, even when one dominant actor enjoys a high degree of hegemonic power.

Section 4: Steering the global economic framework

The title's phrasing in and of itself conjures up interventionism and statist planning. It should not. After all, the postwar international regimes were designed to permit policy makers to 'guide' economic interactions with a view to maintaining stability, full employment, predictability, transparency, and some element of equity, among other objectives. That was 'planning' of sorts. Likewise, governing a society such as in the context of the nation state is a form of 'planning.' Though the latter's content has changed over time, strategic thinking ahead of threats and opportunities has by no means become superfluous. In some respects, it has become *more* important, though perhaps less encompassing, than used to be the case. Primarily because nations have become more intermeshed over the past half century, governance at the higher multilateral level should have assumed greater importance with its focus appropriately fine-tuned. Instead, the commitment to multilateralism has weakened considerably. This may not immediately be obvious to all observers. Because for all practical purposes governance at the higher level depends on the regimes and organs in place, a brief word about the present international economic 'order' is appropriate.

Not everyone is persuaded of the usefulness of the international economic regimes and their custodial IEOs. Some even argue that the postwar infrastructure meant to 'manage' the world economy has been detrimental to the expeditious internationalization of global economic relations. Others fundamentally accept that, in principle, positive benefits derive from having predictable, transparent, and reliable rules for international trade, finance, investment, the monetary framework, and so on. But they may not be completely pleased either with the regimes as originally constituted or with their implementation, including their evolution over time; some see primarily problems with one or more IEOs rather than their underlying regimes. Those commentators do not, however, contest that a search for relevant multilateralism may yield positive benefits, particularly for smaller countries. I share this view. But I also advocate that there is cause for continual honing of the existing *modi operandi*. That is best addressed by taking another look at the origins of the postwar regimes.

During World War II and the ensuing two decades, many foreign policy analysts, and even economists, looked on the whole positively at the opportunities for 'global economic management.' This derived in part from the generally pro-government attitude prevailing after World War II. But also from the profound belief that markets alone could not sustain buoyant growth, stability, predictability, and equity in the world economy. Hence the attempt, in the absence of supranational government, to entrust responsibility for guiding the global economy to IEOs for which 'regimes' were developed. That enthusiasm has since waned considerably. The reasons are legion. They include vastly exaggerated hopes of what can reasonably be accomplished in the context of an essentially intergovernmental body with the membership holding divergent views on what precisely the IEO should accomplish, how the activities of the various IEOs can be co-ordinated, and how each IEO can best be governed internally. But skepticism about global co-operation since the early 1970s also derives from equally mistaken views that IEOs are not particularly useful; some claim they cause more harm than good.

I do not subscribe to either polar stance. I simply assert that the existence of IEOs in which many countries participate and air their own interests, as well as their perceptions of more global issues, forms an essential ingredient of a 'normal' state of affairs in an interdependent global economy. The greater the degree of interdependence, barring higher-level coercive government, the greater the potential role of good governance at that multilateral level. One must recognize that the various actors have their own ideas, values, norms, and assumptions that diverge and even conflict, but influence their behaviour. Needless to say, all this considerably complicates governance of the regimes for which these IEOs act as custodians. Yet there is no alternative no matter how well developed in theory the magic of a more neutral model may be.

We know from experience that the establishment of such regimes tends to be facilitated by the existence of a hegemonic power, but that it is much more difficult to maintain and update those regimes over time. One could easily substitute the notions 'leadership,' 'vision,' and 'responsibility' for 'hegemon,' and I prefer the former combination of terms, as I shall demonstrate below. Whatever one calls it, the commitment to international regimes tends to weaken, thus complicating decision-making in the custodial institutions and neglecting to maintain and update the underlying regime, when the power of the member states gets further diffused with the waning of the leading country's economic vitality (Kindleberger 1986, p. 8) or, one might readily add, its political and moral fibre. Setting up new regimes is almost completely precluded. Working from within the existing regimes and institutions, earlier created largely under impulse of the leading hegemon, tends to be difficult. Yet, the advantages of the regimes should be beyond dispute. More difficult is to ensure that the regime's public good is actually produced and delivered. This conjures up issues about the costs of the regimes and who will defray them. But I shall not deal with those matters here (Brabant 1991, 1997).

Section 5: The advantages of managing the world economy with globalization

An international economic regime can best be thought of as a set of gradually accepted explicit or implicit principles, norms, rules, and decision-making procedures that reflect the common denominator of what actors expect to bring about as far as a given component of the international economic order is concerned (Brabant 1991; Krasner 1982, 1983).[5] To co-ordinate the behaviour of these actors, especially when it has significant external repercussions, this order needs to be endowed with full-fledged organizations or state arrangements through which the agreed-upon rules and conventions can be enforced in a transparent, predictable, and reliable manner. Otherwise an international economic order is likely to fragment quickly into a state characterized by, at best, weak rules and light-hearted breaches thereof as countries adopt entirely at their own discretion policies that have pronounced international repercussions; paralysis in IEOs and 'market anarchy' would be the worst outcomes. A regime's usefulness derives from the fact that it improves the intermeshing of the behaviour of individual states or groups of actors within states upon what can be achieved when the latter all act through uncoordinated individual calculations of self-interest.

Adherence to a particular regime yields benefits and costs. As the degree of interdependence soars the benefits of regime adherence should expand relative to the rising costs of maintaining the regimes, provided the latter are properly governed. *A priori* international regimes benefit smaller countries more than larger ones, whereas their costs are borne in the reverse order. However, if regime benefits accrue to, or costs fall very asymmetrically on, a particular group of countries, it may be best to adopt a regional regime governed by a regional institution (such as the EU within the context of the global trade regime). The point is that there must be some reasonable apportionment of benefits and costs. Otherwise the regime cannot be sustained even though one is manifestly not dealing with a zero-sum game.

The broad benefits and costs of multilateral regimes change over time. This may be so substantial that a revamping of the regime may be in order. The present juncture of 'globalization' may signal just such a chasm between the rationale of the postwar regimes and what they in their largely unadapted format can accomplish at this stage. Rather than focusing Fund activity on exchange-rate surveillance and balance-of-payments assistance, the World Bank on catalyzing development finance, and the World Trade Organization on chiefly trade in manufactured goods, the global regimes should address increasingly the shifts in international interdependence that have been giving rise to discontinuities in the national, regional, and global adjustment processes. For that to materialize, however, positive leadership is required. In principle, this could come from any one participant in the international regime. However, leadership can be effectively exerted only when appropriate resources are mobilized. That is to say, positive leadership must be suitably backed up with resources, even if asymmetrically appropriated. This requires in the first instance vision, responsibility, and commitment on the part of large actors. A readiness to incur the resulting costs, indeed to sustain some sacrifices, in the international interest is indispensable. In the end, such international regimes are desirable to 'protect countries not only from competitive behavior by their peers, but also from their own short-sighted follies' (Williamson 1985, p. 78).

It should be obvious that the regimes in place do not necessarily mirror the ideal that the regime's advocates favoured, the negotiators set out to construct, or the members as stakeholders originally committed themselves to maintain and refine. Nonetheless, there can be little doubt that the regimes targeted in this paper, and the ones usually seen as the pillars of the postwar international economic order, held virtues, hence yielded advantages to the realization of policy objectives, that, as John Williamson (1985, p. 78) remarked for the Bretton Woods institutions, 'were sufficiently real to make that failure [to provide flexibility] a matter of regret.'[6] This has been borne out by a number of events since the breakdown of the 'Bretton Woods system.' One need only recall the debt crises of the 1980s, the Mexican debacle of 1994-1995, and the many instances of disruptive speculative capital flows in many countries. Belatedly, the international community has reacted to these disturbances. The costs incurred by not having provided for these events, and for some it could have been done, has been very large indeed. Endowing the Fund, for example, with extra resources to engage in Mexico-type operations or with the constitutional power to assist countries in setting up institutions and policies to 'manage' better capital flows (in the context of the proposed revision of article IV of the Articles of Agreement so that the Fund can also keep the capital account under surveillance) is useful, of course. But these steps would appear to fall short of a more embracing degree of surveillance and guidance, one that would enable the appropriate international regime to cope with disturbances as they occur rather than only in an improvisational reactive mode.

The test of a good multilateral regime should not be whether its 'constitution' is ideal and it has been adhered to in good faith. Similarly, the criterion for adjudicating the performance of its custodial institution should not be whether it has impeccably fulfilled its role. Rather, the test should be whether it has brought about significant changes for the better in managing the purposes for which it was erected (say, the global monetary, financial, or trade order, or regional integration in the EU) and whether it has shown itself capable of taking action to correct errors and failures, thus promising further gains in the years ahead. I recognize that this is a highly pragmatic rule of thumb. But I simply cannot see the usefulness of continuing the debate on ideal solutions, except as a guiding beacon, while in the meantime the issues one is trying to address are left untended. As the proverb goes, closing the barn door after the horse has bolted is not very useful; shutting only part of the door, preferably the lower one, pending the rehinging of the rest of the enclosure, could have contained the animal.

Section 6: Governing transition and EU integration with globalization

Much the same rationale should prevail with respect to the EU and its governance, on the one hand, and the way in which the broader issues of governing the transition in the eastern part of Europe can best be cast, on the other hand. I can touch upon those issues here only in a very abbreviated format; more extensive renditions can be gleaned from the existing literature (including Brabant 1995a; 1996a, b; 1997 and the references cited there).

Revamping the constitutional make-up of the EU was to have been the principal purpose of the ongoing IGC (Brabant 1996a, b). The objective was a dual one: to forge ahead with 'deepening' integration among the Fifteen by completing the internal market, largely via monetary union (the twin component of Economic and Monetary Union in the much maligned moniker EMU) and entering into other areas of common concern (such as the social sphere, foreign policy, security, and police co-operation), and to permit 'widening.' Deepening requires not only new policies or placing different accents on existing policies. It also calls for modernizing the governance of the EU and perhaps updating its institutions, including the division of powers among the main EU decision-making levels (the European Council, the Council of Ministers, the Commission, the European Parliament, and the European Court of Justice). All this should be accomplished with the goal of improving the way the EU functions among the Fifteen, thus making further enlargement, especially toward the eastern part of Europe, feasible at least in principle.

The poor progress booked to date by the ongoing IGC suggests that at best a minimal set of modifications to the Maastricht Treaty will be ready for approval at the forthcoming Amsterdam European Council (16-17 June 1997). It is not even certain at this stage that the basic changes in governance in the EU will be ready for approval by that time. Failure to enact meaningful shifts in the number of commissioners, in voting rights in the Council, in level of qualified majority, in narrowing the scope for unanimous decision-making to a few crucial constitutional matters, in the size of the European Parliament, and so on will have two consequences. One renders enlargement so much more difficult, unless the constitutional framework of the EU were to be watered down to that of intergovernmentalism – something truly inimical to the very basics of the ambitions on European integration enshrined in the Treaty of Rome. Such a development would indeed impose possibly insuperable barriers to preserving the character and maintaining the pace of integration. One can only pray that such a trend will not come to prevail. Yet failure to resolve to a minimally workable level the governance issues already hampering effective co-operation among the Fifteen is bound to inhibit 'deepening' integration, let alone 'widening' the EU's remit. The latter is particularly ominous for the candidates from Central and Eastern Europe. In consequence, the aspects of globalization referring to the EU are likely to entail conflicts and adjustment pains far exceeding what would prevail with a properly governed EU.

Moreover, the methods and rules of the world the transition economies seek to join more generally are inadequate both to harmoniously accommodate these countries and to assist them in their quest to jump the hurdles that impair their participation in 'regular' international relations. What can be done under prevailing realities? The heart of what multilateral governance should be all about in light of the see-saw changes in the eastern part of Europe now revolves around how the transition economies could usefully participate in these organs, given their present and evolving circumstances. Because these countries are far from being full-fledged market economies, it might be useful to inquire into ways of potentially adapting the international regimes so as to better accommodate the transition economies.[7] Furthermore, because the latter aspire to securing close participation and eventual membership in the EU, how could or should they conform to set norms?

Although there are many similarities between global and regional governance, there are also distinct differences. With fewer actors, regional governance should be less complex than governance in global and near-global organizations based in essence on the principle of full equality among participants. At the same time, the commonality in concerns to be addressed should facilitate the delivery of the 'public good' that multilateral governance is all about. Because the regional regimes that the transition economies desire to join are in a much greater flux than their universal counterparts, this should in principle offer greater opportunities for modifying the regional regimes to reflect the prospective interests of these economies.

An honest attempt to usher the transition economies more fully into the existing international regimes in general and into the EU in particular could therefore benefit from a transition phase. Some modifications in the conventional *modi operandi* of these regimes would therefore seem opportune, at least until the transition economies will have sufficiently matured and be able to play a 'normal' role in these regimes. The benefits would be reciprocal. Insiders would be assured that some realistic measures are taken by countries that cannot fully adhere to the agreed discipline to harmonize their systems with those of the regimes in place and the major actors therein. At the same time, such transitional provisions enable the transition economies to access early on some of the benefits emanating from being associated with the regime. In this way, the international community could avoid undermining support for the ongoing transformation processes in transition economies. It would also provide some assurance that structural transformation will continue as expeditiously as circumstances permit while correcting the economic features of the situation in transition economies that now inhibit fuller participation in the international economy. Because this is a largely uncharted territory, successful conclusion of the deliberations will by necessity depend on creative, imaginative proposals formulated and entertained by all parties involved; once again, pragmatic policy-making in a constructive vein would seem to be required (Cairncross 1985, Weiss 1997).

Conclusions

Looking at the prevailing international economic situation, particularly the place of the transition economies, I have no doubt that Robert Triffin would, in sum, have been appalled by several of its features. One obituary noted that, as far as the stability of the international monetary system was concerned, Robert Triffin was 'proved largely right, his fate was to be a Cassandra, unable to persuade policy makers to make the changes that would have preserved a system in whose underlying principles he strongly believed' (*Financial Times* 1993). That would not have deterred him from riling against the deplorable neglect of the opportunities for global economic management! This has been manifest in terms of revising the *de facto* regimes in place so that the transition economies can extract maximum benefit and the international community can minimize the most negative repercussions of the extraordinary situation in the eastern part of Europe. It has been even more pronounced in terms of revising the *de facto* regimes with a view to enhancing economic co-ordination, thus improving the ways in which the crucial international economic problems of the day and beyond can be tackled.

Infusing realism into the globalization debate is warranted for at least two reasons. One is that it helps to reduce perceived 'threats' to the more realistic dimensions of global interaction. But it also steers the debate on how best to come to grips with some of the threats to the proper discourse: deliberations through multilateral regimes on how best to manage one aspect or another of our global economy; similar comments could be underpinned for other areas of global interdependence, arguably even including culture. *Mutatis mutandis* this has also implications for the EU, particularly as the IGC draws to its close and the process of opening the negotiations for enlargement, perhaps during the Luxemburg European Council (12-13 December 1997), has to be squarely faced by the European leadership.

Whereas it is useful to be aware of the threats that globalization entails for each and every endeavour, I consider it more fruitful to dissect the actual and potential threats carefully with a view to elaborating strategies on how best to cope with the process of change. It is crucial to recall that this entails destruction' of what cannot survive as 'other' partners take the relief as well as 'creation' of what promises a better future and will constitute the springboard for effective participation, including through competition, in the more competitive global framework. In this manner, constructive international responses to the challenges of the transformation of the countries emerging from under communism and of globalization can be provided – if only as an intellectual exercise.

Bibliography

Akbar, Yusaf H. and Bernhard Mueller, 'Global competition policy: issues and perspectives,' *Global Governance*, Vol. 3, No.1, 59-81.

Bairoch, Paul and Richard Kozul-Wright (1996), 'Globalisation myths: some historical reflections on integration, industrialization and growth in the world economy' (Geneva, mimeographed, April).

Brabant, Jozef M. van (1991), *Centrally planned economies and international economic organizations* (Cambridge and New York: Cambridge University Press).

—, (1995a), *The Transformation of Eastern Europe – Joining the European Integration Movement* (Commack, NY: Nova Science Publishers).

—, (1995b), 'Western assistance to PETs, the monetary system, and global integration,' in *The Global Monetary System After the Fall of the Soviet Empire – In Memoriam Robert Triffin 1911-1993*, edited by Miklós Szabó-Pelsőczi (Aldershot: Avebury), pp. 11-33.

—, (1996a), *Integrating Europe: the Transition Economies at Stake* (Dordrecht, Boston, MA, and London: Kluwer Academic Publishers).

—, (1996b), 'The transition economies, the Intergovernmental Conference, and the European Union,' *Banca Nazionale del Lavoro Quarterly Review*, No. 198, 287-312.

—, (1997), 'Managing globalization' *One Europe Magazine*, No. 13, forthcoming.

Cairncross, Alec (1985), 'Economics in theory and practice,' *American Economic Review*, Vol. 75, No. 2, 1-14.

Dahrendorf, Ralf (1990), *Reflections on the Revolution in Europe – in a Letter Intended to Have Been Sent to a Gentleman in Warsaw* (New York: Times Books).

FT (1993), 'Triffin: far-sighted economist,' *Financial Times*, 3 March, 2.

Gray, John (1989), 'Hayek on the market economy and the limits of state action,' in *The Economic Borders of the State*, edited by Dieter Helm (Oxford: Oxford University Press), pp. 127-43.

Harberger, Arnold C. (1993), 'The search for relevance in economics,' *American Economic Review*, Vol. 83, No. 2, 1-16.

Kindleberger, Charles P. (1986), 'International public goods without international government,' *American Economic Review*, Vol. 76, No. 1, 1-13.

Krasner, Stephen D. (1982), 'Structural causes and regime consequences: regimes as intervening variables,' *International Organization*, Vol. 36, No. 2, 185-205.
——, (1983), *International regimes* (Ithaca, NY: Cornell University Press).
Krueger, Anne O. (1997), 'Trade policy and economic development: how we learn?' *American Economic Review*, Vol. 87, No. 1, 1-22.
Krul, Nicholas (1997), 'Hayek and Triffin: fragments on divergence and convergence in policy thinking' (Budapest, March, typescript).
Legro, Jeffrey W. (1997), 'Which norms matter? Revisiting the 'failure' of internationalism,' *International Organization*, Vol. 51, No. 1, 31-63.
Sachs, Jeffrey D. and Andrew M. Warner (1995), 'Economic reform and the process of global integration,' *Brookings Papers on Economic Activity*, No. 1, 1-118.
——, and ——, (1996), 'Achieving rapid growth in the transition economies of central Europe' (Cambridge, MA: Harvard Institute for International Development, July, mimeographed).
Sah, Raaj K. and Joseph E. Stiglitz (1985), 'Human fallibility and economic organization,' *The American Economic Review*, Vol. 75, No. 2, 292-7.
Triffin, Robert (1991), 'The IMS (International Monetary System... or Scandal?) and the EMS (European Monetary System... or Success?)', *Banca Nazionale del Lavoro Quarterly Review*, No. 179, 399-436.
Weiss, Charles Jr. (1997), 'Eurasia letter: a Marshall Plan we can afford,' *Foreign Policy*, No. 106, 94-109.
Williamson, John (1985), 'On the system of Bretton Woods,' *American Economic Review*, Vol. 75, No. 2, 74-9.

Notes

1. I draw here on an earlier elaboration (Brabant 1997) on globalization, building the new Europe, and the implications for multilateral governance.
2. If evidence is needed, one of his last published articles (1991) should corroborate the position I take here. He recalls there his views (together with Fritz Machlup and Jacques Rueff) on the 'ideal' international monetary system. But he leaves no doubt that such a concept would at best be a guiding beacon for concrete policy actions.
3. For one influential advocacy thereof, although it grossly misinterprets the very economic history whose message it seeks to endorse, see Jeffrey D. Sachs and Andrew M. Warner (1995). They have attempted to transfer that message to the transition economies (see Sachs and Warner 1996). But that misses much of the essence of the desired catch-up transformation in these countries.
4. What the precise mandate of the IGC may be has crystallized only under evolving circumstances. For an in-depth analysis of how it meandered between the call for such a conference in the Maastricht Treaty to thoroughly review, consolidate, and update the EU's quasi-constitution and the fall of 1996, see Brabant 1996a, b.
5. This can be suitably rephrased for any multilateral regime when appropriate governance organs and capabilities at *that* level are lacking.

6. Williamson (1985, p. 78) is referring in particular to the failure to 'provide mechanisms capable of maintaining such a satisfactory conjunction of circumstances' as had ensured that the Bretton Woods system could function. The SDR agreement, in his view, provided flexibility with regard to the quantity of reserves but additional reforms (such as limited exchange rate flexibility and asset settlement) that were then perceived to be needed to allow the system to survive, failed to be enacted.
7. Modifications to accommodate other groups of countries with incomplete markets should also be entertained, of course. But they fall out of this paper's compass (see Brabant 1991).

13 From the Marshall Plan to New Balances

Gusztáv Báger and Miklós Szabó-Pelsőczi

A. The Marshall Plan

I. The main elements of the Marshall Plan

There were several elements of the real world and of intellectual perception which have contributed to the creation of the Marshall Plan. Among these, the most important were:

1. a realistic appraisal of the political and military security needs of the United States and of those war-torn European countries which were willing to accept the norms of democracy and of social market economics;
2. a realistic – neither overgenerous nor hard-fisted – appraisal of the economic needs of these countries to receive a mixture of sovereign non-refundable capital transfers; concessionary loans under favourable conditions; as well as asymmetric trading privileges for a limited period of time;
3. the ability of the United States to provide this start-up capital and trading advantages in a sufficient amount;
4. an unusually talented group of American and European policy makers who applied the Plan's relatively limited resources in a pragmatic way based on New Deal and Keynesian economics, and on the whole, succeeded in establishing sound balances among economic and political variables leading to democratic, societal cohesion, recognized by most – if not by all – economic and social players as fair and equitable;
5. a monetary order of adjustable but fixed exchange rates, enshrined in the Articles of Agreement of the IMF;

6. the European Payments Union (EPU 1950-1958);
7. the willingness and the foresight to make way for market forces from the start and even more so as their ability increased to support price stability and growth.

All these elements were highly compatible with the vision of postwar economic, social, and political policy statements from the Atlantic Charter to the Purposes of the International Monetary Fund.

The Marshall Plan was announced in 1947, because simple market forces could not cope with the enormous capital needs of postwar Europe.

Since this announcement fifty years have passed and the world has changed significantly. Most of the elements which have contributed to the creation and the success of the Marshall Plan do not exist, or if they do, we are uncertain of their relevance. Some of these deserve special attention.

II. The international monetary system

The fixed par value system of Bretton Woods (1944) has received a major blow on August 15, 1971 with the suspension of the dollar/gold convertibility, although floating has become general only from early 1973. One of the most distinguished experts on this field, Robert Solomon says: 'It was when inflation was accelerating in early 1973, that the decision was made to adopt floating exchange rates...'.[1] 'A major reason for the move to floating in March 1973 was to put an end to the undermining of monetary policy in Europe...'.[2]

No one would quarrel with the view that various monetary issues, especially the difficulties of sterling and finally its 1949 and 1967 devaluations have exposed the par value system to serious strains for years. This is why the Special Drawing Rights have been developed and that the First Amendment to the Articles of Agreement was made to enter into force on July 28, 1969.[3] It is to be regretted that it was never put to test and that after August 15, 1971 for all practical purposes it has been made inoperative.

Not suprisingly, after August 15, 1971 world inflation has continued, has led to general floating and to the first major oil-price rise of December 23, 1973.

'The quadrupling of oil prices by OPEC at the end of 1973 was probably the most severe shock to the international monetary system – and, more broadly, to the world economy – since World War II', observed Robert Solomon in 1977.[4]

Actually, the basic damage to the world monetary system started with the termination of dollar/gold convertibility. The disintegration of the system continued with general floating: with the first and then the second oil-price explosions in 1973 and 1979; with the debt crisis of the developing countries in 1982; and with the inability of the industrial countries to give a Marshall Plan-type response after 1989 to the structural changes then developing in Central and Eastern Europe.

This chain of events is a major contributor to today's reality. It has basically changed several economic, social, and political balances, which up till August 1971 were relatively stable. As the 1970s, 1980s, 1990s wore on – they became less so.

Without making value judgements at this point, I am observing the above developments as facts. Establishing new balances at satisfactory levels, or in a 'virtuous circle' will be difficult. The explosive development of world liquidity, of offshore currency markets since 1971, as well as of derivative markets during the last decade or so, are making the task even more complex.

III. The security issue (I)

A significant impetus to the development of the Marshall Plan was the political, military danger felt from the aggressive tendencies of the Soviet Empire. Fifty years later, many people feel that with the ending of the cold war, all future dangers for democracy and for free market economies have evaporated. 'The end of history' has become, at least for a while, a popular belief. Its credibility did not last long. The Balkan, the Caucasian wars, the still precarious position of democracy in Russia and in a number of former socialist countries (FSCs) must convince us that while the cold war, as we knew it for close to half a century, is over, its continuation is not peace, but – paraphrasing Klausewitz – a new kind of cold war by other means interspersed with both diplomatic and hot episodes. This situation is not necessarily less dangerous to democracies and free markets in the western hemisphere, or elsewhere than the cold war was.

If this statement is correct, then a Marshall Plan-type of reaction, obviously adapted to the new situation, is called for.

Nature and politics abhor vacua. Therefore, it is important that we recognize that these vacua exist and must be filled at all deliberate speed with democratically inspired free market institutions.

This is why NATO's Eastern extension to sufficiently mature countries is important, this is why NATO's constructive dialogue with Russia and possibly with some of the FSCs is indispensable for the security not only of the Euro-Atlantic Area, but in Marshall's words – used by him in an essentially economic context – 'for the future of the whole world'. Marshall and the Truman Administration in which he served were, especially from 1947 and 1948 on, very conscious of the interrelatedness of the economic and security issues of their age. Therefore, it is entirely appropriate that we discuss these interrelated issues here, from the vantage point of our own times.

By now it is obvious to most of us that our concerns for economic cohesion, diplomatic balance, and military security for all must be global. To, and from, statesmen of even a few decades ago these words might have sounded as Gladstonian or Wilsonian flourishes. Today and for the 21st century, they express the backbone of a Marshallian realpolitik.[5] President Kennedy's dictum: 'Peace is indivisible' was never more true than it is today. The Atlantic Community, or the OECD countries, could not live in peace and amity within themselves and with each other – family quarrels notwithstanding – unless they follow the dictates of a democratic and free economy. Neither could they live in peace and harmony with Russia, China, India, the southern hemisphere, the Islamic world, the Middle East and the Pacific, except by fair principles, supported by strong economies, democratic social cohesion, and clear-sighted realpolitik.

Fifty years ago, on the success of the Marshall Plan 'the future of the whole world' depended. Today, contemplating the future of a global world – which now often looks chaotic and fragmented – we could still learn much from the insights of the Marshall Plan, concerning its underlying search for balances in both the economic and the security sectors.

IV. The socially responsible free economy

One of the elements of success of the Marshall Plan was that it has arrived at a time when postwar Europe was prepared for the state's acceptance of greater responsibility in the creation of a socially more responsible economic order. Schumpeter, already in 1942, has noted, without approving or disapproving, that the 'disintegration of capitalist society has gone' already far on certain fields, and that the implications of these developments 'are being taken for granted both by the business class itself and by (a) large number of economists...(who) accept not only unquestioningly but also approvingly:

1. 'the various stabilization policies which are to prevent recessions, or at least depressions, i.e., a large amount of public management of business situations even if not the principle of full employment;
2. 'the desirability of greater equality of incomes, rarely defining how far short of equality they are prepared to go, and in connection with the principle of redistributive taxation;
3. 'a rich assortment of regulative measures frequently rationalized by antitrust slogans, as regards prices;
4. 'public control, though within a wide range of variations over the labour and money market;
5. 'indefinite extension of the sphere of wants that are now, or eventually, to be satisfied by public enterprise, either gratis or on some post-office principle; and
6. 'of course all types of (social) security legislation.'

A few lines later, Schumpeter adds significantly: 'Capitalism... means a scheme of values, an attitude toward life, a civilization of inequality and of the family fortune. This civilization is rapidly passing away...'.[6]

The social and political conditions of postwar Europe have built the welfare state on the soil of this declining capitalist culture. Its form and content differed greatly from the Beveridge Plan to Erhard's Soziale Marktwirtschaft and from the thinking of Sweden's Myrdal to Italy's Einaudi, and to the United States' countless social programmes.

The net results of these measures were, and still are, rather on the positive side, the numerous unintended consequences notwithstanding. Per capita real GDP growth has shown satisfactory results until 1971, and at a slower space after that. The quality of life improved to a very large segment of the population. Life expectancy increased, a healthy middle-class expanded, which has helped, rather than hindered the work of a cultural and business elite. Democratic societal cohesion became the norm, rather than the exception, at least until the 1970s. The maintenance of economic and social balances became more difficult and more costly after 1971, because of the structural change in the international monetary system (stagflation). The longer life of the population, due to improved healthcare, to higher per capita disposable incomes, and to a better quality of life are not in themselves negative attributes of the postwar system of social responsibility. One should study carefully to what extent the increasing relationship of budgets and budgetary deficits to GDP are the results of the management of the international monetary system during the last three decades; to lax actuarial evaluations, and to plain inefficiencies of social security institutions. During the course of their overdue review, positive elements should not be discarded purely for ideological reasons.

V. The administrative techniques of the Marshall Plan

After World War II, European reconstruction started only with great difficulty. Although by the end of 1947 the Area has received some $10 billion support from various aid agencies like the United Nations Relief and Recovery Agency (UNRA) and the Government Aid and Relief in Occupied Areas (GARIOA),[7] these did not solve the Area's financial problems. At the end of 1947, the gross indebtedness of countries of the Organisation of European Economic Co-operation (OEEC) has reached $9 billion, corresponding to 5 per cent of these countries' annual GDP.[8,9] It was then that the American authorities came to the conclusion that *ad hoc* aid and standard economic practices are insufficient, and that the creation of a new economic institution is needed.

The principles of the Marshall Plan were relatively simple. America has committed itself to help to 'break the cycle of dispair (in Europe) and restore the confidence of the continent... Assistance should be a basic cure, not piecemeal. It should be open to all countries crippled by the war, not just a few. The initiative should be European, not just American... At the same time, any country opposing the programme could not expect help. Efforts to undermine this assistance would be opposed... (On this programme) the whole word of the future (depended)'.[10]

The programme started with remarkable speed. After Marshall's now famous address at Harvard on June 5, 1947, Congress voted the European Cooperation Act[11] into force on April 3, 1948, which made the Marshall Plan operative. Earlier, just a few weeks after the Harvard speech, 16 European countries have created in Paris the Committee of European Economic Co-operation (CEEC) for the purpose of working out a four-year European development programme (European Recovery Programme – ERP). By the fall of the same year, the Committee was reorganized into the Organisation of European Economic Co-operation (OEEC) which after some significant changes in its task and with a new name (Organisation for Economic Co-operation and Development, OECD) still functions. The legislation supporting the Marshall Plan was in force for three and a half years, until June 30, 1951.[12] But during these barely 40 months it 'has changed the course of history' – as it was intended.

Among the most important tasks of the European Recovery Programme was to achieve a fast and strong expansion of production; the re-establishment and maintenance of trade; and of monetary stability; the promotion of intra-European trade and of European economic co-operation. 'Increased production... was to be the touchstone of European recovery.'[13]

The Marshall Plan represented about 1.75 per cent of the United States' GNP between 1948-1951, or $12 billion. Of this amount $9.2 billion were non-refundable grants; about $1.2 billion low interest rate loans, extended on favourable concessionary terms (repayment period 35 years at 2.5 per cent interest; repayment starting in 1952); and $1.6 billion financial assistance to promote inter-European trade.[14]

The outstanding feature of the Marshall Plan was that although it represented a unique departure from the principles of both classical and welfare economics, it has recognized from the start its own emergency and temporary nature. This emergency was the postwar situation. The main trust of the Marshall Plan was the effort to bridge this emergency and once this was accomplished, it lead economic life back to multilaterality and convertibility. There was no specific schedule set when convertibility and multilateralism should be reached. It was, however, assumed, and correctly so, that once the direct and indirect ripple effect of the ERP will run its course, the essential features of free markets: multilaterality and convertibility (at least on current account) will follow in due course.

According to this general thinking, the Second Session of the Committee of European Co-operation accepted a 'Convention for European Economic Co-operation' (Paris, April 16, 1948).[15]

The measures contained in this Convention, aiming at the gradual reduction of quantitative and qualitative trade barriers among OEEC countries are well known. Due to space limitations, they cannot be recounted here. It is, however, worthwhile to call attention to a feature which is almost unique in comparable assistance programmes. The donor country, the United States, while requiring that capital transfers to the recipient countries should be spent mostly in the United States 'for the shipment of goods', it was willing to accept that 'European governments... maintain restrictions on imports from the United States (because it has considered) that freeing inter-European trade... to be an expression of (the Europeans') willingness to cooperate with the United States in keeping Marshall Aid within reasonable limits (and thereby) to minimise the burden on the American taxpayer by reducing the amount of dollar purchases by the participating countries to the greatest extent possible.'[16]

This apparently contradictory American tolerance is understandable if we consider that the Marshall Aid was based on foreign exchange, i.e. USD needs of OEEC countries. The less they imported from the United States, the less were their dollar requirements, hence their need for aid. On the other hand, whatever aid they received was deemed to be spent on the shipment of goods from the United States.

The Marshall Plan was administered by the OEEC in Paris. Recipient Countries worked out their yearly USD requirements on the basis of the ERP. The American Representative at the OEEC naturally had a very important role to play: he had to justify to Congress the way how American taxpayers' money is being spent. His influence was especially great in the determination of how counterpart funds will be used. In the first round, European governments have received their Marshall Plan Assistance in dollars. These were deposited in special accounts. They could dispose of these accounts only with the consent of the American Representative. Once the Recipient Governments have on-lent their share of Marshall Plan transfers to local entrepreneurs, they, for their own account, imported goods from the United States. Then they were obliged to repay the original dollar loans with interest to their national government, in domestic currency, into a counterpart account. This allowed the local government to on-lend the same funds for further development purposes.

'The fundamental interdependence of the flow of goods, services, and ownership titles on the one hand and monetary movements on the other hand, is one of the most obvious and most important aspects of international economic relations' – says Hieronymi.[17]

During the immediate postwar years intra-European trade developed only slowly. European countries had very limited dollar or gold reserves. European goods were not very competitive on American markets in spite of considerable trade concessions. Due to the general shortage of dollars, which many feared to be permanent, European countries were forced to trade among themselves on a bilateral basis and only within strictly established quantitative restrictions. The task was therefore to replace bilateralism with multilateralism in a way which should simultaneously increase the competitiveness of European goods on the world market.

The European Payments Union (EPU)[18] has greatly contributed to the carrying out this task through the creation of a clearing system for the Members of the Union, with monthly settlements. Central banks could settle their surpluses and deficits resulting from clearing balances through accounts opened for this purpose at the BIS. Settlement could be effected up to 40 per cent in gold and convertible currencies and up to 60 per cent within each country's quota in the EPU; the quota corresponded to 15 per cent of each country's 1940 EPU trade. These percentages have changed with time. The net debtor could also pay with any other currency which creditors would accept. Countries with chronic deficits had to undertake either to restructure their economy or to devalue their currency.

The EPU was operative between 1950 and 1958. While its task was not altogether completed, its members increased their intra-European trade from 56 per cent to 89 per cent of total trade during the period 1950-1956; member's national currencies, due to increased trade activity approached convertibility and most of them became convertible by 1958.[19]

The architect, the most distinguished theoretician and advocate of the EPU was Robert Triffin. The Marshall Plan supported this activity. Among others, it contributed $360 million to the start-up capital of the EPU. It can be said with confidence that neither the EPU would have succeeded without the support of the Marshall Plan nor the latter without the contribution of the former.

B. Concepts

I Bridges between then and now

The concept is 'an idea of what a thing in general should be.'[20] Concepts in the economic and social sphere are successful if they establish dynamic balances, 'virtuous circles' energizing constructive forces in the sectors they cover.

The Marshall Plan had such a concept: to help 'the people of the United States escape the danger of isolationism... and to assist all European countries crippled by the war' to get on their feet.[21]

The International Monetary Fund, including its First Amendment, had such concept, facilitating 'the expansion and balanced growth of international trade... (to promote) high levels of employment and real income... (to develop) ...the productive resources of all members... (and) to correct maladjustments in (members') balance of payments without resorting to measures destructive of national and international prosperity...'[22] The success of the Marshall Plan was greatly supported by the concepts of the EPU and the IMF; and have contributed to the balanced growth of the 20-25 postwar years.

These concepts, these visions, were the ultimate sources of the relative peace and societal cohesion of the Euro-Atlantic Community during this period.

It is difficult to see how without a minimum of shared visions and values, democratic global cohesion and a virtuous circle could be obtained in the future. And we shall not forget that globalization today is not a matter of choice, but a technologically given condition.

The ending of the dollar/gold standard has ushered in a period whose economic and societal concepts are different from those of the quarter century following it. The vision of a pragmatically mixed economy of social justice was replaced by a much less sophisticated and much less articulated vision of an essentially profit-driven economic paradigm. A purely profit-driven society does not, cannot, and explicitly refuses to take responsibility for the creation of a socially just society. 'After 10 years of research... I came to the conclusion that the expression of social justice has no sense in the free society of free men... There can be no distributive justice there, where nobody distributes',[23] said Hayek.

Fifty years after the Marshall Plan, we find that the concepts which were the major reasons of its success are not operative any more, and if they are, they are more as survivals of a past age and not as the driving forces of a new century. The forces which brought about a virtuous circle of democratic societal cohesion are slowly but steadily replaced by new technologies and by new and different societal forces with a relatively high probability of bringing about a vicious circle of societal dissent, rather than a virtuous circle of societal cohesion.

The remaining pages of this essay will explore some of the reasons of this change and some of the ways how its most objectionable consequences might be avoided.

C. Toward new balances

I The security issue (II)

Today, the issue of global security is just as important as it was fifty years ago. Then it was soon recognized. This recognition has led to the speedy reconstruction of Western Europe. Today the OECD world, the block of the world's most powerful industrial countries, does not have a realistic concept of the future. It is itself divided by many parochial economic, if not political issues. Although its major actors will likely remain for a while the United States, Europe and Japan, they share the world with many great cultures and power centres: the Russian, for centuries one of the European great powers, the Islamic, the Hindu, the Buddhist, the Confucian, the Hebrew traditions, which are spreading over vast areas and often organized in great states (China, India) or in smaller but still powerful countries (Israel) and covering parts of the northern and southern, eastern and western hemispheres. The opportunities of conflict for military, political, ethnic, cultural and for purely economic competitive reasons are numerous. The daily news is filled with local outbursts, but the restlessness is global and it is tamed only with great difficulty.

It would be inappropriate in our search for virtuous circles to ignore the vast constructive potential inherent in these potentially destructive forces. But the road is dangerous: we are walking on eggs and mines – these latter often wired, in a figurative way, to nuclear capacities, and to other means of destruction.

In a somewhat similar situation the Marshall Plan chose the high road to success. It squarely faced up to the security issue. It mobilized the economic forces of the Atlantic Community with the best monetary and economic tools democratic countries can apply to foster democracy and socially responsible free markets. Thereby, it has initiated virtuous circles which for decades have changed world events for the better.[24]

Thinking in global terms is not our choice. Rapid technological change forced us, in a sense perhaps prematurely, into this mode of thinking. The technical change is there; it has created, it is creating economic, social, political, and military imbalances. Economists and economic policy makers should catch up with the challenge of these imbalances: they should help creating, on the basis of a strong economy, a new balance of a culturally articulated cohesion of free societies where goodwill, amity, and freedom of fear and of want would prevail.

This is a tall order. Its fulfilment depends on a right mixture of idealism and geopolitics. The bringing about of strong economies and of culturally articulated peaceful cohesion on a global scale will be difficult and it will take time. But 'history under no condition will give absolution to eventual failures, simply because of the greatness of the task' – says Kissinger in another context.[25]

The down-to-earth principles and the common sense heritage of George Marshall are suggesting that the seriousness of the security issues should not dampen, but should stimulate the efforts to craft economic, cultural, societal, military security structures bringing about fair and new balances in our increasingly globalized world.

II Monetary, economic and societal coherence

The pragmatically mixed monetary and economic thinking and practice which made the Marshall Plan – in addition to its own attributes – a success, came under heavy attack during the past quarter century. It is in the process of being increasingly transformed into a *laissez faire* economy, in which the monetary, economic, and societal balances of the Marshall Plan era are loosing their countervailing capabilities.

These balances have suffered their strongest shock from the international monetary sector. The *de facto* disregard of the First Amendment of the IMF has led to an unanticipated increase in world liquidity. While official reserves of central banks increased between 1949 and 1968 from $45 billion to $79 billion (an increase of 76 per cent), their increase during the next 20 years, from 1969 to 1988, amounted from $79 billion to $1,147 billion (an increase of 747 per cent). The rate of increase during the second 20 years period was ten times larger than during the first 20 years period. The increase continued during the period 1989-1993 from $1,147 billion to $1,436 billion (an increase of 25 per cent).[26] One should not be surprised that the increase of liquidity at such a rate has led to major structural changes in the global economy, including their negative effects on inflation and high unemployment.

One of the contributing factors of the fast expansion of liquidity is the vigorous growth of the eurocurrency market not even existing during the Marshall Plan era. Eurocurrency, or offshore markets, which contribute the major part of net international bank lending, as annually reported by the BIS, increased from $60 billion in 1969 to $3,780 billion by the end of 1993[27] and to $4,645 billion at the end of 1995.[28]

The speed of international communications, the explosion in the volume of computerized derivative trading gave further opportunities for speculation, especially in currencies and financial instruments, not even dreamt of fifty years ago.

It is no wonder that a disciple of both Hayek and of Karl Popper's 'Open Society', and a successful market participant, came reluctantly to the conclusion that 'if the working of the free market economy is not tempered by the (justified)recognition of the public interest which overrides individual interests, then our current social system, which more or less corresponds to the tenets of an open society, will sooner or later collapse.'[29]

There is no intent here to make irresponsible forecasts. But serious-minded and well-intentioned warnings are to be taken seriously. They are meant to protect, create, recreate a well-balanced, fair and free society, realistically starting from the status quo. They are endeavouring to sketch the outlines of such a society for the last years of the current, and for the first decades of the 21st century.

It is encouraging to note that the BIS,[30,31] the IMF, the FED and other central banks are expanding great energies to maintain the integrity of the system as is now constituted. The World Bank, the EBRD, international organizations like the OECD, and aid programmes like PHARE, are paying to an ever increasing degree attention to the societal effects of global monetary and economic developments.

It is not the task of this paper to judge whether or not these efforts are sufficient to lead automatically to decades of free societal cohesion. But a few pertinent observations are in place.

It is undeniable that because of increased liquidity and fast developing technical innovations, capital mobility during the last quarter century, and especially during the last decade, has grown by an extraordinary degree. This development has many positive effects. But social mobility, by its very nature, did not and could not take up capital mobility's speed. The disparity between the elasticity of capital owners and of labour owners could lead to dangerous social tensions which could increase, rather than decrease as time goes on. On a global scale, this could result in large scale industrial dislocations and in the internal worsening of working conditions. In the future, imbalances within OECD countries could lead to the unnecessary weakening of the constructive forces of OECD countries as a group. Thereby their ability to contribute to the construction of fair and healthy balances pertaining to global societal cohesion would be adversely affected.

It would seem that the first order of business would be the improvement of the global monetary system. Minister Maystadt has made several practical recommendations in 1994 at Brussels, especially with respect 'to the strengthening of the regional approach, as expressed by the current efforts within the European Union';[32] and also to make a greater use of SDR allocations as means to meet 'exceptional needs of the transition countries'.[33]

It is to be welcomed that by now, distinguished market participants of foreign exchange markets express the view that these markets are often exposed to factors which cause unnecessary instability, and might lead to their eventual collapse; they create untoward movements in the real economy and disadvantageously influence public welfare and morality. It is, therefore, justified if public policy intervenes, with well thought-out measures, striving to re-establish stability.[34]

It seems that the striving for price-, and exchange rate stability, growth, and societal cohesion will remain the main issues for decades to come within the OECD area and beyond. Contradictions abound. Rapid technological change does not necessarily lead to higher living standards for broad sectors of the population. High liquidity might be channelled toward non-productive, zero sum games. Savings might have a harder time to find their way into productive investments which could finance legitimate public infrastructural needs like transport and communications, environmental protection and services like schooling, public security, and the support of arts. High level unemployment is high level social waste. A well-functioning modern economy must find ways to spread productivity gains over a wide sector of the population. Healthcare, retirement benefits could be gradually privatized, but only if their increasing productivity is under responsible public supervision. After all, a private pension fund could also collapse just as an ill-managed savings bank can. Acquired rights should be protected. The transition to a more streamlined, more economic, more balanced allocation of resources should be gradual, allowing people time for adjustment to a happier, more constructive life.[35]

III Means

It was the purpose of this paper to call attention to the immense changes which took place in the global societal landscape since the time of the Marshall Plan and, at the same time, to uphold its values.

It could not be the purpose of this essay to formulate specific means through which the above-mentioned values could be translated into today's and the next century's environment. However, it has stressed the importance of the salient points of the Marshall Plan, including Robert Triffin's contributions, which should constructively inspire future economic thought.

The Marshall Plan, under easier circumstances, did provide an institutional model which gave hope, security, and success to several hundred million people in the Atlantic Community.

The message today cannot be as clear and simple as the one of June 5, 1947 was. Today, it is much more difficult to formulate the concept which could lead eventually to new, fair balances on a global scale. It needs to be global. It needs to be acceptable to many nations and communities around the globe. It needs to be both idealistic in the Wilsonian sense but not innocent of realpolitik. It must peacefully co-ordinate many valid cultural, historic, economic, social, and political interests.

Briefly stated: we need a Global Marshall Plan in order to democratically establish the new balances. In view of the obvious difficulties flowing from the unlimited belief in the automaticity of free market forces to establish not only economic equilibria but also to optimize social output and welfare – the Global Marshall Plan could be an idea which will take a long time to develop.

Donald Johnston, Secretary General of the OECD recently wrote in *the International Herald Tribune*: 'The fundamental understanding that economic development depended on co-operation, on the interdependence of trade and investment across the European Community through liberalisation of markets... on the notion of a fully integrated economic community – these were the forces and the philosophy underpinning European unity. It required more: the catalytic role of visionaries in a position to make things happen, among them George Marshall (and) Jean Monnet. The terms of the Marshall Plan... the legacy is the lesson.... Today that lesson serves as a reference point for moving toward an age of true globalization... with good governance ensuring an equitable distribution of that wealth (created through interdependence) within each society.'[36]

Certainly we are looking for a global society in which market and government powers are balanced for optimum social benefit. In order to reach this balance, it is important that the activity of governments currently considered weak should be continued at a much higher intellectual level and that they should place greater stress on the function of education in order to counterbalance the presently almost overhelming influence of the media. If this vision is accepted, the current arrangements of the monetary, economic, and societal order could be peacefully adjusted in due time. This process can be greatly helped by the rich heritage of the countless practical solutions developed during the postwar decades of the socially responsible market economy of which the Marshall Plan is an organic part, and which still underlies the Atlantic Community's current accomplishments.

One of the major areas of importance is the reform of the global monetary system. Increased capital mobility is determined by the unusual privatization of the seiniorage through the offshore markets. This market functions as a politically and internationally almost uncontrolled lender-of-last-resort and hereby provider of world liquidity. The subsidiarization of this function has great advantages but also contains possible dangers. Because of the widespread intellectual and material wested interests attached to the system, its reform cannot be anticipated in the near future.

Immediate concern can be focused on the adaptation of social institutions to the new realities. Whichever way social needs (education, health, pension and unemployment compensation) are financed, the need for these services cannot be denied. The *method* of financing either via the state budget or through private savings is important but almost secondary. In order to maintain democratic societal cohesion the state has a responsibility to give its citizens an opportunity to cover these needs through efficient systems in a historically acceptable measure for every community.

Current efforts to provide these services outside state budgets are abundant. They include President Clinton's recent Philadelphia appeal (April 1997) for voluntary contributions by private corporations and individuals to reintegrate 15 million disadvantaged children with society's mainstream.

The major problem is unemployment. This in itself can be expected to be large especially at the bottom of an economic cycle. Due to technological innovations, per capita productivity in certain sectors can grow much faster than overall growth. This will increase income and wealth differences which could inspire programmes to encourage 'the indispensable synergy between governance systems... (and) social responsibility... Governance reform could be one way of trying to make sure that the active promotion of social inclusion or participation is part of any new and innovative approaches to finding the balance between societal cohesion and economic flexibility'.[37]

Increasingly greater efforts will be made in order to channel resources away from governmental institutions towards 'household, workplaces, voluntary associations...'.[38] While new programmes will recognize universal rights to certain basic social services, they will also encourage the developments of individualized programmes permitting greater choice and self-determination to all market participants. One can imagine systems in which government loan guaranties for education, personal investments and the spreading of decentralized individual entrepreneurship will play a larger role than in the past. The stress is not on disregarding the social interest in self-sustaining and satisfactory individual lives but to provide programmes which will make individuals to achieve these goals only with indirect government assistance.

Many of currently aired solutions might seem to be utopistic and probably some of them are. It should be stressed, however, that the basic theme of these efforts should strive neither at a complete brake with basic principles of Hayekian free enterprise nor with the original, justifiable goals of the welfare state. Instead of confrontation, a constant search 'for Triffinian incommensuribilities among ultimate values, for compatibilities and a tenacious innovative pursuit of simple self-consistent relevant ideas'[39] should be the main strategy for developing social cohesion in a democratic and globally expanding 21st century.

This essay has aimed at extending Triffin's vision to today's problems and to their eventual solution in his spirit.

Notes and references

1. Solomon, Robert, *The International Monetary System, 1945-1976 – An Insider's View*, Harper and Row Publishers, New York, 1977, p. 276.
2. Op. cit. p. 326.
3. For more details of the difficulties of the par value system, see: Solomon, Robert, op. cit. pp. 86-124.
4. Op. cit. p. 290.
5. Kissinger, Henry, *Diplomacy;* Hungarian edition by PANEM-McGraw-Hill-GRAFO, Budapest, 1996.
6. Schumpeter, Joseph A., *Capitalism, Socialism and Democracy*. 3rd edition, Harper and Brothers, New York, 1942, pp. 418-419.

7. Desai, Padma, 'Russian Reform, G-7 Aid and IMF Monitoring: Marshall Plan Lessons', in: *The Global Monetary System After the Fall of the Soviet Empire*, M. Szabó-Pelsőczi (ed.) Avebury, Aldershot, UK in association with the Robert Triffin-Szirák Foundation, 1995, pp. 35-55.
8. Ibid.
9. Triffin, Robert, *Europe and the Money Muddle – From Bilaterism to Near-Convertibility, 1947-1956*. Oxford University Press, New Haven and London, Yale University Press, 1957.
10. Hadsel, Fred L., 'The Marshall Plan from Today's Perspective', in: *Fifty Years After Bretton Woods*, M. Szabó-Pelsőczi, (ed.), Avebury, Aldershot, UK, in association with the Robert Triffin-Szirák Foundation, 1996, pp. 7-10.
11. Desai, ibid. p. 39.
12. Ibid.
13. Desai, op.cit. pp. 38-39.
14. Ibid.
15. Hieronymi, Otto, *Economic Discrimination Against the United States in Western Europe (1945-1958)*, Library Droz., Geneve, Paris, 1973.
16. Hieronymi, ibid, partly quoting William Adams Brown Jr., and Redvers Opie, *American Foreign Assistance*, Washington, DC., The Brooking Institution, 1953.
17. Hieronymi, op. cit. p. 99.
18. 'The Agreement for the Establishment of a European Payments Union. Signed in Paris on September 19, 1950'. The last updated text was published shortly before the Union was dissolved in December 1958. Hieronymi, op. cit. p. 99.
19. Triffin, op. cit. p. 352.
20. Webster's New Collegiate Dictionary. G. C. Merriam Co., Publishers Springfield, Mass. USA, 1959, p. 1174.
21. Hadsel, op. cit. pp. 7-10.
22. *The International Monetary Fund 1945-1965*, Vol. III.; J. Keith, Horsefield, (ed.) IMF, Washington DC., 1969, pp. 187-189.
23. Hayek, Friedrich A. von, 'The Atavism of Social Justice', F.A. von Hayek, *New Studies in Philosophy, Politics, Economics and the History of Ideas*, Routledge and Kegan Paul, London, 1978, pp. 51-70.
24. Kissinger, op. cit. p. 809.: '...Some of the greatest achievements of the 20th century originated from Woodrow Wilson's idealism, like the Marshall Plan...'.
25. Op. cit. p. 837.
26. Witteveen, H.J., 'The Determination and Consequences of International Liquidity', in *Fifty Years After Bretton Woods*. M. Szabó-Pelsőczi (ed.), Avebury, Aldershot in association with the Robert Triffin-Szirák Foundation, 1996, p. 106.
27. Ibid.
28. Based on *Bank of International Settlements, Annual Report*, 1995, pp. 139-140.
29. Soros, George 'The Danger of Capitalism', Hungarian translation in *Magyar Hírlap*, January 25, 1997.
30. *BIS, Annual Reports, op. cit.*
31. Stone, Charles A. and Zissu, Anne eds., *Global Risk Based Capital Regulations*, Vol. I, and II, Irwin, Professional Publishing, Burr Ridge, Illinois; New York, NY., 1994.

32. Maystadt, Philippe: 'The Challenge of Creating Global Economic and Monetary Environment Conducive to a Successful Transition of the Former Centrally Planned Economies', in *Fifty Years After Bretton Woods,* M.Szabó-Pelsőczi, (ed.), Avebury, Aldershot, 1996, pp. 16-26.
33. Ibid.
34. Soros, ibid.
35. See, 'OECD Forum for the Future: Economic Flexibility and Societal Cohesion in the 21st Century', Paris, January 23, 1997, p. 9.
36. Johnston, Donald, 'From the Marshall Plan to Globalization', *IHT,* March 26, 1997.
37. OECD op. cit. p. 4.
38. Op. cit. p. 5.
39. Krul, Nicolas, 'Hayek and Triffin: Fragments of Divergence and Convergence in Policy Thinking', Seventh Conference of the Robert Triffin-Szirák Foundation, May, 1997.

14 The Euro: Hopeful Sign of a New Long Wave Growth

Paul L. Mandy

> *'S'adapter ne consistera plus ici à répéter,*
> *mais à répliquer ce qui est tout différent.'**
> (Henri BERGSON, L'évolution créatrice,
> [1907], Paris, 1939, p. 62.)

Introduction

My paper would like to emphasize the fundamental and unavoidable role that the reshaping of existing monetary institutions, – like the transition from European national currencies to a single currency – plays in order to achieve a long wave of growth and prosperity in the European Economies.[1]

My thesis can be formulated as follows: existing monetary institutions in Europe, much divided because of the existence of the single market on the one hand and of single currencies as the dollar and the yen on the other hand, are not able to efficiently ensure economic growth and full employment. New monetary institutions are required for these purposes, namely to operate the transition from the present downwards Kondratieff-trend to an upwards Kondratieff-movement.

Since the industrial revolution, monetary history shows us clearly that long waves are caused not only by the shift of monetary policies which are mostly related to current business cycles, but by the fundamental changes in monetary institutions themselves. It seems to me that the entry into force of the 'euro' can be considered as such a change in the monetary field in Europe. According to historical evidence, the European single currency is

---

* 'Adapting oneself does not consist here in imitating something, but in making a "retort"; this is very different.'

therefore a hopeful sign for future prosperity on this continent exposed presently to a very high rate of unemployment and, consequently, to the fear of social disorder issued from the 'fracture sociale', from societal fragmentation.

1. European Central Bank: simulacrum of the Bundesbank or a 'new' institution?

Let me begin my approach by a quotation:

> The first task of the European Central Bank will be to try persuade everyone that it's the Bundesbank by another name. I expect it to operate a very tight monetary policy with a bias towards high interest rates.[2]

A few observations are called for.

First. If the author of these lines published in the *Wall Street Journal Europe* should be right, the tight monetary policy of the Bundesbank would be continued by the European Central Bank (ECB). Now, this tight policy, together with the tight fiscal policy required by the Maastricht criteria, would involve and maintain, in the European economy, a very *low growth* accompanied with more and more *unemployment*. For the rate of productivity of labour due to rapid technical and organizational progress, will be constantly higher than the rate of growth of the European economy as a whole. Thus, the macroeconomic goal of the new *Economic and Monetary Union*, i.e. the best trade-off between inflation and unemployment, would not be obtained. Without doubt, there is a fundamental link not only between money and inflation as the monetarists emhasize it, but also between money and employment, between a single currency and the level of output. The purpose of macroeconomics is – according Keynes – to 'progress towards pushing monetary theory back to becoming a theory of output as a whole'.[3] Indeed, the new single currency in Europe, working together with the single monetary policy of the ECB, will give rise to true macroeconomics instead of the fallacious national 'open economy macroeconomics' becoming microeconomics with regard to this European 'Whole Economy'.[4]

Second. If Dornbusch should be right, the new single monetary policy in Europe would deny the opportunity of a *policy mix*. Now, the usefulness of the policy mix being applied in the American economy for a long time and founded upon theoretical considerations,[5] has become evident. Without doubt, in order to cope with business cycles emerging by the nature of a free economy, a country or a region needs to have the ability to mix policies. Thanks to these discerning policies, and the elasticities which go with them we can shift the scenery of a low growth economy – onto a high growth reality.

Third. From the point of view of the peripheral countries applying for membership in the European Union (e.g. Hungary), a *constantly* restrictive monetary policy of the future ECB, as practised by the Bundesbank, would make it difficult to achieve a sufficient rate of growth required to pay the enormous *foreign debt* service. This gross foreign indebtedness of Hungary ($ 3.000/persons, as of end-1995) imposes a huge burden on the growth of the economy and on the welfare of the population. For this country a monetary policy of the ECB copying the Bundesbank, would have disastrous consequences leading to social suffering. In other words, the social cost of such a monetary policy in terms of unemployment and of standard of living would be enormous after the huge cost of the transition process in the early years of the nineties.

For all these reasons, and that is my concern, the ECB should not become a simulacrum of the Bundesbank. There are other models of central banking, like the Federal Reserve System and others. Consequently, there is no reason of repeating merely the Bundesbank. We can and must *change* fundamentally our monetary institutions in order to find again a sustainable long wave growth for the European economy. According to Henri Bergson, the crucial problem consists here in making a 'retort' instead of an imitation. Our newly instituted ECB should not become 'the Bundesbank by another name'.

2. The long waves, or Kondratieff movement

My view is that, presently and since the early 1970s, the European economy moves in a downward long swing, or in a Kondratieff downgrade.[6] This view seems to become more and more confirmed.

We cannot apply this pattern to the same extent to the American economy or to the world economy itself. Indeed, the present floating exchange rate regime with the dollar standard, contrary to the previous gold standard, or the fixed exchange rate system, operates *discontinuities* in the international transmission of business cycles and introduces more or less monetary *independence*, instead of interdependence, between national economies, regions or continents. Therefore, the simultaneity of business cycles in geographic space is not the case.

It is possible that the success of the euro vis-a-vis the dollar could achieve precisely more stable eurodollar exchange rates re-establishing the same sequences in business cycles between the two continents. In this context and thanks to our monetary renewal, the prevailing and almost monopolistic role of the 'eurodollars' in the world economy could be metamorphosed into a more equilibrating 'eurodollar' bilateral monopoly.

The business cycles, both short waves and long waves, are facts which can be recognized only by experience. The pure theory without time and space and founded upon marginalist analysis, does not know business cycles. So, they can be recognized only statistically.

Table 1. Upwards and downwards long waves

Downwards movements	Upwards movements
1790-1815	1815-1850
1850-1873	1873-1896
1896-1914	1920-1940
1945-1973	1973-

Table 1 shows the periods for long wave movements since statistical data were generally available in Europe and in the United States, since the end of the 18th century. They can also be stylized (*Chart 1*).

The *short cycles* i.e. the Kitchin or rather the Juglar movements, recovery and prosperity on one side, recession and depression on the other side, are superimposed on each of them. As *Chart 1* shows, in an upward long wave periods of prosperity are elongated and periods of depression shortened, while in a downward long wave periods of depression are elongated and periods of prosperity shortened.

With respect to the *long waves*, these movements are alternating periods in which either prosperities or depressions predominate. According which predominates, long waves are respectively 'upwards movements' or 'downwards movements'. Contrary to depressions of short cycles, downwards long wave movements do not imply absolute decreases of rates of growth, but *relative* decreases or reduced rates of growth with respect to those observed during upwards movements. At the same time, the price movements in the downwards long waves are characterized by deflation or by disinflation accompanied by high rates of unemployment.

We recognize thus with the greatest ease that, since the seventies, the European economy is marked by a downwards long wave or by a Kondratieff downgrade.

Long wave movements can be explained theoretically. In agreement with Schumpeter, Haberler, Akerman, Wagemann, Marjolin, Guitton, Dupriez, Rousseaux and others, we are convinced that a systematic analysis and explanation of the long waves are highly necessary.

As our problem today is the present Kondratieff downgrade since the seventies, we concentrate on the explanation of the downwards long waves in historical periods. In particular, our main concern consists in explaining the *Kondratieff transitions from downwards to upwards movements*. If our explanation is correct, it can enlighten economic policy-makers on the transition of the present Kondratieff downgrade to a new upwards long wave.

The Euro: Hopeful Sign of a New Long Wave Growth

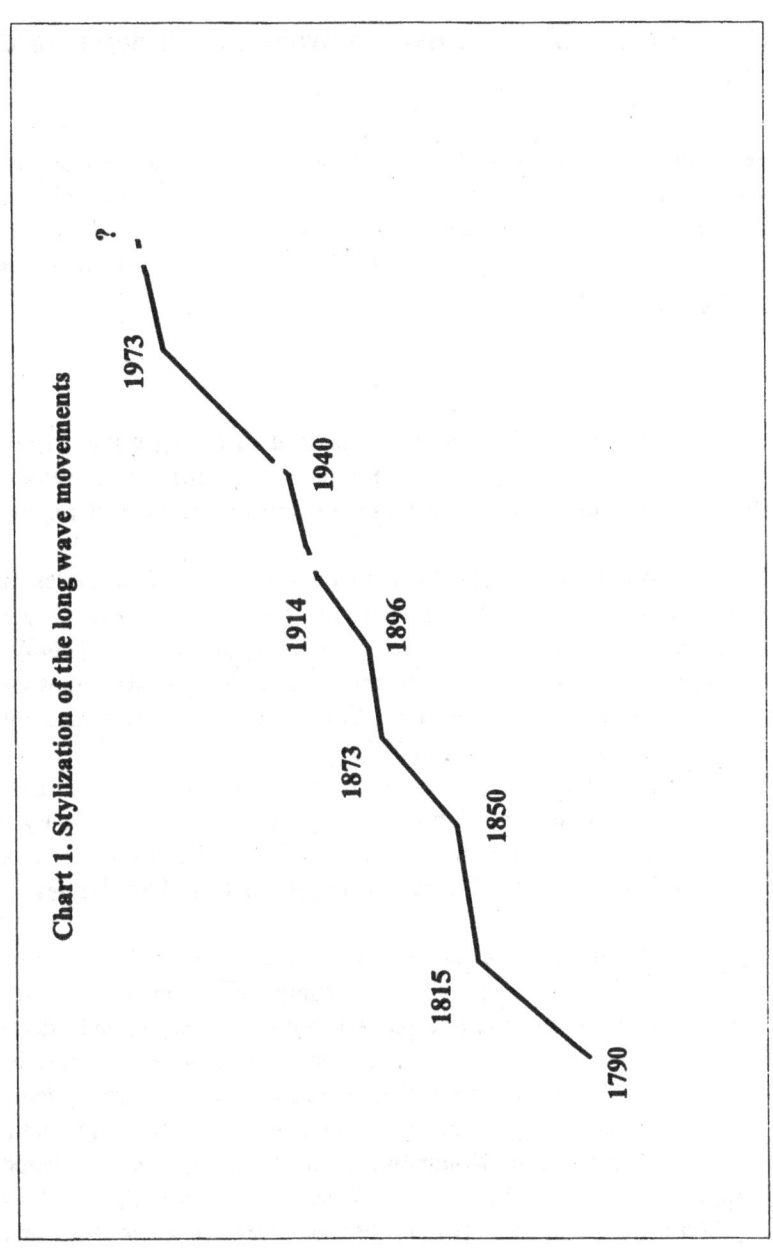

Chart 1. Stylization of the long wave movements

3. How to explain the transition process from downwards to upwards long waves

I agree with the widespread opinion amongst economists that the Kondratieff movements have lost their credibility in our time and the debate in this matter seems to be out of date. But it seems to me that this is the consequence of the dubious or even erroneous explanations that have been given to the *main cause* of these movements.

3.1 Kondratieff

Nicolai Kondratieff was the first who described such long waves in 1926.[7] Schumpeter has thus given the name 'Kondratieff' for the long waves to the memory of this Russian economist executed by the communist regime in 1938.

Kondratieff himself thought that the *main* cause of the long cycles more than other causes of minor importance, can be found in the *discovery of gold mines* producing monetary abundance. Especially, in California (1848) and in Australia (1851) with respect to the transition to the upwards long wave of 1850-1873; then in Transvaal in South Africa at the end of the century with respect to the upwards movement of 1896-1913.

Nevertheless, what is important, is not the discovery of gold mines and their production, but the transformation of the new metal to monetary use. There is no correlation between the increase of the quantity used for money and the Kondratieff upgrade. This view is largely confirmed by Dupriez:

> Let it therefore be clear that the commodious reference to the Kondratieff movement, which Schumpeter proposed, should be construed as an homage to a pioneer, but should not be understood as an acceptance of his theories, not even of his approach. Kondratieff's correlations were circumstantial, within a gold standard system: as such, they cannot be extrapolated. A broader view is necessary, both for the period covered by Kondratieff (1850-1913), the period covered in my book (1789-1939) and for postwar developments. I consider this preliminary statement necessary, because reference to the long wave in English literature pertains largely to the original Kondratieff theory relating long waves to gold production or to the concurring Cassel Kitchin explanation relating long waves to gold stocks. It is largely due

to the reference to such simplistic and circumstantial models that English and American economists looked askance at the long wave itself and dismissed it. But it is altogether too easy to reject a simplistic explanation and to throw the baby away with the bath. Let us therefore re-examine the baby.[8]

3.2 Schumpeter

In his monumental and well-known *Business Cycles*, Joseph Schumpeter viewed *innovations* as the *chief* reason of upwards movements.
Schematically:

– Steam-engines and the iron industry	1790-1815
– Railroadization	1850-1873
– Electrification, automobile industry	1896-1913

This explanation of the transition to upwards long cycles is viewed with scepticism by economists because technical innovations are solely *fortuitous facts* and not systematic phenomena.

3.3 Explanation related to wars

Wars are considered by many economists as the main causes of downwards movements:

– the Napoleonic war	1815-
– the Franco-Prussian war	1870-
– World War I	1918

Nevertheless, wars are also *external factors*. And, after World War II, there was not a Kondratieff downgrade. This fundamental fact disproves this kind of explanation.

In contrast with these explanations, I assume with Leon H. Dupriez,[9] that, the main cause of the Kondratieff transitions from downwards to upswing long waves consists in the *changes of monetary institutions*. The upwards long waves arise not from monetary policies which affect short term movements, but from the institutional transformations in the monetary field. The reshaping of the national central banks into a European Central Bank and the accession to a single currency after centuries of national currencies and hundreds of exchange rate crises, is such a change.

4. Changes in monetary institutions as historical evidence of the Kondratieff-transitions from downwards to upwards movements

In order to depart from the present downwards long wave in Europe and to start an upwards movement of Kondratieff, changes in monetary institutions play a crucial role. The painful accession to the euro, the fundamental change in central banking in Europe and the renewal of European Central Bank policy with respect to the Bundesbank could operate this transition of paramount importance in Europe.

Since the industrial revolution, there were the fundamental transformations of monetary institutions which were able to renew economic dynamism and adequate growth. I would like to demonstrate this thesis as a historical evidence because the three Kondratieff downgrades in the past involved three major institutional changes in the monetary fields, i.e.

1. 1815-1850: from the *Currency Principle* to the *Banking Principle*;
2. 1873-1896: from the *Bimetallism 'boiteux'*[*] to the *International Gold Standard*;
3. 1920-1944: from the *Monetary Disaster of the Great Depression* to the *International Monetary System of Bretton Woods*.

4.1 1815-1850: from the Currency Principle to the Banking Principle

The first Kondratieff downgrade was already characterized by a sharp deflation. After the Napolenic wars whose effects in England were inconvertibility and very high inflation, the gold standard was recovered in 1816. Nevertheless – and it was an enormous error – this return to gold was accomplished at the old prewar parity. The result of this very erroneous

---

[*] 'limping'

The Euro: Hopeful Sign of a New Long Wave Growth

realignment has been the scarcity of money and the substantial fall in the price level (Chart 2).

Chart 2. Wholesale prices in Britain (1865-1885=100)

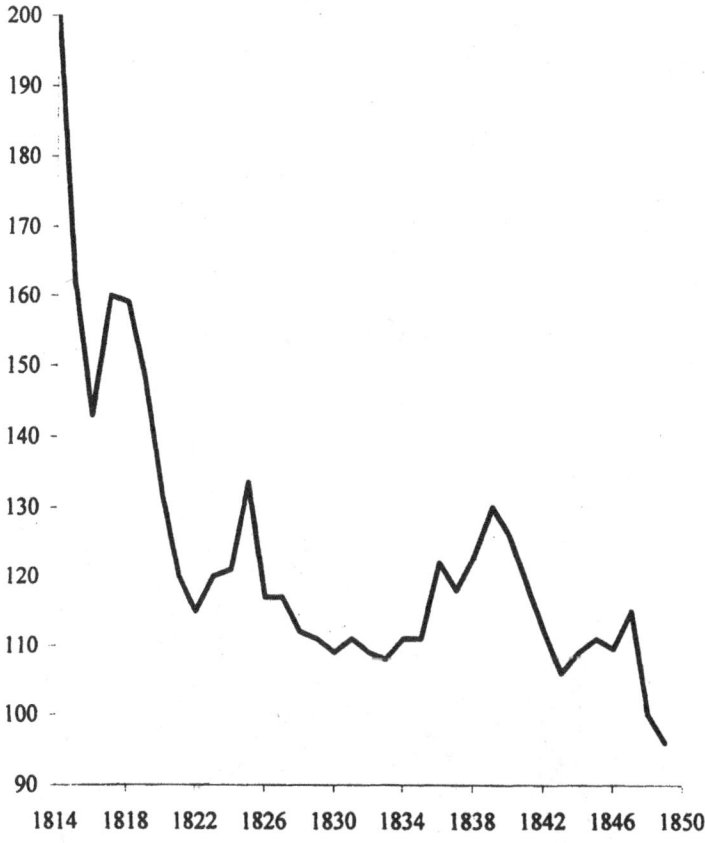

Source: P. Rousseaux, *Les mouvements de fond de l'économie anglaise, 1800-1913*, Louvain, 1938, Cf. Inerties et Révolutions 1730-1840 in P. Leon, *Histoire économique et sociale du monde*, Armand Colin, Paris, 1978, Vol. 3, p. 447.

At the same time full demonetization of silver in England has increased monetary scarcity.

These deflationary circumstances without social laws and without regulated labour conditions entailed an indescribable misery for working people including children as one can see by way of illustration below, children working in a textile factory and fed from the manger of a piggery situated near the workshop.

Misery of factory boys in Britain, 1815-1850

Des enfants, employés dans une usine textile, dévorent des restes dans la mangeoire d'une porcherie proche de l'atelier. Illustration tirée de Life and Adventures of Michael Armstrong the Factory Boy *(1840) par Frances Trollope, qui dénonce dans ce roman les conditions horribles du travail des enfants à l'usine.*

Cf. Inerties et Révolutions 1730-1840 in P. LEON, *Histoire économique et social du monde*, Armand Colin, Paris, 1978, vol. 3, p. 442.

During this downwards long wave, the monetary circumstances have given rise to the huge debate about the respective credibility of the *Currency Principle* and the *Banking Principle*. According to the Currency Principle supported in the Ricardian tradition by the *Currency School* (Torrens, Mc Culloch, Overstone and so on), the banknotes must be strictly covered by the gold reserve assets of the central bank in order to carry out the strict regulation in money supply and to ensure in this manner price stability and external automatic equilibrium. Contrary to this, the adherents of the Banking Principle forming the *Banking School* (Tooke, Fullarton, J. St. Mill and so on) would promote the growth of economy by note issues. In this context, the demand for money responding to the needs of output and trade, is essential. According to this school of thought, the *credit* granted by commercial banks in order to increase the level of output and trade, plays a central role. Following the very discerning statement of Th. Tooke, the increase in bank note circulation would be the effect of the needs of trade and of the higher prices and not their cause.[10]

Unfortunately, during this downwards long wave, the Currency School have predominated and exerted a very deep influence and pressure on money creation. Consequently, the *Bank Charter Act* of 1844 called also Peel's Act after the name of the Prime Minister, was reflecting the spirit of the Currency Principle, established two departments: the *Issue Department* issuing only bank notes and the *Banking Department* creating bank money like a commercial bank. The former, beside only L 14 million fiduciary issues, was obliged to cover other issues 100 per cent by gold, i.e. in one to one proportion to gold reserves. Hence the enormous liquidity shortages in that time.

What is the ultimate meaning of this intensive debate between the two Schools? It is beyond doubt that, in view of following long term economic developments, the Banking Principle had to win the prize. The application of the Currency Principle, – origin and root of all monetarism – induced monetary scarcity for lack of gold, frequent bankruptcies, deflationary pressures and social misery. The fight against inflation predominates economic policy: rules rather than discretion and overall control over money supply without any consideration for the level of output and employment. In this framework and without new discoveries of gold mines and monetization of gold production, the existing monetary institutions are no more able to carry out economic development. The bridge to pass to an upwards long wave growth has broken down. Moreover, as long as the confusion in monetary debates has not been clarified and as the money creation process has been submitted to scepticism, the long wave growth of the economy was paralysed. So, in its effects, 'the *Bank Charter Act* stands as a monument of misguided legislation'.[11]

The transition to such a long wave growth and the achievement of the industrial revolution needed finally the emergence of new monetary institutions founded on the more and more expansive use of *deposits and credits* responding to the needs of trade, according to the teaching of the Banking School. As Table 2 indicates, during this downwards Kondratieff, the decrease of banknotes was the main cause of this scarcity con-comitant with the lack of gold, but also with the increase of deposits.

The victory of the Banking Principle on the Currency Principle changed also the substance of central banking. Especially after the great liquidity crisis of 1857, the Bank of England has become *lender of last resort* in order to avoid bankruptcies. Under the Currency Principle, it has been impossible to act as lender of last resort. Moreover, as the central bank has also become more and more responsible for the *overall liquidity of the economy*, we have to characterize it as a *new* institution without repeating the model of the preceding central banking.

Table 2. Stock of money in Britain

	coins	bill	deposit	total	coins	bill	deposit	total
	(in millions of £)				(in percentages)			
1811	15	45	15	75	20.0	60.0	20.0	100.0
1821	18	32	25	75	24.0	42.7	33.3	100.0
1831	30	29	40	99	30.3	29.3	40.4	100.0
1844	36	28.5	80.5	145	25.0	20.0	55.0	100.0

Source: P. LEON, op. cit. vol. 3, p. 419.

Let us conclude this section with the following striking quotation:

> More fundamentally, if the Act of 1844 had actually fulfilled the expectations of Peel and the Currency School, England's (and Britain's) economic growth would have come to a grinding halt in the middle of the 19th century but, providentially perhaps, the institution of

deposits subject to cheque was already well established. Tooke lost the battle, but his ghost won the war.[12]

4.2 1873-1896: From the Bimetallism 'boiteux' to the International Gold Standard

The American Economy whose role became more and more important in the second half of the 19th century, has already adopted bimetallism in 1792. Within this regime both gold and silver were legal tender and the ratio of their prices was fixed at the mint where coinage became free. France also entered into bimetallism since the beginning of the last century (1803). Moreover, the *Latin Monetary Union* established in 1865 under French leadership, expanded the size of the bimetallic monetary area. England has demonetized silver in 1816 in favour of gold. Prussia and the German States were on a silver standard.

These circumstances have given rise to an intensive controversy between bimetallism and monometallism. The adherents of bimetallism considered that this regime would be a remedy against the scarcity of gold and, at the same time, would provide greater stability for the price level than a monometallic standard.

Events undermined bimetallism. The alternating discoveries of silver and gold mines and, consequently, abundant silver or gold productions disequilibrated this monetary system. Indeed, such events tended to displace the other overvalued metal according to Gresham's law and created alternating silver or gold monometallic regimes.

Other significant events followed. After its victory over France in 1870, the German Empire under the leadership of the former Prussia, exacted reparation payments from France in gold, namely 5000 million gold francs. Consequently, holding huge gold reserves, Germany demonetized silver and passed to the gold standard imitating the prestigious Britain in this way. To make matters worse, the *Latin Monetary Union* was compelled to limit free silver coinage in 1874 in consequence of the overproduction of this metal. The crisis of this fragile bimetallism has thus become unavoidable. In addition, the United States also demonetized silver in 1873, an event that was qualified as a 'crime' by Milton Friedman because this demonetizing legislation was responsible for the sharp deflation of US prices.[13]

Nevertheless, the great depression of this last quarter of the 19th century and the social disturbances that followed it, maintained interest in international bimetallism, considering it as a remedy for monetary disorder. For this purpose, many international Conferences and Commissions were organized between the seventies and the nineties, but without success.

The interest for bimetallism was particularly stimulated in the United States by the threat to pass to the gold standard, like Germany following the example of Victorian Britain. The United States had abundant silver mining, namely in Nebraska. The Free Silver Movement whose leader, William Jenning Bryan, former Nevada Congressman and senatorial candidate has been designated presidential candidate at Chicago in 1896. He loudly denounced the gold standard responsible, according to him, for the deep deflation of prices, for labour troubles and for the suffering of people, notwithstanding the aspiration of many of them for the gold standard:

> Having behind us the producing masses of this nation and the world, supported by the commercial interests, the labouring interests, and the toilers everywhere, we will answer their demand for a gold standard by saying to them: You shall not press down upon the bow of labour this crown of thorns, you shall not crucify mankind upon a cross of gold.[14]

The striking conclusion of the Bryan's speech is well-known in the economic literature under the name of 'cross of gold'. Let this be a word of warning to us in the present Kondratieff downgrade like that occurring at the end of the last century. The making of euro must not be a new cross of gold, a kind of 'cross of Maastricht' involving only sacrifices for people without a hopeful sign for the future. Indeed, why do Maastricht criteria not include also a limiting rate for unemployment or stimulating a high rate of investment as the main variables of adjustment instead of unemployment? Alas, the makers of Maastricht have completely forgotten – or perhaps ignored? – the fundamental macroeconomic 'money-employment' relationship.

The second Kondratieff downgrade was therefore characterized by much controversy on monetary thought and by instability and uncertainty in monetary policy involving lasting deflation. As far as the bimetallism 'boiteux' prevailed in minds if not in facts and without a general agreement about an internationally accepted monetary standard, the transition to an upwards long wave was stopped. Finally, and by surprise, it is the defeat of Bryan in the presidential election of 1896 and the passage, in 1900, of the US to the gold standard which led to an internationally unified monetary system: the international gold standard. Once more, the change in monetary institutions avoiding monetary discrepancies between nations, was necessary for a Kondratieff upgrade.

4.3 1920-1944: From the monetary disaster of the Great Depression to the International Monetary System of Bretton Woods

Even if all of us know too well the economic period characterized by the Great Depression between the two world wars, let us point out a few great policy errors, at least partially responsible for such a downward long wave.

- The enormous and heavy burden of the *German Reparation* amounting to 226 billion of gold marks: 36 times higher than that paid by France in the 1870s. During more than a decade, it contributed to the growing instability of the European monetary situation and to the deepening of the Great Depression.
  As member of the Britain's delegation to the Conference of the Peace at Versailles, Keynes predicted that any amount of reparation will be completely unsuccessful. Indeed, as he disagreed with Lloyd George, chief of the delegation, he resigned without signing the treaty of peace. *The Economic Consequences of the Peace* (1919) has given a full account of his very relevant position.
- The return of Britain to the gold standard in April 1925 once again at *prewar 1913 parity* – as it was the case in 1816 – involved the *overvaluation* of sterling with its harmful consequences not only on deflationary tendencies in force since the end of the war, but also on external balances and on domestic underemployment. Finally, such a misalignment was untenable and entailed the renunciation of the gold standard in September 1931 and the floating of the sterling with more than 30 per cent of depreciation. Given the following depreciation of the dollar in 1933-1934 (more than 40 per cent), the world economy entered in monetary disaster.
- As the Monetary Conference of London in 1933 has been unsuccessful with respect to international monetary co-operation, and after the depreciation of both the sterling and the dollar, France, Italy, Switzerland, Belgium, Poland and others have set up the 'Gold Block'. The political will of these continental monetary authorities to maintain at all cost the parity with gold in spite of the

readjustment or rather the misalignment of other key currencies as the sterling and the dollar, has involved very high costs in unemployment and external inbalances and was finally untenable. Everyone of these countries was obliged to devaluate. Belgium was the first to do so in March 1935 under the leadership of Dupriez and Triffin and whose re-equilibrating adjustment (28 per cent) has been wholly approved by Ohlin and Keynes in a meeting at Antwerpen in July 1935.[15] Belgium was followed by France (1936), by Italy and Switzerland (1936) and by other countries. Nowadays it is no doubt that the Gold Block went the wrong direction.

After these policy errors, I would like to remind you of a few other major monetary events:

- The *collapse of the German mark* and the following *hyperinflation* in the early twenties: consequence of the burden of reparations.
- The Conference of Genoa in 1922 recommending the *gold-exchange standard* owing to the scarcity of gold and introducing once again two competitive currencies, i.e. gold and sterling without learning from the failure of bimetallism.
- *Competitive devaluations* and endless exchange crises with the reinforcement of huge speculative movements.
- The overall emergence of *Economic nationalism* taking into account internal equilibrium only.
- The *shaping of currency areas* like the sterling area and the widespread use of *exchange control* (e.g. Germany in 1936, Britain and France in 1939).

Under these disorderly circumstances, the passage to a Kondratieff upgrade without new monetary institutions, was impossible. The setting up of a new *International Monetary System* at Bretton Woods with new international monetary institutions like the *International Monetary Fund*, was unavoidable. This was followed by the *European Payments Union* within the Marshall Plan, responding to the need for multilateral trade between European countries.

The outstanding merit of these institutional changes after World War II, when one might have expected a downwards long wave, the functioning of the new monetary institutions was able to carry out the transition to a

Kondratieff upgrade. The institutional change in the monetary field was the main cause of the upwards long wave transition.

Conclusion

The comparison of the present economic evolution in Europe since the seventies with the three Kondratieff downgrades, convinces us that presently the European economy stands once again in a downwards Kondratieff movement. Indeed, we can easily draw parallels between them.

- The later collapse of the Bretton Woods system founded upon the dollar gold-exchange standard, recalls the failures of the gold-standard, of the gold-exchange standard, and the weakness of bimetallism in the last quarter of the past century.
- Misalignments in exchange rates, competitive devaluations and depreciations, floating regimes dominated by huge speculative movements, characterize all downwards long wave.
- The intensive but confuse debate between Keynesianism and Monetarism recalls the great debates about bimetallism and mono-metallism, and a few decades earlier, about the Banking principle and the Currency Principle. The debate from Ricardo to Hayek and Friedman did not result yet in a satisfactory solution concerning the international monetary order.
- With regard to monetary policies in downwards long waves, they are generally restrictive, involving deflation or disinflation in one side, depression and unemployment in the other side.

We tried to demonstrate in three stages as historical evidence that fundamental changes in monetary institutions are required to pass from a downwards Kondratieff to an upwards Kondratieff swing.

The transition from national currencies to a single currency within most countries in the European Union and the setting up of the European Central Bank are, without doubt, turning points in the European economy. We can therefore ask a question of paramount importance: Are the expected changes in our monetary institutions able to bring about this transition within the European economy while coping with low growth and high unemployment for more than two decades?

The answer to this question depends on the future functioning of our European Central Bank. This is therefore faced with a crucial choice: to become 'Bundesbank by another name' or to innovate like a 'new' institution. Several models are available for this choice. On of them is that of the Federal Reserve System which tries to harmonize efficiently both 'money-prices' links and 'money-employment' relations according to business cycles. Anyone who comes in the Federal Reserve Building at Washington, can read at the left wall of the entrance:

> In the Federal Reserve Act we instituted a great and vital Banking System not merely to correct and cure periodical financial debacles, not simply indeed to aid the Banking Community alone, but to give vision and scope and security to commerce and amplify the opportunities as well as to increase the capabilities of our industrial life at home and among foreign Nations.[16]

In this prospect, the future single currency can be a hopeful sign. It is no easy matter to set up a new continental central bank. Nevertheless, both theoretical arguments and historical evidence teach us that neither deflationary policies of the future ECB, nor overvaluation of the euro will be able to manage successfully the transition towards a long wave of high growth and of full employment. The case seems to me absolutely clear-cut in order to avoid 'la fracture sociale' or societal disorder, within the European community, the new European Central Bank should not become 'the Bundesbank by another name'.

Notes and references

1. I am indebted to Professor Ronald Anderson and to Professor Philippe Monfort for their helpful comments. The author alone is responsible for this analysis.
2. Roger Bottle, 'EMU May Pose Traumas If Preparation is lacking', *The Wall Street Journal Europe*, Nov. 11, 1996, p. 4.
3. John M. Keynes, *The General Theory of Employment, Interest and Money*, MacMillan, London, 1936, Preface, p. VI.
4. Cf. the astonishing title and analysis of R. Dornbusch, *Open Economy Macroeconomics*, Basic Books, New York, 1980.
5. Cf. the writings of Robert Mundell on this subject.
6. Léon H. Dupriez, '1974 a downturn of the long wave?' *Banca Nazionale del Lavoro Quarterly Review*, September 1978, No. 126.

7. Cf. *Archif für Sozialwissenschaft and Sozialpolitik*, 1926.
8. Léon H. Dupriez, ibid., pp. 199-200. The related book is *Mouvements économiques généraux*, Louvain, Nauwelaerts, 1947, Vol. 2.
9. Cf. above all, *La monnaie dans l'économie*, Cujas, Paris, 1976, pp. 292-311.
10. Tooke and Newmarch, *History of Prices*, Vol. 4, p. 194, quoted by Dupriez, ibid., p. 249.
11. Bank Charter Act of 1844 (by Rondo Cameron), in *The New Palgrave Dictionary, of Money and Finance*, I, Macmillan, 1992, p. 124.
12. Ibid. p. 125.
13. Cf. 'Crime of 1873', *Journal of Political Economy*, 98, pp. 1159-1194.
14. 'Cross of gold' (by Richard Sylla), in *The New Palgrave....*, I, p. 549.
15. Cf. Léon H. Dupriez, *Les réformes monétaires en Belgique*, Office International de Librairie, Bruxelles, 1978, pp. 105, 111-112.
16. Carter Glass, *An adventure in Constructive Finance*, Inscription upon Bronze Bas-Relief, Left Wall, Entrance to the Federal Reserve Building, Washington D.C.

Part III

East-West Convergences

15 Investment and Growth in the Transition Process

Nicholas Stern and Hans Peter Lankes

1. Introduction

The stimulation of growth in investment and income are central aims of the transition process. While some countries in the region, in particular in Central Europe but also in parts of the former Soviet Union, are beginning to reap the benefits of reform – often after a painful period of income collapse – others have so far been less successful. In this presentation, we shall draw some lessons from the first five to eight years of transition in particular in terms of the relationship between economic reforms and investments. The focus will be on private investment because of its central role in generating growth in an open market economy, and also because it is at the heart of the EBRD's activities – and therefore, an area in which we can draw on some direct experience. The relationship between investment and trade is obviously very important in this context, and we shall provide some evidence on how reform, trade and investment interact in the transition process.

The paper is structured around two lessons of experience. First, for rapid growth in the transition economies the 'right' *kind* or quality of investment is at least as important as increase in the *amount* or quantity of investment. Second, the 'right' kinds of investments require a favourable investment climate. Although these points appear to state the obvious, in practice they are not always well understood. Differences in understanding and in acting on that understanding go some way towards explaining the uneven economic performance among the transition economies. We shall also suggest that progress in transition is associated with a greater outward orientation of investments.

We shall draw extensively on research published in successive Transition Reports and on surveys into foreign investment conducted by the EBRD.[1]

2. Growth and the 'right' kind of investment

An important, but of course not the only, source of growth is the accumulation of factors of production through fixed investment in plant and equipment (increasing physical capital) and through education (increasing human capital). However, factor accumulation alone is insufficient to sustain high rates of growth. In the former Soviet Union, for instance, there was a narrow focus on this particular mechanism during what Kornai has described as 'the age of forced growth'. We will emphasize this point because it holds the key to what investment during the transition to a market economy is all about, namely a focus on the efficiency of factor use, on demand-orientation particularly in sectoral allocation and on the exploitation of complementarities with inherited but now heavily depreciated factors of production.

Capital accumulation under central planning

Among the characteristics of the 'age of forced growth' in the Soviet Union were: (i) that consumers had little voice in determining overall investment rates in a system primarily controlled by agents whose interests or inclinations lay in expansion; (ii) that investment priorities were geared heavily towards investment and producer goods; and (iii) that incentives were not linked to efficiency, with prices, costs and economic returns playing only a minor role in guiding the structure and technology of the capital stock.

As a result of the first of these characteristics investment rates as a share of national income were consistently and impressively high, while consumption was suppressed. As a result of the second, a capital stock was built up over time whose sectoral and technological structure was far removed from that generated in market economies and from consumer demand. The third characteristic finally accounts for an extremely low efflciency of capital in generating value added (even if valued at the distorted prices of the old system). A particularly stark example of inefficiency is the energy coefficients in GDP. Compared with the OECD area, the energy intensity of GDP in 1992 was about four times higher in the Eastern European countries, and more than six times higher in many countries of the former Soviet Union.[2] While the command system was wasteful of all resources, its lack of attention to prices and opportunity costs made it especially wasteful of resources in which it was particularly well endowed. It is in this sense an unfortunate accident of history that some of the command economies were also those with very large resources of oil, gas, and coal.

Chart 1 plots investment shares in GDP against GDP growth rates of six centrally planned economies (CPEs) from 1974 to 1989, as well as those of 20 countries that are broadly comparable in terms of population growth (as a proxy for labour force growth) and income per capita (US$ 2,000-6,000 annually in 1974). It is evident from this comparison that the CPEs were singularly unable to translate high investment rates into growth. In fact, fitting lines that relate these two variables, as is done in Chart 1, suggests a 'rightward' shift in the functional relationship between them in CPEs. It appears that CPEs were not showing the kind of productivity growth that arose from both human and physical capital accumulation in other countries.[3]

Sources of productivity gains and growth in transition to a market economy

Given a history of extensive factor accumulation, a priority in the transition economies is to generate significant and sustained gains in productivity. Such gains arise in a market economy through the ways in which markets, enterprises and financial institutions function and interact. Three channels are identified here which are playing an important role in the transition economies.

First, both within (through restructuring and better management) and across enterprises (through functioning markets for mobile factors) more effective use can be made of the factors of production which have already been accumulated. The transition experience so far has shown that improved management and incentives can extract greater and higher quality output from existing factors of production, in some cases spectacularly so. Successful restructuring must be driven by a strong commercial orientation within an enterprise (by which we mean a sharp focus on customers and costs) which in turn arises largely from competition and hard budget constraints. This restructuring often requires both the release of resources that no longer fit with an enterprise's new commercial orientation and the investment in new plant and equipment (and in training) which is complementary to those factors which are retained or newly acquired by the enterprise. Relatively modest amounts of the 'right' investment can sometimes build on idle or inefficiently employed capacity to generate significant returns. In practice, this has led, for instance, to a temporary shift in the structure of investment away from (still valuable) plant to (often technologically obsolete) equipment. Chart 2 demonstrates this in the case of Poland.

The second channel for productivity growth is the transfer of new commercial skills and technologies from one enterprise to another through commercial (or other) interactions. These interactions can be among local producers. They can also involve trade and foreign direct investment. The latter interactions are particularly important where gaps in technology between the transition economies and Western market economies are wide. Empirical evidence reveals that total factor productivity of developing countries is significantly and positively related to the research and development in their industrial country trade partners and to their imports of machinery and equipment from the industrial countries. Since technology lags behind Western countries in many sectors – and is now often commercially available to companies in the region – substitution of new processes or products for technologically obsolete old ones will allow productivity to rise even when only replacement investment takes place.

Finally, the process of structural change has caused capital scarcity or bottlenecks in high value-added sectors such as services and certain parts of the infrastructure and investment in these can have a high yield and thus a substantial effect on growth.

These sources of productivity gains should make it possible for transition economies to grow faster than OECD countries in the medium term even in the absence of very high investment rates. New investment can also potentially generate higher value added than in most developing countries because the skilled operators and engineers are there to make it work (often with limited retraining investment). Since much human and social capital is currently 'structurally unemployed' as a result of economic dislocation, the opportunity cost in the short run may be small.

Each of the channels of productivity growth identified above is promoted by an environment which consists of commercially driven enterprises operating in open economies with competitive markets and hard budget constraints. We now turn to the challenges in generating this kind of environment.

3. Investment and the business environment

Evidence on the relationship between investment and transition

It is instructive to relate levels of investment to the transition process. We find that investment levels, for both domestic and foreign direct investment

(FDI), are positively associated with progress in transition. Table 1 shows the results of a study that the EBRD conducted during 1995 with the data then available. It compares the timing of the first major steps towards liberalization with developments in fixed investment to GDP ratios in countries in transition. Investment data in the region are notoriously unreliable, but the Table can nevertheless be used to indicate some broad trends.

Table 1. Sequence of price liberalization and changes in the share of fixed investment in GDP

		Investment share picks up after/stabilizes after				
		Same year	1 year	2 years	> 2 years	Continues to fall throughout period covered
Investment share drops (years before liberalization)	> 2 years	Uk				Ar, Ge, Mo, Ta
	2 years	La	Es		Ki	
	1 year	Al, Po	Li, Ro, Ru		Bu, Cr	Uz
	same year	Sl (no change)	Hu, Cz	Sk		
	n. a.					

Note: Acronyms refer to the first two letters of the countries, except for Slovakia (Sk). Three countries are missing from the Table due to insufficient information: Azerbaijan, Kazakhstan and Turkmenistan.

Table 1 shows that the cumulative fall in the investment share was less severe in fast liberalizers, and the subsequent recovery was stronger. Those countries that were at an advanced stage of transition in mid-1994 experienced on average a fall of 3.4 percentage points in their investment/GDP ratio between 1989 and the trough. The average recovery from the investment trough represented almost two thirds of the previous fall by 1994. For countries that were at an intermediate stage of transition, these figures were 16 per cent and a quarter respectively, while in countries at earlier stages of transition the fall represented 14 percentage points and recovery had not yet been reported.

Table 2. Transition indicators, country risk and levels of FDI
(Only countries covered by EBRD survey)

	Average transition indicator in 1996 (4 is advanced transition)	Country risk rating, 1 is low risk (number of raters in brackets)	Cumulative FDI inflows 1989-96 (mill US$)	Cum, FDI inflows per capita 1989-96 (US$)
Czech Republic	3.5	1.11 (99)	6,606	642
Hungary	3.5	1.28 (95)	13,266	1,288
Estonia	3.4	2.05 (73)	707	459
Poland	3.3	1.44 (99)	4,957	128
Slovak Republic	3.3	1.76 (80)	767	144
Croatia	3.1	2.73 (44)	564	118
Latvia	3.1	2.18 (73)	585	234
Lithuania	3.0	2.25 (71)	308	83
Slovenia	3.0	1.49 (57)	731	366
Russia	2.9	3.07 (74)	5,600	38
Kirghizia	2.7	3.14 (21)	132	29
Romania	2.6	2.68 (77)	1,434	63
Bulgaria	2.5	2.70 (71)	420	50
Kazakhstan	2.5	2.95 (39)	2,761	165
Ukraine	2.4	3.16 (61)	1,167	23
Turkmenistan	1.1	3.22 (23)	444	111

Sources: EBRD Transition Report 1996, survey data, IMF and EBRD estimates.

Additional evidence on the transition-investment relationship comes from data on FDI. The first column in Table 2 presents simple averages of the EBRD's nine transition indicators for 1995, ranging from 1 (little progress) to 4 (advanced transition).[4] The second column presents country risk assessments by a sample of foreign investors surveyed as part of an EBRD research project.[5] Interviewees were asked to rate the countries they felt confident assessing into four risk-groups, with 1 referring to a relatively low risk (comparable with risk in OECD countries) and 4 referring, to an unacceptably high level of risk. The data reported here represent the average of ratings. The Table indicates that FDI flows, as recorded in the balance of payments, have tended to be relatively high on both an absolute and per capita basis in countries at an advanced stage of transition and whose country risk is perceived to be low. The rank correlation coefficient between the average transition indicator and country risk on the one hand, and cumulative FDI per capita on the other is 75 per cent and 78 per cent, respectively. However, there is no evidence of a smooth functional relationship between FDI and transition level/risk (one factor that may be distorting the picture is natural resource investment, in which first-mover advantage to secure reserves is very important and which is, therefore, apparently less risk-sensitive than investment in other sectors).

Elements of a favourable investment climate

There are good reasons to suggest that progress in economic transition is an important determinant of private investment decisions, and so the evidence discussed above is unsurprising. The investment climate is created in large part by government policies, institutions and behaviour. A favourable investment climate is one which imparts a strong commercial orientation to investment decisions, which allows investors to realize the returns on sound investments and which limits the risks to investment arising from government policies and practices. The strengthening of this climate in many countries of the region requires significant further progress in macroeconomic stabilization and in tax reform. It requires structural reforms that strengthen the functioning of markets, enterprises and financial institutions. And it requires consistent, transparent and market-oriented behaviour from the authorities (often policies and institutions leave considerable discretion to the authorities). In our experience, governments that have gone furthest on the formal aspects of transition, such as liberalization and privatization have also recognized the importance of more qualitative aspects of the investment climate.

Perhaps the most fundamental lesson from the EBRD's experience with private investment in the region is its severely limited scope in the absence of macroeconomic stabilization and of basic structural reforms (such as price and trade liberalization, privatization of small-scale enterprises and elimination of directed credits and interest rate controls in credit markets). In such a climate for investment, financially viable private investment projects tend to be restricted to those which operate as enclaves within the local economy. Such projects are often capital intensive projects in the natural resource sector, where the capital inputs are sourced from abroad, and the output is exported. The main locally provided inputs are labour and transportation services. This type of private investment, while it can be of real value, has only limited linkages to the local economy and is unlikely to generate the types of commercial interactions that yield significant spillovers on the productivity of the local private sector.

The investment environment improves with progress in macroeconomic stabilization and structural reforms. However, the success of reforms in stimulating investment depends crucially on the way in which they are implemented and on the capacity of private institutions to respond to improvements in the business environment. Effective implementation of reform requires of governments the development of institutions which ensure that the application of laws and regulations conforms with legislative intentions and that the scope for arbitrary and capricious behaviour by the authorities is strictly checked. Similarly, the effective response of the private sector requires well-functioning enterprises and financial institutions that have market-oriented skills and effective corporate governance and incentive structures.

These deeper institutional and behavioural issues are important dimensions of transition, going beyond the passage of the required reforms by legislatures. However, change of this nature is also very complex. Since it involves fundamentally a learning process, it does not depend on simple fiat but draws on the gradual build-up of experience and therefore requires time. This explains why progress in transition has been particularly obvious in fields where the necessary development of institutions and behaviours, be they in government or the private sector, is less demanding. Accordingly, as countries move closer towards market economies, it is these institutional and behavioural factors that are becoming increasingly prominent items on the reform agenda.

Survey evidence reported by the World Bank suggests that shortcomings in the implementation of reforms, and in particular in the way the business of government is conducted, remain a deterrent for private investor activity.[6] The evidence relates to the CIS, but is consistent – though to a lesser extent – with EBRD experience even in the more advanced economies in transition. Key messages from the survey include:

- Taxes and tax administration are seen as a major problem. The firms interviewed felt that they face too many taxes and very high rates. They feel that the tax burden is not equitably shared across enterprises. Tax laws are perceived as vague and nontransparent.

- Laws and regulations are seen as complicated, ever-changing and burdensome, demanding considerable management time to 'discover' and negotiate with public officials, and providing opportunities for them to extract payments.
- The continuing uncertainty about the legal, institutional and regulatory regime increases the risk of business and deters investment.
- There is not much confidence in the legal administration to enforce basic property rights and contracts, or to control crime and corruption.

The survey was conducted among enterprises worldwide and therefore allows comparisons of the severity of these investment deterrents with other regions. The results reproduced in Table 3 confirm that the transition economies of the CIS still face significant challenges in improving their investment climate – for domestic investors but even more so if they are to compete successfully with other locations for FDI. In fact, the survey also reports some evidence that the situation has been deteriorating rather than improving in recent years.

Table 3. Obstacles for doing business – Survey results
(percentage of respondents reporting a 'strong obstacle')

	CIS	World	Developing countries	Developed market economies
High taxes/tax regulations	80	59	62	50
Policy instability	52	32	36	12
General uncertainty on costs of regulations	44	29	30	17
Crime and theft	48	38	43	11
Corruption	84	47	54	18

Source: World Bank (see footnote 6).

4. Transition, foreign investment, and trade

As we have argued external trade and investment are potentially important channels for productivity gains in the transition economies. The trade regime is also a key determinant of the investment climate, often determining the volume and nature of foreign investment in particular. It is, therefore, not surprising that we find strong empirical correlations between trade-related aspects of foreign investment in the transition economies and progress in economic reform.

While trade and FDI are sometimes approached separately in both economic theory and policy, they are in fact strongly interrelated, not least since they tend to be undertaken by and often within the same multinational enterprise. It has been estimated that in 1990 multinational enterprises were responsible for 80 per cent of world trade, while a third of worldwide exports took the form of intrafirm trade. Trade and FDI can be substitutes, as happens when FDI is undertaken to jump import barriers or to reduce transport costs in serving a particular market. On the other hand, they can be complements, for instance when a company invests in distribution systems or in trade-related services to boost exports to a foreign market. FDI can create trade, where it is undertaken to serve world or regional markets from a low-cost production base, and conversely the opportunity to trade can cause FDI while restrictions may dissuade it. Lastly, FDI can contribute to trade diversion in the context of rules of origin within free trade areas or quota restrictions on imports from certain locations but not from others.

All of these motives and patterns of FDI can be found in the transition economies. Since this is a vast area, we focus on two aspects that are particularly important, namely the extent to which the trade orientation of FDI is associated with the process of economic transition and the importance attached by investors to obstacles to trade. In this section, we present some results from a survey of foreign investors conducted by the EBRD in 1995.[7]

Progress in transition is associated with greater outward orientation of FDI

The majority of investments in the sample, which covered 16 of the EBRD's countries of operations, were undertaken or planned to serve the domestic market of the host country as opposed to regional or world markets – this was true for 96 out of a total of 145 (potential) investments. However, it is striking how the relative share of export-oriented investment increases as one moves from early to more advanced transition economies.

In a statistical analysis of the interview sample, controlling for various other host country characteristics including income and size, a one point increase in the EBRD's transition indicator raises the odds that investments are of the export, relative to the domestic market type by 224 per cent. This suggests that progress in transition (and therefore a more favourable investment climate) strengthens integration into the international economy and allows countries to better exploit their comparative advantage. 'Export-oriented' investors stress the importance of production cost reduction in general and availability of cheap *skilled* labour in particular – this is the single most important motivating factor in their investment decision.[8] In light of our earlier discussion of the investment climate it is useful to note that a country's level of transition relates also to the likelihood of success. One point 'up' in the transition indicator of a country is associated with an 80 per cent fall in the chance of a project being eventually abandoned/postponed.

The result would imply that the share of cost-motivated, export-oriented investments into any particular transition economy will increase over time, while that of market-oriented will recede.

A further result throwing some light on the process of integration into international production networks – especially if viewed in conjunction with the association between transition and export orientation – is that a project's position within the production chain of its multinational parent corporation differs by project function. Export investments are somewhat more 'upstream' within the multinationals' production chain and sell almost half of their product within the corporation (i.e. to the parent company or other subsidiaries), while for market investors the share is only 3 per cent. In both cases input supply is roughly one-third from within the corporation (imports).

Trade policy and foreign investment

The survey suggests that barriers erected by trade policy are a significant impediment for foreign investors in some countries of Eastern Europe and, in particular, in the CIS. For purposes of the analysis, countries which had broadly comparable characteristics in the respondents' eyes were classified into three groups, with group 1 containing Hungary and the Czech Republic, group 2 the rest of Eastern Europe and the Baltics, and group 3 the CIS. Very few investors in group 1 report barriers of significance to the procurement of imported inputs. For group 2 countries (which include Poland) and for the CIS countries, almost half of respondents report a problem.

In group 2 countries, tariffs on imports from the EU are viewed as the relatively most important trade barrier (38 per cent of respondents), which suggests that the situation will improve as implementation of the Association Agreements proceeds. In group 3 countries, tariffs are less of an obstacle but foreign exchange and related controls are viewed as significant (30 per cent of respondents). Our impression is that the increased macroeconomic stability achieved over the past 2-3 years in many CIS countries will have reduced the importance of this issue.

Barriers affecting exports are a negligible problem for group 1 investors, but are a significant impediment for one quarter of group 2 and one third of group 3 investors. For projects in group 2, the only export barriers reported with any frequency are import tariffs imposed by other transition economies, while for projects in group 3, there are considerable intra-CIS trade frictions (taking the form both of import barriers and other controls in the country of sale, and export barriers and foreign exchange controls in the host country).

It is interesting to note, given the frequent public discussion of contingent protection in the EU, that only 12 per cent of export investors in group 3 countries perceive non-tariff barriers on EU/EEA markets to be problematic and view them as a significant variable in their investment decision (and virtually none in group 1 and 2 countries). Non-tariff barriers covered by the survey included measures such as anti-dumping investigations and licensing. But in interpreting this result, one should be careful not to play down the issue – the survey covered a broad cross-section of manufacturing industries, and contingent protection has been concentrated in a small number of 'sensitive' industries. In some of these industries the transition economies of the CIS enjoy a potentially significant comparative advantage – if not, it is unlikely that the protection would have been requested.

5. Conclusions

If there is one clear implication from this presentation, it is that transition in the region still has a long way to go if the potential for investment and growth is to be realized. Particularly important in the next stages are the difficult administrative and behavioural factors that are fundamental to a favourable investment climate. In some countries, as demonstrated by the results on the role of trade policy, there also remains scope for completing some of the more basic steps in liberalization.

It is important to share these conclusions and analyses with policy makers. However, we can also contribute directly to improving the investment climate. From the perspective of the countries in the region and the market perspective, finance (be it internal or external) that is directly associated with quality investments and which involves commitments for the medium term can help boost the growth potential in a number of different ways.

The EBRD has a clear role and responsibility in this regard. The purpose of the EBRD is to 'foster the transition towards open market-oriented economies and to promote private and entrepreneurial initiative in the Central and Eastern European countries' (from Article 1 of the Agreement Establishing the EBRD). The EBRD promotes transition through the investment projects which it helps to finance. We look particularly for projects which as well as being 'additional' to the market also have transition impact ('additionality' refers to the Bank's impact on the project, and transition impact to the project's influence on the economy and transition process). Thus by choosing projects which are directed to adressing the transition and refusing to participate in projects which do not advance the transition, the Bank is pursuing its mandate.

We have developed an approach that allows us to guide project selection and design towards key areas of the transition process in a country by way of a 'transition impact checklist', built around demonstration effects (including behavioural), institutional change and competition enhancement. This is still a relatively new approach and there are no clear precedents, nevertheless, it may be a useful tool for other institutions and analysts and we, therefore, append the checklist to this paper. We would welcome your comments.

Qualitative aspects of transition impact of projects: a checklist

Note: The checklist covers only those potential effects of a project on the host country that relate to the conversion from a command economy to an economy driven by well-functioning markets. It does not cover direct income and resource effects of a project and environmental impact only indirectly to the extent that it is a consequence of the broadening and deepening of markets. Applications of the checklist should, therefore, preferably be viewed in conjunction with an analysis of the financial and economic rate of return and of the wider environmental impact of a project. The checklist is 'generic' in the sense that, in principle, its categories fit all project types (e.g. SMEs, infrastructure projects, technical assistance). Sector-specific guidelines are available for financial sector and infrastructure projects.

Project contributions to the structure and extent of markets

1. *Greater competition in the project sector.* A project can promote greater competition in its sector of activity. Increased competitive pressure is likely to improve the efficiency with which resources are utilized, demand is satisfied, and innovation is stimulated. However, in some circumstances a project might lead to a slackening of

competitive pressure on market participants, including the project company itself.
2. *Expansion of competitive/market interactions in other sectors.* A project can help to set business relationships in other markets on a more competitive basis. The benefits for the transition process would be similar to those described under the impact discussed above. There are two important ways in which markets can be extended and their functioning improved by projects:
   a) through interactions of the project entity with suppliers and clients;
   b) through project contributions to the integration of economic activities into the national or international economy, in particular by lowering the cost of transactions.

To have a structural effect, these contributions should not be 'one-off' but enhance competitive market interactions on a sustained basis. This would generally be achieved either through the formation of actors, methods of work, policies and institutions which last, or through interactions that have a strong demonstration effect.

Project contributions to the institutions and policies that support markets

3. *More widespread private ownership.* A project may result in increased private ownership through privatization, or new private provision of goods and services. This can generally be expected to strengthen market-oriented behaviour, innovation, the pool of entrepreneurship and, more generally, commitment to the transition. Private ownership is also in itself part of the transition objective. With the right kind of business standards, regulation and legal environment private ownership is complementary to, and often a condition for, the expansion and improvement of markets.
4. *Institutions, laws and policies that promote market functioning and efficiency.* A project may help to create or reform governmental or private institutions, policies and practices whose function is to enhance entrepreneurship and the efficiency of resource allocation. This is particularly relevant where not only the project entity itself but also other economic activities benefit. Four types of contribution are of particular importance here:

a) the creation/strengthening of public and private institutions that support the efficiency of markets;
b) improvements to the functioning of regulatory entities and practices;
c) project contributions to government policy formation and commitment, promoting competition, predictability and transparency;
d) contributions to laws that strengthen the private sector and the open economy.

Project contributions to market-based conduct, skills, and innovation

1. Other economic actors what is feasible and profitable and thereby inviting replication. There are three types of demonstration effect which are of particular importance here:

   a) demonstration of products and processes which are new to the economy;
   b) demonstration of ways of successfully restructuring companies and institutions;
   c) demonstration to both domestic and foreign financiers of ways and instruments to finance activities.

2. *Setting standards for corporate governance and business conduct.* By implementing high standards of corporate governance and business conduct in entities supported by the Bank, projects may contribute to the spreading of behaviour and attitudes that enhance the legitimacy and functioning of the market economy. This is a form of demonstration effect which functions by establishing reference points for other firms and individuals concerning businesses that they wish to invest in or interact with. Where role models for business conduct and corporate governance are rare, such pressures are less likely to materialize. A difference with institutional change as discussed under point 4 is that such behaviour may not be codified in a formal way.

Notes and references

1. Survey results are presented in Lankes, H.P. and A. Venables 'Foreign direct investment in economic transition: The changing pattern of investment,' *Economics of transition*, Volume 4 (2), pp. 331-347, 1996; and Lankes, H.P. and A. Venables, 'Foreign direct investment in Eastern Europe and the former Soviet Union', working paper, EBRD.
2. A cross-country comparison of energy (in)efficiency in production can be found in the EBRD Transition Report 1995, Table 4.1.
3. The regression lines are defined in terms of the rate of growth (dependent variable), the investment share in GDP (independent variable) and a shift factor. This is obviously a simplification of what is in reality a very complex relationship, and there are a number of possible underlying theories. However, an analysis of the roots of low productivity growth under central planning is not our main focus here.
4. The EBRD transition indicators as reported in the EBRD's Annual Transition Reports measure progress in privatization, enterprise restructuring, the scope and openness of markets, financial sector reform and the creation of legal and institutional frameworks supporting private sector activity.
5. A fuller presentation of the survey is contained in Lankes, H.P. and A. Venables (1996) (reference in footnote 1). 11,000 firms world-wide were contacted in January 1995. 1,435 responded, of which 628 indicated they were willing to be interviewed at senior executive level. Executives from 117 of these firms with 145 investments in Eastern Europe and the former Soviet Union were interviewed between June and November 1995. To qualify for the survey, the company needed to have an operational, planned, postponed or abandoned project in the mining or manufacturing sectors of an EBRD country of operations; in addition, its headquarters had to be in Western Europe. The 145 surveyed investments cover 16 economies in transition, employ 39,000 workers and have a total foreign equity contribution of US$ 2.8 billion.
6. Evidence taken from a background paper by the World Bank presented at a seminar on Conditions for Growth in the CIS at the EBRD's Annual General Meeting, April 13, 1997: 'Improving the environment for business and investment in the CIS and Baltic countries: Views from entrepreneurs and World Bank country economists'.
7. A brief description of the survey can be found in footnote 5, references in footnote 1.
8. In the sample, salaries of skilled workers in export investments are at 16 per cent of their Western (parent company) level, while productivity is reported to be, on average, 72 per cent of the Western level. Since other, unspecified cost factors are less advantageous, overall unit costs of exporters represent 67 per cent of those in Western Europe.

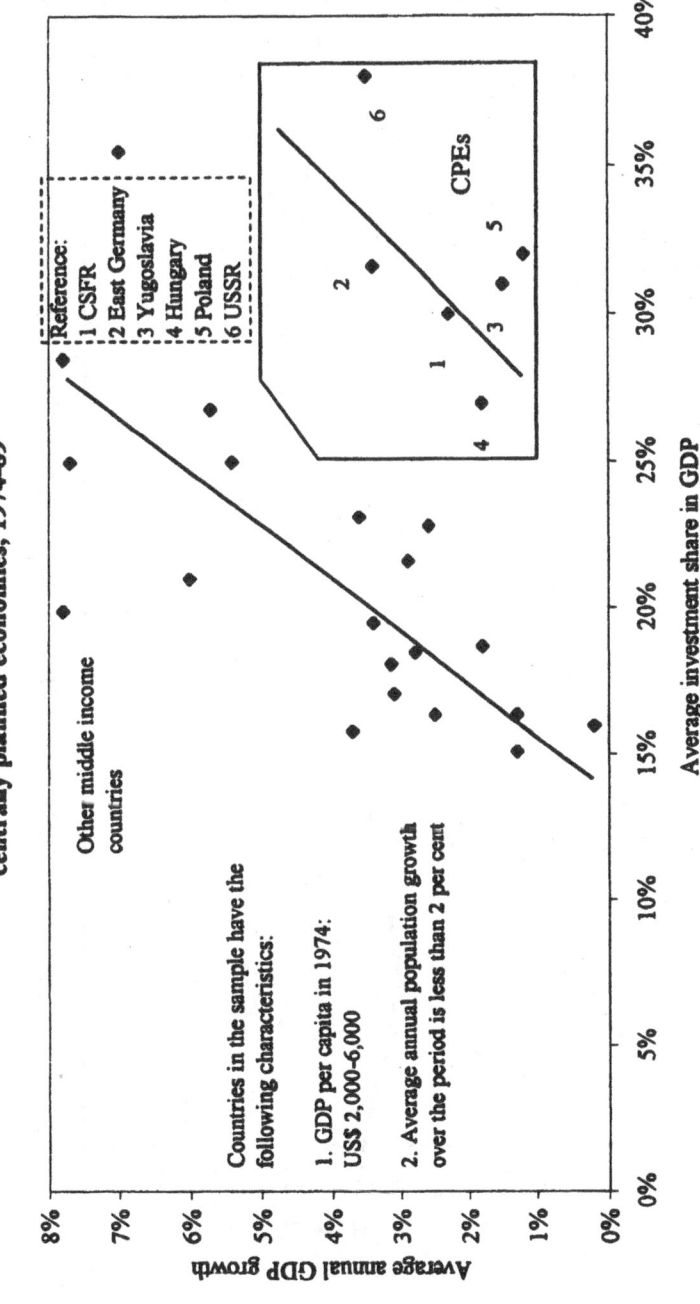

Chart 1. Growth and investment in middle income countries and centrally planned economies, 1974–89

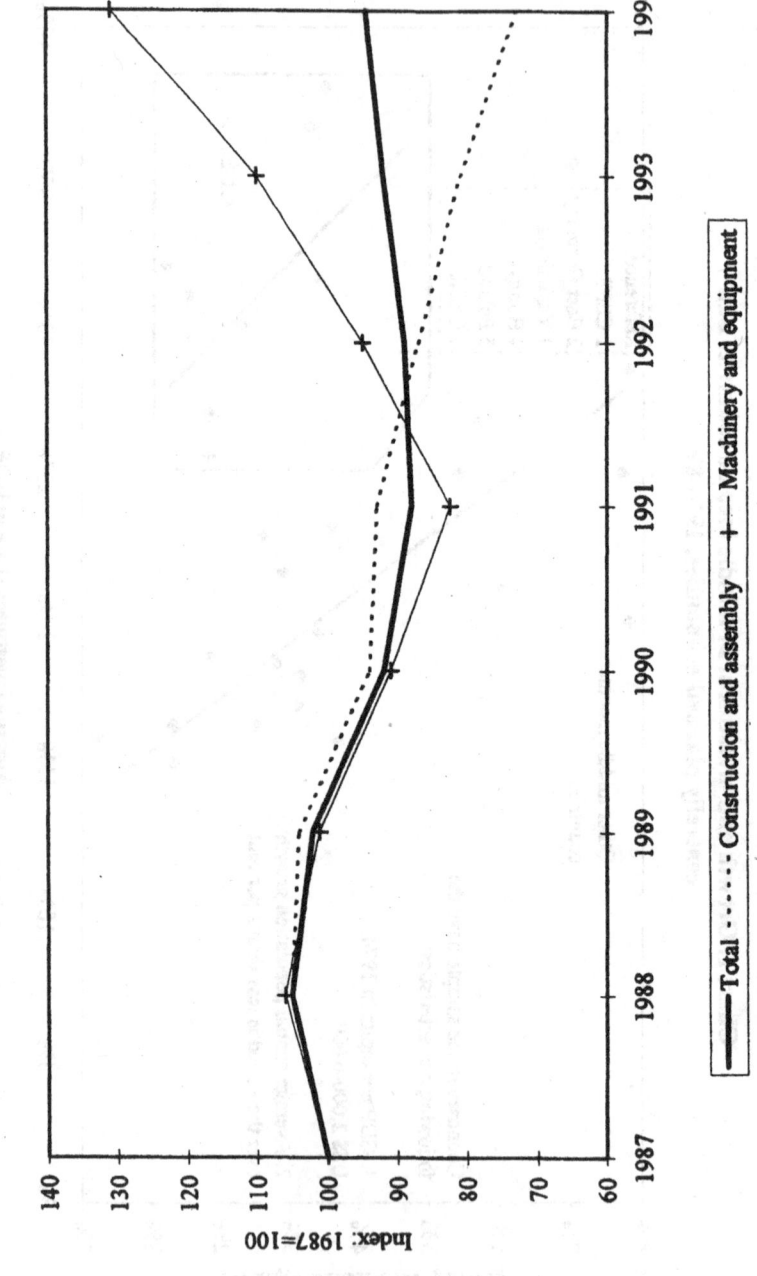

Chart 2. Poland 1987-94: Investment in construction and machinery

16 Monetary Governance in Selected Transition Economies – What Has Been Achieved?

Maciej Krzak and Aurel Schubert[*]

1. Introduction

Monetary governance refers to the combination of the legal framework, the strategy and the operational framework of monetary policy-making in a particular country. In the economies in transition of Central and Eastern Europe, the institutional framework of monetary policy was practically created from scratch from the beginning of transformation. Six years of transition inspire us to ask what has been achieved. In this study, we intend to highlight the shift from direct instruments to indirect instruments of monetary management. Furthermore, the paper gives a comparative overview of the different institutional set-ups of monetary policy in the countries examined. Our study is restricted to the CEFTA-5[1] countries, the Czech Republic, Hungary, Poland, Slovakia, and Slovenia, which appear most advanced in their respective degrees of monetary transition.[2] These countries also aspire to join the European Union along with five other transition economies. Sooner or later, they will also voice an interest in becoming members of the prospective European Economic and Monetary Union (EMU). Though this perspective is still very remote – especially since the third and final stage of monetary union has not even started yet – we believe it is useful to examine the monetary frameworks in these countries in comparison to the monetary framework prepared for the conduct of monetary policy by the European

---

[*] Foreign Research Division, OeNB; Krzak also: The Vienna Institute for Comparative Economic Studies. The views contained herein do not necessarily coincide with those officially held by the institutions with which the authors are affiliated.

System of Central Banks in EMU as published by the European Monetary Institute (EMI) in early 1997.[3]

In this study, we focus on targets and instruments of monetary policy-making and dwell only briefly on the question of central bank independence.[4] We discuss exchange rate policy only within the context of monetary policy, concentrating mainly on the impact of capital flows on the effectiveness of monetary management. We do not go into a description of the centrally planned episode and of the first steps of Transition, as the topic has already been discussed comprehensively by Duchatczek and Schubert (1992 and 1993) nor do we touch on the issues of regulation and supervision of the banking industry. Specifically, we do not discuss the impact on monetary policy-making of bail-outs of commercial banks by central banks.

The paper consists of five sections. After the introduction, in Section 2, we briefly outline the tenets of the modern monetary framework in market economies with particular reference to the monetary framework developed by the EMI. In Section 3, which is the core part of the paper we analyse the evolution of the monetary framework in the five CEFTA countries. In Section 4, exchange rate policy and regimes are briefly discussed in the context of monetary policy issues. Section 5 starts with a brief summary of the paper to proceed to the main conclusions.

2. Theoretical underpinnings of sound monetary policy

The theoretical standard for the institutional set-up of monetary policy in developed market economies includes recommendations for central bank independence, monetary policy targeting, instruments, and the interdependence of monetary and exchange rate policy. The literature on these issues is still developing, with new studies steadily adding to our knowledge.

2.1 Central bank independence

According to the empirical evidence,[5] a strong negative correlation can be observed between the degree of central bank independence and the inflation rate. Central bank independence from political institutions is believed to allow and encourage the bank to focus monetary policy on long-run issues, especially on price stability. In this way, it is free from political pressures to generate political business cycles by running expansionary policies before elections in order to support the incumbents' re-election efforts.[6] Independence has several facets: functional, personal and financial. Personal independence, for instance, is ensured by fixing longer terms of office for the governors of the central banks than the political election cycle or by diminishing the government's role in appointing the governor and by explicitly limiting the possible reasons for the removal of a governor to very few and transparent cases, all unrelated to monetary policy decisions. Functional independence refers to the central bank's autonomy in defining the intermediate goals of monetary policy and in implementing monetary policy. Financial independence includes, among other aspects, independence from the fiscal authority. This way the central bank cannot be forced to contribute to the financing of budget deficits, either by directly purchasing government debt instruments or by simply printing money.

Whether a higher degree of central bank independence results in 'a free lunch', that is, lower inflation without the cost of wider output variability, is still hotly debated. Alesina and Summers (1993) and Walsh (1994) report no association between central bank independence and output variability, whereas Rogoff (1985) as well as Debelle and Fischer (1994) find evidence that higher central bank independence leads to stronger recessions during disinflationary processes. They suggest that a central bank should be granted *only instrument* independence, but not *goal* independence. If evidence swayed toward the latter view, then the current strong trend would require mitigation and a critical evaluation of numerous banking acts in advanced and emerging market economies. At this stage of the debate, our stance is that the bank should be independent, but accountable. Accountability means that information about central bank targets and instruments is publicly available together with up-to-date information on the achievement of the targets.

2.2 Targets

In the medium to long run, a central bank is accountable for its adherence to the ultimate objective. Targeting has the advantage of enabling the central bank to recognize where it wants to go; it also has informational merit as it lets the private sector know what to expect in the future. Targeting obviously makes central banks accountable for their actions. Outsiders obtain a chance to discuss the announced targets and whether they are aimed at the right direction. It has become standard to describe central banks' goals by classifying them as ultimate goals and as intermediate and operational targets.

The ultimate goal could be an economic variable whose development is very important for the economy, such as price stability, the inflation rate, the rate of unemployment, the development of real GDP or the stability of financial as well as foreign exchange markets. Multiple targets are likely to be incompatible and to create conflicts for the central bank concerned. The trade-off between some of them can be described with a welfare loss function of the government. A number of these targets, e.g. the unemployment rate or the GDP growth, were proposed within a framework of an anti-cyclical role of monetary policy. Progress in targeting theory as well as empirical evidence have led to the widespread conviction that ensuring price stability – maybe in combination with financial stability – should be the only goal of monetary policy.[7] Disillusion with monetary policy as a means to dampen business cycles rests on three important results of economics theory: 1) monetary policy is unable to affect real variables in the long run, but can do so only in the short run; 2) there are long and variable lags between policy implementation and its impact on the economy, so at the time the policy becomes effective, it may become counterproductive; 3) a time inconsistency problem arises, i.e. if inflationary expectations are low and thus the marginal cost of additional inflation is low, policy-makers are tempted to pursue expansionary monetary policies to push output above its normal level. The public will recognize and anticipate that behaviour and adjust its expectations accordingly. Consequently, output will not change, but inflation will rise.

Price stability is a primary candidate for a final goal of monetary policy. Economic theory establishes and explains the links between money and inflation depending on the time framework. In the long run, there is a systematic relationship between money and inflation, which is a purely monetary phenomenon. The quantity theory of money is valid and money is neutral, i.e., it does not influence real variables. Thus, in the equilibrium (dynamic steady) state, monetary policy can at best achieve price stability or, as the next best outcome, a desired rate of inflation.

In the short to medium run, central banks need other performance criteria than the achievement of the final goal as monetary policy works with long (and variable) lags. Assessment can be based on monitoring the central bank's performance relative to its announced strategy, a set of procedures specifying how to act to achieve the final objective. Pure discretion would imply no strategy and no possibility of evaluating a central bank's behaviour in the short run. From a different angle, the need for credibility of actions and the time inconsistency problem decisively weaken the case for discretion. Most central bank strategies[8] are based on indirect targeting. However, one strategy that has recently gained importance – the United Kingdom, Sweden, Finland, and Canada are among the countries whose central banks have adopted it – directly targets the inflation rate without a traditional intermediate stage.

The rationale for intermediate targets rests on the argument that instruments available for central banks affect the ultimate goals of monetary policy only with a long lag. This makes it hard to correct mistakes before they show up when the ultimate target is missed. Therefore, central banks use different (intermediate) variables which have strong and predictable links with ultimate goals and are easily observable. These variables are either under the direct or indirect control of the monetary authorities. As a consequence, central banks distinguish between intermediate and operational targets.

In principle, the choice of an intermediate target should be based on its measurability, controllability and its ability to predict its own effect on ultimate goals. The perfect intermediate target is a variable that a central bank can control and that, at the same time, has an exact relationship with the ultimate target of the policy. Economic theory has suggested a number of intermediate targets. The most popular are the short-term interest rate, nominal GNP (GDP), different monetary aggregates and the exchange rate. Nominal GNP has only been a theoretical alternative so far, especially due to shortcomings of statistical data. The criteria for choosing intermediate targets were first proposed in a seminal work by Poole (1970) and developed by follow-up research. Basically, the choice between an interest rate and a measure of the money supply as the appropriate intermediate target depends on the nature of the aggregate demand shocks occuring in that particular economy. A prevalence of monetary shocks calls for interest rate targeting, whereas a prevalence of real shocks calls for monetary targeting. In the case of supply shocks, the theory does not offer unambiguous answers.

Problems with monetary targeting at an early stage of economic transition mainly due to uncertainty concerning money demand and the monetary transmission mechanism led to a preference for the exchange rate as an intermediate target. Since exchange rate targeting has become popular in many of the economies studied here, we will dwell a little on its merits as a target. Fixing the exchange rate implies that the money supply becomes endogenous, and the central bank can only directly control its domestic component. All other nominal variables, like the price level, the nominal wage rate or the quantity of money, have to adjust to the exchange rate. Preferably, a country should peg the exchange rate to the currency of an important trade partner country with a good price stability track record. This approach is particularly attractive to countries whose monetary authorities and policies lack credibility either because they have established a bad reputation as inflation-prone or because they have no track record yet, as is the case of the transition economies. The exchange rate target gives them a way to acquire credibility via the partner institution if the commitment is supported by the necessary conservative monetary policy.

The other advantage of the exchange rate fix as a target is its high visibility and transparency to the public. It is evident that exchange rate targeting is mostly applied in the high inflation countries aiming at a significant reduction of inflation or in countries which enter multilateral exchange rate agreements, like the EMS. Crawling exchange rate pegs or crawling exchange rate bands are looser commitments. They are recommended for countries with moderate and persistent inflation which have stabilized their economies but still need support for further disinflation and desire flexible monetary arrangements. These forms of crawling devaluation at preannounced rates during a given period are aimed at anchoring inflationary expectations and at the same time protecting the balance of payments. Flexibility is required to absorb various shocks (external or domestic, demand or supply) of different magnitudes which hit the economy. In particular, movements of portfolio capital can exert pressure on the exchange rate which a band of feasible fluctuations can help to offset without changing the exchange rate regime or large-scale intervention.

For the choice of an *operational* target, it is important that the target have a strong and predictable impact on the chosen intermediate target. This implies that if a monetary aggregate is the intermediate target, a reserve aggregate such as the monetary base would be the preferred operational target. On the other hand, if the desired intermediate target is an interest rate or an exchange rate, then a short-term interest rate will be the preferred operational variable. Among the most broadly used operating targets are reserve aggregates such as reserves, non-borrowed reserves, the monetary base or the non-borrowed base and short-term money market interest rates, which are more directly responsive to the instruments of central banks (open market operations, changes in the discount and/or lombard rate and changes in reserve requirements).

Direct inflation targeting does not fit the traditional division into intermediate and operating objectives.[9] It has not been used by the reviewed economies in transition yet, but it is mentioned in the framework report of the EMI as a possible alternative to a strategy based on monetary targeting.[10] The alternatives, nominal GNP targeting, interest rate, and exchange rate targeting, are dismissed in the report as not viable for the conduct of monetary policy in EMU.

2.3 Instruments

Modern central banks' tool kits consist of the discount and/or lombard rate, reserve requirements, and open market operations. Access to the discount window is typically rationed by quantity restrictions (quotas) if the discount rate is below comparable market interest rates. At present, a general tendency away from below-market-rate discount and lombard lending toward open market operations at market interest rates can be observed. Theorists have long proposed a penalty discount rate. The lombard rate concept, which acts as a cap in interbank market rates, is based on this idea.

Reserve requirements are too unwieldy a tool to be used in the everyday conduct of monetary policy. Small changes potentially produce large swings in base money. Extremely small changes in mandatory reserve ratios to overcome this problem are too costly to engineer. The tendency is to assign them solely the role of a prudential norm which should guarantee a minimal solvency of financial institutions. Reserve requirements usually do not pay interest and act as a tax on bank deposits. In a stable economy with low interest rates and relatively low reserve requirements this is not a problem, but in inflationary economies with relatively high requirements, such as the economies in transition, non-remunerated minimum reserves create a considerable wedge between deposit and credit rates.

Open market purchases and sales of securities have been the most important tool of monetary policy in advanced economies for years. Open market operations occur at the initiative of a central bank, which can completely control their volumes. They are flexible and precise enough to fine tune the conduct of monetary policy. They can be easily reversed when necessary and they can be implemented quickly without administrative delays. Broad use of open market transactions is conditional on the development of money markets and the availability of marketable securities. Usually, government securities are used. Repurchase operations, rather than outright purchases, predominate, as they allow for more flexibility and precision.

2.4 EMU framework

The positive and normative knowledge of central banking is reflected in the framework for monetary policy conduct that has been proposed by the EMI report.[11] The proposed institutional set-up can be treated as a benchmark towards which the monetary frameworks of countries aspiring to enter the European Union, among them the ones examined in this paper, should evolve. The role and importance of central bank independence is emphasized in the report. The final goal is the achievement of price stability. The report leaves open whether monetary targeting or direct inflation targeting should be used by the European System of Central Banks. It rightly points to the fact that the differences between these two types are largely semantic, as both strategies place monetary aggregates at the centre of the set of variables to be monitored.[12] The debate at the EMI exemplifies the current stage of controversy. The EMI stopped short of recommending direct inflationary targeting, leaving the option open. The second president of the EMI, Wim Duisenberg, strongly opposes the idea of direct inflation targeting on the grounds of the unclear signals such a strategy produces for monetary policy. In his view, it is a 'look-at-everything' approach.[13] The difference between intermediate and final-target approaches may be more apparent than real as intermediate targets are used to promote the final target of price stability. In fact, projected inflation plays the role of the intermediate target for direct inflation targeting. A country pursuing a pure intermediate monetary target places a 100 per cent weight on money growth relative to its target, while a country pursuing direct inflationary targeting uses several indicators, one of them being money supply growth.

In order to allow and enable the public to assess the performance of the future European System of Central Banks, its targets will be announced and published. To make the ESCB more accountable, analyses and data relevant to monetary policy will also be regularly published. Explanations of deviations from targets and of policy responses by the ESCB will also become part of the communication with the public.

The ESCB will use open market operations to steer interest rates, manage the liquidity of financial markets and signal the stance of monetary policy. It will have at its disposal five types of open market transactions: while reverse transactions will play the biggest role, also outright transactions, the issuance of debt certificates, foreign exchange swaps and the collection of fixed-term deposits will be possible.

A marginal lending facility will allow eligible counterparts to obtain overnight credit on their own initiative (like the current lombard loan in several countries). Deposit facilities will be available to absorb excess liquidity. The interest rate on the marginal lending facility will provide a ceiling for the overnight market interest rate while the deposit rate will provide its floor. The access to both facilities will be unlimited under normal conditions.

The framework for the monetary policy of the ESCB includes the possibility of imposing minimum reserves on financial institutions.[14] The ESCB may apply a uniform reserve ratio to the whole reserve base or differentiate reserve ratios across categories and maturities of eligible liabilities. The possibility of remuneration of the reserves held is not excluded.

In the following part of the paper we will discuss how institutional setups of monetary policy conduct in the CEFTA countries square with these normative propositions. The brief description of the evolution of monetary conduct will precede it to give a broader perspective on prevailing tendencies. We begin with a short account of the starting.

3. Present monetary policy framework

3.1 The initial conditions

The organizing principle of the economy as a whole was based on the classical directive Soviet-type model to run the whole economy like one factory, where all externalities are internalized. The reality of centrally planned economies, including the monetary environment, has been described in numerous articles and books. We intend to refresh the readers' memory of the basic features of monetary environment to underscore the point of departure of the countries reviewed.[15] It does not, however, apply to Slovenia, which as a part of former Yugoslavia experienced a system that was labelled market socialism at the time. At a small risk of simplification, it can be said that, under socialism, monetary policy in the (proper) sense of Western economics did not exist. With the exception of household decisions about savings and consumption, money was accorded a passive role.[16] Its issuance was subordinated to central economic plans expressed *de facto* in physical units, since money was used as a unit of account only. Financial markets played no role in the allocation of scarce resources. As a consequence, the central bank provided firms with funds in order to enable them to fulfil central planner's production targets. The state credit plan mirrored the central plan, which directly allocated credits to firms and sectors. The interest rate only played a marginal role in the allocation of financial resources and did not reflect market conditions; investment credit and housing credit were usually subsidized. Thus, credit was rationed on the basis of state investment and production plans. Bankruptcy was excluded; firms always obtained the funds they needed, without a proper screening of profitability of output or investment projects, so they worked under a soft budget constraint.

The structure of the financial system was rudimentary. The only financial assets were currency, bank deposits and, rarely, government bonds. Banking was a state monopoly, and the banking system has been termed a monobank system because all banks were state-owned and directly or indirectly depended on the central bank, which was usually involved in commercial activities. The two-tier structure of the banking system did not exist. The existence of so-called specialized banks – investment, foreign trade, and savings banks – blurred this picture only on the surface, as they were not allowed to lend funds to enterprises or, in particular, to channel individuals' savings into commercial loans. Central banks had little autonomy and were dependent on the government in their decisions. Their *raison d'etre* was to implement various elements of the central plan, e.g. the state foreign trade bank executed the state monopoly of foreign exchange and handled all foreign trade transactions. In centrally planned economies, households used cash, while the enterprise sector made payments through bank accounts. These two circuits were separated; firms held cash to pay wages, but were allowed to keep only insignificant amounts of cash otherwise.

Central banks targeted credit plans, which in detail assigned financial funds to economic entities. They used instruments of direct monetary control, i.e. credit ceilings and interest rate ceilings. The exchange rate was mainly an accounting device to translate foreign prices into domestic prices. Often, a multitude of so-called conversion ratios for specific item groups was used. Domestic currency was practically nonconvertible. Foreign exchange controls were imposed not only on capital transactions, but also on current account transactions. There was no official foreign exchange market, so the need for foreign exchange intervention did not arise. The demand for foreign currency was rationed by administrative measures.

This account outlines a rigid model of central planning. It should, however, be made clear that long before the end of communism, some of the reviewed countries, in particular Hungary and to a lesser extent Poland, started discarding features of the model. Former Yugoslavia had a two-tier banking structure and market principles to allocate credit.

We proceed to the analysis of the current frameworks of monetary policy in the countries examined.

3.2 Status of the central bank

In this section, we touch on only the most important issues related to central bank independence in the CEFTA countries. We did not go into most details of legal acts.[17] It is evident that these countries draw on the experience of Western European countries and attempt to harmonize their central bank acts with the requirements of the Maastricht Treaty. The central bank acts were adopted relatively early in the transition process. Poland, whose central bank act already originated in the late 1980s, is an exception, although the old law is due to be replaced soon. Hungary modified its act in 1996.

3.2.1 Legal status

The legal status of the CEFTA central banks is such that they are independent in four of the countries. In Poland, the central bank act does not specify this issue, but the new central bank law pending introduction will explicitly use the term independence. Central banks are free to develop instruments of monetary policy and conduct monetary policy, for which they are accountable. Three of the central banks are responsible for exchange rate policy. The National Bank of Poland has to consult the Ministry of Finance before any exchange rate policy changes are introduced. The National Bank of Hungary (NBH) makes decisions jointly with the government, though the initiative rests with the NBH. In Poland, monetary policy guidelines are approved by parliament, which restricts the autonomy of the central bank in shaping monetary policy. In other countries, parliaments are not involved in this process. In Hungary, monetary and fiscal policy are reconciled before their implementation. All acts will have to be modified to exclude an option of central bank financing of budget deficits, should these countries join the EU.

3.2.2 Personal independence

The governor's terms are 6 years in each of the countries, longer than the respective political cycle. In the Czech Republic, Hungary, and Slovakia, the governor is appointed by the president of the state. In the latter two countries, it is done on the basis of the government's recommendation. In Poland and Slovenia, he or she is appointed by parliament on the proposal of the republic's president. Slovenia is the only country which does not specify the rules of dismissal of the central bank governor. In all other countries, the governor may voluntarily resign his or her office and can only be dismissed on the basis of a criminal act or the inability to perform his/her function.

3.2.3 Financial independence

All banks are meant to be self-financing institutions. They act as agents of the public. Central banks in these countries should transfer their profits after replenishment of reserves or statutory funds to the state budget. A shortfall of these profits may jeopardize the conduct of monetary policy, as was the case in Poland in 1996. Sterilized interventions proved so costly that profits fell to one sixth of the projected amount in the state budget so that the central bank had to change course and let interest rates drop despite earlier announcements excluding their reduction. Central bank acts containing plans covering all contingencies in the case of potential losses are not as common as regulations on the transfer of profits to the state budget. They exist in Slovenia, where losses are to be covered first from the reserve fund and then from the state budget, and in Hungary, where the state covers all losses. In Poland, they are to be covered from the reserve fund, but a contingency for higher losses has not been specified. Apparently, losses are not expected in the Czech Republic and Slovenia as these countries have made no relevant provisions.

3.2.4 Financing budget deficits

The weakest part of the central bank statutes is their leniency as regards direct financing of budget deficits by credit extended by the central bank. While the potential amounts are limited, they nevertheless enable governments to seek cover for a substantial part of their deficits. In the Czech Republic and Slovakia, the government is allowed to sell short-term Treasury bills of up to 5 per cent of previous year's revenues. In Slovenia, the government can draw up to one fifth of the planned deficit. In Hungary, the government may borrow up to 2 per cent of planned budget revenues, while in Poland it can sell government securities totaling no more than 2 per cent of the planned state expenditure. In practice, these regulations are respected. The Czech and the Slovenian governments did not need a recourse to inflationary financing, as these countries have run balanced budgets. Poland and Slovakia have respected the regulations so far. Hungary's government once overrode the regulation and borrowed more than the 2 per cent specified by the law.

3.3 Strategy

At the outset of transition in 1990 to 1991, central banks in former socialist countries had no experience or technology to apply monetary strategies based on indirect instruments of monetary control, as practiced by advanced market economies. Money markets did not exist; the relevant instruments had yet to be created. Since then, the monetary environment has changed dramatically. The change was fostered by central bank activity, which helped construct interbank and foreign exchange markets in these countries.

3.3.1 Targeting

Targeting plays a prominent role in monetary strategies of the group of countries analysed here. A division into ultimate, intermediate, and operating targets has been adopted across our sample of countries. At the beginning of transition, the separation was not obvious and it took several years before this division clarified and became comprehensible for the public. For example, the NBH started distinguishing among these targets for the first time in its Annual Report of 1993. Poland formally stated this division for the first time in the guidelines for monetary policy in 1996.

The ultimate goal of monetary policy in these five countries is price stability. Over the last years, there have been no changes in the formulation of the final goals. The formulations used in the offcial acts vary from internal and external stability of the domestic currency in the case of Hungary to just currency stability in the remaining countries, though the wording in Poland is different, stating that the central bank is obliged to pursue the goal of 'strengthening the currency'. Hungary initially interpreted the goal of external stability of the forint in terms of a sustainable position of the current account. This was the case between 1990 and 1992 and later in 1994. In 1993, the stress was put on disinflation. In the Czech Republic, Poland, and Slovakia, the central bank is also explicitly obliged to support the economic policy of the government if this does not interfere with the final goal. Since all these countries experience high inflation compared to the European Union or North America, the goal should be interpreted as a reduction of inflation.

Internal and external currency stability can conflict under certain conditions as external stability in fact pertains to exchange rate policy. This stability can be interpreted in real or nominal terms. The choice of a real exchange rate anchor would leave the price level indeterminate. The fixity of the nominal exchange rate is congruent with the goal of domestic stability of the currency, if the exchange rate is pegged to the currency of a country with a good inflation record.

The stipulated support of government policy opens another area for conflict, as in an inflationary environment the central bank could endorse a more counter-inflationary strategy than the one welcomed by the government. The government may point to the rule requiring support for government policy so that the central bank could face pressure to soften its stance. The result is slower disinflation. It is evident that the world wide recognition of the limits of counter-cyclical monetary policy is reflected in the formulation of the final goals in our sample of countries. None of them openly lists full employment as a final goal.

At the beginning of transition, four of the countries (Slovenia was the exception) resorted to exchange rate targeting. The exchange rate had the appeal of a transparent anchor in a period of sweeping systemic change. Over the years of transition, three out of four countries have shifted to monetary targeting as one of the intermediate targets. Setting monetary targets in an economy in transition poses numerous difficulties. As the number of economic agents rapidly grows and liberalization and privatization proceed, the money demand function becomes unstable. No historical data which would give reliable grounds for the estimation of parameters of such a function have become available. Strong shocks, including supply shocks (e.g. liberalization of prices), hit the real economy so Poole's (1970) analysis has only limited merit in the selection of targets. On the money supply side, changes in the money multiplier may be pronounced even when the reserve requirement is constant and the monetary base is fixed. The time lags with which the changes in money supply affect the real economy are unknown. It is no wonder that central banks changed their targets quite often in such a monetary policy environment. A dose of experimenting was also necessary to gain experience.

The evolution of adopting intermediate and operating targets proceeded in step with the shift from direct monetary management to indirect monetary management. The Czech Republic, for instance, initially set a target for an increase in the domestic credit volume in 1990, then switched to net domestic assets of the banking system and from 1992 on, has tracked the broad money indicator (M2), which has been announced to the public. Poland also targeted net domestic assets of the banking sector until the end of 1992. In 1994 to 1995, Poland switched to targeting interest rates, apparently ascribing more relevance to monetary shocks than to real shocks; a large denomination of the zloty had been planned at the end of 1994 and shifts in money demand had been expected.

Table 1. Changes in intermediate targets in the period of transition

	1990	1991	1992	1993	1994	1995	1996
Czech R[18]	Increase in the domestic credit vol.	Exchange rate and net domestic assets in the banking sys..	Exchange rate and net domestic assets in the banking sys..	Exchange rate and M2	Exchange rate and M2	Exchange rate and M2	Exchange rate and M2
Hungary	Real exch. rate and net domestic loan stock	Real exch. rate and net domestic loan stock	Real exch. rate	Real exch. rate and net domestic assets	Real exch. rate and net domestic lending	Exchange rate	Exchange rate
Poland	Exchange rate and net domestic assets	Exchange rate and net domestic assets	Exchange rate and net domestic assets	Exchange rate and net domestic assets	Exchange rate and interest rates	Exchange rate and interest rates	Exchange rate and broad money
Slovakia	n.a.	n.a.	n.a.	Exchange rate and M2	Exchange rate and M2	Exchange rate and M2	Exchange rate and M2
Slovenia	n.a.	M1	M1	M1	M1	M1	M1

The intermediate targets of the countries in question vary little more than final goals. The countries which target the exchange rate have usually adopted another target as well. The Czech Republic, Slovakia, Hungary, and Poland have more or less stringent versions of fixed exchange rates (see Annex), so they have to adjust monetary growth accordingly. Therefore, monetary targets can only be supplementary as total money supply becomes endogenous under a fixed exchange rate regime, and the central bank can control only its domestic component. The Czech Republic, Slovakia, and Poland track broad money aggregates. In the Polish case, monetary targeting is more meaningful than in the Czech Republic or Slovakia, which have fixed exchange rates due to the looser exchange rate system of a crawling band. Slovenia, which formally had a managed floating system, is an exception as it uses a narrow money aggregate: it has been targeting M1 since 1991. This choice is based on the empirical evidence that the money demand for M1 is stable enough to warrant such a policy. Hungary does not supplement its preannounced exchange rate devaluation target with explicit targets for monetary aggregates, as money demand is believed to be too unstable to credibly validate such an announcement.[19] In the past, it targeted domestic credit expansion along with the real or nominal exchange rate when the current account constraint was less binding (in 1993).

In all of the countries with the exception of the Czech Republic, *operational targets* are compatible with monetary intermediate targets. Monetary intermediate targets call for reserve aggregates as operating targets, such as the monetary base, the non-borrowed base or bank reserves. Poland and Slovenia adopted base money, while the Czech Republic targets the interest rate, namely the one-week PRIBOR (Prague interbank offered rate), which endogenizes central bank money and thus potentially conflicts with the M2 target. Since the fixed exchange rate takes precedence over the monetary target, this does not necessarily have to be problematic for monetary policy coherence. Hungary targets the interest rate differential vis-a-vis the main financial markets to influence short-term capital flows. It thus monitors the repo rate. In the past, it targeted open market operations (limits on repurchase agreements were set in 1993 to 1995) and refinancing by the central bank (1990 to 1992). Slovakia does not announce its operational target, but monitors the monetary base. The NBS is of the opinion that foreign exchange inflows compromise its ability to control the operational target, therefore it stops short of announcing the formal target.[20]

Day-to-day central banking practice shows that central banks in these countries monitor other variables, in particular, interest rates, the trade balance, the current account or domestic credit expansion. For example, the National Bank of Poland monitored short-term interest rates in the first half of 1996 and in the autumn of 1996 became sensitive to domestic credit expansion in the context of the rapidly worsening trade balance, despite formally meeting its intermediate and operational targets.

3.3.2 Instruments

Perhaps with the exception of Slovenia, all of the examined economies started with transitory and inadequately developed financial systems.[21] For this reason, at the beginning of transition, direct instruments of monetary management played a prominent role to guarantee that monetary developments remained under control. All these countries experienced a decline in the GDP as well as a surge of inflation during the period of price liberalization. Therefore, they needed monetary restraint to eliminate excess liquidity. Since then, direct instruments such as interest rate ceilings or credit ceilings have been abolished in all countries reviewed here (see Table 2).

Table 2. Removal of direct controls

	Interest rate ceilings	Credit ceilings
Czech Republic	1992	1993
Hungary	1991	1990
Poland	1990	1993
Slovakia	1992	1995
Slovenia	1991	1991

Since the onset of transition, central banking in the group of countries analysed in the paper has been evolving to meet standards of the advanced Western economies. All sampled central banks use standard instruments from the tool kit of monetary control so that the classification of instruments into discount rate, reserve requirements, and open market operations is applicable to each of them (see Table 3). The shift to give greater importance to 'supply'-driven instruments relative to 'demand'-driven instruments is noticeable. Discount and lombard facilities have been losing significance relative to open market operations over the course of transition.

The gradual approach to the removal of direct controls dominated. Slovenia was an exception as it eliminated direct controls immediately after the declaration of independence from Yugoslavia. Poland phased out such controls in 1993. The Czech and Slovak Federation phased them out in 1992, but Slovakia reintroduced them in 1993 – to finally eliminate them at the end of 1995. Auctioned credit and repurchase tenders, which are indirect control procedures, have become common procedures instead.

Table 3. Introduction of indirect instruments of monetary management

	Open market operations	Discount rate	Reserve requirements
Czech Republic	1993	1990	1990
Hungary	1990	1989	1987
Poland	1992	1990	1990
Slovakia*	1993	1990	1990
Slovenia	1992	1991*	1991*

* Inherited from the disintegrated Federation.

Open market operations

Open market operations (OMOs) did not exist at the beginning of transition, and the creation of the necessary infrastructure could not happen overnight. They had to be implemented from scratch and their importance has risen considerably. Over the years, the evolution of instruments was moderated by changing problems of monetary policy. Commonly, central banks had to inject liquidity in the first years of transition. Only later on did they have to cope with the excess liquidity of the banking sector, after foreign exchange inflows had increased and after banks, having accumulated bad loans and having learned from the failures of the first years, restricted credit to the economy. OMOs were installed rather as defensive operations, i.e. to offset the impact of other factors on the monetary base, then as dynamic operations, i.e. to change the level of monetary base or bank reserves permanently. Hence, new instruments were sought to mainly respond to the new challenges, in particular to the challenge of capital inflows, but the search also proceeded in accordance with a 'vision' of what modern central banking should be.

A distinct feature of these countries is a proliferation of central-bank-issued papers to help withdraw excess liquidity and contain the domestic loan expansion of banks – as state (Treasury) papers are not available in suffficient volumes. The auction system has become a method of choice to introduce market principles, i.e. ration liquidity by means of the interest rate. There is a visible shift to use OMOs to affect only the short end of the yield curve (Czech Republic, Hungary, and Poland), where the markets are most liquid and directly exposed to central bank policy changes. The following table of refinancing in Slovakia illustrates trends which are common to all CEFTA countries: central bank refinancing exhibits a downtrend, while OMOs have gained considerable significance. The issuance of central bank securities has also dramatically increased.

Table 4. Relative use of monetary instruments in Slovakia
(average volume SKK billion)

	1993	1994	1995	1996
Discount loans	4.4	2.0	0.8	0.9
Other refinancing	39.5	33.2	32.6	31.7
OMOs	0.0	0.4	2.1	13.0
Central bank bills	0.0	0.0	5.1	21.9

Source: National Bank of Slovakia.

In the *Czech and Slovak Republic,* OMOs were started on a very small scale in 1992, when the expected dissolution of the monetary union lowered money demand and a stronger inflow of foreign capital led to unwanted increases in money supply. Since a broader use of state securities for open market operations was not possible because the country had run budget surpluses for years, the CNB had to issue its own bills in 1993 to supplement repurchase operations in Treasury bills. That year, seven CNB bond issues with a two-week maturity each were effected. In 1994, the CNB offered one- and three-month bills on the primary market. Repo tenders were introduced in secondary trading. Since 1994, the operational monetary management of the CNB has been based on repo operations, which replaced the hitherto auctioned refinancing credits. The recourse to repo operations was propelled by the need to sterilize foreign currency inflows. In 1996, repo tenders of one- and two-week maturities were used to influence the one-week PRIBOR. The following Table – reproduced from Hrncir (1997) – presents evidence on the rapidly increasing relevance of OMOs for the monetary policy of the CNB.

Table 5. Liquidity drainage by open market operations of the CNB
(CZK billion)

	1990	1991	1992	1993	1994	1995	1996
Reverse OMOs	0.0	0.0	-11.8	-26.4	-70.4	-89.4	-138.4
Refinancing	17.4	21.1	15.1	6.5	7.1	7.3	13.4

Source: Hrncir (1997). Note: (-) drainage and (+) injection of liquidity.

In Poland, during the middle of 1990, the *NBP* started to auction one-week NBP bills in an attempt to drain the excessive liquidity of the banking sector. Thus, rudimentary open market operations were started. The NBP diversified its sales of bills to three- and six-month maturities in 1991. It started to auction one- and three-month Treasury bills in May 1991, and due to the growing supply of Treasury bills, it suspended auctioning of NBP bills in early 1992. The launching of one- and three-year government bonds in 1992 enabled the central bank to conduct repurchase agreements and reverse repurchase transactions for the first time. In 1994, open market operations took off as the country's international reserves began to grow rapidly. The NBP stood ready to sterilize their impact on the money supply. The role of one- to fourteen-day reverse repurchase agreements became dominant. Outright operations of Treasury bills involved smaller amounts as the NBP was getting rid off its portfolio of short-term Treasury securities. In November 1994, as the excess liquidity of the banking system became chronic, the NBP resumed auctions of its own bills. The introduction of the book entry form of government securities in 1995 boosted outright sales of Treasury bills since their physical denominations were large and non-marketable, while the book entry form has made it possible to break them into smaller amounts.

In *Hungary*, OMOs are conducted by means of outright sales/purchases of government securities, repurchase/reverse repurchase agreements, and foreign currency exchange swaps. Starting in 1993, the significance of open market operations increased steadily. Until 1993, the NBH had influenced a large part of the yield curve with posted interest rates, but later on withdrew and focused solely on the short end of the curve. Currently, one-day, one-week and overnight facilities exist. The one-week, repo rate has been quoted since January 1994. In 1994, foreign exchange deposit swaps of one to three years were also actively used to ensure the medium-term liquidity of banks with foreign currency deposits. They were phased out in 1995 as they created too much liquidity and were replaced by foreign exchange deposit swaps available only for the purpose of project financing. Repurchase agreements were another plentiful source of banking sector liquidity in 1994. At the end of 1995, reverse repurchase agreements were activated in order to drain the excessive liquidity of the banking sector caused by the unexpected inflow of foreign currency. Outright sales were also an important sterilization tool. In 1995, outright sales of government securities from the NBH portfolio were the main instrument, but this changed in 1996, when the reverse repo replaced them in significance. In 1995, to tighten monetary policy, daily limits on repo transactions were introduced, but they do not apply to a special overnight facility designated to ease unexpected liquidity problems. In return for this availability, the NBH charges a prohibitive rate of interest. Compared with standard lombard loans, it is a very expensive facility, especially if the loans are rolled over (everyday compounding interest rate).

As has been already mentioned, the development of open market instruments in *Slovenia* was catalysed by the need to sterilize the inflow of foreign currency into the country, which in the 1992 to 1994 period averaged over 4 per cent of the GDP annually. In 1991 to 1993, the current account posted substantial surpluses, while in 1995 to 1996, the capital account posted a large surplus; in 1995, short-term capital inflows were estimated at nearly 10 per cent of the GDP.[22] This excess supply of foreign currency conflicted with the counter-inflationary policy of the Bank of Slovenia (BS) in pursuing the ultimate goal of domestic currency stability. The BS wants to reduce the Slovenian inflation rate to the levels recorded in the European Union. The variety of available instruments makes Slovenia distinct not only among transition economies.[23] Since the government has conducted a prudent fiscal policy of surpluses or a balanced budget throughout the period of transition, too few government securities exist, so that the central bank cannot rely on them to conduct open market operations. To fill this vacuum, it had to introduce its own securities driven by the need to reduce the monetary base. Foreign currency reserves have become practically the only channel of creating the monetary base since late 1991.

The central bank issues tolar bills with various maturities ranging from 2 to 60 days, so-called 'twin' bills denominated in tolar and German mark, bills with warrants and foreign currency bills. Tolar bills indeed have characteristics of certificates of deposit as they are non-marketable. In contrast, foreign exchange bills with maturities between two months and one year are transferable. Such bills with maturities of less than 120 days can be used to comply with minimum requirements for foreign exchange cover (see below). The most sophisticated instrument is the tolar bill with warrants which has a maturity of six months and bears a fixed nominal interest rate. The attached warrant, which can be stripped, makes the paper attractive as it gives an option to buy additional bills at a discount, which is in turn positively related to an excess of actual inflation and domestic currency depreciation over the officially projected ones. It is evident that this instrument is a bridge between instruments based on real and on nominal rates. Thus, it offers a hedge against adverse developments. Twin bills with maturities of between three and six months comprise tolar and foreign currency parts, which can be traded separately. They are sold at a discount and priced in tolar. Both instruments were broadly used in 1994 and 1995. Repurchase agreements concluded at daily auctions, in which the BS buys its own foreign currency bills from banks for four weeks, are actively used to inject high-powered money. Reverse repurchase agreements have never been introduced.

Table 6 below illustrates the relative importance of different instruments in Slovenia over the course of transition. The figures display the significant role of foreign currency bills and repurchase agreements. Short-term loans have been the most actively used financing facility lately.

Table 6. Relative use of selected instruments in Slovenia
(SIT billion)

	1992	1993	1994	1995
Lombard loans*	6.2	18.6	4.3	3.7
Liquidity loans**	n.a.	14.6	15.8	11.2
Short-term loans**	-	-	1.2	3.0
BS bills issued:				
F/X bills***	-	-	87.3	120.0
tolar bills	-	4.3	74.3	168.0
twin bills	-	19.9	7.3	14.7
bills with warrants	-	-	33.1	13.9
Repurchase agreements F/X bills p		7.0	91.9	108.3
r		5.6	94.6	92.2

* Total volume approved;
** daily average volume;
*** outstanding balance on December 31:
p = purchase; r = reverse operation.

Strings attached to instruments, such as a requirement that a participating bank has to purchase a certain amount of foreign exchange from non-banks or that it has to accept exchange rates given by the BS are administrative distortions in disguise.

In *Slovakia*, OMOs were first used in 1993. In the beginning, repurchase transactions were conducted and Treasury bills were traded. NBS bills were introduced in 1995 at a time when the state budget deficit turned into a surplus. The current account surplus coupled with the capital account surplus, the latter due to improved confidence in the Republic's fundamentals, triggered strong foreign currency inflows. The bank stood ready to sterilize their impact on the monetary base, therefore it attempted to reduce the excessive liquidity of the banking sector. Sporadic auctions of NBS bills were conducted in January to July 1995, and regular auctions have been launched since August 1995. Outright purchases and sales of instruments are another type of instrument which is available. No data on the relative use of OMO instruments are available, but the central bank puts great emphasis on repurchase transactions with maturities of up to seven days. Due to the inflow of foreign currency, reverse repo transactions have had a high significance.

Table 7. Slovakia: instruments and transaction volumes
(SKK billion)

	1993	1994	1995
Primary auctions of treasury bills	n.a.	128.9	50.8
NBS bills sold	0	0	127.8
Volume of OMOs	n.a.	35.0	586.0

Source: NBS Annual Report 1995.

Standing facilities

The decommercialization of central bank activities involved redefining central bank lending facilities, making them available to banks rather than businesses. This process has taken place gradually as the central banks inherited the financing of large public investment projects, a commitment they could dismantle only over time. Forms of preferential financing have been scaled down, though they still exist in all countries examined. For example, the NBH has schemes for investment project financing and export credit. All countries have discount rates and, with the exception of Hungary, also lombard rates. The structure of NBH interest rates is the least transparent as it announces the so-called base rate to which all other rates are related. The discount rate is one of them and stands a few points above the base rate. The relevance of the discount window as a facility to inject liquidity has declined over the years. There is a tendency to eliminate discount loans as a form of a subsidized credit, and access to the discount window is limited. Slovenia discontinued discount loans in 1992.

The lombard rate, which at the beginning marked the price of another important source of liquidity, has been assigned the role of a ceiling on market rates and is used when central banks want to perform the role of a lender of last resort. This tendency is best exemplified by the evolution in Slovakia, where the lombard rate had originally been pegged to the discount rate, then tied to the discontinued auctioned refinancing credit rate, and finally set autonomously. In Poland, access to the lombard facility is unlimited, and the lombard rate serves as a cap on interbank market rates. Forms of refinancing credit other than discount and lombard lending were used extensively at the beginning of transition. They were gradually subjected to a greater degree of market principles, e.g. auction refinancing credit in the Czech Republic. The lombard rate could not have been used from the beginning in any of these countries, as a portfolio of assets which could be provided as collateral was almost non-existent. In Hungary, the overnight repurchase facility replaced the lombard window.

Reserve requirements

Reserve requirements were adopted early in the transition process and given the role of an operational instrument. Their initial levels were quite prohibitive to lending as the reviewed countries wanted to check inflation, which accelerated in the wake of price liberalization. Less important in the beginning was the issue of the prudential impact of high minimum reserve requirements.[24] After the initial phase, a tendency to reduce these ratios has been visible. However, this tendency has been frustrated at times by the need to use required reserve ratios as operational instruments to control liquidity of the banking sector. The Czech Republic, Hungary, Poland, and Slovakia resorted to this instrument in order to tighten monetary policy, even when they were well advanced in transition. Slovenia has left minimum reserve requirements unchanged for almost two years now and seems to be in the best position among these countries to approach Western standards in this field.

Table 8. Number of changes in mandatory reserve ratios

	1990	1991	1992	1993	1994	1995	1996	1997*
Czech R.[25]	1	0	2	2	1	1	1	1
Hungary	1	1	0	1	2	4	6	0
Poland		1	1	0	1	1	1	2
Slovakia	1	0	2	0	0	1	1	0
Slovenia	n.a.	3	1	0	0	1	0	0

* Until April 15, 1997.

The use of minimum reserve requirements to contain unwanted money supply growth is evidence that financial markets are still somewhat immature in these countries. Open market instruments to cope either with excess liquidity (reverse repos) or with shortages of liquidity within the banking system (repos) still have to be supplemented with 'blunter' tools in situations of stress. Each of the countries realize that required reserve ratios are still too high by Western European standards and will have to be lowered in order to reduce the cost of financial intermediation, which will help domestic banks compete with their foreign rivals. This need presents a challenge to monetary policy, as money supply tends to grow when reserve ratios are lowered due to a higher money multiplier; this increase is hard to offset. These reserves are not commonly remunerated. Only Hungary and Slovakia provide interest, but interest rates are fixed well below the respective inflation rate.

In *Czechoslovakia,* minimum reserve requirements were introduced in 1990, but until 1992, they were the same for demand and time deposits. Since 1992, minimum reserve requirements have played the role of an operational instrument. They were raised for the first time in November 1992 in conjunction with the removal of credit ceilings. When the country split, the Czech Republic introduced a further increase, which was later reversed. Thus 1993 marked the year in which reserve requirements became an active instrument of monetary management. They were again raised in the Czech Republic in reaction to high capital inflows in 1994. Most recently they were raised in August 1996 to 11.5 per cent from 8.5 per cent and are scheduled to be lowered in May 1997 to 9.5 per cent on deposits with commercial banks.

Unlike in the other countries in transition, the central bank in *Slovakia* did not use in the earlier years minimum reserve requirements as an operational instrument of monetary policy. It had maintained reserve requirements at 9 per cent on demand deposits and 3 per cent on time deposits through August 1, 1996, when the latter was raised to 9 per cent as well, but savings deposits earmarked for dwelling construction were excluded, so that the required reserve ratio remained at 3 per cent on these deposits. The increase represented one of the NBS's efforts to tighten monetary policy.

The *Hungarian* central bank has used reserve requirements as an operational instrument. In 1987, it introduced a uniform requirement on liabilities of commercial banks. The mandatory reserves were gradually reduced until the launch of the stabilization programme in March 1995 in order to make Hungarian banks more competitive. Subsequently they were raised in a few successive steps, as monetary policy needed to be tightened. They were relaxed again following the success with disinflation. At present, they are still high enough (12 per cent for all deposits with commercial banks and 8 per cent for deposits with savings banks) to create a wedge between deposit and credit rates. To narrow this wedge, the NBH pays interest on mandatory reserves, which distinguishes Hungary from the other countries reviewed in the paper. This interest rate is relatively high in nominal terms, but negative in real terms. The remuneration policy took twists, as this interest rate was drastically reduced in 1993 to 1994, to be increased again in 1995.

Reserve requirements were put in place in *Poland* in 1990 and have been actively used since then. The NBP introduced separate reserve requirements on foreign currency deposits, which accounted for more than 70 per cent of total money supply in 1990. Different ratios were also imposed on demand and time deposits. At the beginning of transition, the NBP frequently manipulated the minimum reserve requirements on domestic deposits. They were raised to the legal limit of 30 per cent in 1990 and then slowly decreased. Yet these ratios[26] are still very high by OECD standards. The declared course is to gradually align these ratios to the levels that will enable domestic banks to compete with foreign banks from OECD countries once their entry to the Polish market has been liberalized by the end of 1998. So far it has been more a verbal commitment than a fact. To the contrary, the minimum reserve ratio on foreign currency deposits has been raised twice since 1995 to lower their attractiveness relative to domestic ones. The NBP believes that banks are more sensitive to changes of the reserve ratio than to changes in headline interest rates. The mandatory reserves do not pay any interest, which under the condition of high inflation is a penalty tax for banks and drives a considerable wedge between deposit and credit rates. Poland reduced the requirements on demand deposits in 1996 to establish a downward tendency ahead of the planned liberalization of financial services in 1998, but raised them again in February 1997 as an attempt to slow down domestic credit expansion by banks. Following this move, reserve requirements on time deposits were raised in May. Reserve requirements on foreign currency deposits were increased on the same dates in an effort to realign them with the requirements on domestic deposits.

Reserve requirements were in place in former Yugoslavia. In *Slovenia*, they gained operational meaning between October 1991 and April 1992. Since then they have played a passive role, consistent with their prudential function. The general tendency has been to reduce this requirement to levels consistent with standards in more advanced economies. In this respect, minimum reserves on deposits with maturities of over one year were eliminated. From April 1992 to April 1995, the requirements remained unchanged. The most recent changes were introduced in April 1995. The scheme of reserve requirements is more complex than in other countries, where discrimination between demand and time deposits is standard, because Slovenia distinguishes among more categories of deposits.[27]

There are no reserve requirements on foreign currency deposits in Slovenia, instead there are foreign exchange cover regulations. In the initial stage of independence, the lack of foreign currency reserves prompted the BS to adopt a regulation requiring banks to maintain 35 per cent of the average monthly inflow and outflow in foreign currencies in the preceding three months in the form of liquid assets denominated in foreign currencies. This foreign reserve minimum was additionally imposed on household deposits to guarantee their safety and to boost the confidence of the public. The scale of the coverage ranges from a high of 100 per cent on demand deposits to 5 per cent on foreign exchange deposits of over one year. A slightly different scale applies to the accounts of non-residents.

4. Exchange rate system and monetary policy

At the beginning of transition, the reviewed countries in general favoured more rigid exchange rate regimes compared to more flexible ones. With the exception of Slovenia, they introduced fixed exchange rates. Hungary chose the softest version, the adjustable peg, which explicitly allowed for discretionary devaluations. Slovenia adopted managed floating right from the start of independence. Their respective choices were motivated by a number of considerations.[28] Since then, a tendency toward more flexible exchange rate regimes can be observed in response to substantial inflows of foreign currency, which started interfering with the central banks' disinflation-oriented monetary plans. Fluctuation bands have been either introduced or widened to create more uncertainty as to the possible course of the exchange rate. Intra-band intervention has been allowed and used. In parallel to this process, the tendency to introduce more transparency, pegs can be recorded as well: the Czech Republic, Hungary, and Slovakia reduced the number of currencies in their respective baskets. These general conclusions are supported by detailed facts.

The *CNB* sets the exchange rate. The regime of a fixed peg against a basket has been maintained since the start of the reforms. The original basket of five currencies was replaced by the basket of only two currencies, the DEM (65 per cent) and the USD (35 per cent), after the split of the Federation in 1993. In March 1996, the band for feasible fluctuations was widened to +/- 7.5 per cent from +/-0.5 per cent on either side of the central rate. Since the Czech koruna has been subject to upward pressure from the beginning of transition, the CNB mainly bought foreign exchange to meet its exchange rate target and sterilized its impact on the money supply to a considerable extent. It resorted to unconventional methods as well, since the deposits of the National Property Fund and Telecom were moved to the central bank from commercial banks, which meant draining liquidity as they stopped supporting the process of multiple deposit creation. To curb excessive liquidity, the maximum limit on short-term (up to one year) open positions against non-residents was set at 30 per cent above claims against them with an overall limit of CZK 0.5 billion, effective August 3, 1995. To discourage trading with the CNB and to stimulate trading among banks, a 0.25 per cent fee is charged on foreign exchange transactions with the CNB. Such transactions have no effect on money supply. Sterilization of capital inflows cost the CNB 0.3 per cent of the GDP in 1994 and 0.5 per cent of the GDP in 1995.

The central bank is responsible for exchange rate policy in *Slovakia*, which maintains a system of a pegged exchange rate against a basket of currencies that was streamlined from five currencies to two, i.e. USD (40 per cent) and DEM (60 per cent). The growing external disequilibrium in 1993 led to a discretionary devaluation of the koruna by 10 per cent against the basket, but since then the currency has been stable. The band has been gradually widened, like in the other countries of the region; it was expanded from +/-1.5 per cent to +/-5 per cent. After the dissolution of the Federation, Slovakia temporarily reintroduced certain limits on currency convertibility due to a drop in international reserves. Considerable inflows of foreign currency led to major purchases of foreign currency by the NBS by means of outright purchases, and the NBS conducted sterilization operations on a large scale in 1995 and 1996.

Both the central bank and the Ministry of Finance are responsible for exchange rate policy in *Hungary*. The initiative rests with the government, but its proposals are subject to the approval of the NBH. Hungary maintained an adjustable peg until March 13, 1995. Before the introduction of the crawling peg, the forint was frequently devalued in rather moderate to small steps. After a 9 per cent devaluation in March 1995 against the basket, that system was replaced by the preannounced crawling peg with an initial monthly devaluation rate of 1.9 per cent versus the basket, which later was reduced to 1.1 per cent. The composition of the basket was modified several times. The most important change was the reduction of the number of basket currencies to two. Other changes were driven either by disinflation considerations or by the competitiveness issue. Since January 1997, the basket has comprised DEM (70 per cent) and USD (30 per cent), which is intended to signal a strong forint policy and the determination to curb inflation. The width of the band within which the forint is allowed to fluctuate is relatively small at +/-2.25 per cent. This reflects the fact that upward pressure on the currency is a relatively new phenomenon which has not been accounted for yet. Sterilized intervention policy started in late spring 1995.

The evolution of the exchange rate system in *Poland* from a rigid to a more flexible one went through several stages: the abolition of a fixed peg against a single currency (the USD) and the shift to a basket, the introduction of a crawling peg and then of a crawling band of 7 per cent on either side of the central rate. In 1990 to 1993, the balance-of-payments constraint acted as a catalyst for changes aimed at striking a balance between anchoring for inflationary expectations and securing the necessary competitiveness to protect a sustainable current account position. In 1994 to 1995, the current account surplus and capital inflows put upward pressure on the zloty. The endogenity of money supply under the crawling peg started frustrating NBP targets, so the central bank opted for more monetary independence. The crawling band was widened to 7 per cent on either side of the central rate, which at the end of 1995 had to be revalued. The crawling devaluation rate was reduced to 1 per cent monthly against the basket in January 1996. Sterilization by means of purchases of foreign currency from commercial banks was only partial and very costly due to wide interest rate differentials. It is estimated that it was 0.6 per cent of the GDP in 1995 and 0.8 per cent of the GDP in 1996.[29] Poland's basket of five currencies has not been modified since 1991.

According to law, the *Bank of Slovenia is* in charge of exchange rate policy. The country adopted a managed floating system from the beginning of independence after an intellectually interesting debate between adherents of a fixed and a flexible regime.[30] For much of the period, Slovenia implicitly targeted the real exchange rate, actively using the option of managed floating. In 1994, large sterilizations of currency inflows were necessary. This intervention proved very costly, as evidenced by the fall in the BS's operating surplus from SIT 17 billion in 1992 to SIT 1 billion in 1994. Total sterilization costs were estimated to reach 2.6 per cent of the GDP in 1992 to 1994 with the percentage spread evenly in 1992 and 1993 and jumping to 1.4 per cent in 1994. The BS intervenes on the foreign exchange market by means of purchases of foreign currency called 'temporary repurchase agreements.' Their construction resembles that of a foreign currency swap and purchase of foreign exchange with the right to repurchase by the counterparty. In 1995, the bank launched a new instrument, i.e. the sale of foreign exchange against a purchase of foreign exchange bills. Starting in April 1996, the BS simultaneously offered a triple combination of existing instruments – foreign currency purchases, foreign exchange swaps, and purchases of its own foreign exchange bills – to arrest appreciation of the tolar. Outright purchases played a smaller role. Sales of foreign currency and purchases of own foreign exchange bills were introduced in 1995 when the upward pressure on the tolar reversed in the second half of the year after the introduction of a series of administrative controls on inward capital movements.

Capital controls were reinstated in early 1995 and strengthened in 1996. A 40 per cent non-interest-bearing tolar deposit on financial borrowing from abroad up to seven years was put in place in 1995. In 1996, 10 per cent retention deposits have been imposed on all foreign credits, and portfolio investors are required to open a fiduciary account with a Slovenian bank through which all transactions are performed. According to anecdotal evidence, this regulation induced enterprises to arrange longer maturities of loans (e.g. borrowing for 7 years and one day) and was gradually circumvented, which renewed tension on the forex market in 1996.

5. Summary and conclusions

In this paper, we have sketched and analysed how monetary governance has changed in the five Central and Eastern European economies which have advanced most in their transition from centrally planned to market systems. They all managed to progress from direct instruments of monetary control to indirect instruments in a relatively short period of time, i.e. at most within three years. Their starting points were characterized by a lack of infrastructure for indirect monetary policy. Interbank markets did not exist. Open market operations were impossible because there were no marketable Treasury or central bank securities. Since then, significant progress has been made. The basis for modern central banking has been established. All countries have the necessary infrastructure for open market operations, and their use has dramatically risen from zero levels. This change has been successful as no major retreat was observed. The search for new instruments mainly responded to arising challenges, in particular to the challenge of very large capital inflows and the need to contain the excess liquidity of the financial sector. But the developments were also in accordance with these countries' understanding of modern central banking.

The shift to indirect instruments of monetary policy-making could not proceed without a parallel development of financial markets, as experience clearly shows. Poland's early move away from direct instruments in 1990 was not successful, and it had to return to the use of credit ceilings, because it could not cope with the excess liquidity of the banking sector in any other way.

However, financial markets remain still underdeveloped, which determines specific features of monetary governance in the countries analysed. The central banks of these countries have developed instruments to cope either with excess liquidity (mainly reverse repurchase agreements) or with shortages of liquidity within the banking system (repurchase agreements). As the markets are immature, these operations have to be supplemented with 'blunter' tools in the situation of stress, e.g. with required reserves. Required reserves still play a role as an operational instrument to control liquidity within the banking sector in Hungary, the Czech Republic, Poland, and Slovakia. Slovenia is in the best position to soon approach Western standards in this respect. Required reserves are still relatively high compared with those in Western European economies and will have to be reduced to lower the cost of financial intermediation and to improve local banks' international competitiveness. The (gradual) reduction of required reserves poses a challenge for monetary policy-makers, as the money supply will tend to grow and liquidity enhancing effects will have to be offset. The proliferation of securities issued by the central banks in order to help withdraw excess liquidity and contain domestic loan expansion and because state (Treasury) securities cannot fulfil this function is another common phenomenon in the countries reviewed.

The following tendencies, which are consistent with tendencies observed in the more advanced countries, are observable: open market operations have become the most important monetary instrument. The tendency to reduce amounts of central bank lending is visible. Tenders of repurchase agreements are popular. A shift to affect only the short end of the yield curve by open market operations is also evidenced by shortened maturities. A move toward monetary targeting has occurred. However, a relative ineffectiveness of monetary targets similar to that in advanced economies can be noted, as the targets are exceeded most of the time, e.g. in Slovakia, in the Czech Republic, in Hungary, and to a lesser extent in Poland. Even if they are met, the course of inflation may prompt the central bank to attempt to influence interest rates, the exchange rate or simply to use moral suasion (e.g., Poland in 1996).

With the notable exception of Slovenia, all other countries in the group analysed here started with a policy of exchange rate targeting. Hungary, however, did not commit itself to a nominal peg but chose a looser form of an adjustable peg. The trend toward more flexibility in the exchange rate system followed has set in, as the countries are striving to free their monetary policies from external constraints resulting from large capital inflows. Poland exemplifies this path best with its shift from a peg to the US dollar to a crawling peg to a basket of currencies and then to a crawling band. Thus, at present exchange rate policies are not converging toward the Western European standard of increasing monetary integration which requires fixed exchange rates.

The evolution of monetary governance will continue in the present direction to rely mostly on OMOs, albeit at slower pace concomitant with the widening and deepening of financial markets, whose development will boost the reliance on open market operations. The significance of central bank lending facilities will continue to diminish. Mandatory reserves will be lowered to levels compatible with Western Europe and will stop functioning as an operating instrument. The elimination of forms of preferential credits is indispensable to stop subsidized central bank credits. Discount credit can, in fact, be a form of such a subsidized credit, like the remnants of socialist state investment projects and other schemes such as export or agriculture financing. Lines of credit in the context of privatizations will probably be the last to be eliminated.

An attempt to use direct inflationary targeting as a monetary strategy cannot be excluded, as the difficulties of monetary targeting remain pronounced despite a certain stabilization of the demand for money compared to the early stages of transition. We do not foresee a reversal of the trend toward more flexible exchange rate regimes anytime soon. In the future, a reversal toward more stable exchange rate arrangements will be necessary when these countries start seriously contemplating and preparing for a participation in the European Economic and Monetary Union. For now, it appears more reasonable for these countries to enjoy a somewhat higher degree of monetary autonomy in order to be able to deal with the problem of excessive capital inflows and to avoid (real) exchange rate developments which would contribute to unsustainable external imbalances.

References

Alesina, Alberto and Lawrence H. Summers (1993), 'Central Bank Independence and Macroeconomic Performance: Some Comparative Evidence.' *Journal of Money, Credit and Banking* No. 25, pp. 151-162.
Bank for International Settlements, (1997), 'Mr. Tosovsky Gives the Czech Republic's Perspective of Transition in Central and Eastern Europe', *BIS Review* 25, pp. 1-11.
Bank of Slovenia. Various issues of Annual Reports 1992-1996.
Begg, David K. H. (1996), 'Monetary Policy in Central and Eastern Europe: Lessons After Half a Decade of Transition' *IMF Working Paper*, p. 108.
Bod, Péter, (1994), 'Targets and Instruments of Monetary Policy in Hungary', In: Baliho, Tomas and Carlo Cottarelli, eds., *Frameworks for Monetary Stability, Policy Issues and Country Experiences*. IMF, Washington D.C., pp. 423-441.
Bohnec, Darko and Joze Bradesko, (1996), 'Monetary Operations – The Case of Slovenia.' Paper delivered to the Joint Conference of the Centre for Central Banking Studies at the Bank of England and Czech National Bank. (November), pp. 4-8.
Clarida, Richard and Mark Gertler, (1996), How the Bundesbank Conducts Monetary Policy'. *National Bureau of Economic Research Working Paper 5581* (May).
Cukierman, Alex, (1992), *Central Bank Strategy, Credibility and Independence: Theory and Evidence*. Cambridge, Mass. MIT Press.
Czech National Bank. Various issues of Annual Reports 1992-1996.
—, (1994), Monetary Policy Implementation 1990-1994 (June).
Debelle G. and Stanley Fischer, (1994), 'How Independent Should a Central Bank Be?' In: Fuhrer J.C., ed., *Goals, Guidelines and Constraints Facing Monetary Policy-makers*. Federal Reserve Bank of Boston.
De Melo, Martha and Cevdet Denizer, (1997), 'Monetary Policy during Transition.' *Policy Research Working Paper 1706* (January).
—, (1992), Monetary Policy Issues in Selected East European Economies. *SUERF Papers on Monetary Policy and Financial Systems* 11.
Duchatczek, Wolfgang and Aurel Schubert, (1993), 'Monetary Policy Issues and Monetary Integration in Selected East European Countries.' In: Fair, Donald E. and Robert J. Raymond, eds., *The New Europe: Evolving Economic and Financial Systems in East and West*. Kluwer Academic Publishers, Dordrecht.
European Monetary Institute, (1997a), *The Single Monetary Policy in Stage Three, Specification of the Operational Framework* (January), pp. 14-23.
—, (1997b), *The Single Monetary Policy in Stage Three: Elements of the monetary policy strategy of the ESCB*, February.
Fischer, Stanley, (1994), 'Modern Central Banking.' In: Forest Capie, Charles Goodhart, Stanley Fischer and Norbert Schnadt, eds. *The Future of Central Banking*, The Tercentenary Symposium of the Bank of England, Cambridge University Press, pp. 262-308.
Friedman, Benjamin M., (1996), 'Does Monetary Policy Affect Real Economic Activity? Why Do We Still Ask This Question?' In: Siebert, Horst, ed., *Monetary Policy in an*

Integrated World Economy, Symposium 1995, J.C.B. Mohr (Paul Siebeck). Tübingen, pp. 3-31.

Gomulka, Stanislaw, (1997), 'Managing Capital Flows in Poland' Paper presented at the seminar on Managing Capital Flows in Central and Eastern Europe, Brighton, mimeo, March.

Green, John H., (1996), 'Inflation Targeting: Theory and Policy Implications.' *IMF Staff Papers* 43 (4) (December),: 779-795.

Haldane, Andrew, (1995), 'Inflation targets', *Bank of England Quarterly Bulletin* 35 (3) (August), pp. 250-59.

Hochreiter, Eduard and Sandra Riesinger, (1995), 'Central Banking in Central and Eastern Europe – Selected Institutional Issues' *ECU Journal* 32, pp. 17-20.

Hochreiter, Eduard, (1995) 'Central Banking in Economies in Transition'. In: Willett, T., R. Burdekin, R. Sweeney and C. Wihlborg, *Establishing Monetary Stability in Emerging Market Economies*, Westview Press.

Hrncir, Miroslav, (1997), 'Exchange Rate and Monetary Policies in the Czech Republic'. In: *Monetary Policy in Transition in East and West: Strategies, Instruments and Transition Mechanisms*, Oesterreichische Nationalbank.

IMF, (1995), *Economic Review of Czech Republic* (April).

Janackova, Stanislava, (1996), 'Dilemmas in Czech Monetary Policy'. *Eastern European Economics* (September-October), pp. 78-92.

Kohútikova, Elena, (1995), 'The Exchange Rate Policy of the Slovak Republic'. In: Havilk, Peter and Olga Radzyner, eds., *Monetary Policy in Central and Eastern Europe: Challenges of EU Integration*. Vienna, pp. 116-134.

Kominkova, Zora and Viktoria Muckova, (1996), 'Restructuring of the Banking Sector of Slovakia'. Paper presented at the OECD/WIIW Seminar on Restructuring of the Banking Sector in Transition Countries, Vienna, December 9-10.

Kokoszczynski, Ryszard, (1995), 'Monetary Policy Instruments: The Case of Poland in the 1990s'. In Havilk, Peter and Olga Radzyner, eds., *Monetary Policy in Central and Eastern Europe: Challenges of EU Integration*. Vienna, pp. 196-198.

——, (1997), 'Monetary Policy in Poland: Strategies, Instruments and Transmission Mechasnisms.' In *Monetary Policy in Transition in East and West: Strategies, Instruments and Transmission Mechanisms*, conference proceedings, Oesterreichische Nationalbank.

Kokoszczynski, Ryszard and Stopyra, Jerzy, (1996), 'Dylematy wyboru celow posrednich i operacyjnych w polityce pienieznej Narodowego Banku Polskiego'. *Bank i Kredyt* 27 (6), pp. 36-49.

Kosak, Janez, (1995), 'Directing Monetary Policy towards EU Integration: The Case of Slovenia.' In Havilk, Peter and Olga Radzyner, eds., *Monetary Policy in Central and Eastern Europe: Challenges of EU Integration*. Vienna, pp. 106-116.

Kranjec, Marko, (1995), 'Introduction of a New Currency: The Case of Slovenia'. *Development and International Cooperation* XI (20-21) (June-December), pp. 127-142.

Krzak, Maciej, (1995), *Experience of East European Countries with Different Exchange Rate Regimes*. The Vienna Institute for Comparative Economic Studies. Vienna (April), p. 217.

Lavrac, Vladimir and Peter Stanovnik, (1996), 'Monetary Policy under a Flexible Exchange Rate in Slovenia'. *Banking Newsletter – A Journal for Money and Banking.* Special Issue, pp. 37-46.

Lavrac, Vladimir, (1996), 'Some Characteristics of the Slovenian Banking System'. Institute for Economic Research, Lubljana (June), mimeo.

Leiderman, Leonardo and Svensson, Lars E., (1995), *Inflation Targets.* Center for Economic Policy Research, London.

Makúch, Jozef and Marian Nemec, (1997), 'Monetary Policy in Slovakia: Strategy, Instruments and Transmission Mechanisms'. In: *Monetary Policy in Transition in East and West: Strategies, Instruments and Transmission Mechanisms,* conference proceedings, Oesterreichische Nationalbank.

Mencinger, Jozef, (1993), 'How to Create a Currency – the Experience of Slovenia.' *Weltwirtschaftliches Archiv,* pp. 418-31.

—, (1997), 'Monetary Policy under Flexible Exchange Rate Regime, the Case of Slovenia.' Paper presented at the ACE Conference Monetary Problems in Transition Economies. Budapest, February 7-8.

Mishkin, Frederic, (1997), 'What Monetary Policy Can and Cannot Do'. In: *Monetary Policy in Transition in East and West: Strategies, Instruments and Transmission Mechanisms,* conference proceedings, Oesterreichische Nationalbank.

Narodna Banka Slovenska, (1996), various issues of Annual Reports, 1994-1996.

—, (1996), *Monthly Monetary Survey,* various issues.

National Bank of Hungary, (1996), Annual Reports 1990-1995, Budapest.

Neményi, Judit, (1997), 'Monetary Policy in Hungary: Strategy, Instruments and Transmission Mechanisms'. In: Monetary Policy in Transition in East and West: Strategies, Instruments and Transmission Mechanisms, conference proceedings, Oesterreichische Nationalbank.

OECD, (1997), *Slovenia,* OECD Economic Surveys (April).

—, (1996), *The Czech Republic,* OECD Economic Surveys (July).

—, (1994), *Economic Survey of the Czech and Slovak Republics* (February).

Pietrewicz, Jerzy and Andrzej Slawinski, (1996), 'The Role of the Money Market in Managing Liquidity.' *Bank i Kredyt.* Occasional English Issue of Reprints from 1994-1995, pp. 43-53.

Poole, William, (1970) The Optimal Choice of Monetary Policy Instruments in a Simple Macro Model. *Quarterly Journal of Economics* 84 (May), pp. 192-216.

Radzyner Olga and Sandra Riesinger, (1997), 'Central Bank Independence in Transition: Legislation and Reality in Central and Eastern Europe'. *'Focus on Transition',* 1, National Bank of Austria.

Ribnikar, Ivan, (1995), 'The Monetary System of a Small Currency Area: The Case of Slovenia'. *Development and International Co-operation.* XI (20-21) (June-December), pp. 143-157.

Riecke, Werner, (1995), 'Final Goals, Intermediate Targets and the Use of Instruments of Monetary Policy within a Changing Exchange Rate Regime'. In: Haviik, Peter and Olga Radzyner, eds., *Monetary Policy in Central and Eastern Europe: Challenges of EU Integration.* Vienna, pp. 177-195.

Rogoff, Kenneth, (1985), 'The Optimal Degree of Commitment to a Monetary Target'. *Quarterly Journal of Economics*, 100, pp. 1169-90.

Saje, Janez, (1996), 'Monetary Policy under a Flexible Exchange Rate in Slovenia'. *Banking Newsletter – A Journal for Money and Banking*. Special Issue, pp. 47-50.

Schubert, Aurel (1997), 'Unabhangigkeit sichert Stabilitat – Notenbank ünabhängigkeit in modernen Europa', *SWS Rundschau*, Heft 1, pp. 119-124.

Stiblar, Franjo, (1996), 'Restructuring of the Banking Sector of Slovenia.' Paper presented at the OCED/WIIW Seminar on Restructuring of the Banking Sector in Transition Countries. Vienna, December 9-10.

Strzelec, Agnieszka, (1996), 'The Independence of the National Bank of Poland 1989-1994', Empirical Test based on research by Cukierman, Webb and Neyapti (1992), *Bank i Kredyt*. Occasional English Issue of Reprints from 1994-1995, pp. 9-21.

Ugolini, Piero, (1996), 'The Road to indirect Instruments,' IMF Occasional Paper 144 (October).

Walsh, C.E., (1994), 'Central Bank Independence and the Short-run Output Trade-off in the EC'. Working Paper 1.35, University of California at Berkeley, Center for German and European Studies.

Notes

1. CEFTA stands for Central and Eastern European Free Trade Agreement; the CEFTA-5 countries are currently the same as the CEEC-5.
2. Romania is not object of this study as it will join CEFTA in July 1999.
3. See European Monetary Institute (1997a).
4. For a detailed discussion of the present state of central bank independence in Central and Eastern Europe, see Radzyner and Riesinger (1997).
5. See Cukierman (1992), Alesina, and Summers (1993).
6. For a short summary of the arguments for an independent central bank see Schubert (1997).
7. See Mishkin (1997) for the relevant arguments.
8. The EMI (1997a) identifies five key elements of any monetary strategy: 1) a quantified definition of the final objective; 2) a communication policy; 3) the availability of a broad set of indicators; 4) detailed information on monetary aggregates; 5) tools to allow forecast for inflation and other economic variables.
9. An explicit inflation target is set, as are the index, its target level, the tolerance interval, the time frame, and possibly the situations under which the target can be modified or even disregarded. In a useful simplification, inflation targeting is a monetary framework under which monetary policy decisions are guided by expected future inflation relative to an announced target. Inflation targeting has been explicitly adopted by New Zealand, Canada, the United Kingdom, Sweden, Spain, and Finland. See Leiderman and Svensson (1995).
10. See EMI (1997a).
11. See EMI (1997a) and (1997b).

12. See Haldane (1995) for more information on this topic.
13. See *The Financial Times*, March 22, 1997.
14. It is interesting that only their traditional role in the conduct of policy is mentioned in the document, i.e., stabilizing money market interest rates and possibly contributing to the control of monetary expansion by creating or enlarging a structural liquidity shortage.
15. This stylized description extensively draws on Duchatczek and Schubert (1992).
16. In the pure model, consumption is also rationed by administrative instruments and prices only register trades.
17. This would involve a study in its own right, whereas the purpose of this paper is to give an overview of the monetary policy frame in the reviewed countries. We recommend readers interested in details of central bank independence in Central and Eastern Europe to refer to the latest study by Radzyner and Riesinger (1997) or earlier work by Hochreiter and Riesinger (1995).
18. See Neményi (1997).
19. 1990 to 1992: Czechoslovakia.
20. See Makúch and Nemec (1997).
21. See Section 3.1.
22. See Mencinger (1997).
23. This description draws on the Annual Report of the Bank of Slovenia (issues from 1991 to 1995), on OECD (1997), and on Kranjec (1995).
24. None of these countries ever wanted to follow a recommendation of a 100 per cent reserve requirement.
25. 1990 to 1992: Czechoslovakia.
26. As of the date at which this paper was written, they stood at 20 per cent for demand deposits, 11 per cent for time deposits and 5 per cent for foreign exchange deposits.
27. As of the date at which this paper was written, they stood at 12 per cent for deposits up to 1 month, 6 per cent for deposits between 1 and 3 months, 2 per cent for deposits between 3 and 6 months and 1 per cent for deposits between 6 and 12 months.
28. See Krzak (1995) and Radzyner and Riesinger (1997) for a more detailed analysis.
29. See Gomulka (1997).
30. See, e.g. Lavrac and Stanovnik (1996) or Mencinger (1993) for an exposition of arguments.

Annex (closing date May 1, 1997)
Status, targets and instruments of central banks in the CEFTA countries

	Czech Republic	Hungary	Poland	Slovakia	Slovenia
Central bank status					
a) state budget fiancing	a) short-term loans, upper limit of 5% of budget and no more than 20% of anticipated budget deficit	a) short-term lending, limited to 2% of planned annual central budget revenues	a) may buy T-bills of up to 2% of state budget expenditures	a) purchase of T-bills (maturity up to 3 months), upper limit of 5% of previous years' budget revenues	a) short-term loans, upper limit of 5% of budget and no more than 20% of anticipated budget deficit
b) term of the governor; electoral cycle; appointer of the governor; grounds for dismissal	b) 6-year term; appointed by president; criminal act, resigns or is unable to serve	b) 6-year term; appointed by president upon proposal of prime minister; sentenced guilty by court, resigns or is unable to perform function	b) 6-year term; appointed by parliament on proposal of the president; convicted, unable to serve or resigns	b) 6-year term; appointed by the president on government proposal after parliament's approval, sentenced guilty by court, unable to serve or resigns	b) 6-year term; appointed by parliament upon proposal of the president; no reference on dismissal
c) responsibility for monetary policy	c) sets monetary policy and its instruments	c) sets monetary policy and its instruments	c) defines monetary policy, its instruments, but guidelines are subject to approval by parliament	c) sets monetary policy and instruments of its implementation	c) sets goals and instruments of monetary policy
d) competence for exchange rate regime and its management	d) determines the exchange rate	d) government determines the exchange rate in agreement with the central bank	d) determines the exchange rate with the co-operation of the Ministry of Finance	d) determines the exchange rate	d) initiative on exchange rate law

Monetary Governance in Selected Transition Economies

	Czech Republic	Hungary	Poland	Slovakia	Slovenia
Targets					
a) ultimate	a) to safeguard the stability of the domestic currency	a) internal and external currency stability and support the government's economic policy	a) strengthen the stability of domestic currency and support economic policy of the government	a) safeguard the stability of domestic currency and support the economic policy of the government	a) currency stability and the general liquidity of the payment
b) intermediate	b) fixed exchange rate, M_2	b) exchange rate, M_2	b) broad money (a proxi for M_2) exchange rate	b) fixed exchange rate M_2	b) M_2
c) operational	c) 1 week PRIBOR	c) interest rate differential	c) monetary base	c) no official target	c) base money
Instruments					
a) direct controls	a) phased out in 1993	a) phased out in 1991	a) phased out in 1993	a) terminated in 1996	a) none since 1992
b) indirect controls	-	-	-	-	-
1) interest rates	1) discount rate lombard rate	1) discount rate, base rate	1) discount rate lombard rate	1) discount rate lombard rate	1) lombard rate
2) reserve requirement	2) in place, no interest	2) in place, pays interest below market (and below CPI inflation) rates	2) in place, no interest	2) in place, required reserves pay small interest	2) in place, no interest
3) open market operations	3) CNB bills, 1W and 2W tenders	3) repurchase and reverse repurchase agreements, outright sales of government securities, forex swaps	3) reverse repos transactions, outright sales of T bills, NBP bills	3) repos tenders, outright purchases and sales, issues of NBS bills	3) purchase agreements, foreign exchange bills, twin currency bills, BoS forex bonds, BoS bond sales, forex swaps

	Czech Republic	Hungary	Poland	Slovakia	Slovenia
Exchange rate system					
a) type	a) fixed peg	a) crawing peg	a) crawing band	a) fixed peg	a) managed float
b) basket	b) 65% DEM, 35% USD	b) 70% DEM, 30% USD	b) basket: 45% USD, 35% DEM, 10% GBP, 5% HCF, 5% FRF	b) 40% USD, 60% DEM	b) not applicable
c) band	c) ± 7.5%	c) ±2.2%	c) ±7%	c) +7%	c) not applicable

CNB = Czech National Bank
NBS = National Bank of Slovakia
BoS = Bank of Slovenia
NBP = National Bank of Poland

17 Has the European Union the Right Strategy for Central and Eastern Europe?

Marie-Paule Donsimoni

Introduction

Within the confines of Europe, the development of the political and economic structures of the EU, and since 1989, the extension of free market beliefs to Central and Eastern Europe, represent a striking example of the process of global convergence which forms a key theme of this conference. While many of the changes which have taken place in Western, Central, and Eastern Europe have been driven by political ideals, not least by the wish to prevent further wars between nation states, the desire for greater political integration is matched and indeed driven by the stronger trade and investment ties which have developed across Europe from the coasts of Ireland and Portugal in the West right across to the borders of Russia and beyond.

This paper analyses these developments first by examining the security rationale which underlies EU policy towards the countries of Central and Eastern Europe. This rationale creates tensions with NATO, the guardian for so many years of Western Europe's military security. The paper then goes on to examine the real economic integration which has taken place between the two regions, and the political process which is designed to see EU enlargement institutionalize these real economy developments. The problems generated by the at times differing agendas of key participants are also highlighted, yet our key conclusion is that support in both EU countries and aspiring EU members is sufficient to ensure that enlargement ultimately will happen, not least because enlargement reflects real economic integration. Enlargement is more likely to be destroyed by existing arguments within the EU over issues such as EMU and institutional reform than it is by direct disputes between the countries of Eastern and Western Europe. To paraphrase this, the answer to the question 'Has the European Union the right strategy for Central and Eastern Europe?' would be that the EU's enlargement approach is not perfect, but it will probably work, given patience and a resolution of the EU's existing internal problems.

The rationale of EU enlargement

The first and most important point which must be emphasized at the beginning of any discussion about the enlargement of the EU towards the Central and Eastern European countries is that the key overwhelming motive is the need to enhance security and stability across the continent. Inevitably, this overwhelming motive overlaps with the rationale of NATO, Europe's other great international institution. The enlargement of one cannot therefore be considered without examining the enlargement of the other.

The timetable for NATO expansion has currently overtaken the timetable for EU expansion. The EU's enlargement process will be explained in more detail later, but a broad consensus of opinion believes that new members will not actually join the EU until at least the year 2002. In contrast, NATO will declare the identity of its 'first wave' of new members this summer, who will then join in 1999. This first wave is expected to comprise Poland, Hungary, and the Czech Republic. Romania, supported by France, is also a possibility, as is Slovenia, which is backed by Italy. Some sceptics believe there will not be a second wave, particularly in light of Russian antipathy to Baltic state membership.

There are tensions between these two enlargement processes. It has been a truism since 1989 that security derives more from economic, political, social, and environmental factors than from military strength. In addition, the cold war demonstrated that the creation of insecurity in one's neighbour merely fuelled insecurity at home. In this context, it can be claimed that EU enlargement can offer greater security benefits than NATO enlargement, since it can improve economic, political, social, and environmental conditions in new member countries without directly threatening those left outside the enlarged entity. The hostility of Moscow to NATO's enlargement, which can be contrasted with its wish to build ties with the EU, supports this claim. If Russia feels threatened or encircled by the process of NATO enlargement, then collective security is not enhanced, particularly among Russia's neighbours.

Yet the claim that security is better secured through EU rather than NATO membership does not accord with the wishes of NATO's aspiring members. There is little doubt that most Central and East European countries have always believed that NATO membership would consolidate their security more effectively than EU membership. Nor is there any enthusiasm among them for an increasing security role to be played by the EU or WEU, even though all applicant countries have become WEU associates.

Inevitably, the motives of NATO's existing European members also differ, both with regard to EU and NATO enlargement:

- Germany has been the driving force in Europe behind both enlargement processes, both because it wants to move the 'front line' as far to the east as possible and because it wishes to take a leading role in Europe, which will enhance its status with Russia and the United States. Geographically, it also wishes to give top priority to its immediate Central European neighbours, Poland, Hungary, and the Czech Republic.
- France backs both processes, though for different reasons. Paris wants to build a European security policy and identity which is independent of US influence. As a Mediterranean power, it has also publicly pressed the case of the southern states, particularly Romania and Turkey.
- The United Kingdom's support for EU enlargement seems primarily motivated by an unspoken belief that it will prevent further EU integration and will also be good for trade. In contrast, London has also been most negative about enhancing the security role of the WEU. However, these attitudes could change under the new Blair administration.

For the moment, these different agendas and perspectives do not appear to threaten the coherence of the EU's collective drive for enlargement, though inevitably, if enlargement occurs, the formulation of foreign policy between twenty member states will prove more problematic than between fifteen. The recent accession of the European Free Trade Area countries to the EU suggests that new members sometimes do not accept the strategic assumptions of the original members. In the area of security, there is suspicion about the real purpose of a EU-based security entity and a quasi-instinctive reliance on the United States for a military lead.

In managing the two enlargement processes, the EU also faces the prospect of disruption in the eastern Mediterranean. Turkey has threatened to veto NATO enlargement if its application to join the EU is not considered more actively, while Greece could block eastward enlargement of the EU if Cyprus does not join as well. Neither of these issues looks likely to block enlargement in the end, but their political management will be difficult and they could stall the process at key points.

The simplest and least divisive scenario would be for EU and NATO enlargement to take place in parallel and en bloc. Unfortunately, this is also the least likely outcome, given the tensions between the two processes and the different motives of the various parties.

Real economic integration

Yet while these tensions exist over the future form of enlargement of these two institutions, it is important to remember that a considerable degree of integration between the various parts of Europe has already taken place on the ground. This is particularly the case at the economic level which many believe is the real basis of lasting security. The integration of EU economies with those in Central and Eastern Europe has proceeded quickly since 1989, particularly on the back of ten bilateral Association Agreements. Since 1991, these have set a timetable for trade liberalization.

The outlook for further rapid growth in flows of both trade and foreign direct investment between Western, Central, and Eastern Europe prior to formal EU enlargement is good, though its pace will depend on how quickly the EU removes remaining barriers and how successful are the different applicants in reforming their economies. Central and Eastern Europe provides faster growing markets than the EU and lower production costs. The former are even more attractive given improving access back into EU markets. Within Central and Eastern Europe, trade policy regimes and the investment climate have also been improving because of efforts to match EU single market standards. Though the EU is still focusing on ensuring that new policies and rules are implemented, the improved policy environment has supported higher levels of trade and investment even before EU enlargement would take place.

The EU's enlargement process

The EU's enlargement process is due to begin in earnest after this summer's Intergovernmental Conference. The European Commission is due to produce a package to be known as Agenda 2000, which will include assessments of individual applications and an evaluation of the impact of enlargement on EU policies, notably the Common Agricultural Policy and the regional funds policy. Thereafter, preliminary negotiations could start by the time of the Luxembourg summit in December 1997, although the formal start is more likely under the UK presidency in the first half of 1998.

However, the start of negotiations will not ensure a smooth ride to enlargement. There are many issues to be resolved in the negotiations and there are also a host of other items on the EUs agenda which could disrupt and even destroy the timetable for enlargement, not least the need first to conclude the IGC and the on-going EMU project. The year 2002 is probably the earliest realistic date for the first accessions, even if the whole process runs smoothly.

The key unresolved procedural issue for the EU is whether to start negotiations with all of the applicant countries, or only the front-runners. The United Kingdom and Germany would like to begin formal negotiations only with the top four or five countries – probably the Czech Republic, Hungary, Poland, Slovenia, and possibly Estonia – as would the European Commission. But the Nordic and Scandinavian countries want to ensure that the Baltic states are included, so they favour opening negotiations with all ten East and Central European applicants. France has argued for a common start, which will bring in all the applicants, including Turkey. The most likely outcome is a political fudge incorporating a nominal common start and an on-going consultative process for all aspiring members, coupled with a screening process which leads to more detailed negotiations for the favoured few.

The EU as a body faces two key strains in pursuing enlargement. The first is the budget – countries have already begun jockeying for position on the new EU budget, which is due in 1999. Enlargement implies reforms of the Common Agricultural Policy and the structural fund budgets. A major political mobilization of EU farmers and structural funds recipients in opposition to enlargement cannot be ruled out.

The second area of strain is institutional reform and flexibility. EU institutional structures are already under strain with just 15 member states. If the IGC results in only minimal reforms to EU structures, there will be increased pressure from the more integrationist countries to introduce more flexibility into EU decision-making.

This could have both positive and negative effects for enlargement. Without some form of flexibility, it seems unlikely that an enlarged EU would be able to function if we consider the diversity of members' opinions. However, applicant countries are concerned that flexibility could result in their becoming second-class members of the EU. Set against an upper tier of more closely integrated states, the new member states could be forever relegated to a lower tier and unable to participate in initiatives they would like to join.

However, this prospect is unlikely to be sufficient to cause applicants to walk away from the EU. Adopting EU regulatory and policy models undoubtedly has had economic benefits for the countries of Eastern and Central Europe by speeding up the process of transition and boosting trade and investment. Hanrmonization is a prerequisite for joining the EU, which is a key foreign policy goal for all the applicants. Thus, governments have been able to overcome sectoral and other interests when forcing through painful economic reforms, and have gained new bodies of legislation more quickly. This is despite the occasional inappropriateness of EU economic models for economies in transition, and the incompleteness and anomalies of EU policy, which reflect the historic peculiarities of members' national interests.

There is some concern that a rapid move by applicants to adopt EU environmental and social standards could harm their international competitiveness by causing a rapid rise in labour costs. However, this will not necessarily be a direct consequence of moves towards EU membership. Changes in environmental regulations and social costs are likely to cause only a slow rise in production costs, and accession negotiations are likely to result in transitional periods for phasing in EU social regulations. Moreover, Central and East European governments are in any case already under pressure to clean up environmental damage and to use resources, particularly energy, more efficiently. This process will improve their long-term competitiveness by developing sectors based on higher added value rather than just low costs. Thus, while relations with the EU are set to becoming an increasingly important issue in the domestic politics of the Central and East European states, the balance of domestic political forces is likely to remain pro-, rather than anti-EU for the foreseeable future. The official abandonment of EU membership as a policy goal is unlikely.

Conclusion

To conclude, it is our belief that the security rationale which underlies EU policy towards the countries of Central and Eastern Europe creates tensions with NATO, but the process of enlarging either body need not stymie the other. In terms just of EU enlargement, the political process which will drive this policy is in tune with real mechanisms of economic integration, which are already taking place. Naturally, in a negotiation of the magnitude which will characterize discussions between current and aspiring EU members, there will be difficulties, stand-offs, and delays, but we do not believe that one of these will ultimately destroy the process. The problems which already exist within the EU over issues such as institutional reform and EMU are more likely to be fatal. Yet provided these internal EU problems are overcome, support in both EU countries and aspiring EU members will be sufficient to ensure that enlargement ultimately will happen, not least because enlargement reflects real economic integration.

18 Seven Years of Financial Market Reform in Central Europe

Gerhard Fink and Peter Haiss

Abstract

The paper deals with the question whether banks in Central Europe are in a position to exert a positive influence on enterprise performance. Effective, market-driven corporate governance by banks is discussed along the following four questions: are banks sound enough, large enough, strong enough, and skilled enough to have an impact on improving the efficiency of firms? Data on financial sector reform in those 10 formerly communist Central European countries (Bulgaria, Czech Republic, Estonia, Hungary, Latvia, Lithuania, Poland, Romania, Slovakia, and Slovenia) that signed association agreements with the European Union forms the basis of analysis.

With regard to skills, it is argued that the widespread banking crisis in the CE-10 is not a consequence of communist heritage any more, but of the weak, slow, and sometimes contradictory policies of the post-communist governments.

While 'bad debt' constitutes the banks' most visible problem, it is argued further that two other problems really endanger the reform process not only of the financial sector, but of the entire reform countries' economies. Firstly, the size of these financial markets is about equivalent to the rounding error of US financial statistics, causing an inherent volatility bomb. For investors, this implies diversification strategies, short-termism and risk-adjusted return on investment goals. For the respective regulators, this recommends co-ordination strategies for the various capital markets, and setting up financial markets that serve not only a small number of speculators but industry and population at large.

Secondly, using a stakeholder approach, it is argued that strong tendencies prevail for nonprudent banking. Therefore, supervisors, foreign investors and bankers should analyse the 'degrees of freedom' of local bank owners and bank managers by dependence analysis. For supervisors and regulators it is also important to consider the links between reliable corporate governance practices, foreign direct investment, and the stability of the countries' currencies.

The conclusion is drawn that due to asymmetric information, small high-risk 'bubble' markets, uncertain bank privatization, capitalization and supervision, it is not easy to see how banks which have difficulties to manage themselves can exert a positive influence on the management of corporations and increase the efficiency of firms. However, even if the more general answer is negative, this does not imply that individual banks or financial institutions may not be in a position to positively influence enterprise performance.

Seven years of financial market reform in Central Europe[1]

1. Introduction

After seven years of transformation, it is getting more and more difficult to blame the communist heritage for the state of the financial markets in the CE-10.[2] Governments and Central Banks mostly took measures half-heartedly, hesitantly, and often too late. Thus, the banking sector in most of the CE-10 still can be considered as a sector where capital disappears. Depositors and the state, i.e. the taxpayers, are losing money in most CE-10 countries. However, it would be exaggerated to speak about a general banking crisis in Central Europe. In many of the CE-10, after several recapitalizations, the still dominating fully or partly state-owned banks provide some stability in the local financial markets, while newly created private banks suffer from a weak capital endowment and are much more prone to fraud and bankruptcy. Recent attempts of bank managers to gain control over former state banks pose new challenges to bank supervision, require new and enhanced rules of prudential banking and efficient deposit insurance systems. However, it is of major importance to the future economic development of the CE-10 to be in a position to exert a positive influence on enterprise performance. In the following, effective, market-driven corporate governance by banks is discussed along the following four questions: are banks sound enough, large enough, strong enough, and skilled enough to have an impact on improving the efficiency of firms?

2. How healthy is the financial sector in the CE-10?[3]

Bulgaria

In 1990, the Bulgarian banking system was split into 75 mostly small-sized banks (including 3 private institutions), savings banks, and the Foreign Trade Bank (Bulbank). A process of restructuring was hesitantly implemented with significant delay and bank supervision took insufficient measures. In 1996, the situation aggravated. Due to a decline in the rate of inflation, while nominal interest rates were still kept high, the real interest rates soared up to 30 per cent in early 1996. This proved disastrous for many enterprises (Podkaminer 1996, p. 10). According to a report by the Bulgarian National Bank only 21 per cent of credits extended could de classified as sound, 64 per cent were doubtful, and 15 per cent non-performing (*NZZ* 30/04/1996). Only after a structural reform of the banking sector was made a precondition for the IMF's standby agreement of 1996, the Bulgarian government took some action. An amendment of the banking law now makes bankruptcy of banks possible. A law for protection of deposits secures 100 per cent of private personal deposits denominated in lev, which will be made available in instalments. Personal deposits denominated in foreign currency will be blocked for two years. Enterprise deposits are protected only up to 50 per cent, deposits denominated in foreign currency will be converted into lev.

In 1996, the extremely high interest rates made several banks falter. When the government tried to prevent capital flight by trebling the interest rate to about 300 per cent it had to put 15 privately and state-owned banks under state control, among them the First Private Bank, AgroCredit-Bank, and Mineralbank. Closing Mineralbank affected foreign lenders with $252 million, among those the Industrial Bank of Japan with $140 million. Until January 1997, 14 banks were filed for bankruptcy or filing was prepared (*NZZ* 27/01/1997). The cost of the bank crisis was estimated at $1.7 billion, about 12 per cent of the GDP (*HB* 06/04/1996). Bad claims of banks should be replaced by $400 million foreign exchange denominated bonds issued by Bulbank, while the state takes over the bad claims on corporations (*NZZ* 27/01/1997).

In early 1997, the end of the crisis is not visible. Important legal regulations about collateral, creditor protection, and bank privatization are still missing (*NZZ* 27/01/1997). After restructuring, some 20 banks may remain. Bulbank, the Bulgarian foreign trade bank, is the largest bank (dollar equivalent of assets 3.1 billion in 1995), ranks 15th in Central and Eastern Europe (*The Banker* 7/1996).

Table 1. Top 10 CE-10 banks in terms of assets in EU-associated Central Europe in 1995

Bank Rank in USD billions of assets 1995	Land	Assets $bn	Share in countries aggregate assets	RoA in %	Equity tier 1 capital $mn	Capital assets ratio
1. Komercni banka	CZ	14.652	26.1%	1.58	988	6.74
2. Ceska Sporitelna	CZ	13.828	24.7%	0.07	636	4.60
3. Powszechna Kasa	PL	11.292	21.3%	1.71	297	2.63
4. Bank PeKaO	PL	8.212	15.5%	1.59	391	4.76
5. Investicni a Postovni banka	CZ	7.841	14.0%	0.73	494	6.30
6. OTP Bank	H	7.670	37.9%	0.87	265	3.45
7. Ceskoslovenska obchodni b.	CZ	7.152	12.8%	1.64	537	7.51
8. Vseobecna Dverowa banka	SK	5.430	49.1%	1.81	403	7.41
9. Slovenska sporitelna banka	SK	5.300	47.9%	0.77	185	3.49
10. Bank Handlowy s Warszawie	PL	4.310	8.1%	5.60	725	16.82
Total		85.687			4,921	
Avrg.		8.569			492	
Comparisons*						
4 Citicorp	US	256.853	4.6%	2.18	19,239	7.49
50 Internationale Nederland Bank	NL	154.049	21.7%	0.65	6,254	4.06
116 Bank Austria (before acquisition of Creditanstalt)	A	68.165	17.1%	0.39	3,059	4.49

Data: *The Banker* 07/96 'Top 1.000 Banks' fiscal year 1995.
Source: Fink/Haiss (1996).
Note: In the above ranking only banks from EU-associated transition countries are included. The following Serbian bank would make the CE top ten in terms of total assets:

| 8 Beogradska Banka | YU | 6.159 | n.a. | 4.37 | 278 | 4.51 |

*(in order of world's 1000 largest banks - 1995)

Czech Republic

Besides Plzen-based Kreditni Banka (with debt amounting to 12 billion koruna, i.e. surpassing the 1995 budget deficit by 4 billion koruna), until mid-1996, major problems in the Czech banking field could be avoided by several recapitalizations handled by the fully state-owned Consolidation Bank and the debt collection agency Ceska Inkasni which took over non-performing loans at repeated occasions (Mejstrik 1995, Chudzik 1995). In 1994, the three largest banks were quasi-privatized, with the state holding an important share directly (25.7 per cent in 1994) and indirectly by the National Privatization Fund (33-47 per cent). However, managers of some of the former state banks tried to gain control over their banks by increasing the holdings of own shares and setting up a network of weak shareholders consisting of major debtors to the banks (*HB* 31/05/1996). At Investicni Banka the share of own holdings was at 17 per cent in 1994 (Mejstrik 1995, p. 127; OECD 1996, p. 49). This poses a major challenge to bank supervision to keep the banking system functioning smoothly while new industry bank-clusters are emerging. Jointly with the top management, major debtors are gaining influence on the business strategies of banks.

During 1993-1996, 12 banks were in distress. In August 1996, Kreditni Banka Plzen reported the largest open debt so far ($500 million). In September 1996, Agrobanka was put under National Bank control, the same bank which showed negative capital in its balance sheet for 1993 and was rescued by government intervention in 1994. After the first failures of private banks by a licence stop in 1994 the Czech National Bank hoped to induce foreign banks to buy already established small but undercapitalized private banks. Since this policy showed little success, the bank licence stop was temporarily lifted in December 1995 when Bayerische Vereinsbank got an upgrade to a full licence (*NZZ* 02/12/1995) and in May 1996 when Midland Bank and Westdeutsche Landesbank were granted new licences (*NZZ* 25/05/1996). In December 1996, the acquisition of Interbanka by Bayerische Landesbank was announced (*ST* 10/12/1996). Out of the 55 banks, 22 are controlled by foreign banks. However, a concept was aired that the state controlled banks should be privatized, too. ING and Nomura reportedly showed interest for Investicni a Postovni Banka, Ceska Sporitelna, and CSOB, which report losses, should be merged before privatization (*FAZ* 06/11/1996).

Due to the large interest rate differential with West European and US markets and a perceived low exchange rate risk, enterprises and banks were increasingly turning to loans denominated in foreign currency (OECD 1996, p. 521). As far as local banks were offering foreign currency denominated loans to prime clients and befriended shareholders, while borrowing abroad in foreign currency, banks were getting increasingly vulnerable as continued deterioration of the balance on current account enforced a significant nominal depreciation of the Czech koruna.

Komercni banka ($14.7 billion assets) and Czeska Sporitelna ($13.8 billion assets) are the two largest banks in Central and Eastern Europe. Together they account for roughly 50 per cent of aggregate total bank assets of Czech banks. Investicni a Postovni banka is at rank 5, Ceskoslovenska obchodni banka at rank 7 in Central and Eastern Europe (*The Banker* 07/1996).

Estonia

Soon after the currency stabilization in 1992, the first private bank of Estonia (Tartu Bank) collapsed. Clients lost about $14 million (Dillon and Vensel 1995). Since then a significant number of banks folded, among others Social Bank in 1994. The enhanced capital adequacy standards could not be met by numerous banks which consequently were closed or merged with other banks. At the beginning of 1996, the number of local banks had declined to 14 from 40 in 1992. In addition, two foreign banks maintain branch offices and seven foreign banks operate representative offices in Estonia (Bank of Estonia communication January 1996). Hansa Bank with assets of $550 million is the largest Estonian bank (*NfA* 06/11/1996).

Hungary

Hungary prevented failures of all large banks with repeated recapitalizations, which raised the share of the state in the banks' equity to more than 80 per cent. After the breakdown of communism the number of banks increased quickly and reached 42 at the end of 1993. While a few smaller banks and savings associations collapsed, the larger banks were recapitalized in a first round during 1993-94 (Chudzik 1995). Finally, privatization of the larger state-owned banks is making progress. Only after the government poured further capital into the banks, and after the EBRD took direct equity participations like in Poland, and the Foreign Trade Bank (MKB) started to sell significant shares to Bayerische Landesbank, and Budapest Bank to General Capital Services in 1995, did the government decide in July 1996 to sell a 25 per cent share in Trade and Creditbank (K+H) to a 'strategic' investor, before the end of 1997. An offering is planned for May 1997 (*FT* 06/12/1996). In November 1996, ABN AMRO-Bank could acquire a 89.23 per cent share in Magyar Hitel Bank (*HE* 1996, vol. 24, No. 4). While OTP is still controlling most of the retail business of Hungary, more and more foreign-owned banks begin to develop branch networks. At the end of February 1997, a run on Postabank raised concerns about the stability of the banking system (*Kurier* 01/03/1997).

The largest Hungarian bank is the former state savings bank OTP, which was privatized by stock exchange operations. With assets of $7.8 billion, this is the sixth largest bank in Central Europe (*The Banker* 07/071996). The market is highly concentrated. OTP alone accounts for roughly 38 per cent of aggregate bank assets (similar to the situation in Slovenia with Nova Ljubljanska Banka accounting for about 34 per cent). The market share of the top 6 Hungarian banks is 75 per cent (*HNB* 1995).

Latvia

In 1993 and 1994, 23 smaller banks folded. Since the government took little action, six more banks including the largest Latvian bank (Banka Baltija) collapsed in May 1995. These banks disposed of 40 per cent of all deposits (*FT* 30/01/1996). The collapse caused a decline of the GDP by 2.3 per cent in 1995 (*NfA* 19/01/1996). Because of delayed action, the government failed to prevent asset stripping by the top management of Banka Baltija (*NZZ* 03/08/1995). In 1996, only 11 banks of 35 still have a licence to take deposits (*HB* 12/09/1996). A significant improvement of banking supervision is needed which takes more efficient measures at earlier stages (*FT* 11/07/1995 and *NfA* 10/01/1996). The largest bank is Pareks Bank with assets of about $230 million, closely followed by Latvian Union Bank (*HB* 12/09/1996).

Lithuania

At the end of 1995, the two largest private banks folded (Innovation Bank and Litimpex Bank) which together held 23 per cent of all deposits. Out of 28 banks 11 were filed for bankruptcy (*WSJ* 21/12/1995 and *NfA* 19/01/1996) and more banks suffer from inadequate capital endowment and insufficient reserves (*NZZ* 29/01/1996). Weak and inefficient bank supervision, insider privatization and large lending to dominant shareholders are the main reasons for the difficulties in the banking sector. The crisis of 1995-96 hit the taxpayers. $325 million capital injection was needed. This was about 10 per cent of government spending (*HB* 11/03/1996). The required amount could only be raised abroad and contributed to an increase in foreign debt (*NfA* 22/03/1996). In June 1996, an amendment to the National Bank law and the law on the creation of a deposit insurance fund were adopted by parliament. It is expected that only a few private banks and the state controlled banks with a market share of about 60 per cent may survive. The largest bank is Vilnius Bankas, which is 87.5 per cent foreign-owned (*WSJ* 05/02/1997).

Poland

Poland avoided an open banking crisis, but bank restructuring and privatization was delayed with numerous twists and turns of the government and the Sejm (parliament) about bank reorganization programmes, which so far were not fully implemented. In 1995, Agrobank was filed for bankruptcy. Contrary to public announcements, during the last three years only five banks were privatized with foreign participation: Bank Slaski with ING, Wielkopolski Bank with Allied Irish Bank, Bank Rozwoju Eksportu with Commerzbank and Petrobank with LG Group of South Korea (*WSJ* 28/06/1996) and Bank Handlowy during 1997. At the end of 1995, a bank consolidation programme was adopted. Under the leadership of Bank Handlowy and Bank PeKaO S.A., two bank-clusters should be created (*NZZ* 30/11/1995 and *HB* 16/04/1996), but the programme was changed again. Now only one group of banks should be created under the leadership of Bank PeKaO S.A. Bank Handlowy and the previously partly privatised state banks should remain independent (*NZZ* 29/05/1996). The privatization of Bank Handlowy by a public offering took effect in June 1997. However, foreign banks could not gain control over Bank Handlowy (*WSJ* 27/03/1997) and, thus, have little impact on bank modernization. Bank PeKaO will be privatized only in small steps until the year 2000 (*FAZ* 28/12/1996).

The largest banks in Poland are the previous savings bank PKO ($11.3 billion assets) and the Bank PeKaO S.A. ($8.2 billion assets). These banks are at rank 3 and 4 in Central Europe and account for roughly one third of aggregate assets. With roughly 16 per cent, the next two largest banks, Bank Handlowy s Warszawie and Bank Gospordarki Sywnosciewej, show the highest capital assets ratio among CE-10 banks (*The Banker* 07/1996).

Romania

The market is dominated by the state banks. Restructuring and privatization of the former state-owned banks is not visible. The government attempted several times to restrict activities of foreign banks because of soaring foreign exchange denominated loans. Until 1995, 19 private banks were founded. Since 1992, a large part of the state budget deficit is financed by the state savings bank, consequently the government has to guarantee savings deposits.

In November 1995, the private bank Dacia Felin was put under central bank supervision due to problems caused by large lending to its major shareholder. After having received government support of $335 million, the bank still needed more funds (*FT* 29/05/1996). A few weeks later the government decided neither to support Dacia Felin nor the also troubled Credit Bank any longer. The banking licence for the inactive Banka Fortuna was withdrawn. Problems became also visible in the investment fund sector. After new rules of asset valuation were implemented, some of the funds reported a decline in value down to 50 per cent (*NZZ* 12/07/1996).

Business of foreign banks was restricted in March 1996, when the licence for foreign exchange trading was withdrawn from 18 of 22 banks. After IMF grumbling, a relicencing of some of the foreign banks was announced in May 1996 but apparently implemented only in February 1997 (*FT* 03/05/1996, *WSJ* 21/06/1996, *HB* 07/03/1997). Before that, in July 1996, further restrictions were imposed in order to stop the fast growth of foreign exchange denominated credits supplied by the commercial banks (*NfA* 19/07/1996). The three largest Romanian banks are not found among the top 20 in Central Europe (*The Banker* 07/1996).

Slovakia

Several recapitalizations by the State Consolidation Bank and Slovenska Inkasni kept the banking sector stable although it still is a sector 'where capital disappears' (Chudzik 1995, Sobek 1995). For example, Consolidation Bank itself was in financial difficulties in 1994. Due to twists and turns in the various programmes, privatization made little progress. Finally in June 1996, parliament classified the largest banks with a joint market share of about 75 per cent as 'strategically important' enterprises (*NZZ* 29/06/1996). Therefore, Slovenska Poistovna, Slovenska Sporitelna, Vseobecna Uverova Banka, and Investicni a Rozvojova Banka must not be privatized before 2003 (*NZZ*

15/02/1997). Thus, political influence on the large banks seems to prevail (Sobek 1997). 28 commercial banks (including engagements of 10 foreign banks) and two specialized banks are servicing the market.

The two largest banks Vseobecna Uverova Banka ($5.4 billion assets) and Slovenska Sporitelna ($5.3 billion assets) rank eight and nine in Central Europe (*The Banker* 07/1996).

Slovenia

After initial recapitalizations of the quasi-state banks (Borak 1995), presently there are 30 banks and 7 savings banks active in Slovenia. Komercialna Banka Triglav, a private bank, was closed. Attempts to reorganize the banking sector in four larger and twelve smaller banks made little progress so far. Bank of Slovenia is in charge of deposit insurance until the agency for deposit insurance will assume its activities. An amendment to the banking law is under discussion in parliament.

In 1995, Nova Ljublianska Banka had a market share of about 34 per cent with assets of $3.6 billion. It ranked 12 in Central and Eastern Europe (*The Banker* 07/1996).

General observations

Perhaps with the exception of deposit insurance (Groszek 1995), most countries have established all the *institutions* needed to perform the financial market *functions*. However, there remains much to be done to make the financial system function in a way that it contributes to economic growth, which so far is generated by factors outside the banking system, and to 'create an effective and stable framework for monetary policy' (Kozinski 1995, Groszek 1995). The financial sector in the CE-10 is ridden by troubles, state-owned and newly founded private banks are in distress. Bank supervision is weak due to lack of adequate rules and lack of efficiency. Asset stripping of faltering banks could not be avoided. Initial recapitalizations could not prevent moral hazard. Privatization is hardly progressing. In the Czech Republic, where formally quasi-privatization was pushed forward, a lack of adequate rules is weakening bank supervision and raising concerns about more widespread moral hazard. There are hardly any signs that the banking sector of any of the CE-10 could be opened to EU competition after 1999 as envisaged in the association agreements with the

EU. The weak financial sector may become a stumbling block for EU membership.

Thus, it is not easy to see how banks which have difficulties to manage themselves can exert a positive influence on the management of corporations and increase the efficiency of firms. One can rather expect tinkering around with debt. More likely withdrawal from troubled enterprises, and predominant balance sheet cosmetics, to avoid problem-solving as long as possible will occur. Supported by policy makers, banks are making use of market imperfections: high spreads of interest rates and increasing refinancing abroad, while governments keep domestic interest rates high and the domestic currency overvalued (except in Poland).

3. Is the financial sector large enough to exercise significant corporate governance?

The banking sector

Assets of the banking system in the Czech Republic amount to $56 billion, in Poland $40 billion, in Hungary $20 billion, and in $Slovakia, Slovenia and Romania about $11 billion each. The size of these markets is approximately as large as the rounding error in US financial statistics: the Czech and Polish markets account for roughly a percentage point of the US market, the others are way below. But even the financial markets of less developed European Union member countries like Portugal or small EU members like Austria are three to 80 times larger than national financial markets in CE-10.[4] The Visegrád Five (Czech Republic, Hungary, Poland, Slovakia, and Slovenia) roughly match the Portuguese financial market. In fact, Bank Austria (1995 assets $68.2 billion, largest in Austria) is roughly 20 per cent larger than the aggregate Czech financial market, Citicorp as the leading US bank (assets $256.9 billion) about five times (Table 2). With assets of $85.7 billion, the top ten CE-10 banks together are about half the size of Internationale Nederland Bank.

Table 2. Size of financial markets, assets in bn $

	Average 1989-91	Average 1992-94	Year 1995
Estonia	0.728	0.949	
Latvia	0.496	1.103	
Lithuania	0.893	1.396	
Romania	28.708	11.150	9.680
Slovenia	5.737	6.717	10.869
Slovakia	32.048	17.967	12.494
Hungary	21.082	22.135	20.216
Poland	23.418	36.215	53.040
Czechia	32.048	36.138	56.090
Portugal	72.524	104.442	152.529
Austria	275.980	313.824	404.015
Spain	643.213	653.936	803.748
Italy	1,206.230	1,201.869	1,392.322
UK	2,152.872	2,175.458	2,648.609
Germany	2,311.230	2,928.130	3,924.158
USA	4,782.133	5,002.100	5,545.300
Japan	9,726.164	13,566.768	15,902.752

Data: IFS 06/96.
Source: Fink/Haiss (1996).
Note: Latvia & Lithuania: data available from 1993 on; Slovenia & Estonia: data available from 1991 on; CSFR for Czech and Slovak Republics up to 1992.

Financial markets in the transformation economies are small due to three reasons: the neglect of financial intermediation under communism and to varying degrees also during the first years of transition; low level of GDP per capita; and mostly, because only a small number of the population participates in financial markets. This is posing a major problem. Economically weak markets are prone to highly speculative activities. Foreign actors can easily influence asset prices on the financial markets of the economies in transition and exercise a disturbing influence on the real economy (*HB* 28/07/1995). Thus, a careful approach towards liberalizing international capital transfers seems to be advisable.[5]

Compared with established market economies, a low level of financial intermediation can be observed in Estonia, Latvia, and Romania (about 30 per cent of the GDP), Poland (46 per cent), and Hungary (51 per cent). In the Czech Republic, the level of financial intermediation was relatively high throughout the transition period (more than 110 per cent of the GDP) and is close to the level observed in Italy (see Table 3).

Table 3. Degree of financial intermediation

Country	1995 Bank assets in $ bn	In % of line above	In % of USA
Japan	15,902.752	100.0	286.78
USA	5,545.300	34.9	100.00
Germany	3,924.158	70.8	70.77
UK	2,648.609	67.5	47.76
Italy	1,392.322	52.6	25.11
Spain	803,748	57.7	14.49
Austria	404.015	50.3	7.29
Portugal	152.529	37.8	2.75
Czech Republic	56.090	36.8	1.01
Poland	53.046	94.6	0.96
Hungary	20.216	38.1	0.36
Slovakia	12.494	61.8	0.23
Slovenia	10.869	87.0	0.20
Romania	9.680	89.1	0.17
Lithuania	1.396	14.4	0.03
Estonia	1.355	97.1	0.02
Latvia	1.103	81.4	0.02

Comparisons

Bank	Bank assets (1996) in $ bn	In % of Czech Banks	In % of USA
Citicorp	256.853	457.9%	4.6%
Bank of Boston	47.397	84.5%	0.9%
Bank Austria	68.165	121.5%	1.2%

Data: IFS 06/96.
Source: Fink/Haiss (1996).

During 1994 and the first half of 1995, the unsound speculative effect of foreign engagement in small financial markets was observed in Poland and in the Czech Republic (*HB* 28/07/1995). Because of high rates of inflation in most of the economies in transition that are compressing the financial sector as a whole (Stypulkowski 1995) and due to the crowding out of private investors by government debt (Bonin and Shaffer 1995), the ratio of domestic credit to the GDP is very low in Estonia, Latvia, and Romania (10 to 20 per cent), Poland and Slovenia (below 35 per cent) and Hungary and Lithuania (around 60 per cent). In the Czech Republic where inflation is relatively low and the government does not run a deficit on the state budget, the decline in the ratio may be due to the debt consolidation in 1993 (Table 4).

Table 4. Domestic Credit relative to GDP
Domestic Credit in % of GDP

	Average 1989-91	Average 1992-94	Year 1995*
Estonia	60.6%	10.2%	11.0%
Latvia	n.a.	20.4%	14.5%
Romania	81.1%	23.7%	23.6%
Poland	29.0%	39.1%	28.2%
Slovenia	36.8%	29.3%	35.9%
Hungary	82.5%	67.4%	55.7%
Lithuania	n.a.	19.2%	60.8%
Slovakia	110.0%	83.5%	62.4%
Italy	78.1%	86.1%	85.7%
Czechia	110.0%	92.3%	91.5%
Portugal	74.0%	87.9%	93.2%
Spain	104.6%	101.1%	104.5%
UK	120.2%	119.1%	125.8%
USA	116.6%	120.5%	129.6%
Germany	115.8%	133.1%	148.7%
Austria	124.6%	140.1%	149.7%
Japan	140.9%	138.8%	136.0%

Data: IFS 06/96.
Source: Fink/Haiss (1996).
Note: CSFR for Czech and Slovak Republics up to 1992 data; for Slovenia and Estonia is available from 1991 on, for Latvia from 1993 on, for Lithuania from 1994 on.
* For Slovakia & Portugal: latest figures for 1994.

Even when taking into account that the degree of internationalization of financial markets is small in large economies (USA 1.9 per cent, Japan 5.9 per cent) and larger in small open economies, the shares of foreign assets and liabilities in the transition economies (Table 5) are rather small (Czech Republic and Poland 9 per cent each, Slovakia and Romania 11 per cent each), compared e.g. to Portugal or Austria (about 23 per cent; Table 5). The high figure for Latvia represents the capital inflows from Russia, the low figures of Hungary may go up through the participation of foreign banks in the ongoing privatization efforts.

Table 5. Internationalization of financial intermediation
Foreign assets and liabilities in per cent of total assets and liabilities

	Average 1989-91	Average 1992-94	Year 1995*
USA	2.8%	2.3%	1.9%
Hungary	3.6%	5.2%	5.5%
Japan	8.0%	5.4%	5.9%
Lithuania	n.a.	7.3%	7.9%
Czech Republic	5.1%	6.0%	8.6%
Poland	17.5%	11.6%	8.9%
Slovakia	5.1%	7.4%	10.7%
Romania	4.9%	8.9%	11.7%
Germany	12.0%	12.6%	13.5%
Italy	12.6%	14.9%	14.4%
Spain	7.7%	14.5%	16.3%
Slovenia	9.5%	20.5%	17.9%
Estonia	7.3%	20.2%	21.0%
Portugal	16.1%	19.6%	22.1%
Austria	24.7%	23.8%	23.9%
Latvia	n.a.	21.7%	38.8%
UK	47.6%	49.5%	50.1%

Data: IFS 06/96.
Source: Fink/Haiss (1996).
Note: Latvia and Lithuania: data available from 1993 on; Slovenia and Estonia: data available from 1991 on; CSFR for Czech and Slovak Republics up to 1992.
* Latest figures for Portugal: 1994.

From the relatively small degree of financial intermediation, one has to draw the conclusion that banks could not have an overall strong impact on economic efficiency of the economy even if the banks were strong, healthy and well-organized. This observation goes parallel with the observation of continuos trouble in the banking sector. Since most people do not trust the banks, they do not keep their money with banks, thus the degree of financial intermediation is low.

The stock markets

While basic banking structures did exist prior to transformation, capital markets and respective institutions (stock exchange, investment houses etc.) needed to be re-established after the collapse of communism. There was considerable amount of political and media attention towards stock exchanges as visible symbols. The above mentioned small order of magnitude applies to the stock and bond markets, too, and is aggravated by low liquidity. On the one hand, the CE-10 report a relatively small GDP, and on the other hand, in those countries where governments so far have shown little commitment to privatization, stock and bond markets remained small even with respect to the GDP level: in Hungary and Poland about 4 to 5 per cent of the GDP. However, in the Czech Republic the stock market capitalization of $16 billion amounts to 35 per cent of the GDP due to the fast voucher privatization. By international comparison the Czech Republic is showing a higher ratio of stock market capitalization to the GDP and also to total bank assets than Austria, Italy, and Germany. That is, in the Czech Republic the stock market is more important to company finance than in those countries in spite of their higher per capita GDP and their long-established capital markets (although the Prague Stock Exchange is heavily bank-driven as discussed below). Still, the Visegrád Five capital markets match roughly 75 per cent of the Vienna Stock Exchange. Moreover, the largest single values at the major stock exchanges of the world are significantly larger than total market capitalization of the stock exchanges in transition economies. Thus, again, foreign investors can easily drive the stock exchanges of Bratislava, Budapest, Prague, Warsaw, etc. either to bubble or to bust at any time they like (Table 6).

Table 6. Stock markets
Stock Market Capitalization (SMC) 1995

	In $ bn	In % of the GDP	In % of total bank assets
Slovakia	1.53	8.8	13.8
Hungary	2.19	5.0	10.8
Poland	3.59	4.0	6.8
Czechia	15.98	35.0	28.5
Austria	30.57	15.5	7.7
Spain	196.76	35.2	25.7
Italy	200.85	18.0	14.4
Germany	582.02	27.6	15.3
UK	1,347.79	122.0	50.9
Japan	4,426.53	86.0	28.3
USA	6,401.00	90.0	67.0
Comparisons:			
Visegrád Four	23.29	8.8	16.6
In % of Austria	76.2	56.6	215.8

Source: Fink/Haiss (1996).
Data: Federation of European Stock Exchanges (07/1996); Patrick/Bank Austria (1996); Economist, May 4 and 13, September 14, 1996.

At the *Ljubljana Stock Exchange* (LSE), the delay in privatization led to a stalemate of the equity market in terms of shares listed and trading volume. In early 1997 confidence was shaken by a central bank decision that foreign investors (accounting for roughly 20 per cent of turnover) must route transactions through custody accounts in local banks, which might increase transaction costs by 15 per cent for foreigners (Hopper et al. 1997). In 1996, the Ljubljana SBI-index lost about 30 per cent in dollar terms, making it the worst CE-10 performer.

With a 1996 BUX rise of roughly 130 per cent in dollar terms, the *Budapest Stock Exchange (BSE)* was last years' star performer, and not only among emerging markets. A major reason was the return of foreign investors. While there are shares of 38 companies traded, the small total market size of about $4.7 billion (market capitalization 1996) and the low turnover rate of roughly 14 per cent, it does not take much demand to boost prices, however. As much as 70-80 per cent of all equity transactions are estimated to originate from foreign investors. In comparison to the other capital markets in Central Europe, the *Warsaw Stock Exchange (WSE)* has a bigger domestic investor base, which are trading in a smaller number of stocks, but with a high turnover rate. About 40 per cent of market capitalization in Poland is in bank stocks. Warsaw's trading volume on a daily basis is 40 times that of the Bratislava Stock Exchange, 12 times the Budapest daily volume and three times higher than Prague's. During 1996, the Warsaw WIG-index gained roughly 60 per cent in dollar terms, making up for a mere 0.3 per cent in 1995. For 1997, initial public offerings of the 15 Polish national investment funds were announced. In Poland, monthly reporting by listed corporations is required and the domestic investor base is much broader than in other CE-10. Thus, in the small segment of listed stocks (4.3 per cent of the GDP) corporate governance by the stock markets is much more effective in Poland than e.g. in the Czech Republic.

According to estimates, at the official *Prague Stock Exchange* (PSE) about 60-80 per cent of trading is driven by foreign investors. One attraction is the sheer number of tradable stocks in Prague. While in Poland and Hungary, stock markets came first and privatization second, the Czech Republic took the opposite track in the transition. Due to two waves of privatization there were 1.725 stocks traded in Prague compared to 38 in Budapest and 68 in Warsaw at the end of 1995; most of them, however, in the unlisted section. Since most of this stock is hardly traded, about 1000 were delisted from PSE during 1997. Due to the role big banks are playing as privatization fund managers, the lack of transparency of the capital market, and of proper protection for minority shareholders, foreign investors have pulled about $500 million out of the Czech stockmarket in 1996. In early 1997, shareholders in two investmentfund groups, Trend and CS Fondy, have been fleeced of assets worth nearly $80 million (*Economist* 03/29/1997). The Prague PX-50-index rose by about 25 per cent in dollar terms, but PSE-prices are rather meaningless as the real action takes place off-exchange (Jones 1997; Kapoor 1997; Koth 1997). Hesitantly, the government tries to improve the situation. From March 1, 1997 all stock trading (also off-stock exchange transactions) must be reported and new quarterly disclosure rules are implemented. To escape that rule, several Czech investment funds converted into more loosely regulated holding companies.

In spite of the fact that trading volume on the *Bratislava Stock Exchange* remained fairly small, with only 23 officially listed and 528 unlisted (i.e.

OTC-traded only) stocks, the Bratislava options exchange (BOE) was opened as the first derivatives exchange in Central Europe. While the Bratislava Stock Exchange performed quite well in 1994, the halt to privatization gave it a slide in 1995 with a fall in the SAX-index of 25 per cent in dollar terms, in 1996 it gained about 9 per cent. The SAX was mainly driven by power struggles between parliament and the president about privatization and amendments to the securities law allowing shareholders to be secret, i.e. banks to be bought by state-controlled steel conglomerates.

The Prague and the Bratislava stock exchanges have to compete with another stock trading system, derived from the voucher privatization procedure. While the members of a stock exchange decide who is to enter the market either as new member or via the services of the established member, the RM-S system is directly accessible to anyone who wants to buy or to sell a dematerialized share registered with the Centre for Securities. Buyers have to deposit advance payment in full, and suppliers have to transfer disposal over registered shares to the RM-S system. These measures keep the capital requirements of the RM-S very small. The RM-S system seems to be of particular importance to small share-holders, since all registered shares can be traded, and not only the shares listed by the stock exchange authorities. Prices at the RM-S system are reportedly lower than at the stock exchange (Triska 1995, Meistrik 1995, Palenik 1994, Koth 1997). About 80-90 per cent of trade takes place outside the official markets (stock exchange and RM-S) as registered by the Centres for Securities in Prague and Bratislava, respectively. Mostly, it is trade among the Investment Privatisation Funds which are streamlining their portfolios (Triska 1995, Mejstrik 1995).

Table 7. Visegrád stock exchanges

	Stock indices 1994-96, Changes in per cent points dollar basis			Cumulative trading volume in millions of dollars		Market turnover in % SMC	Number of stocks listed					
							1993		1994		1995	
	Index	1994	1995	1996	1994	1995	1995	l	nl	l	nl	l	nl
Czech R.	PX-50	-41.0	-19.9	+24.1	894.3	1,105.4	22.0%	3	950	23	989	56	1,671
Hungary	BUX	+3.6	-13.9	+128.6	255.0	868.0	14.0%	28	28	41	n.a.	38	n.a.
Poland	WIG	-47.4	+0.3	+63.0	5,020.6	3,598.7	60.0%	21	7	27	5	55	13
Slovakia	SAX	+110.2	-25%	+8.8	43.1	258.0	n.a.	8	499	15	497	23	528

l = listed, nl = OTC/unlisted/parallel quoted/RM-S.

Source: Fink/Haiss (1997) updated.
Data: Patrick/Bank Austria, 1996; Hopper et al (1997); Federation of European Exchanges 7/1996, *The Economist* (04/05/96; 13/05/96; 09/14/96).

While the emerging capital markets in Central Europe have been booming since mid-1993, some analysts argued already before the Mexican crisis has hit the emerging markets in general, that in many cases, those stock market prices bear no relation to the fundamental values of companies. The lack of market transparency and information disclosure, the comparatively low trading volume and liquidity, the narrow market focus, the high share of OTC trading, the composition of market participants, the fact that many laws and supervisory institutions are only now in the making, the low capitalization of many securities houses, on top of the secondary emphasis that was given to the recreation of a vivid commercial banking market remain as unsolved structural problems (Blommenstein and Spencer 1993, Haiss 1995).[6] For example, during the first round of privatization, the Czech stock market remained still extremely narrow, since 75 per cent of total trading volume was concentrated on 1 per cent of those firms. Lasting effects of the second round still need to be seen. Moreover, of the 1,001 stocks initially traded, only five were officially listed while 996 were unlisted. Investment funds owned by banks (which are in most cases still nationalized) also happen to be members of the Prague Stock Exchange. By the privatization methods applied in the Czech Republic, large sectors of the economy have been handed over to mutual fund managers. From the companies on offer in the first round of privatization, 75 per cent of all the shares designated for voucher purchase were attracted by the over 300 funds available (Meth-Cohn 1993). The top 14 funds control almost 70 per cent of voucher shares and just over a quarter of the entire equity of these companies. The Czech voucher funds are also given a privileged view of companies' inner workings through seats on their boards. Throughout the last two years, there has been a huge consolidation of corporate ownership and investment funds began to convert themselves into holding companies. The move liberates these new companies from the supervision of the finance ministry as well as legislation covering investment funds.

Corporate governance through anonymous securities markets, therefore, has not been possible in the early stages of transition (Stern 1995). While theoretically the stock exchange is a market with perfect information for both investors and capital seeking corporations, in fact, it is not in the CE-10. In the economies in transition 'stock markets with their distinct shareholder structure are not capable of circumventing the negative effects of asymmetric information which are prevalent with debt financing' (Linne 1995).

4. Are banks supervised enough?

Banks have to be geared towards prudent banking. Positive effects of prudent banking are a public good (Coffee 1996). Economic stability generated by prudent banking leads to an increasing propensity to save. The increasing savings will be channelled by the banks into efficient investment and thus contribute to growth and increase the prosperity of nations. The production of public goods justifies government action.

Short term gains from non-prudent banking mainly accrue to insiders (dominant owners, managers, high-rank employees). If bank supervision is inefficient, there is a strong tendency that insiders shift to non-prudent banking to internalize quick and large gains from (risky) opportunities, while losses from these undertakings have to be borne by outsiders. With bank supervision not existing 'new banking licences may initially be nothing more than a licence to steal' (Akerloff and Romer 1994, quoted by Baer and Gray 1996).

If efficiency and strength of supervision fluctuates, there will be a tendency that insiders show a preference for holding liquid assets. These assets can easily be taken away by insiders or diverted to high risk ventures to the benefit of insiders when supervision is getting weaker.

Thus, weakly supervised banks will tend to

a) hold over-proportionately high liquid assets (Myers and Rajan 1997);
b) provide credit for high risk ventures if the profit of these ventures accrues to insiders and to strong stake-holders, but in case of failure the loss has to be covered by depositors, naive minority equity holders, or the public.

Although the negative effects of insufficient bank supervision are well known in general, Baer and Gray (1996, pp. 107-8) conclude after their analysis of corporate governance in Hungary and Poland: 'For reasons we do not fully understand that countries liberalizing chartering policies almost always fail to follow up with reforms mandating adequate disclosure and creating a well-functioning supervisory system.' Similar observations were also made for some developing countries (Lewis and Stein 1997). An answer can be found by analysing the direct gains from prudent and non-prudent banking which accrue to important stakeholders.

Table 8. Possible gains from prudent and non-prudent banking

Stakeholder	Possible gains from prudent banking		Possible gains from non-prudent banking		Effects in case of bank failure
	direct effects (short term)	indirect effects (spillovers)	direct effects (short term)	spillovers (long term)	
general public	none	highly positive economic and political stability, efficient institution building	none, if dirty money is not reinvested locally	highly negative	highly negative in particular in case of large retail bank
depositors (predominantly small depositors)	small positive interest rate safe deposit	increasing trust in banking system, increasing propensity to save	target interest income	risk of loss of non-insured deposits	sizeable loss
national bank	good reputation for top management	increasing trust in monetary and financial policy-making	none, tendency of capital flight	general accusation of insufficient supervision, bail out requirements repeated recapitalizations	general accusation of insufficient supervision, bail out requirements loss of high rank post
political circles (individuals close to power)	none	none	personal access to large credit		
political parties (organizations)	ruling: stability opposition: none	ruling party: good reputation	access to financial funds, finance for election campaigns	large bank collapse may trigger later loss in elections	with large losses risk of political turmoil
financially sound private owners	easy access to financial funds	safe capital investment	diversion of own equity to other people's advantage	limited investment opportunities	loss of equity
financially weak private owners	restricted access to new finance	none	easy access to financial funds	larger investment opportunities	loss of equity: likely smaller than open credit
state as owner	none	increasing trust in monetary and financial policy-making	none	general accusation of insufficient supervision, bail out requirements	general accusation of insufficient supervision, bail out requirements
privatization agency	higher privatization revenue	privatization faster	privatization slower	low privatization revenue, privatization not possible	
managers	reasonable salary	safe job (but political pressure not excluded)	easy access to finance and large property, large salary, political protection by beneficiaries of non-prudent banking	loss of position in case of severe bank crisis, dependence on political circles (beneficiaries)	loss of position in case of bank failure
employees	reasonable salary	safe job	easy access to large credit	loss of position	loss of job

Most of the short-term effects of non-prudent banking accrue to politically weak stakeholder groups (depositors) or to insider groups whose individual members as an alternative could generate significantly larger direct gains from non-prudent banking (managers, employees, individual shareholders of banks).

The state as an owner is rather weak in exercising corporate governance (Fink and Schediwy 1992) since other interests, e.g. 'protecting jobs' and avoiding political trouble, override the interest in reasonable profits of banks and state-owned corporations. In addition, the direct gains of the state from prudent banking are small (if not negligible) in comparison with tax revenues. Some element of non-prudence may even be welcome to political rulers since nonprudence gives leeway in exercising power. It helps to get access to finance for political purposes and to serve the politicians' clientele. Reportedly, the 1992 election campaign of Mr Klaus was largely funded through a 60 million koruna loan from the then state run Investicni Banka, in 1994 to be merged into Investicni a Postovni Banka (*WSJ* 27/12/1996). Thus, there may be also a lack of political will to have exercised strong bank supervision (Baer and Gray 1996, p. 78).

The political pressure for establishing reasonable disclosure rules and bank supervision is weak in transition economies since the major preoccupation of all people is with the redistribution of wealth by privatization. People are much more concerned about getting rich quickly by redistribution of property than by regular work. As long as privatization is not settled and its outcome broadly accepted by the general public there is a political dominance of those people who expect to gain from the redistribution of wealth, over those, whose major interest is stable economic and political conditions and ordinary economic growth.

The use of instruments for corporate governance by banks is influenced by the way banks are governed and supervised. Corporate governance can be exercised through four channels: control by equity rights (share holding), by admitted rights (proxies for small shareholders and dominant institutional investors), by financial rights (claims of creditors), and by assumed stakeholder power of outsiders.

In the European context of the 1990s the strongest impact on corporate governance of banks so far was generated by international organizations. A successful approach towards future EU membership is regarded as an important element for internal legitimisation of governments in the CE-10. Becoming a member of the Council of Europe, the WTO, the OECD, and finally of the EU is indicating the steps which have to be taken in order to become a full member of the ivy-league of prosperous European nations. These steps require the adoption and application of rules and codes of conduct which are constituting elements of the common body of values among the members of these organizations.

The association agreements with the EU foresee that the CE-10 will open their financial markets to foreign banks and financial institutions five to ten years after the agreements went into force. Another precondition for EU membership is the adoption and application of the acquis communautaire also in the field of banking, including bank supervision, deposit insurance etc. (Commission 1995 – White Book). If the CE-10 do not comply with these rules EU-membership will not be possible. Thus those countries which consider themselves as the first-round candidates for enlargement hesitantly begin to comply. The Hungarian parliament, for example, adopted the draft law on deposit insurance by November 1996 (*HE* 1996, Vol. 24, No. 4).

As for direct industrial ownership of banks, i.e. holding shares in industrial corporations, there are two features to be mentioned: a) debt for equity swaps of enterprises which had to undergo restructuring in a bankruptcy procedure and b) acquisition of shares in order to exercise control rights. Many of the industrial conglomerates controlled by banks in Europe are a consequence of earlier weak corporate governance by banks or capital markets.[7] Banks assume controlling stakes in the course of bankruptcy workouts. Acquisition of controlling stakes in enterprises by purchasing shares seems to be the exception. Mostly this instrument is used with the intention to resell later, e.g. the purchase of Tungsram by the Austrian Bank GiroCredit. Tungsram was later resold to General Electric (for the complete case see Marer and Mabert 1996).

When bank supervision is weak, insiders have a preference for getting credits from the bank to purchase equity. The purchased shares can be used as a collateral. If the venture is successful the benefits accrue to the insider. If the venture fails the downside risk is with the bank and ultimately with its depositors and equity holders. Otherwise, banks seem to use shareholdings for defensive purposes. In the Czech Republic significant cross holdings among banks and own share holdings of banks were accumulated. These measures also aim at preventing more strict corporate governance by strong outside shareholders (Dittus and Prowse 1996, pp. 60-63, OECD 1996).

Based on research by Bonin, Shaffer, Belka, McKinnon and others, Baer and Gray (1996, p. 72) depict a preference for equity financing under the conditions of a weak legal framework for debt collection, weak monitoring competencies of creditors, large downside risks, and weak control powers of creditors. In addition, when interest rates are high (this may coincide with large downside risks), corporations depend more on retained earnings for financing new investment (McKinnon 1991). This is basically due to the fact that managers and owners can strip assets at the expense of creditors, just as managers can do at the expense of owners (Beer and Gray 1996, p. 74). This is the point where banks are neither willing nor geared to exercise corporate governance unless it is in the direct interest of some insiders of the bank.

5. Are bankers strong and skilled enough to exercise corporate governance?

In their decision-making, East European bankers have to consider the interests of major stakeholders. These include the minister of finance, the national bank, privatization agencies, own bank staff, depositors, large state-owned corporations, sometimes also shareholders and new private investors. Timing and intensity of bank reform are determined by the vested interests of these groups.

- The minister of finance: often the major debtor, but also representative of the state as the owner of large banks.
- The national bank: often the major supplier of funds. Both together play a role in banking supervision, nomination of bank managers, and decision on bank recapitalization. Both share an interest in 'as little trouble as possible'.
- Privatization agencies: influence if, when and to whom banks' are privatized, and also if, when and to whom the banks' major corporate clients are privatized, that is, which corporations can web ties with banks and vice versa – and at what debt level.
- Bank staff: employees want to keep their positions, and for their career often they are rather slow and hesitant in their decision-making. They tend to delegate decision-making to their superiors (risk avoidance).
- Depositors: the providers of retail refinance have little impact on bank management. They have a relatively weak position, can exert influence only indirectly as voters in parliamentary elections. This again enhances the interest of the minister of finance in 'as little trouble as possible'.

- Large state owned corporations: in particular corporate debtors have some influence on bank managers' behaviour. They can cause trouble by deciding on how, when and what credit to honour.
- New private investors: have little influence, but they want to get access to bank credit. They are seeking to gain influence on the bankers' decision-making. They feel crowded out by the state as a debtor and by large (still or formerly state owned) corporations.

In this framework, the question was raised, whether the banks did not only inherit nonperforming loans (the stock problem), but also continue to extend their credit portfolio with bad debtors (the flow problem) while presumably good debtors were crowded out? According to Bonin and Shaffer (1995) and Belka et. al. (1995), banks were not the major financiers of companies' losses in Poland and Hungary. Based on empirical data on the largest 200 manufacturing companies in these countries, they conclude that severely financially-distressed firms, most of which are state owned, finance their losses mainly by running up tax arrears, i.e. a deterioration of tax and social security discipline.[8] The analyses of the Shaffer-group further suggest that banks slowly moved toward more prudent banking, but bankers had to make a decision how much 'bad debt' they could afford to reveal. Given the dependence of bankers on political decision making, they have to be obedient to the minister of finance and the governor of the central bank, and 'avoid trouble'. However, bank profitability is not high enough to depreciate at once all debt which might be considered as 'bad'. Thus bankers fiddle around with bad debt. Given their desire to stay in office and to make a career, and the necessity to clear the books only in the medium term they chose a selective approach and determine their 'optimum level' of bad debt to be shown in the balance sheet, while withdrawing slowly from bad debtors in real terms and shifting their portfolio piecemeal to new private clients.

By implementing more stringent rules of prudential banking since the early 1990s, more of the outstanding credits of banks had to be classified. However, the level of 'bad debt' to be shown in the balance sheets, e.g. in terms of overdue payment of interest and redemption to some extent is easily handled by the banks. Without increasing the actual amount outstanding delays in payments by clients can be avoided simply by granting new credits to these clients sufficiently in advance of payment due. This policy seems to serve best in the interest of all major stake holders. When after long hesitation governments mingled into this process without analysis of the background, overestimating the potential of bureaucratic procedures (as under communist planning) and underestimating the abilities of firms and banks for stepwise adjustment (Bonin and Shaffer 1995) things became really bad. As in the case of Bulgaria (Dobrinsky 1995) the first wave of selective recapitalization raised expectations of a general clean up. Having got rid of only part of the 'true' bad debt, because of the selective approach chosen by political considerations, banks easily adjusted and restored the previous level of 'bad debt' in their books within shortly after recapitalization (Buch 1995, Bonin and Shaffer 1995, Dobrinsky 1995).

Similar to the 'bad debt' problem, the 'inter-enterprise credit issue' may have been the other reason why ill-conceived policies were pursued. Politicians and central bankers were very much concerned about the 'soft budget constraint' of state owned firms and 'low payments discipline'. When central banks tried to impose ceilings on bank lending to large state-owned firms, it became known that credit among enterprises amounts to more than 30 per cent of GDP. Such a level is not excessively high when compared with data from established market economies (Belka et al 1995, Bonin and Shaffer 1995). It nevertheless raised major concerns in some of the countries. In Hungary the so called 'automatic trigger' was implemented by the bankruptcy law of 1992. Enterprises in delay with a single payment had to file for bankruptcy automatically. By these measures banks lost control about what and how much to declare as 'bad debt' and the small equity capital base was completely eroded. Most of the major banks reported negative equity. Despite the previous announcements that recapitalization was a once, and for all action, further official and/or unofficial bailouts became necessary (Buch 1995, Bonin and Shaffer 1995, Chudzik 1995, Dobrinsky 1995, Mejstrik 1995). Being burdened with a variety of indirect and direct taxes, the undercapitalized Hungarian banks as a consequence charged a much higher spread (9.4 per cent in 1994) than banks in Western Europe, Poland and the Czech Republic (IFS 1995, Marer 1994). Because of the capital injections the share of government in equity is increasing (Chudzik 1995). Liability side operations put a brake on privatisation efforts, as is clearly seen in the case of Poland and Hungary (Buch 1995). Thus, illconceived recapitalization rather delayed than promoted the privatization of banks, at least in Hungary and Poland, thus hindering effective corporate governance as discussed below.

Table 9. Interest rate spreads
Spread between lending and deposit rates

	Average 1989-91	Average 1992-94	Year 1995
Latvia	n.a.	37.9%	19.8%
Lithuania	n.a.	39.1%	18.7%
Slovenia	n.a.	26.9%	9.5%
Estonia	n.a.	n.a.	7.3%
Slovakia	4.4%	6.1%	7.1%
Hungary	6.6%	8.5%	6.5%
Czechia	4.4%	6.5%	5.8%
Poland	142.5%	1.6%	1.7%
Average CE	n.a.	18.1%	9.6%
Av. Visegrád	39.5%	5.7%	5.3%
Germany	3.2%	6.7%	7.1%
Portugal	8.4%	6.0%	6.6%
Italy	7.3%	6.6%	6.0%
Austria	4.8%	3.5%	4.3%
USA	4.1%	2.9%	3.6%
UK	2.0%	1.9%	2.8%
Spain	5.2%	1.7%	2.4%
Japan	3.7%	2.5%	2.3%
Average	4.8%	4.0%	4.4%

Data: IFS 6/96.
Source: Fink/Haiss (1996).
Note: Latvia and Lithuania: data available from 1993 on; Slovenia and Estonia: data available from 1991 on; CSFR for Czech and Slovak Republic up to 1992; best figures for Portugal: 1994.

While above the impact of stakeholders on corporate governance was discussed from an agency-theory point of view, it is also revealing to elaborate on the outcome to asset/liability management. Whether banks are strong enough to exercise corporate governance is discussed by reviewing the room to manoeuvre of bank management in various positions of the balance sheet and the presumed strength of relevant stakeholders which have an impact on the respective items.

Table 10. Stakeholders influences

Type of liability	External stakeholders' interest and strength	Power of external stakeholder
Due to credit institutions (interbank finance)	save deposits, strong position in refinancing the bank, interest of other bank owners	strong
Due to Central Bank	keeping the bank afloat, permanent threat on bank managers, strategy: to avoid trouble	very strong
Due to private savers	save deposits, reasonable interest, position weak, mostly dispersed and politically not organized. Proof: lack of deposits insurance in some CE-10	very modest
Due to companies	save deposits, reasonable interest, strong position only when deposits are significant	modest/strong
Securitized liabilities	save investment, reasonable interest, depending on holder of securities	modest/strong
Subscribed capital	state as owners, strategy: to avoid trouble	very strong
	private owners with significant share	very strong
	private owners with dispersed ownership	very modest
	managers as owners	strong
	employees as owners	strong
	increase leeway of managers and employees	none
Contingent liabilities from circulated bills of exchange	position varying by investor and issuer	
from guarantees and collateral	position varying depending on partners	

Type of asset	Stakeholders' interest and strength	Power of external stakeholder
Cash	bank managers' leeway increased	none
Balance with Central Bank	bank managers' leeway increased	modest
Debt instruments issued by public authorities	government, financing government deficits reduces power of government, increases leeway of bank managers	modest
Claims on credit institutions	strong position of bank management, dependence on good will of other banks	modest/strong
Claims on private customers	small amounts, widely dispersed clients	very weak
Claims on corporations	the larger the amount the weaker the bank management	strong/modest
Own shares	strong position of bank management	none
Shares in other banks and corporations	strong position of bank management with respect to small companies, weak position with respect to large debtor corporations	weak/strong

This analysis reveals the dilemma in bank politics. As long as banks are state owned, repeatedly capitalized and/or refinanced by the Central Bank, the interest of the minister of finance and the governor of the Central Bank in 'as little trouble as possible' prevails. Corporate governance by banks can only assume modest moves to withdraw slowly from major debtors, otherwise the bank itself may be threatened in its existence and due to the collapse of large corporations unemployment would soar.

As soon as the state is not involved in a bank, the managers theoretically get more room to move towards stricter corporate governance. However, powerful asset-side stakeholders often get in a position to dominate the bank by purchasing a reasonable share in the bank. Since private depositors have little impact on bank management, the pressure to exercise corporate governance on major debtors remains weak if these debtors become owners of a bank. Thus, bank mangers again have little power to exercise efficient corporate governance. In several instances managers formed coalitions with preferred borrowers. These coalitions opened the opportunity of asset stripping in case of financial distress.

During the last seven years of economic transition, thousands of bank managers and employees enjoyed training provided by West European and American commercial banks, Central Banks, and international institutions. In the framework of the PHARE programme the EU still is providing assistance in training and in research on banking. Considering these efforts we have two possibilities in our assessment. Either the training or the legal conditions and property structures are inadequate in the CE-10. In the light of our analysis we come to the conclusion that training was enough. Since both state-owned banks and the new private banks repeatedly are in financial distress, the widespread banking crisis in the CE-10 during 1995 to 1997 is not a consequence of communist heritage, but of weak, slow, and sometimes contradictory or ill-conceived policies of the post-communist governments.

The weak position of bank managers with respect to corporate governance of major debtors is due to significant weaknesses in regulation and supervision of banking. In many of the CE-10 standard rules and procedures (capital adequacy requirements, risk assessment, asset valuation rules, deposit insurance, etc.) are not yet fully implemented. There is also missing a code of conduct in case of financial difficulties and bankruptcy procedures. In many instances of bank failures asset stripping by owner/mangers could not be prevented. There is also a lack of stable rules for bank privatization.

In addition, more attention has to be paid to specific shareholder/stakeholder relations. It seems appropriate to enhance the general 'single borrower rules'. These rules should limit lending not only to individual corporations, but also to clusters dominated by a single or a few owners. Single borrower rules should also comprise a bank's holdings of bonds and shares of companies. Significant limits should be imposed on lending to shareholders, on holding of own shares, on cross share holdings among banks, and among banks and enterprises. Among banks and among banks and enterprises only one-way share holding should be permitted. Share holdings in other banks and enterprises should be subject to additional capital requirements. A temporary relief may be granted only when a bank acquires a stake in an enterprise through a debt for equity swap in course of a bankruptcy procedure.

In the case of the CE-10 the issue of bank-company clusters comes up as an 'agency problem of privatized firms' (Blommenstein and Spencer 1993). Only a few of the (still nationalized) commercial banks charge risk spreads based on market criteria. The situation is even worse considering the often narrow, illiquid capital markets and the influence of information asymmetries on these markets (Mayer 1992, Smith and Walter 1992). Therefore, those countries' people cannot trust the newly established capital markets. Most of the privatisation vouchers and company coupons the people had received from privatization funds were usually handed over to investment funds mostly managed and controlled by commercial banks since the banks seem to be the more safe and trustworthy financial intermediaries. In the Czech Republic two thirds of the people involved entrusted investment funds with their vouchers (Meistrik et al. 1995).

In those countries where investment funds were established in the process of privatization the role of the investment funds and their possible conversion into direct holding companies should be reconsidered. Of particular concern are the opportunities of banks managing these funds to manipulate asset prices by stock market operations and the possible consequences of extended bank lending to enterprises controlled by investment funds which are in turn controlled or managed by the lending bank.

There is possibly an exception to the rule. Subsidiaries of West European or American banks are subject to governance by their parent banks and thus much better designed for exercising corporate governance also in the CE-10. If effective reporting systems are established at the stock exchange (as. e.g. in Poland and Hungary) then foreign owned investment banks can have a significant impact on the conduct of corporations with listed stocks. Thus, in these small segments of the CE-10 economies corporate governance by banks can be effective. The policy advice for bank supervision is to promote access of well-established foreign banks to the CE-10 financial markets (opposite to the predominant attitude in the CE-10).

As to the distribution of foreign exchange and solvency risks, there are several options available depending on the setting of actual transactions. If banks take credits in foreign exchange and convert those into local currency which is then provided at competitive interest rates to enterprises, the banks earn most of the interest rate differential, but carry also the full exchange rate risk. If the order of magnitude of this kind of business is getting large, banks will get into difficulties after a consequent depreciation of the currency.

Banks may also act as intermediaries and offer foreign exchange denominated credits to their clients which are refinanced abroad. Then the borrowing enterprise is converting the foreign exchange into local currency and carries the full exchange rate risk. However, if the higher local market interest rate would be too high a financial burden for the borrowing enterprise, then a future depreciation of the currency in the order of magnitude of the interest rate differential, too, cannot be borne by the borrower. Thus borrowing enterprises and consequently the lending banks will get into trouble. Therefore, some banks try to avoid direct involvement into such transactions, but advise and handle the issue of global depository notes on financial markets abroad. In this case the bank acts as an advisor to the issuing company and earns an appropriate fee while the full solvency risk of the issuing company is to be borne by a third party, i.e. the foreign investor.

Given the typical risk of these transactions, policy makers are advised to keep exchange rate adjustments and interest rate differentials in line. As long as the real interest rate differentials reflect differentials in productivity gains they could be maintained since the current account remains in surplus, reflecting better earning opportunities in economies with faster productivity gains and inducing capital inflows into the real sector of the economy.

In times of increasing or rapidly falling rates of inflation, governments (central banks) are also advised to keep interest rates in line with price movements. Negative real interest rates (mostly observed in periods of soaring inflation) put a brake on real investment and real economic activity. Too high positive real interest rates, which may occur when inflation goes down and the interest rates are not adjusted accordingly, destroy even very productive enterprises which are credit financed. It is hardly possible to earn 20-30 per cent real interest in competitive product markets. Thus the advice is to keep real interest rates positive at modest levels of about 2-5 per cent.

6. Conclusions

Seven years of financial market reform in Central Europe is a sufficiently long time to put the house in order. Thus, the recurring banking crises in the CE-10 are not a consequence of communist heritage any more, but of weak, slow, and often contradictory policies of postcommunist governments. Even after the European Union had listed the minimum requirements for financial market reform in the White Book of 1995 an appropriate preaccession strategy of many of the CE-10 is only slowly forthcoming. New industrial-political clusters are apparently strong enough to prevent the establishment of a strong bank supervision and of adequate rules of prudent banking. Strong tendencies for non-prudent banking prevail.

Recently the Hungarian government is coming to the conclusion that sound banking can hardly be established without experienced banks from the EU or the US entering the market at a larger scale, thus privatization of the large former state-owned banks is taking place with strong involvement of renowned foreign banks. The largest bank in Lithuania is largely foreign owned. In Poland and the Czech Republic signs for a greater involvement of renowned foreign banks in the formerly state-owned banks are mixed. There seems to be resistance against majority shares of foreigners in the large domestic banks. In all the other CE-10 countries privatization of state-owned banks is hardly progressing.

Given the strong tendencies towards non-prudent banking in most of the CE-10, the small size of the financial markets, asymmetric information, as well as uncertain bank privatization, capitalisation and supervision, it is not easy to see how banks at large will exert a positive influence on the management of corporations and increase the efficiency of firms. However, this does not imply that individual banks or financial institutions may not be in a position to exert a positive influence on enterprise performance when rules of disclosure at the stock exchanges are tight enough as is the case for example in Poland and Hungary.

Notes

1. Earlier work was presented at the 19. SUERF Colloquium in Thun, Switzerland, October 1995 and published in Fink and Haiss (1996a, 1996b and 1997). The opinions expressed are the authors' personal views and do not necessarily reflect those of Bank Austria, the Institute of European Affairs or the Institute of European Studies. The

authors wish to thank Paul Marer, Bloomington, Indiana and Blue Ribbon Commission, and the following co-ordinators of PHARE ACE projects for extremely helpful support in providing information about their ongoing research and working papers published by their research institutes: D. Bailey, London, M. Fry, Birmingham, G. Fuolega, Venice, C. Green, Loughborough, Y. Katsoulacos, Athens, B. Kavic, Ljubljana, M. Koparanova, Sofia, R. Macdonald, Strathclyde, E. Miklaszewska, Krakow, V. Palenik, Bratislava, U. Plowiec, Warsaw, J. Sgard, Paris, M. Shaffer, Edinburgh.

2. CE-10: Bulgaria, Czech Republic, Estonia, Hungary, Latvia, Lithuania, Poland, Romania, Slovakia, Slovenia, i.e. the ten EU-associated Central European countries which eventually will become members of the European Union.
3. For the history of post-communist banking 1988-1995, see Fink/Haiss (1996a, 1996b and 1997).
4. Total assets of the top 10 CE-10 banks (85.7 billion dollar 1995) are of about the same size as Royal Bank of Scotland, a bank of only regional importance in Europe. The top 7 banks in CE-10 together match about Bank Austria (68.2 billion dollar 1995). However, it is not the level of concentration that matters here (which is actually quite high in some of the CE-10). It is rather the small size of financial markets in these countries that poses a general problem, as further discussed in section three.
5. Buch (1995) provides a good classification scheme for recapitalization programmes.
6. At the Vienna Options and Futures Exchange OTOB, 'traded indices' covering 50 to 85 per cent of the respective individual Visegrád stock exchanges and a composite index (CECE) were introduced in July 1996. In early 1997, trading in options and futures on those indices was partly started, thereby easing liquidity problems to a certain degree.
7. The second reason is the fact that in continental Europe banks not just financed the industrial revolution, but to a certain degree also initiated it.
8. While emerging private firms have little in the way of outstanding tax liabilities relative to total debt, and hold more in the way of bank credit, corporatised and state-owned enterprises owe a much higher proportion to the government. In the case of Hungarian firms, the Bonin and Shaffer data (1995, 21) suggest a flow of tax arrears towards low profitable-firms of the magnitude of two per cent. In the case of Polish firms in financial distress, roughly 50 per cent of the losses were financed by an increase in tax and social security liabilities (Belka et al 1995, 17). Lower reserve requirements and selective lending policies, on the other hand, led to excess liquidity within the Polish banking sector, with the government as the main benefactor (Schrooten 1994).

References

Abbreviations used for Newspapers and Journals:

BdW *Blick durch die Wirtschaft*
DP *Die Presse*, Vienna
DS *Der Standard*, Vienna
FAZ *Frankfurter Allgemeine Zeitung*
FT *Financial Times*, London
HB *Handelsblatt*, Frankfurt
HE *The Hungarian Economy*
IFS *International Financial Statistics*, IMF, Washington D.C.
IHT *International Herald Tribune*, Paris
NfA *Nachrichten für den Aussenhandel*
NZZ *Neue Zuricher Zeitung*, Zurich
WSJ *The Wall Street Journal*, Europe
The Banker, London
The Economist, London

Akerloff, George A., and David M. Romer (1994), *Looting: the Economic Underworld of Bankruptcy for Profit*, Brookings Papers on Economic Activity. The Brookings Institution, Washington D.C. (quoted by Baer and Gray 1996).

Baer, Herbert L. and Cheryl W. Gray (1996), 'Debt as a Control Device in Transitional Economies: The Experiences of Hungary and Poland', in: Roman Frydman, Cheryl W. Gray and Andrzej Rapaczynski (eds), *Corporate Governance in Central Europe and Russia*, Volume 1, Central European University Press Budapest, London, New York 1996, pp. 68-110.

Bank of Slovenia (1994), *Monthly Bulletin* 6-7, Ljubljana 1994.

Belka, Marek, Saul Estrin, Mark Shaffer and I.J. Singh (1995), *Enterprise Adjustment in Poland: Evidence from a Survey of 200 Private, Privatized, and State Owned Firms*, London School of Economics, Centre for Economic Performance, Discussion Paper No. 233, April 1995.

Blanden, Michael and Anthony Rowley (1996), 'The Top 1000', *The Banker* 7, pp. 96-207.

Blommenstein, Hans and M. Spencer (1993), 'The Role of Financial Institutions in the Transition to a Market Economy,' *IMF Working Paper* 93/75. Washington: IMF.

Bonin, J. P. and Mark Shaffer (1995), *Banks, Firms, Bad Debts and Bankruptcy in Hungary 1991-94*, London School of Economics, Centre for Economic Performance, Discussion Paper No. 234, April 1995.

Borak Neven (1995), Slovenian Banking Reform: Searching for the Bank Model, in: Ewa Miklaszewska (ed), *Competitive Banking in Central and Eastern Europe*, Jagellonian University Krakow 1995, pp. 293-302.

BREE (1995) Bank Research Eastern Europe: 'Gute Noten für Tschechiens Banken', in *HB* 1995/07/10.

Buch, Claudia (1995), *Bad Debt and Foreign Support - the Experience of Central Europe,* PHARE ACE Conference on The Role of the Banking System in the Economic Transformation of Central European Countries, Organizer Urszula Plowiec, Warsaw May 18-20, 1995.

Chudzik, Robert (1995), 'Comparative Analysis of the Bank Restructuring Programs in the Czech Republic, Hungary and Poland.' In Ewa Miklaszewska (ed), *Competitive Banking in Central and Eastern Europe.* Krakow: The Jagiellonian University Press 1995, pp.131-149.

Coffee, John C. (1996), 'Institutional Investors in Transitional Economies: Lessons from the Czech Experience, in: Roman Frydman, Cheryl W. Gray and Andrzej Rapaczynski (eds), *Corporate Governance in Central Europe and Russia,* Volume 1, Central European University Press Budapest, London, New York 1996, pp.111-186.

Commission (1995), *White Paper: Preparation of the Associated Countries of Central and Eastern Europe for Integration into the Internal Market of the Union,* Brussels, Commission of the European Union, May 1995.

Dillon, Patricia and Vello Vensel (1995), *Claremont Policy Brief,* mimeo 1995.

Dittus, Peter and Stephen Prowse (1996), 'Corporate Control in Central Europe and Russia: Should Banks Own Shares?' in: Roman Frydman, Cheryl W. Gray and Andrzej Rapaczynski (eds), *Corporate Governance in Central Europe and Russia,* Volume 1, Central European University Press Budapest, London, New York 1996, pp. 20-67.

Dobrinsky, Rumen (1995), *Bad Enterprise Debt in Bulgaria,* WIIW-Research Reports No. 211, Vienna, January 1995.

Federation of European Stock Exchanges (1996), *European Stock Exchange Statistics, July 1996,* Bruxelles.

Fink, Gerhard and Peter Haiss (1996a), *Finanzmarktreform in Osteuropa,* Teil 1: Erbschaft und organisatorischer Aufbau, in: *Bankarchiv* 6/1996, pp. 429-440.

Fink, Gerhard und Peter Haiss (1996b), *Finanzmarktreform in Osteuropa,* Teil 2, Transformationsprobleme und Lösungsansatze, in: *Bankarchiv* 7/1996, pp.1-9.

Fink, Gerhard and Peter Haiss (1997), Financial Market Reform in Eastern Europe, in: Lucjan Orlowski and Dominick Salvatore (eds.), *Trade and Payments in Central and Eastern Europe's Transforming Economies,* Greenwood Press, pp. 1997.

Fink and Schediwy (1992), 'Weak Ownership: Lessons for Eastern Europe', in: H. Siebert (Hrsg.), *The Transformation of Socialist Economies,* J.C.B. Mohr (Paul Siebeck) Tubingen 1992, pp. 81-93.

Frydman, Roman, Cheryl W. Gray and Andrzej Rapaczynski (eds), *Corporate Governance in Central Europe and Russia,* Volumes 1 and 2, Central European University Press Budapest, London, New York, 1996.

Groszek, Mieczyslaw (1995), *Role of Banks in Financing of Economic Development,* PHARE ACE Conference on The Role of the Banking System in the Economic Transformation of Central European Countries, Organizer Urszula Plowiec, Warsaw May 18-20, 1995.

Haiss, Peter (1995). 'Western financial markets offer choices for the East', In: Christopher Saunders (ed), *Eastern Europe in Crisis and the Way Out.* London, Macmillan 1995, pp. 180-196.

Haiss, Peter and Gerhard Fink (1996), Seven Years of Transformation of the financial markets in Central Europe, paper presented at the PHARE-ACE Conference 'Restructuring Transnational Economies in the 90's: Enterprise Behaviour and Financial Intermediaries,' Sofia, October 1996, Organizer Malinka Koparanova.

Hopper, Laura, Henning Esskuchen, Florian Hellmich and Lance Owen (1997), 'Börsen Reformstaaten' in *Bank Austria Investment Focus* 2, pp. 22-23.

IMF (1995), *International Financial Statistics 5.* Washington, D.C., IMF.

Jones, Colin (1997), 'Prickly in Prague' in: *The Banker* 2, pp. 41-48.

Kapoor, Michael (1997), 'Self-destruction' in: Business Central Europe 1, pp. 55-56.

Koth, Adalbert (1997), 'Der Kalkulationszinsfuss zur Berechnung von Ertragswerten' in *RWZ Rechnungswesen-Zeitschrift*, 1, pp. 21-26.

Kozinski, Witold (1995), *The Role of the Banking System in the Transformation Process of the Polish Economy,* PHARE ACE Conference on The Role of the Banking System in the Economic Transformation of Central European Countries, Organizer Urszula Plowiec, Warsaw May 18-20, 1995.

Lewis, Peter and Howard Stein (1997), 'Shifting Fortunes: The Political Economy of Financial Liberalization in Nigeria'. *World Development,* vol 25, No. 1, 1997, pp. 5-22.

Linne, Thomas (1995), *Limits of the Banking System and Potential Chances for Stock Markets in Transformation Economies,* PHARE ACE Conference on The Role of the Banking System in the Economic Transformation of Central European Countries, Organizer Urszula Plowiec, Warsaw May 18-20, 1995.

Marer, Paul (1994), *Hungary During 1988-1994; A Political Economy Assessment in East Central European Economies in Transition,* Study paper submitted to the Joint Economic Committee of the U.S.A., Washington D.C., Congress of the United States 1994, pp. 480-505.

Marer, Paul and Vincent Mabert (1996), 'GE acquires and restructures Tungsram: The first six years (1990-1995)', in: CCET-OECD, *Trends and Policies in Privatisation,* Vol III., No. 1., Paris 1996, pp. 149-185.

Mayer, Colin (1992), *In the Image of the West: Creating Financial Systems in Eastern Europe,* SUERF Colloquium on The New Europe: Evolving Economic and Financial Systems in East and West, October 8-10, 1992, Berlin.

McKinnon, Ronald (1991), 'Financial Control in the Transition from Classical Socialism to a Market Economy', *Journal of Economic Perspectives* 54, pp. 107-22.

Mejstrik, Michal (1995), 'The Banking and the Non-Banking Financial Sectors: Their Role in Privatization of the Economy', in: Ewa Miklaszewska (ed), *Competitive Banking in Central and Eastern Europe.* Krakow: The Jagiellonian University Press 1995, pp. 113-130.

Mejstrik, Michal, Anton Marcincin and Radek Lastovicka (1995), *Privatization in the Czech Republic: Resulting Ownership Structures and Emerging Capital Market.* Paper for the World Congress for Central and East European Studies, Warsaw, August 6-11, 1995.

Meth-Cohn, Danila (1993), 'Directors in Waiting,' *Business Central Europe 5,* pp. 58-59.

Myers, Stewart C. and Raghuram G. Rajan (1997), *The Paradox of Liquidity,* paper presented at the 1997 annual conference of Allied Social Sciences Associations, New Orleans 1997 (MIT School of Management, Cambridge, MA, and Graduate School of Business, University of Chicago, IL).

OECD (1996), *The Czech Republic,* OECD Economic Surveys, Paris.

Palenik, Viliam, (1994), 'The Capital Market in the Slovak Republic After the First Year of its Existence' in *BIATEC,* vol. 2 (1994) No. 8.

Patrick, Suzanne (1996), 'Creating Efficient Capital Markets - Commentary' in Bank Austria (ed) *Perspectives* - Bringing Central and Eastern Europe to Market, Vienna, pp. 65-74.

Podkaminer, Leon (1996), 'Slow Growth in Central and Eastern Europe', WIIW-*Forschungsberichte* 228, 7196.

Schrooten, Mechthild (1994), *Performance of the Banking Sector and Stabilization Problems in Poland,* PHARE ACE Conference on The Role of the Banking System in the Economic Transformation of Central European Countries, Organizer Urszula Plowiec, Warsaw May 18-20, 1995.

Shaffer Mark E. (1990), 'State Owned Enterprises in Poland: Taxation, Subsidization and Competition Policies', *European Economy,* 43, pp. 183-201.

Smith, Roy and Ingo Walter (1992), *Bank Industry Linkages: Models for Eastern European Economic Restructuring,* SUERF Colloquium on The New Europe: Evolving Economic and Financial Systems in East and West, Berlin October 8-10, 1992.

Sobek, Otto (1995), *The Banking System in Slovakia,* PHARE ACE Conference on The Role of the Banking System in the Economic Transformation of Central European Countries, Organizer Urszala Plowiec, Warsaw May 18-20, 1995.

Sobek, Otto (1997), 'Slovak Banking in the Year 1997', *Naronda Banka Slovenska Banking Journal,* Vol. V, January 1997, p. 36.

Sporg, Volker (1995), 'Hohe Renditen bei hohem Risiko,' *Bank Austria Investment Focus 6,* 1-7.

Stern, Nicholas (1995), *Transition Report Update.* London, European Bank for Reconstruction and Development, 1995.

Stiblar Franjo (1994), *Banking in Slovenia,* WIIW-Mitgliederinformation 1994/1.

Stypulkowski Cezary (1995), *Counteracting the Depreciation of Banks' Equity in the Inflationary Environment Versus Fiscal Obligations,* PHARE ACE Conference on The Role of the Banking System in the Economic Transformation of Central European Countries, Organizer Urszula Plowiec, Warsaw May 18-20, 1995.

Triska Dusan (1995), 'Post-Privatisation Securities Markets in the Czech Republic', in: Stilipon Nestor (ed), *Mass Privatisation - An Initial Assessment,* Paris: CCET-OECD 1995, pp. 87-105.

19 Disinflation, Fiscal Positions, and Seigniorage – A Comparative Analysis of the EU Countries and Some Remarks on Economies in Transition

*Peter Brandner and Eduard Hochreiter**

1. Introduction

After high and strongly differing inflation rates in the EU-15 in the 1970s, price pressures have subsided and inflation rates in the EU have converged at the level of 2 per cent in early 1997 with little dispersion. In 1997, all EU countries except Greece may fulfil the Maastricht inflation criterion.[1] Disinflation, however, has been accompanied, at least in the early stages, by sluggish real growth and mounting unemployment, as well as high public deficits and rising government debt. The latter, in some cases, has reached very high, or, indeed, unsustainable levels.[2] After the fiscal 'excesses' of the 1970s, governments during the 1980s have begun to respond to these negative trends and have embarked (often unsuccessfully)[3] on fiscal consolidation programmes. While there might be some correlation between the timing of fiscal retrenchment in the 1990s with the requirement to fulfil the Maastricht fiscal convergence criteria in 1997 in order to qualify for participation in the first wave of EMU, these retrenchment measures have become necessary, regardless of Maastricht. Yet, progress in most cases (with

---

* The views expressed are those of the authors and do not necessarily reflect those of the Oesterreichische Nationalbank or of the Austrian Institute of Economic Research. We are grateful for helpful comments by Georg Winckler, and for efficient research assistance by Daniel T. Dickler and Gert Wehinger; and for secretarial assistance by Angela Berger.

the notable exception of Ireland) has been slow despite multiple efforts. At the end of 1996, only 3 countries (Denmark, Ireland, and Luxembourg) were not subject to the Excessive Deficit Procedure (Art. 101 of the Treaty of Maastricht) and hence, at that time, fit to join EMU on this score.

The paper investigates the links, if any, between disinflation and the evolution of fiscal balances in the EU countries covering the period 1970-1996. The focus is both on the longer-term effects of disinflation on fiscal balances and the role of interest rates and seigniorage in this process and on short-term cyclical relationships. We concentrate on the government's bookkeeping relation as a starting point to consider the conditions under which 'Keynesian' (sticky price model) or 'neoclassical' (flexi price model) effects dominate the disinflation episodes.

The paper also explores if the concomitant reduction in seigniorage income has been large enough to seriously affect fiscal consolidation. Finally, it also tries to shed some light on the question if there are systematic differences between the disinflation consequences in EU countries and selected economies in transition (EIT)[4] for the period 1990-1996.

The paper is organized as follows: Section 2 describes the theoretical and develops the framework for the empirical analysis. In Section 3, the data sources and the methods to identify the disinflation periods are presented. Section 4 reports the results of the empirical analysis. Section 5 very tentatively discusses the lessons, if any, EIT might draw from the experience of the EU countries. Section 6 offers some conclusions.

2. Theoretical background

2.1 The model

Consider first a standard AS-AD model[5] of an open economy, where disinflation induced by monetary contraction reduces real GDP. This works via the interest rate channel provided the country is large enough to influence world interest rates. Under this assumption, the recessionary effects are smaller under fixed than floating exchange rates. Expectations are static, and wages and prices react only sluggishly to changes in demand and supply. Fiscal policy is exogenously given.[6] If, however, government revenue (including seigniorage) and/or government expenditure varies with GDP and employment, fiscal policy becomes endogenous. This worsens the fiscal balance with disinflation unless fiscal policy counteracts with discrete measures. This effect may be exacerbated if real interest rates rise during the disinflation period.

In contrast, in a 'neoclassical world' where wages and prices are flexible and where there is a credible long-run commitment by policy makers to disinflation, real interest rates need not rise, real GDP and employment need not contract and fiscal balances need not worsen. Disinflation induced by monetary contraction is transmitted in this model via the wealth and expectations channel.

Dornbusch (1988) in his study on Ireland did indeed find support for a link between disinflation, rising real rates of interest, output and employment losses, and deficit and debt explosion in the 1980s.[7] Instead, McDermott and Wescott (1996), when analysing twenty OECD countries have found that credibility effects may offset the recessionary disinflation impact effects quite early in the process. Hence, real interest rates need not rise, no output losses and budget deficit increases need to occur, especially over the medium term. If fiscal positions do deteriorate, this must be due to other factors, e.g., discretionary expenditure programmes or revenue cuts.

Consider the government's bookkeeping relation in discrete form:

$$(B_t - B_{t-1}) = r_t B_{t-1} + D_t - H_t \qquad (1)$$

where B_t denotes the level of real public debt at time t, D_t the real primary public deficit excluding seigniorage revenue and H_t real seigniorage. The primary deficit is split up into

$$D_t = G_t - T_t \qquad (2)$$

where G_t denotes real public expenditure and T_t real public revenue excluding seigniorage revenue.

Seigniorage is proxied by

$$H_t = i_t M_{t-1} \qquad (3)$$

where M_{t-1} is the lagged real monetary base and i the nominal rate of interest.

By substituting (2) and (3) into (1), we obtain

$$(B_t - B_{t-1}) = r_t B_{t-1} + (G_t - T_t) - i_t M_{t-1} \tag{4}$$

and expressing the appropriate variables in terms of GDP yields

$$(b_t - b_{t-1}) = \Delta b_t = (r_t - y_t)b_{t-1} + (g_t - t_t) - i_t m_{t-1} \tag{5}$$

Ideally, we would need a model explicitly taking into account the interactions among the variables in equation 5. As a first rough approximation, we assume that the growth rate of GDP y, g and t are a function of π, and that r and i depend both on π and π^e.[8] We rewrite equation 5 as a behavioural equation, each argument being a function of π and π^e respectively, except b_{t-1} and m_{t-1}, which are predetermined.

$$\Delta b_t(\pi_t) = \{r[\pi^e_{t+1}(\pi_t)] - y_t(\pi_t)\}b_{t-1} + g_t(\pi_t) - t_t(\pi_t) - i_t[(\pi^e_{t+1}(\pi_t)]m_{t-1} \tag{6}$$

Differentiating equation 6 (discrete approximation) with respect to π and π^e yields:

$$\frac{\Delta b_t}{\Delta \pi_t} = [\frac{\Delta r_t}{\Delta \pi^e_{t+1}} \cdot \frac{\Delta \pi^e_{t+1}}{\Delta \pi_t} - \frac{\Delta y_t}{\Delta \pi_t}]b_{t-1} + \frac{\Delta g_t}{\Delta \pi_t} - \frac{\Delta t_t}{\Delta \pi_t} - [\frac{\Delta i_t}{\Delta \pi^e_{t+1}} \cdot \frac{\Delta \pi^e_{t+1}}{\Delta \pi_t}] \cdot m_{t-1} \tag{7}$$

The effect of disinflation on public debt depends on the numerical value of the various parameters. Depending on the assumptions adopted ('Keynesian-type' or 'neoclassical'), *a priori* restrictions may be placed on these parameters.

$\frac{\Delta i}{\Delta \pi^e} \leq 1:$ If the nominal interest rate i changes proportionately to the expected inflation rate, i.e., $\frac{\Delta i}{\Delta \pi^e} = 1:$, the real interest rate r, cet. par., remains constant: $\frac{\Delta r}{\Delta \pi^e} = 0$, otherwise it changes.

$0 \leq \dfrac{\Delta \pi^e}{\Delta \pi} \leq 1$: If, say, disinflation is fully credible and perceived as being permanent, expected inflation changes *pari passu* with actual inflation, i.e., $\dfrac{\Delta \pi^e}{\Delta \pi} = 1$, otherwise $\dfrac{\Delta \pi^e}{\Delta \pi} \neq 1$.

$\dfrac{\Delta y}{\Delta \pi} \geq 0$: Phillips curve relationship. If $\dfrac{\Delta y}{\Delta \pi} = 0$, the Phillips curve is vertical.

$0 \leq \dfrac{\Delta G}{\Delta \pi} \leq 1$ and $0 \leq \dfrac{\Delta T}{\Delta \pi} \leq 1$: Denotes the reaction of government receipts and expenditures to changes in the inflation rate. If $\dfrac{\Delta G}{\Delta \pi}$ and $\dfrac{\Delta T}{\Delta \pi} = 1$, government revenues and expenditures are fully indexed.

The following *a priori* conclusions emerge:
'Keynesian' short-run effects are to be expected if one or more of the following assumptions hold:

(1) $\dfrac{\Delta \pi^e}{\Delta \pi} < 1$: less than fully credible permanent disinflation, *cet. par.*, implying a rise in the real rate of interest, i.e., $\dfrac{\Delta r}{\Delta \pi^e} > 0$.

(2) $\dfrac{\Delta y}{\Delta \pi} > 0$: there is an inflation/growth trade-off.

(3) $\dfrac{\Delta G}{\Delta \pi} > \dfrac{\Delta T}{\Delta \pi}$: The degree of indexation of government expenditure is higher than that for revenues (taxes), i.e., expenditure reduction needs discretionary measures.

Hence, the fiscal balance will deteriorate the more in a disinflation episode, the more r rises (i.e., the less i falls), the more y contracts, the higher the initial level of debt b_{-1} and the more seigniorage declines.

In contrast, if we make 'neoclassical' assumptions, (flexible wages and prices) and assume a fully indexed fiscal system we get:

(4) $\dfrac{\Delta i}{\Delta \pi^e} = 1$: the nominal rate of interest changes proportionately with π^e.

(5) $\dfrac{\Delta \pi^e}{\Delta \pi} = 1$: fully credible policies, which are permanent (i.e., no reneging).

(6) $\dfrac{\Delta y}{\Delta \pi} = 0$: vertical Phillips curve.

In this case the term: $\dfrac{\Delta b_t}{\Delta \pi_t} = [\dfrac{\Delta r_t}{\Delta \pi^e_{t+1}} \cdot \dfrac{\Delta \pi^e_{t+1}}{\Delta \pi_t} - \dfrac{\Delta y_t}{\Delta \pi_t}]b_{t-1} + \dfrac{\Delta g_t}{\Delta \pi_t} - \dfrac{\Delta t_t}{\Delta \pi_t}$ of

equation 8 equals zero, provided the budget is initially balanced and

$$[\dfrac{\Delta i_t}{\Delta \pi^e_{t+1}} \cdot \dfrac{\Delta \pi^e_{t+1}}{\Delta \pi_t}] \cdot m_{t-1} > 0$$

or, expressed differently:

(7) $\quad \Rightarrow \quad \Delta b = -(\Delta \pi) \cdot m_{t-1}$

Equation 8 contains an important result. It states that under neoclassical assumptions, and a constant r, y remains unaffected by disinflation, and fiscal expenditure and revenue are fully indexed, public debt increases, because of seigniorage revenue losses. Note that this result is due to the fact that the central bank accounts are not consolidated with the government. This is justifiable because central banks are (as yet still by differing degrees) independent in the EU, and thereby seigniorage generation and its appropriation to the government are logically independent.[9] As a result, successful disinflation[10] requires accompanying fiscal consolidation.

2.2 Effects of disinflation on the cyclical component of the fiscal balance

In general terms, equations 4 to 6 relate the reaction of the debt to GDP ratio b to the respones of i, the credibility effect, and y, the Phillips curve trade-off, to disinflation. The stronger these effects are, the more debt accumulates. Both short-term, cyclical and longer-term effects may be expected.

In order to investigate the cyclical relationship between the budget deficit, inflation and disinflation as well as other variables of interest, we consider the following equation:

$$(b - b^*) = \beta_1 DP + \beta_2 DM + \gamma X \tag{8a}$$

The cyclical budget $(b - b^*)$ is measured as the difference between the actual budget balance d and its trend d^*. d^* is calculated with a Hodrick Prescott (HP) filter ($\lambda = 100$) and may be interpreted as the structural component of the fiscal deficit.[11] It is explained by two dummies DP and DM and a vector X of variables, representing, i.a., real growth y, its lagged value y_{-1}, the lagged level of the public debt to the GDP ratio b_{-1} and the real rate of interest r. Dummy DP represents periods when inflation exceeds trend inflation, i.e., periods when $(p > p^*)$, whereas dummy DM represents periods when inflation is below trend inflation (disinflation), i.e., $(p < p^*)$. Again, the HP filter provides a measure of trend inflation.

The numerical values of β_1 and β_2 measure that part of the budget deficit (in percentage points) that is due to the fact that the economy is in an inflation or disinflation state as defined above. In case the two coefficients β_1 and β_2 are statistically different from each other, the fiscal balance reacts asymmetrically to inflation and disinflation episodes as defined above. The coefficient γ denotes the influence of the other variables on the cyclical budget balance.

We also estimated the following equation

$$(b - b^*) = \beta_1 DP * (p > p^*) + \beta_2 DM * (p < p^*) + \gamma X \tag{8b}$$

In this multiplicative-dummy-specification, β_1 and β_2 measure the influence of 'disinflation' or 'excess-inflation' on the cyclical budget balance.

3. The data

The sample comprises the 15 EU countries and selected European economies in transition (EIT). The time coverage for the EU countries is 1970-1996, that for the EIT 1990-1995. Data are taken from OECD, EUROSTAT, WIIW and BIS sources and are contained in Tables 1 and 1a in the annex.[12] Whenever possible, the fiscal variables and long-term interest rates are selected according to 'Maastricht standards', although this often implies a break in the time series. The inflation measure is the consumer price index CPI as published by the OECD for reasons of time coverage.[13]

3.1 Identification of disinflation periods

There are several ways to identify disinflation periods. In their study on the UK inflation cycle, Artis et al. (1995, p.1146) use the monthly year on year retail price index to identify disinflation episodes. Ball (1994, p. 157) calculates trend inflation from $(t - 4)$ to $(t + 4)$ quarters to smooth short-term oscillations of the inflation rate.

An HP filter is employed to extract the long-term movements in the inflation rate. Overall, the differences between the three methods are minor as far as the length of the period is concerned. However, the absolute peak/trough values may differ substantially (e.g. Germany). To disregard extreme values may be quite warranted as thereby the oil price-induced peaks are cut off (see Neely and Waller 1997, p. 58).

As the purpose of this study is to investigate the effects of *deliberate disinflation* on fiscal positions, the focus of interest is on longer lasting durable disinflation periods, not the ones that occurred because of price/wage controls. The latter, in general, unwind quickly once the controls are removed. In the 1970s such behaviour could be observed frequently (e.g., Greece 1974-1976).

Table 1. Basic disinflation data

Country	Disinflation periods (DI) (monthly data; HP-filtered)			Fiscal positions (change start-end in x-points; % of GDP)				Interest rates (change; start-end)			Seigniorage (SE) (% of GDP)		
	Start end	Inflation maximum (in %)	DI (in %-age points)	Duration (No. of months)	gross debt change	budget deficit change	primary balance excl SE change	primary balance excl SE av. level	nominal rate of interest change	real rate of interest change	real rate of interest av. level	average SE inflation periods	average SE DI inflation periods	average SE loss
1. Austria														
period 1:	9/74-11/78	9.2-3.5	5.7	46	16.3	-4.1	-2.8	-2.0	-1.5	+4.4	2.2	1.0	1.1	-0.1
period 2:	3/81-2/87	6.7-1.4	5.3	71	21.4	-2.6	-0.7	-1.5	-2.3	+3.1	4.1	1.0	0.9	0.1
period 3:	8/92-8/96	3.9-1.9	2.0	48	13.5	-2.4	-3.6	-1.3	-1.9	+0.1	4.1	0.7	0.7	0.0
2. Belgium														
period 1:	2/75-12/78	13.4-4.3	9.1	46	7.9	-1.2	-0.2	-3.4	0.0	+8.4	0.8	1.1	1.1	0.0
period 2:	9/82-5/87	8.5-1.1	7.4	56	39.1	+5.2	+4.1	-1.9	-6.0	+0.3	5.4	1.3	1.0	0.3
period 3:	8/90-9/95	3.5-1.7	1.8	61	0.0	+3.1	+0.8	+3.0	-2.1	-0.2	5.5	0.7	0.5	0.2
3. Denmark														
period 1:	n.a.	n.a.	n.a.	n.a.	n.a.	n.a.	n.a.	n.a.	n.a.	n.a.		0.7	n.a.	n.a.
period 2:	8/80-4/86	12.0-3.8	8.2	68	8.8	+10.3	+11.5	-1.1	-8.7	+0.4	8.0	0.6	0.6	0.0
period 3:	10/88-5/93	4.6-1.5	3.1	55	20.5	-6.3	-7.3	+2.0	-4.7	-0.4	7.3	0.6	0.5	0.1
4. Finland														
period 1:	3/75-1/79	17.8-7.5	10.3	46	3.2	-1.9	-3.0	+4.2	+0.7	+12.8	-3.1	0.3	0.3	0.0
period 2:	2/81-9/86	12.2-3.3	8.9	67	5.2	-1.1	-0.2	+1.0	-0.7	+8.1	5.0	0.5	0.6	-0.1
period 3:	9/89-12/96	6.6-0.5	6.1	87	44.7	-10.6	-8.3	-5.2	-5.4	+1.4	6.8	0.8	0.9	-0.1

Table 1. Basic disinflation data (cont.)

Country	Disinflation periods (DI) (monthly data; HP-filtered)			Fiscal positions (change start-end in x-points; % of GDP)				Interest rates (change; start-end)			Seigniorage (SE) (% of GDP)		
	Start end	Inflation maximum (in %)	DI (in %-age points)	Duration (No. of months)	gross dept change	budget deficit change	primary balance excl SE change	primary balance excl SE av. level	nominal rate of interest change	real rate of interest change	real rate of interest av. level	average SE inflation periods	average SE DI inflation periods	average SE loss
5. France														
period 1:	11/74-2/78	13.0-9.2	3.8	39	n.a.	-2.4	-1.3	-1.6	-0.4	+5.2	-0.3	1.0	0.9	0.1
period 2:	3/81-2/87	13.6-2.8	10.8	71	11.3	-2.7	-1.1	-1.6	-4.7	5.9	3.8	0.8	0.7	0.1
period 3:	2/90-9/94	3.5-1.7	1.8	55	17.4	-3.6	-2.2	-1.2	-1.3	0.5	5.7	0.6	0.4	0.2
6. Germany														
period 1:	12/73-6/78	7.2-3.0	4.1	54	10.5	-1.1	+0.8	-3.6	-4.7	-0.1	3.1	0.9	0.6	0.3
period 2:	7/81-12/86	6.2-(-0.1)	6.3	65	6.0	+2.4	+3.6	-1.0	-4.5	+2.4	5.0	0.8	0.8	0.0
period 3:	6/92-12/96	4.9-1.3	3.6	54	16.7	-1.2	0.0	-1.0	-1.7	+1.2	3.8	0.7	0.7	
7. Greece														
period 1:	4/74-2/77	24.1-11.9	12.2	34	7.6	n.a.	-0.6	-2.7	-0.5	+10.2	-4.5	1.6	1.8	-0.2
period 2:	12/80-10/88	24.9-13.4	11.5	94	39.5	-6.0	+2.3	-7.6	-1.1	+7.4	-1.8	2.5	3.3	-0.8
period 3:	1/91-12/96	20.5-7.9	12.6	71	18.3	+3.6	+5.9	-1.4	-7.7	5.7	6.5	2.5	2.8	-0.3
8. Ireland														
period 1:	5/75-7/78	20.3-9.1	11.2	38	4.2	-2.7	-7.5	-6.8	-1.8	+2.9	-3.6	2.0	2.1	-0.1
period 2:	6/81-2/88	20.2-2.5	17.7	80	39.7	+4.3	+7.4	-6.5	-6.0	+11.1	4.9	2.1	1.4	0.7
period 3:	11/89-12/96	3.8-1.5	1.5	87	-28.4	-0.1	-2.5	+2.2	-1.5	+0.7	6.1	0.9	0.7	0.2

Table 1. Basic disinflation data (cont.)

Country	Disinflation periods (DI) (monthly data; HP-filtered)				Fiscal positions (change start-end in x-points; % of GDP)				Interest rates (change; start-end)			Seigniorage (SE) (% of GDP)		
	Start end	Inflation maximum (in %)	DI (in %-age points)	Duration (No. of months)	gross debt change	budget deficit change	primary balance excl SE change	primary balance excl SE av. level	nominal rate of interest change	real rate of interest change	real rate of interest av. level	average SE inflation periods	average SE DI inflation periods	average SE loss
9. Italy														
period 1:	12/74-8/78	19.1-13.0	6.1	44	10.0	-2.2	-0.8	-9.7	+3.8	+12.1	-4.4	1.9	2.6	-0.7
period 2:	10/80-7/87	19.9-4.7	15.2	81	32.5	-2.4	+1.0	-7.4	-4.8	+10.7	3.1	2.6	2.4	0.2
period 3:	7/90-11/96	6.5-3.3	3.2	77	25.4	+4.4	+4.4	-2.3	-3.9	-1.8	6.4	1.9	1.9	0.0
10. Luxemb.														
period 1:	8/75-9/78	10.9-3.5	7.4	37	n.a.	+3.5	n.a.	n.a.	-0.1	+6.6	-0.2	-	-	-
period 2:	9/82-3/87	9.4-(-0.2)	9.6	54	n.a.	+5.6	n.a.	n.a.	-1.7	+8.3	3.7	-	-	-
period 3:	4/90-7/96	3.7-1.4	2.3	75	1.3	-3.5	n.a.	-0.1	-2.5	+0.7	4.3	-	-	-
11. Netherl.														
period 1:	4/75-11/78	10.2-4.1	6.1	43	0.2	+0.5	+0.3	-0.7	-1.1	+4.6	1.4	0.6	0.6	0.0
period 2	5/81-4/87	6.8-(-0.5)	7.3	71	29.3	-1.7	+1.1	-1.9	-4.3	+2.3	5.6	0.6	0.6	0.0
period 3:	12/91-1/96	3.3-1.9	1.4	49	1.2	-1.1	-0.6	+0.6	-1.8	+0.5	4.2	0.6	0.7	-0.1
12. Portugal														
period 1:	n.a.	n.a.	n.a.	n.a.	n.a.	n.a.	n.a.	n.a.	n.a.	n.a.	n.a.	2.0	n.a.	n.a.
period 2:	3/84-9/87	28.4-9.0	19.4	42	10.4	+0.6	+5.5	-2.6	-12.9	+5.9	4.0	3.7	4.0	-0.3
period 3:	5/90-12/96	13.2-3.0	10.2	79	0.0	+2.7	+1.3	-1.1	-9.4	0.0	5.2	n.a.	2.7	n.a.

Table 1. Basic disinflation data (cont.)

Country	Disinflation periods (DI) (monthly data; HP-filtered)				Fiscal positions (change start-end in x-points; % of GDP)				Interest rates (change; start-end)			Seigniorage (SE) (% of GDP)		
	Start end	Inflation maximum (in %)	DI (in %-age points)	Duration (No. of months)	gross debt change	budget deficit change	primary balance excl SE change	primary balance excl SE av. level	nominal rate of interest change	real rate of interest change	real rate of interest av. level	average SE inflation periods	average SE DI inflation periods	average SE loss
13. Spain														
period 1:	10/77-12/8	23.2-17.6	5.6	38	3.8	-2.0	-1.9	-3.3	+5.6	+13.4	(-7.8)	1.3	1.4	-0.1
period 2:	10/77-3/88	23.2-5.0	18.2	125	31.8	-2.5	-0.5	-5.1	+2.4	+20.2	0.3	2.5	2.4	0.1
period 3:	2/90-12/96	6.8-3.3	3.5	82	24.6	-1.6	-0.4	-2.7	-4.7	-1.7	6.1	n.a	1.7	n.a
14. Sweden														
period 1:	n.a.	n.a.	n.a.	n.a.	n.a.	n.a.	n.a.	n.a.	n.a.	n.a.	n.a.	0.7	n.a.	n.a.
period 2:	12/80-2/87	12.9-4.0	8.9	74	25.1	-2.8	+5.0	-3.5	-1.4	+7.2	2.7	0.8	0.9	-0.1
period 3:	10/90-12/96	10.1-(-0.4)	10.5	74	25.1	-2.8	-4.8	-7.7	-3.6	+5.3	5.5	n.a	1-0	n.a
15. UK														
period 1:	8/75-8/78	22.3-9.9	12.4	36	-3.9	+0.3	+0.6	-2.9	-1.9	+12.5	-2.4	1.0	1.0	0.0
period 2:	5/80-1/87	16.8-3.7	13.1	80	3.9	+0.6	+1.3	-0.3	-4.1	8.4	4.0	0.8	0.5	0.3
period 3:	5/90-8/93	8.9-1.9	7.0	39	14.7	-4.2	-3.7	-3.9	-1.8	+3.2	4.0	0.4	0.4	0.0
16. EU														
period 1:	2/75-9/78	14.3-9.5	4.8	43	-	-	-	-	-	-	-	-	-	-
period 2:	10/80-6/87	12.9-3.2	9.7	80	-	-	-	-	-	-	-	-	-	-
period 3:	7/90-12/96	5.7-2.3	3.4	77	-	-	-	-	-	-	-	-	-	-

Table 1a. Basic disinflation data

Country	Disinflation periods (DI) (monthly data; HP filtered)			Fiscal positions (change; start-end in x-points; % of GDP)			Interest rates (change; start-end)			Seigniorage (SE) (% of GDP)		
	Start end	Inflation maximum (in %)	DI (in %-age points)	Dura-tion (no of years)	Gross debt change	Budget deficit change	Budget deficit average level	Nominal rate of interest change	rate of interest change	Nominal rate of interest av. level	average seignioriage Disinfla-tion tax	oppor-tunity cost
Czech Republic	1991-1996	56.7-8.8	47.6	5		+2.0	-0.7	n.a.		n.a.	3.0ˣ	2.9ˣ
Hungary	1991-1994	35.0-18.8	16.2	3		-0.9	-5.6	+3.0		23.6*	7.4	7.6
Poland	1990-1996	585.8-19.9	565.7	6		+1.3	-2.9	-9.0		33.8*	3.8ˣˣ	3.6ˣˣ
Romania	1993-1996	256.1-38.8	217.3	3		-3.4	-3.8	-80.2		67.6*	1.8ˣ	1.5ˣˣˣ
Slovakia	1991-1996	61.2-5.8	55.4	5		-4.2	-4.0	n.a.		n.a.	1.1ˣˣˣ	1.4ˣˣˣ
Slovenia	1992-1996	207.3-9.9	197.4	4		-0.2	0.1	-46.4		31.0**	18.2ˣˣˣˣ	

* base rate   ** interbank rate
ˣ 1993-1995   ˣˣ 1992-1995   ˣˣˣ 1993-1994   ˣˣˣˣ 1992-1994

To qualify as disinflation period the following requirements must be satisfied:

1. The length of the disinflation period must be at least 36 months. This is longer than the periods used in other studies.[14] The rationale for this choice is that we are looking for a period that is long enough to cover both possible impact and second round effects of disinflation on fiscal balances, when fiscal countermeasures become effective. Moreover, we want to eliminate movements in the inflation rate that are due to short-term wage/price controls.
2. The turning points are defined as the maximum and minimum values of the CPI inflation rate.
3. In cases where there are more than one identical maximum/minimum values, those values which maximize the disinflation period were chosen.

The identified disinflation and inflation episodes are reported in Table 1. In cases where the episodes overlap, 'decenia boundaries' (i.e., 1970s, 1980s and 1990s) were either split up or considered in that decennium, to which more observations belong.

4. Empirical results

In this section, we study the empirical evidence to draw conclusions if, and to what extent, 'Keynesian' sticky price or 'neoclassical' flexi price reactions dominate the effects of disinflation on fiscal balances (see section 2.1).

4.1 Short-term, cyclical developments

As a first step equations (8a, 8b) are estimated by OLS. We are aware that due to endogeneity problems, a simultaneous equation bias may arise. However, we think that only in cases when contemporaneous growth enters the equation this is a serious problem when an IV approach should be used. The sign of γ depends on the variable considered.

Table 2a. Short-term determinants of the cyclical budget balance
(equ. 8a)

Country	DP	DM	GDPAGR	GDAGR (-1)	FISBAC (1)	R2	DW
AT	-0.38 (-0.97)	- 0.97**		0.24* (2.77)		0.24	1.72
BE	-0.54 (-1.36)	-0.72 (-1.61)	0.28** (2.34)		0.47** (5.02)	0.33	1.68
DK	- 2.06**	- 0.83**		0.66** (4.30)	0.64** (7.51)	0.72	2.67
FI	- 1.09**	-0.66* (-1.73)		0.34** (4.93)	0.49** (3.38)	0.47	1.54
FR	- 0.69**	- 0.82**	0.31** (3.34)		0.46** (3.53)	0.34	1.68
DE	-0.12 (-0.32)	0.12 (1.04)			0.21** (2.71)	-0.03	1.88
IE	-0.43 (-0.99)	0.42 (1.28)			0.48** (2.44)	0.24	1.68
IT	-0.58* (-1.68)	- 1.18**	0.33** (3.29)		0.34** (2.81)	0.31	1.64
NL	-0.63* (-1.90)	- 0.54**		0.24** (2.27)		0.12	1.88
PT	- 1.82**	-0.64 (-1.28)		0.30** (2.98)	-0.37** (-2.41)	0.13	1.98
ES	-0.56* (-1.79)	-0.39 (-0.75)		0.17** (2.20)	0.33* (1.86)	0.20	1.94
SE	- 1.70**	-1.73* (-1.90)	0.70** (2.56)	0.37** (2.14)	0.77** (9.80)	0.64	1.38
GB	-0.52* (-1.83)	-0.54 (-1.34)		0.23** (2.21)	0.60** (5.18)	0.48	1.46

** Significant at 5%.
* Significant at 10%.

Table 2b. Short term determinants of the cyclical budget balance
(equ. 8b)

Country	DP	DM	GDPAGR	GDAGR(-1)	FISBAC(1)	R2	DW
AT	0.34** (2.30)	0.23 (1.10)		0.22** (2.92)		0.27	1.51
BE	0.11 (0.88)	-0.13 (-0.97)	0.27** (2.40)		0.43** (4.30)	0.31	1.65
DK	-0.27** (-2.02)	-0.93** (-2.16)		0.56** (3.93)	0.71** (9.29)	0.76	2.93
FI	-0.31** (-2.97)	0.41* (1.84)		0.37** (4.96)	0.49** (3.31)	0.51	1.56
FR	-0.05 (-0.50)	0.06 (0.41)		0.27** (3.62)		0.13	1.58
DE	-0.45** (-2.78)	0.02 (0.09)		0.12 (1.61)	0.16 (1.53)	-0.00	1.94
IE	-0.27* (-1.68)	0.03 (0.30)			0.36** (2.05)	0.21	1.57
IT	-0.02 (-0.26)	0.15 (1.39)	0.31** (3.05)		0.31** (2.57)	0.24	1.91
NL	-0.26 (-0.85)	0.14 (0.43)		0.24** (2.14)		0.11	1.79
PT	-0.41 (-1.61)	0.27 (1.05)		0.42** (2.51)	-0.44** (-2.69)	0.16	2.03
ES	-0.01 (-0.16)	0.23 (1.01)	0.24** (2.41)		0.41** (2.80)	0.17	2.00
SE	-0.49* (-1.94)	0.66 (1.32)	0.84** (4.08)		0.89** (12.33)	0.64	1.33
GB	-0.01 (-0.18)	0.56** (6.41)	0.24** (3.00)	0.20** (2.27)	0.72** (7.97)	0.66	1.42

** Significant at 5%.
* Significant at 10%.

As can be seen, we are unable to find significant positive effects of inflation and negative effects of disinflation on the cyclical balance position. Inflation/disinflation does not appear to have an asymmetric influence on the short-term cyclical balance. This is not necessarily at variance with the results we achieved for the longer-term interrelationships (see section 4.2).

4.2 Longer-term developments

According to equation (6) the level of public debt increases if real interest rates rise, real growth contracts, the primary balance worsens and seigniorage declines. Under these conditions, debt accumulates until corrective action is taken, real growth picks up or real interest rates decline again.

4.2.1 The relationship between disinflation and changes in general government debt

Graph 1 relates disinflation, as measured in percentage points from the identified inflation peak to the trough, with the percentage point change in the debt/GDP ratio for the same period.[15] Proceeding this way allows us to focus on the movement of public debt *over the whole* of the disinflation episodes. Note, however, that we are not in a position to say anything about particular movements *during* disinflation or regarding the sustainability of debt or deficit levels.

Graph 1

Disinflation (DI) and general government debt (GGD)
(change in percentage points)

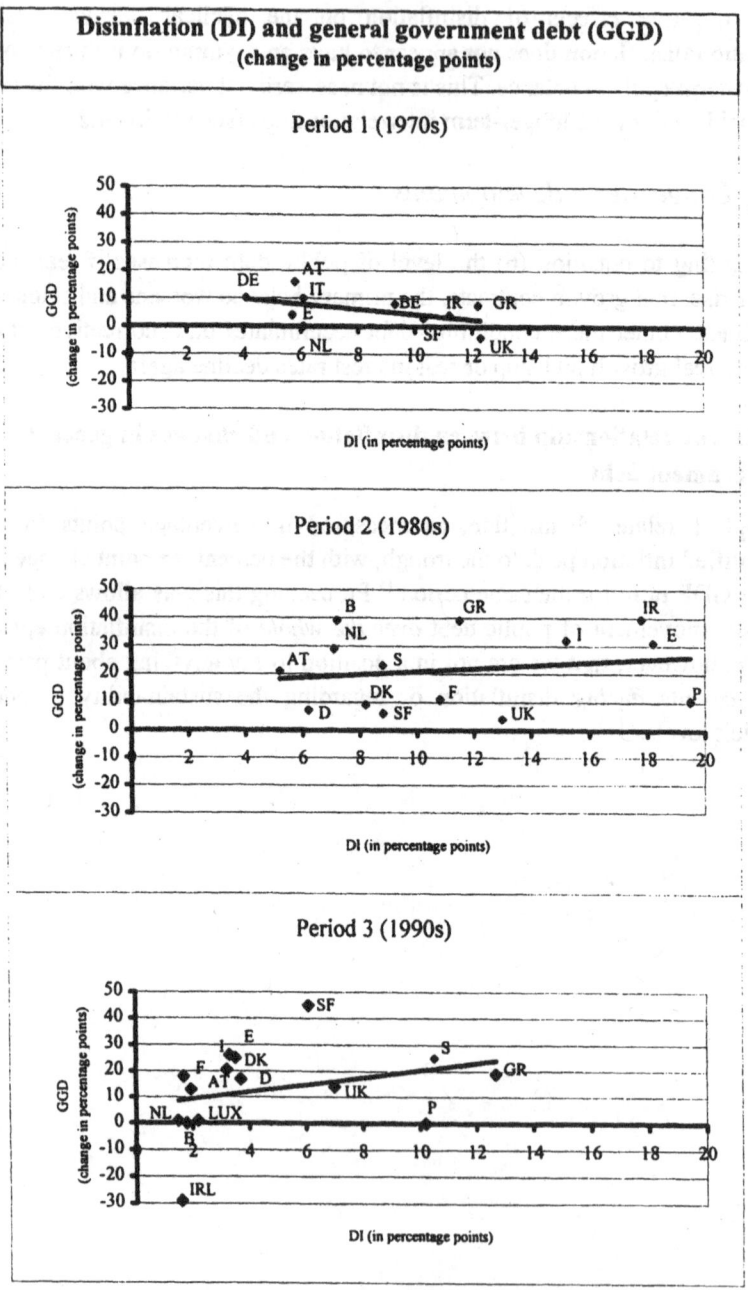

The graph underlines the sharply different general developments in the three periods under consideration: the 1970s, 1980s and the 1990s. Debt in the disinflation episodes in the 1970s did rise with the exception of the UK, but the rise was comparatively small (less than 10 percentage points of GDP except Austria) and disinflation and debt accumulation were negatively correlated, the correlation coefficient being -0.5 (see Table 3).

Table 3. I. Disinflation (DI) and general government debt (GGD)
(change in percentage points)

period	DI mean	CORR coefficient	GGD mean
1	8.3 (3.1)	-0.50	6.0 (5.7)
2	11.3 (4.7)	+0.20	21.5 (13.8)
3	4.7 (3.7)	+0.30	13.0 (16.7)

Note: Standard errors in parenthesis.

II. Disinflation (DI) and real rate of interest change (RIR)
(change in percentage points)

period	DI mean	CORR coefficient	PBeS mean
1	7.8 (3.1)	-0.41	7.8 (4.5)
2	11.2 (4.5)	0.72	6.8 (5.1)
3	4.7 (3.7)	0.73	1.0 2.2

III. Disinflation (DI) and primary balance excluding seigniorage
(change in percentage points)

period	DI mean	CORR coefficient	PBeS mean
1	7.9 (3.2)	-0.25	-1.5 (2.4)
2	11.3 (4.7)	0.07	2.9 (3.6)
3	4.9	0.20	-1.5 (4.0)

In contrast, disinflation and debt accumulation do not appear to be systematically related in the 1980s, when debt accumulation reached 21.5 per cent on average and hence was sharply higher than in the 1970s. Yet, while the absolute amount of disinflation in period 2 surpassed that of the 1970s in all but four countries, (i.e., Austria, Belgium, Finland, and Greece), more disinflation does not necessarily imply more debt accumulation. While in Belgium or in the Netherlands, the decline in inflation during the disinflation periods of the 1980s was less or slightly above that of the 1970s, debt accumulation was low in the earlier but extremely high in the later period. In contrast, in Italy and Ireland, both the amount of disinflation and debt accumulation rose significantly.

In the 1990s, disinflation converged in most EU countries to a range between 1.5-3.5 per cent[16] with vastly differing debt developments. While public debt in Ireland declined by nearly 30 percentage points, it rose in Italy by 25 percentage points. Again, care has to be taken in interpreting the results. Debt might still have increased *start-end*, while, at the same time, the increase might have been halted or reversed *during* the episode, as indeed was the case in Italy or Greece. The dramatic reversals in Ireland (debt declined in the disinflation phase in the 1990s by nearly 30 percentage points) on the one hand and in Finland and Sweden (debt jumped by 45 and 25 percentage points respectively) on the other hand, are clearly borne out in the data.

Having these developments in mind, let us now examine the evolution of seigniorage, real interest rates, and primary balances.

4.2.2 The relationship between disinflation and changes in seigniorage

Recall that the fiscal position in a disinflation period, *cet. par.*, also deteriorates under flexi-price or 'neoclassical' assumptions (equation 7). This result is due to the decline in seigniorage associated with the fall in the inflation rate. We have to ask to what extent has seigniorage income declined and, if so, if this fall was large enough to seriously impede fiscal consolidation and, hence, significantly contributed to the increase in public debt.

Following Drazen (1984), seigniorage (h) using the opportunity cost concept ($h=i \cdot m$) is calculated[17] (see also equation 3). Thereby a rough estimate of the amount of seigniorage generated both over time and across countries[18] is obtained. Disregarding remunerated and non-remunerated reserve requirements and foregoing a more detailed measure of opportunity cost such as in Hochreiter et al. (1996) does not affect the general conclusions. The simplification adopted does, however, overestimate the loss in seigniorage revenue due to disinflation of countries which earlier had relatively high reserve requirements with low or no remuneration.

Regarding the appropriate measure of opportunity cost, we opted for the long-term benchmark rate of interest of 10-year government bonds[19] (or equivalent). This choice can be justified on the grounds that as an alternative to financing (part of) the public deficit by appriopriated seigniorage, many governments usually prefer to issue long term-bonds.[20]

The results obtained are summarized in Table 4 below. With the exception of Ireland, Italy and Spain, our results are broadly in line with those of other studies, e.g., Gros (1992) or Rovelli (1994). Seigniorage in the 1970s and 1980s is, however, overestimated for the three countries mentioned above, because of the exclusion of remunerated minimum reserves, which were sizeable.

For the 'low seigniorage countries' the range of seigniorage was between 0.4 and 1.3 per cent of GDP over the whole period (1970–1996). For the 'high seigniorage countries' Greece, Italy, Portugal and Spain, seigniorage up to the late 1980s/early 1990s ranged between 1.3 and 4.0 per cent of GDP and was indeed a non-negligible source of revenue for the government in these countries.

Yet, in general, seigniorage does not differ significantly between inflation and disinflation periods. This is especially true for the low seigniorage countries. This somewhat surprising result is due to the fact that the observation period starts in 1970, when inflation was on a strong upward trend, while financial markets in most countries under study were still highly regulated and interest rates controlled. The first disinflation period, which started around 1974, coincided with (slow) moves to deregulate interest rates allowing the level of interest rates to respond to high levels of inflation. This interest rate effect has been even stronger in the 1980s in a number of countries. As a consequence, seigniorage did, in fact, *increase* in the disinflation episodes in the 1970s and 1980s, when interest rates were high and rising. This phenomenon predominantly occurred in high seigniorage countries, e.g., Greece and Italy, where seigniorage generation in disinflation periods rose around 0.7–0.8 per cent of GDP.

Table 4. Low seigniorage countries

Country	period	Seigniorage (SE) (period averages, % of GDP)		
		SE inflation period	SE disinflation period	SE loss
Austria	1970s	1.0	1.1	-0.1
	1980s	1.0	0.9	0.1
	1990	0.7	0.7	0.0
	1995	-	0.6	-
Belgium	1970s	1.1	1.1	0.0
	1980s	1.3	1.0	0.3
	1990	0.7	0.5	0.2
	1995	-	0.4	-
Denmark	1970s	0.7	n.a.	n.a.
	1980s	0.6	0.6	0.0
	1990	0.6	0.5	0.1
	1995	-	0.4	-
Finland	1970s	0.3	0.3	0.0
	1980s	0.5	0.6	-0.1
	1990	0.8	0.9	-0.1
	1995	-	0.9	-
France	1970s	1.0	0.9	0.1
	1980s	0.8	0.7	0.1
	1990	0.6	0.4	0.2
	1995	-	0.3	-
Germany	1970s	0.9	0.6	0.3
	1980s	0.8	0.8	0.0
	1990	0.6	0.7	0.0
	1995	-	0.6	-
Netherlands	1970s	0.6	0.6	0.0
	1980s	0.6	0.6	0.0
	1990	0.6	0.7	-0.1
	1995	-	0.6	-
Sweden	1970s	0.7	0.9	-0.2
	1980s	0.8	1.0	-0.2
	1990	-	-	-
	1995	-	1.1	-
UK	1970s	1.0	1.0	0.0
	1980s	0.8	0.5	0.3
	1990	0.4	0.4	0.0
	1995	-	0.3	-

Table 4. High seigniorage countries

Country	period	Seigniorage (SE) (period averages, % of GDP)		
		SE inflation period	SE disinflation period	SE loss
Greece	1970s	-	-	-
	1980s	2.5	3.3	-0.8
	1990	-	-	-
	1994	-	3.0	-
Ireland	1970s	2.0	2.1	-0.1
	1980s	2.1	1.4	-0.7
	1990			
	1995	-	0.7	-
Italy	1970s	1.9	2.6	-0.7
	1980s	2.6	2.4	0.2
	1990	-	-	-
	1993	-	1.4	-
Portugal	1970s	2.0	n.a.	-
	1980s	3.7	4.0	-0.3
	1990	n.a.	2.7	-
	1994	-	0.9	-
Spain	1970s	1.3	2.4	-1.1
	1980s	2.5	1.7	0.7
	1990	-	-	-
	1995	-	1.4	-

Over time, however, seigniorage has fallen significantly in both types of countries and by 1995 converged around 0.5 per cent of GDP in the low seigniorage countries except in Finland and Sweden. In the high seigniorage countries, seigniorage has declined to 1 and 1.5 per cent of GDP. (For Greece only data up to 1994 were available.)

Moreover, but not explicitly considered in this paper, in the 1990s reserve requirements, have been substantially reduced following financial market liberalization, financial market integration and in preparation EMU.[21] Considering also that part of the seigniorage generated is being retained by the central bank[22] and that according to the accounting rules laid down in the European System of Accounts only that part of seigniorage that is transferred to the government counts as government revenue, the contribution that seigniorage appropriation can make *today* to financing the public deficit in EU countries is very small.

Inasmuch as the decline in seigniorage has been due to disinflation rather than financial market integration, disinflation has indeed made fiscal consolidation more difficult for formerly high inflation countries. But, given the overall size of the fiscal problem in these countries, most of the difficulties originated elsewhere.

In general, seigniorage has been a less important source of revenue for the government than is sometimes argued. Seigniorage did, however, appreciably contribute to financing public deficits in high inflation countries in the 1970s and 1980s. Yet, the difference between seigniorage generation between inflation and disinflation phases *within* decades has been small and did even (in most cases only marginally) rise in the 1980s in some countries, despite overall falling inflation rates.

4.2.3 The relationship between disinflation and real interest rate changes

Under 'neoclassical' assumptions, we would expect that real interest rates, *cet. par.*, remain unaffected by disinflation, while under 'Keynesian' assumptions, we would expect an increase, at least initially, until prices adjust.

In fact, *ex post* real interest rate developments tended to be positively associated with the absolute amount of disinflation in all three periods,[23] although the overall increase during disinflation periods varies sizeably both over countries and periods. Similarly, levels of average real interest rates and their dispersion differ sharply, again with a tendency to converge in the third period to a range of 4-6 per cent in most countries.

Graph 2

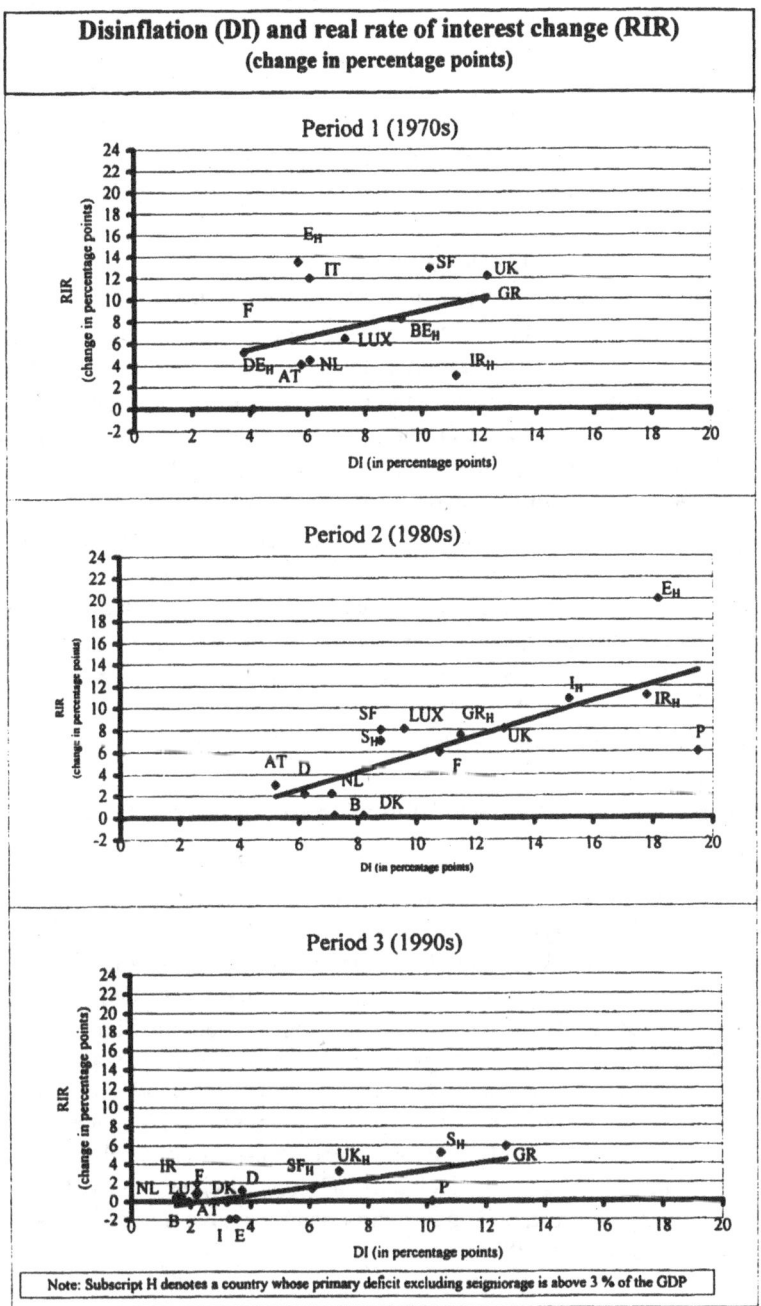

During the 1970s and 1980s there were some spectacular increases in real interest rates in a number of countries. These sharp rises may reflect the combined effect of interrelated developments: (1) the worldwide rise in interest rates after around 1980 increasingly reflecting expected inflation, (2) (sometimes hesitant) moves from direct to indirect monetary control which required interest rate deregulation and (3) a general shift to more stability-oriented economic policies, which, at least initially, may have raised risk premia.

These stylized facts contain prima facie evidence for the existence of 'Keynesian-type' interest rate reactions, at least in periods 1 and 2. Yet, high fiscal deficits have not necessarily implied large increases in real interest rates in disinflation periods, measured start-end, except, perhaps, in period 2 (e.g., Italy, Ireland and Spain). At the end of the disinflation period of the 1990s, real interest rates were at about the same level as at the beginning, and, in some cases, such as Italy and Spain, and marginally in Belgium and Denmark, real interest rates actually declined as measured start-end. Only in three countries they actually rose by more than 2 percentage points.

The results of the 1990s may have been associated with the small amount of disinflation by comparison with earlier periods, the greater credibility of the disinflation process as the increase in public debt could be contained or reversed and, perhaps most importantly of all, the fact that corrective fiscal measures have been introduced and sustained.

Let us now examine the development of primary balances.

4.2.4 The relationship between disinflation and changes in the primary balance

Graph 3 gives us an overall picture of the interrelationship between disinflation and primary balances. Again, very different developments during the three periods emerge. In the 1970s disinflation and the change in primary balances were negatively correlated. More disinflation tended to weaken primary balances. In the 1980s no correlation is apparent, while in the 1990s disinflation and the change in the primary balance as measured start-end were positively correlated (see Table 4). Yet, it is precisely in the 1980s when average primary deficits were the largest (save Finland and Sweden) and had reached unsustainable levels.[24] Public debt exploded by at least 40 per centage points of GDP in Belgium, Greece, Ireland, Italy, and the Netherlands. By contrast, average primary balances have moved into surplus in four countries in the 1990s.

Graph 3

Disinflation (DI) and primary balance excluding seigniorage (PBeS)
(change in percentage points)

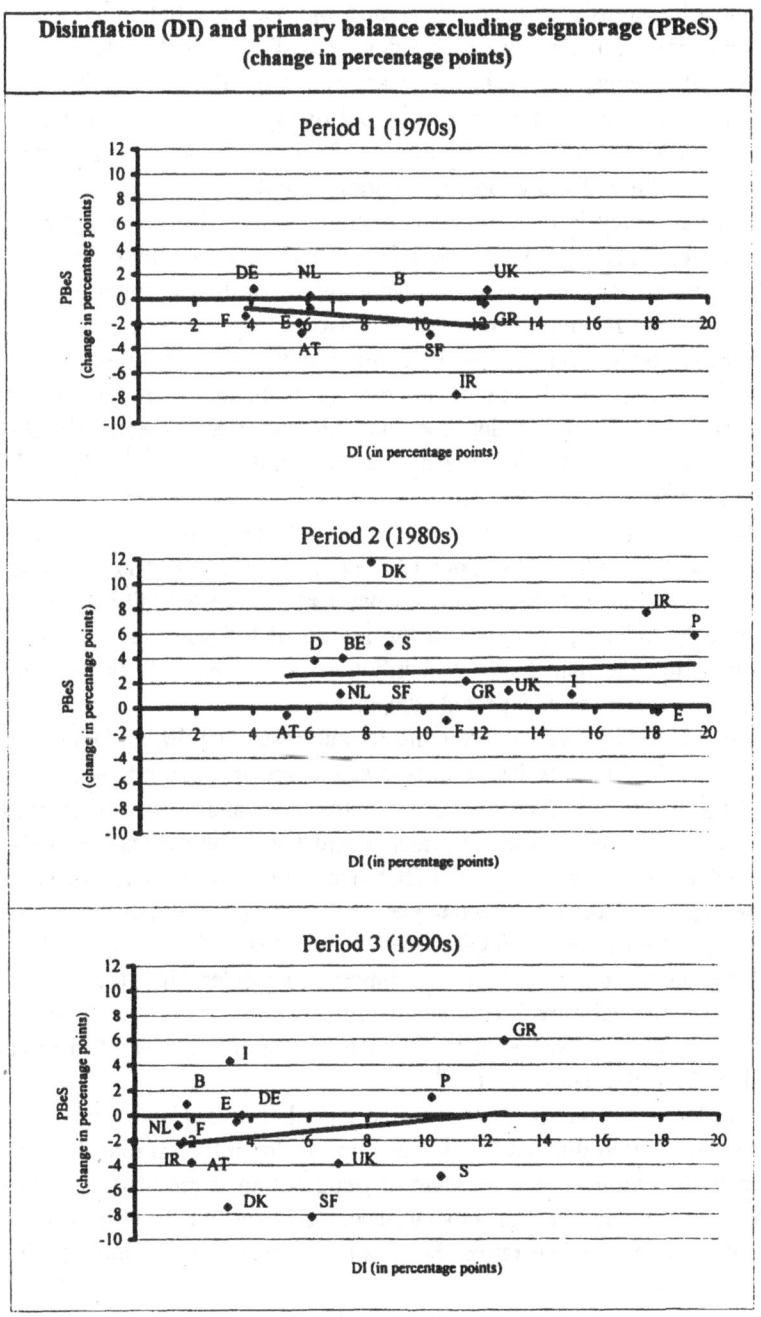

Analysing the effects of disinflation on government revenue and expenditure, we may distinguish between *direct* and *indirect* disinflation effects. The former depend on the degree of indexation of the fiscal system, i.e., the reaction of revenues and outlays to changes in the inflation rate, the latter on the response of government revenues and outlays to (disinflation-) induced changes in GDP growth. Furthermore, discrete policy measures may be introduced both in disinflation and inflation periods.

If fiscal policy is exogenous, as assumed in the 'Keynesian-type' fixed price model in section 2.1, government revenue and expenditure are invariant of disinflation. This assumption is inappropriate for the EU countries, at least as far as fiscal revenues are concerned. Government outlays are, save any contingency budget provisions, determined by the budgetary process, passed by parliament and fixed in nominal terms for the budget year. An unexpected change in the rate of inflation does not directly affect expenditure. On the other hand, revenue is at least partly (de facto) indexed (e.g., VAT), yielding a certain fiscal asymmetry in disinflation episodes. We are not yet in a position to quantify the importance of these effects. But, given that total indirect tax take in the EU is around 10 per cent of the GDP and assuming the elasticity of π to T to be 1, then a 1 per cent unexpected fall in π worsens the primary balance, *cet. par.*, in the region of 0.1 percentage point. It is important to note that it is not disinflation *per se* that affects the primary balance but rather the unexpected component.

More generally, we have to consider automatic stabilizers. Hoeller et al. (1996; pp.17, 57) show that automatic stabilizers are very important for EU countries, most so in Sweden and the Netherlands and lowest in Greece and Portugal. Hence, economic performance and fiscal balances are interrelated. In Sweden, a 1 per cent change in GDP and the tax share affects government borrowing by 0.7 per cent. On the other end of the spectrum, the same change affects government borrowing in Greece by less than 0.4 per cent.

Regarding indirect effects, we have to consider first the effects of disinflation on real growth and then the effects of these changes in real GDP on fiscal balances. One common approach to quantify the cost of disinflation on the GDP is the sacrifice ratio.[25]

We define the sacrifice ratio as the cumulative loss of output during a disinflation period divided by the reduction in the inflation rate. In order to estimate the output loss, a measure of trend output is required. The way of measuring trend output is the crucial issue. Neely and Waller (1997) show the fragility of the sacrifice ratios. Since all the assumptions employed in the literature are more or less ad hoc, we calculate trend output using the HP-filter.[26]

Table 5. Sacrifice ratios

country	period		
	1	2	3
Austria	2.14	1.42	2.54
Belgium	-4.42	4.89	3.85
Denmark	-	1.35	3.42
Finland	1.12	1.07	-0.32
France	3.22	0.84	0.06
Germany	3.12	0.44	1.56
Italy	3.13	0.87	0.69
Netherlands	0.37	1.47	2.23
Spain	-0.58	0.83	-1.14
Sweden	-	0.99	0.72
UK	0.61	2.08	2.40

The results reported in Table 5 indicate that the sacrifice ratio varies widely among the EU countries and over time. France, Italy, and Finland show declining sacrifice ratios over the three periods. In contrast, in Denmark, the Netherlands and the UK the sacrifice ratio rose over time indicating increasing costs of disinflation. There seems to be no systematic relationship between the level of inflation and the sacrifice ratios.

Therefore, the most important effect on fiscal balances over the observation period must originate from discrete fiscal policy actions. We may, in principle, logically distinguish two phases of fiscal effects during a disinflation episode. First, an *impact effect*, where changes in the fiscal balance are, *cet. par.*, dominated by direct disinflation effects and automatic stabilizers. The argument is that even if fiscal measures are introduced at the beginning of a disinflation period, it is assumed that the time necessary to formulate, pass and implement such discretionary (counter)measures, in general, is too long to have an impact at least in the first disinflation year.

Second, there are *second round effects* where, *cet. par.*, discrete policy measures dominate the fiscal outcome.

The prime example for the existence of such effects is Austria, where each of the three disinflation periods coincides with, at times, dramatic fiscal worsening in the first one or two years, which is – still during the disinflation phase – reversed later. We found similar experiences in some episodes also in other countries, e.g., Denmark, Finland, the Netherlands and Sweden. The evidence, how much of these effects can be traced to explicit policy action is mixed. Using the results obtained by Neeley and Waller (1996), there is some evidence, but it is weak. This is most likely due to the rather strict conditions set by Neeley and Waller to qualify as a period of fiscal stimulus or consolidation. But, using OECD country reports to study expansionary and contractionary fiscal policies, one can accumulate more anecdotal evidence.

4.2.5 A first evaluation of the relative importance of various factors

We first consider the evolution of seigniorage and the sacrifice ratio. Then, in order to get an indication regarding the relative weight of real interest rates and the primary balance to the development of public debt, we estimate the following equation:

$$GGD = \alpha 1 + \beta 1 DI \qquad (9a)$$

$$RIR = \alpha 1 + \beta 1 DI \qquad (9b)$$

$$PBeS = \alpha 3 + \beta 3 DI \qquad (9c)$$

where GGD stands for the change in public debt, *RIR* the change in real interest rates and *PBeS* the change in primary balances excluding seigniorage, estimated for each of the three periods and measured start-end. DI stands for disinflation (see section 3.1)

Having in mind that we examine the effect of π on the above variables only (see equation 6) and that we have only 15 observations at most, extreme care has to be taken in interpreting the results reported below.

Table 6.

I	Regression of disinflation (DI) on general government debt (GGD) (changes in percentage points)		
period	DI coeff.	Constant coeff.	R^2
1	-0.919	13.589	0.247
	(2.723)		
2	(-1.618)	14.742	0.042
	0.601	(1.463)	
3	(0.725)	6.545	0.093
	1.371	(0.931)	
	(1.154)		

Note: t-values in parentheses.

II	Regression of disinflation (DI) on real rate of interest change (RIR) (changes in percentage points)		
period	DI coeff.	Constant coeff.	R^2
1	-0.180	-0,077	0,060
	(-0,759)	(-0,039)	
2	0,050	2,312	0,004
	(0,228)	(0,863)	
3	0,209	-2,520	0,039
	(0,698)	(-1,381)	

Note: t-values in parentheses.

III	Regression of disinflation (DI) on primary balance excluding seigniorage (PBeS) (changes in percentage points)		
period	DI coeff.	Constant coeff.	R^2
1	0,590	3,129	0,166
	(1,413)	(0,895)	
2	0,803	-2,205	0,520
	(3,753)	(-0,857)	
3	0,429	-1,005	0,530
	(3,826	(-1,517)	

Note: t-values in parentheses.

Nonetheless some tentative conclusions may be drawn:

1. There has been a secular decline in seigniorage in all countries. This decline has been small, less than 1 per cent of GDP since 1970 in the low seigniorage countries. It has been more pronounced in Greece, Ireland, Italy, Portugal, and Spain. Yet, looking at each period in isolation, we did not find sizeable seigniorage losses in disinflation periods. In the disinflation episode in period 2 (the 1980s) seigniorage even rose in some countries. We may very tentatively conclude that the disinflation effect on seigniorage and hence on public debt is small.
2. Sacrifice ratios vary widely among EU countries. No systematic influence between disinflation and output loss was found in equations 9b and 9c.
3. The statistical significance of the β coefficient is low or hardly existent and the explanatory power is very low. In periods 2 and 3 the coefficient in equation 9a is statistically significant, yet, in absolute terms, real interest rates hardly rose (1 per cent on average; in four countries they actually declined). Hence, this result is not at variance with the credibility literature. Overall, the effect of disinflation on public debt appears to be relatively small.

Being extremely tentative, we may conclude that over all EU countries and all three subperiods periods 'Keynesian type' effects are more likely to have been present than 'neoclassical' flexi price ones. The fact that in the 1990s the increase in debt came to a halt or, by now has been reversed, can be traced back to fiscal adjustment measures, having brought the primary balances into surplus on average. With inflation being as low as it is now, disinflation appears to have come to an end. The challenge now is to keep inflation around current levels. In this context fiscal policy has an important role to play.

5. A fragmentary extension of the analysis to EIT

The opening up of former centrally planned economies implied a systemic change which has important bearings on our analysis.

First, the introduction of market price structures, the lifting of price controls and the outphasing of subsidies resulted in a once-and-for-all jump in the general price level. Under conditions of economic restructuring, this shock has tended to turn into inflation. In some cases, e.g., Poland and Romania, very high rates of inflation ensued, while the price shock was much more subdued in (then) Czechoslovakia. This initial shock set the stage for the following disinflation process, which has to be seen in a much broader sense than disinflation in an EU context. Hungary stands out, because price liberalization had started well before 1990, and hence no such shock occurred.

Second, fiscal policy had to be newly designed. Efforts to contain budget deficits have been central to macroeconomic stabilization. In fact, the countries under consideration have exerted strongly varying degrees of control over budget deficits (see Table 1a). While the Czech Republic maintained the budget close to balance over the whole disinflation process up to now, and Poland succeeded in bringing the deficit quickly down, and Hungary by 1996, Romania still lags.

Third, financial markets also had to be developed from scratch. But, by 1993 (in Romania later) money markets were in place and functioning on the basis of money market interest rates.

Fourth, after the initial output decline, real growth strongly rebounded in all EIT considered, except Hungary.

Fifth, the data problem. Still, not all necessary data are available over the whole observation period with a periodicity of less than one year. No data are available for primary balances. The lack of sufficiently long time series excludes a more rigorous econometric analysis. Hence, we are, at this point, restricted to rather descriptive data mining. Yet, we believe that some interesting provisional results emerge.

Disinflation did start after the initial shock and has been sustained up to now except for a hiccup in Hungary in 1995 and in Romania in 1996. The total amount of disinflation has been much more pronounced than in the EU and has varied widely from a high 560 percentage points (Poland) to less than 50 percentage point, with the exception of Hungary. Today, inflation appears to be converging in the 5-10 per cent range in three of the six countries under consideration. Did this swift disinflation process have negative consequences for the fiscal balance?

Recalling equation 6, we ought to analyse the relationship between disinflation, interest rates, real growth, the primary balance, and seigniorage. Yet, in a transition economy, disinflation and fiscal consolidation measures are a prerequisite for reigniting real growth. Hence, we would expect disinflation and fiscal retrenchment to be positively correlated. In fact, it is discrete fiscal measures which appear to be most important. Similarly, measures to ensure positive real interest rates are central to improve resource allocation and to finance the fiscal deficit via financial markets. Given the problems of fiscal expenditure control and of expanding the revenue base as well as tax collection, we would also expect, at least in the initial period, the appropriation of seigniorage to finance the budget to be of considerable importance.

Having the issues sketched above in mind, we now examine the empirical evidence (see Table 1a). It is not surprising that we do not find a systematic relationship between disinflation and the budget deficit. The central government deficit – measured start-end – worsened sizeably in Romania and Slovakia and marginally so in two other countries while it improved in the Czech Republic and Poland. It is impossible to find any influence of disinflation on the outcome, all the more so, as in Poland the start-end improvement coincided with by far the strongest disinflation and in the Czech Republic with the lowest.

Real *ex post* interest rates were strongly negative at the beginning of the observation period, but by 1996, short-term real interest rates in all EIT considered turned positive. This development – while having an effect on the cost of servicing the debt – has been an explicit aim of economic policy and hence the result of policy action. At the same time, it cannot be excluded that disinflation might have contributed. Yet, it is impossible to quantify this contribution or to label it as a cost of disinflation.

This leaves us with the issue of seigniorage which we will consider in somewhat more detail. We employed the same calculation method as in section 4.2.2 but report in Table 7 not only the results achieved by using the opportunity cost but also the inflation tax concept.

Table 7. Seigniorage selected EIT in %

Country	1990	1991	1992	1993	1994	1995	1996
Czech Republic							
inflation tax	n.a.	n.a.	n.a.	3.8%	2.2%	3.1%	2.3%
opp. cost seigniorage	n.a.	n.a.	n.a.	2.1%	2.4%	4.2%	3.7%
Hungary							
inflation tax	7.3%	11.2%	7.0%	6.5%	5.1%	7.8%	n.a.
opp. cost seigniorage	7.6%	11.1%	6.9%	5.0%	7.2%	8.8%	n.a
Poland							
inflation tax	89.2%	9.5%	5.6%	3.6%	3.0%	2.8%	1.9%
opp. cost seigniorage	n.a.	n.a.	5.7%	3.4%	2.7%	2.5%	1.9%
Romania							
inflation tax	1.9%	30.7%	30.0%	25.9%	10.5%	2.7%	3.2%
opp. cost seigniorage	n.a.	n.a.	n.a.	n.a.	n.a.	n.a.	4.2%
Slovakia							
inflation tax	n.a.	n.a.	n.a.	2.5%	1.5%	1.5%	n.a.
opp. cost seigniorage	n.a.	n.a.	n.a.	1.9%	1.7%	1.0%	n.a.
Slovenia							
inflation tax	n.a.	n.a.	7.6%	1.2%	0.9%	0.6%	0.5%
opp. cost seigniorage	n.a.	n.a.	2.2%	1.4%	1.3%	0.6%	0.7%

Note: The main difference between our results and those achieved in Hochreiter et. al (1996) are due to the fact that remunerated reserve requirements were not deducted here. This difference can be substantial, e.g. for the Czech Republic and Hungary 0.75%-points of the GDP in 1993.

Seigniorage, indeed has been an important source of government revenue in most of the EIT considered, at least at the beginning of the transition process. At the time of the Polish hyperinflation it reached nearly 90 per cent of GDP and in Romania around 30 per cent of GDP. It is striking how quickly seigniorage declined and in 1996 converged to 2-4 per cent of the GDP. In addition, the difference between seigniorage measured as inflation tax and as opportunity cost has been quite small. This is a reflection of near zero or slightly positive real short-term interest rates. Of course, the results critically depend on the interest rate and inflation measure used. In general, however, measured seigniorage at the present time tends to converge regardless of the measurement method employed. In those countries where remunerated minimum reserves have been in force, our results overstate the amount of generated seigniorage. In the case of the Czech Republic and Hungary this overestimation amounted to about 0.75 per cent of GDP (1993).

In fact, as far as the EIT are concerned, this is the only robust result we have arrived at. We were not in a position to quantify the relationship between disinflation *per se* and real interest rates, and that between disinflation and the fiscal balance. The main reason for that is the interrelationship between macroeconomic stabilization and the building of market structures in a transition economy. Yet, the bottom line is the same as that reached for the EU countries. Successful disinflation requires fiscal stringency.

6. Conclusions

Disinflation is no new phenomenon. Since the mid 1970s there have been numerous attempts in the EU countries to disinflate but it took until the 1990s that inflation rates converged at very low levels with little dispersion. The paper argues that the effect of disinflation on fiscal balances depends on whether the economy reacts more according to 'Keynesian-type' fixed price or flexi price 'neoclassical' models. In the former, disinflation coincides with rising real interest rates and rising fiscal deficits and public debt, while in the latter case there need not be an increase in real interest rates or debt. It is shown that also under the latter assumptions fiscal balances worsen with disinflation because of the decline in seigniorage.

The paper – very tentatively – finds that at least in the disinflation episodes of the 1970s and 1980s disinflation is accompanied by rising real interest rates and mounting public debt in a number of EU countries (measured start-end). Yet, it appears that the contribution of the decline in seigniorage and that of disinflation on the change of interest rates cannot explain the debt explosion observed. In fact, the major effect has to be attributed to discrete fiscal policy. Disinflation cannot be sustained and hence successful, unless accompanied by fiscal retrenchment.

In a very fragmentary extension of the analysis to selected European EIT, we found that seigniorage was an important source of government finance at the beginning of the transition process and its rapid decline might have posed problems. However, if so, the effects were (to a large extent) counterbalanced by fiscal measures. The bottom line is the same as the one found for the EU countries.

References

Artis, Michael M. J., Bladen-Hovell, R. C., Osborn, Denise R., Smith, Graham and Zhang, W. (1995), 'Prediciting Turning Points in the UK Inflation Cycle', *The Economic Journal*, 105, September, pp. 1145-1164.

Ball, Laurence (1994), 'What Determines the Sacrifice Ratio?', in Mankiw, Gregory N. (ed.), *Monetary Policy*, Studies in Business Cycles, Volume 29, NBER, The University of Chicago Press, Chicago and London, pp. 155-181.

Buiter, Willem H. (1995), 'Macroeconomic Policy During a Transition to Monetary Union', CEPR, Discussion Paper No. 1222, London, August.

Burda, Michael and Wyplosz, Charles (1993), 'Macroeconomics: a European Text', Oxford University Press, Oxford and New York.

Chiarini, Bruno (1996), 'Disinflation in the Italian Economy in an Optimal Setting', *Open Economies Review*, Vol. 7, No. 4, October.

Dornbusch, Rudiger (1988), 'Credibility, Debt and Unemployment: Ireland's Failed Stabilization', *Economic Policy*, 8, April, pp. 173-210.

Drazen, Allan (1985), 'A General Measure of Inflation Tax Revenue', *Economic Letters* 17, pp. 327-330.

Frenkel, Jacob and Razin, Assad (1992), 'Fiscal Policies and the World Economy', MIT Press, Cambridge, MA.

Gros, Daniel (1992), 'Seigniorage and EMU: The Fiscal Implications of Price Stability and Financial Market Integration', *CEPS Working Document*, No. 69, Brussels.

Hochreiter, Eduard; Riccardo Rovelli and Winckler, Georg (1996), 'Central Banks and Seigniorage: A study of Three Economies in Transition', *European Economic Review* Vol. No. 40, pp. 629-643.

Hoeller, Peter; Louppe, Marie-Odile and Vergriete, Patrice (1996), 'Fiscal Relations within the European Union', *Economics Department Working Papers*, No. 163, OECD, Paris.

Klein, Manfred and Neumann, Manfred (1990), 'Seigniorage: What is It and Who Gets It?, *Weltwirtschaftliches Archiv*, pp. 205-221.

McDermott, John C. and Wescott, Robert F. (1996), 'An Empirical Analysis of Fiscal Adjustments', *International Monetary Fund Staff Papers*, Vol. 43, No. 4 (December), pp. 725-753.

Missale, Alessandro (1991), 'Debt Maturity: The Evidence', Ph.D. dissertation, MIT.

Neely, Christopher J. and Waller, Christopher J. (1997), 'A Benefit-Cost Analysis of Disinflation', *Contemporary Economic Policy*, Vol. XV, January, pp. 50-64.

Rovelli, Riccardo (1994), 'Reserve Requirements, Seigniorage and the Financing of the Government in an Economic and Monetary Union', *European Economy*, Notes and Reports, No. 1, pp. 11-55.

Sachs, Jeffrey D. and Larrain, Felipe B. (1994), 'Macroeconomics: A Global Perspective'; German Version, R. Oldenbourg Verlag, München, Wien.

Notes

1. A country fulfils the inflation criterion if its annual inflation rate does not exceed 1.5 percentage points of the (unweighted) average rate of (harmonized) consumer price inflation of those 3 countries which have the lowest inflation rate. The data are taken from Deutsche Bank Research (*EWU-Monitor* No. 26, February 7, 1997; p. 2).
2. Dornbusch (1988; p. 198) feared just that for Ireland: '...it is entirely clear that a period of high real interest rates in the world would make Irish debt certainly unsustainable.'
3. McDermott and Wescott (1996) studied twenty OECD countries and found that between 1970-1995 there were 74 consolidation episodes of which only 14 could be considered as successful. The unsuccessful cases in the EU countries are due to the failure of the debt ratio to decline.
4. Bulgaria, the Czech Republic, Hungary, Poland, Romania, and Slovakia. The choice of countries was motivated by the desire to mix countries with different economic adjustment policies, different inflation history and the expectation that most of the reform countries included in this paper will be in the first wave of EU East enlargement.
5. See, e. g., Burda and Wyplosz (1993; 218).
6. See also Sachs and Larrain (1994; 465 in the German version).
7. McDermott and Wescott (1996) classified the Irish fiscal consolidation programmes of 1983 and 1984 as failures while they concluded that those of 1987-1989 were successful.
8. Of course, the variables in equation 6 depend on other factors than π and π e as well. Yet, for the purposes of this study, it suffices to explicitly formulate π only.
9. Cf. Klein and Neumann (1990) or Rovelli (1994).
10. Successful disinflation is defined as one that does not have negative effects on fiscal balances.
11. See European Commission (1995).
12. Not all data were available for Denmark, Luxembourg, Portugal and Sweden for period 1 and for Luxembourg in period 2.

13. As we are interested in disinflation periods only, and for some variables such as fiscal variables, only annual data are available, estimation problems emerge. This is particularly true for the EIT.
14. Cf. Artis et al. (1995) and Ball (1994).
15. Note that there is some asymmetry in the time coverage because disinflation is identified using monthly data, while for the other variables only annual data were available.
16. The exceptions being Greece, Portugal, and Sweden where disinflation surpassed 10 percentage points.
17. For a good survey of the literature, see Rovelli (1994).
18. To countercheck, seigniorage using the inflation tax concept (h= Πm) has also been calculated. As could be expected, sizeable quantitative differences emerge in high inflation countries with not so well-developed financial markets.
19. Burda and Wyplosz (1993, p. 300) report work by Missale (1991) who found that the average maturity of outstanding government debt at the end of the 1980s ranged from 0.6 years (Greece) to 9.4 years (UK) with government debt in Germany and the Netherlands having an average remaining maturity of 5.0 and 5.9 years respectively.
20. Gros (1992) also used a long-term rate of interest as opportunity cost measure in this context.
21. Gros (1992) in analyised the effect of moving to EMU on seigniorage assumed that the ratio reserve requirements to GDP would converge at 2% by 1995 and that interest payments on reserve requirements would be gradually reduced to zero.
22. See Hochreiter et.al. (1996).
23. See Table 3.
24. Following Winckler et al. (1996) we calculated the primary positions necessary to stabilize debt levels in the respective years.
25. See, e.g., Dornbusch (1988) or Neelcy and Waller (1994).
26. Being aware that sacrifice ratios are very sensitive to selection of the empirical approach, a more detailed analysis to check the robustness of the results would be useful.

20 The Integration of Russia into the World Monetary System: Macroeconomic Consequences and Problems

Dmitry Smyslov

The course for achieving an openness of the economy in relation to the outer world, its integration into the world economy is the foreign economic aspect of the profound market transformations realized in Russia. In particular, this course presupposes a convergence of the national monetary machinery with the world monetary system, its joining the existing international monetary and financial institutional structures and its entry into the International Monetary Fund (IMF) and the International Reconstruction and Development Bank (World Bank). This latter steps were already taken in 1992.

Up to the present, the national monetary mechanism of Russia has been generally formed as an integral part of the world monetary system. This mechanism corresponds to the demands of the market economy and is defined by rules and aims accepted by the world community. The reformation of the national monetary machinery was going according to well-defined basic directions.

Firstly. A monetary market was formed. Actually, its formation had been started even during the period of the existence of the USSR. It means that the participants of foreign economic transactions do not sell their foreign exchange earnings in a compulsory way at a fixed-rate to the state as it was during the period of the existence of the state monetary monopoly, but they are either reselling them in the market or keeping them on accounts in commercial banks. They have to sell a half of these earnings in the market during a fixed term. An institutional infrastructure of the monetary market, consisting of commercial banks, foreign currency exchanges and non-exchange interbank markets was formed. A more detailed monetary legislation defined the operations in foreign currency.

Second. The formation of a full scale gold market is in process. In the near future, it is expected to issue legislation and regulations which will enable commercial banks and physical persons to buy and sell gold at freely formed market prices and, within certain limits to export it.

Third. In accordance with IMF requirements, multiple currency practices were abolished and rates were unified. Since July 1992, a single ruble/dollar exchange rate for all internal calculations in connection with current international transactions was introduced.

Fourth. The free convertibility of the rouble was introduced for current transactions. In the beginning, it was of an internal character only. However, in 1996, Russia officially notified the IMF and accepted from June 1, this year obligations imposed upon member states according to the Article VIII of the IMF Agreement. This means a complete removal of currency restrictions on persons in Russia. The establishment of premises for a gradual transition towards the practice of free quotations and free circulation of the rouble in foreign currency markets is underway.

Fifth. An Agreement on the Formation of the Payments Union of CIS member states was signed in 1994. At the beginning, it was supposed that an interstate clearing mechanism would be formed within the frameworks of this Union. This then would have become the sole and compulsory channel of clearing between all subjects of foreign economic activity, as it was in the postwar European Payments Union. Projects of this kind were proposed by a number of participants of conferences of the Robert Triffin-Szirák Foundation (Miklós Szabó-Pelsőczi, Jozef van Brabant, and others). However, in reality, a 'soft' version of the payments union was formed, based on free convertibility of the currencies of the member states. Therefore, difficulties emerged in connection with the functioning of the Interstate Bank, formed by CIS member states in 1993, and which has no authority for operations with commercial banks. There are provisions for realizing measures concerning the formation of a multilateral system of transactions in a 'collective currency', but the achivement of this goal is postponed for a more remote future.

In the beginning of the 1990s, numerous Russian and foreign economists suggested a more gradual and smoother way of realizing market transformations including an attainment of the external openness of the economy. The well-known international AGENDA Group of experts (Jan Kregel, Egon Matzner, Gernot Grabher, and others) in *The Market Shock* expressed apprehensions that the market transformation programmes accepted for actions are focused mainly 'on abstract targets such as economic stabilization, balanced budgets, balanced current account, convertible currency, etc., irrespective of the consequences of their policies on output, investment, employment and private consumption'.[1] In particular, they recommended an introduction of free convertibility of domestic currencies firstly only for purchasing means of production which would favour the investments and economic growth while preserving currency limitations for a certain period on the import of consumer goods.[2]

In Russia, the warnings of the supporters of a 'gradualist' approach were not taken into account. The views of such foreign advisers as, for example, Jeffrey Sachs and Anders Äslund gained the upper hand which were for a speedy realization of the 'shock therapy'. A realization of this strategy in the sphere of the foreign economic and currency relations led inevitably to a number of negative consequences, which are mentioned in the following sections.

Changes of the import structure

The rash liberalization of prices, the total removal of protective barriers in foreign trade, the introduction of rouble convertibility – all these measures led to a number of negative changes in the import structure. These steps opened the doors for the importation of foods and other consumer goods in high demand, providing a high level of commercial profits. Table 1 shows that the share of foods and raw materials doubled in total imports from great distances during 1995 in comparison with 1990. These, together with manufactured commodities (clothes, foot-wear) make up about one-third of the imports. At the same time, a sharp rise of the rate of exchange of the dollar in relation to the rouble (more than by 50-fold from the beginning of 1992) reduced the opportunities of importing investment goods in sufficient quantities. As a result, the share of machines, equipment, and means of transport, which was over 40 per cent in 1990, decreased to near one-third of total imports. At this level it corresponded approximately to the share of foods and commodities produced by the light industry.

An inflow of more competitive imported commodities naturally contributed to the aggravation of the economic crisis. The output of the gross national product in 1995 was 62.1 per cent and that of manufactured goods

48.5 per cent of the level of 1990. As regards a reduction of the import of the industrial equipment, K. Bush, one of the authors of the research work devoted to problems of a transitional economy in the countries of the for the former USSR, warned correctly that this fact 'could have a deletrious effect on investment plans and long-term growth prospects.'[3] It is not surprising then that capital investment in 1995 was only 21.0 per cent of its 1990 level.

Table 1. Commodity structure of the import from the far-beyond-the-border countries (in per cent of a total value)

Commodity groups	Years						
	1990	1991	1992	1993	1994	1995	1996 (Jan-June)
Foods and agricultural raw materials	15	24	26	22	30	29	27
Manufactured consumer goods (fabrics, raw hide, furs and articles made of them)	4	5	14	17	8	5	4
Machines, equipment and means of transport	41	33	38	33	38	38	36
Others	40	38	22	28	24	28	33

References: Data for 1990-1991: Benedicte Vibe Christensen, 'The Russian Federation in Transition: External Developments', *Occasional Paper*, No.111; The International Monetary Fund, Washington, 1994, February, p. 39.
Data for 1992-1996; 'Russia in Figures', *Finances and Statistics*, Moscow, 1996, pp. 147-148.

Rate of exchange and 'imported' inflation

As a result of a sharp expansion of food and consumer goods import, the share of imports in the total amount of consumption increased more than two fold in 1995 in comparison with 1992, and exceeded by 50 per cent the total volume of commodities in this market. This circumstance raised severely the vulnerability of the national economy to imported inflation. This caused a decline of the rubel/dollar exchange rate. This became apparent during the events of the autumn of 1994, and culminated in the well-known 'Black Tuesday', on October 11, 1994.

A lag of the fall of the rouble's market rate of exchange in relation to the dollar from its internal depreciation has caused an avalanche of decline of the rate of exchange of the rouble in the fall of 1994. The latter had as its direct consequence, an uneven rise of prices of imported commodities, a derangement of the financial stabilization, which began to show by the middle of 1994.

The 'Black Tuesday' served as a signal to a sharp change of all the landmarks of Russian macroeconomic policy. As a result, the suppression of inflation became a priority aim. Its attainment at any price was regarded of paramount importance. This course was pursued in close co-operation with the International Monetary Fund, and its demands were unconditionally fulfilled.

In the monetary sphere, the change of reference points manifested itself from the middle of 1995 in establishing the so-called 'currency corridor', the limits of variations of the current rate of exchange of the rouble on the exchange and interbank monetary markets. From the middle of 1996, the 'horizontal' currency corridor was changed, stipulating a consecutive reduction of the limits of allowable fluctuations of the rate of exchange. This machinery, called 'a crawling peg to the dollar within the limits of the currency corridor' by the former permanent representative of the IMF in Russia, T. Woulf, is still functioning in 1997.[4] It means an attempt to ensure an admissible balance between contradictory purposes: on the one hand to retain an anti-inflationary anchor of the economy, and to favour export expansion and the attraction of foreign investments, on the other.

As a result of the introduction of the currency corridor in 1995, a stabilization of the rate of exchange was really attained, but in some months even the trend towards a decline of the rate of exchange of the dollar in relation to the rouble prevailed. This fact gave the authorities an opportunity to increase the amount of foreign reserve assets by two fold as a result of which they amounted to nearly 20 billion dollars at the end of the first quarter of 1996. However, during the summer months of 1996, the trend for a more rapid growth of the rate of exchange of the dollar in relation to the rouble in comparison with the growth of domestic prices appeared again. Owing to currency interventions, the administration managed to break an uneasy situation and to retain the control over the rate of exchange of the rouble. But it cost a loss of over 5 billion dollars as a result of which the level of gold and currency reserves was reduced to about 14 billion dollars. Net reserves were reduced to 600 million dollars by February this year.

The ability of the administration to support a very high degree of saturation of the market with consumer goods and services, to restrain the growth of prices, and to retain control over the dynamics of the exchange rate, largely depends on the balance of payments. Here, there are both positive and negative developments. Acute problems requiring cardinal strategic decisions exist.

What is hidden behind the trade balance surplus?

One of the supports of the currency and the entire macroeconomic policy of the administration is a permanent large-scale trade balance surplus. In 1995, it was 22.8 billion dollars and during the first 9 months of 1996, 17.5 billion dollars.

A stable excess of receipts over payments in the trade balance opens certain opportunities for the administration for macroeconomic manoeuvring. However, in the case of Russia such a state of affairs does not indicate the economic health of the country, as it is accompanied by economic recession, a direct result of import restriction, the reduction of investment activity, and the decrease of consumer demand. This is an equivalent of a mere outflow of real economic values during a given period of time when internal investments and personal consumption are lost.

In what way the trade balance surplus is being formed is of a fundamental importance. As it follows from the data shown in Table 2, in Russia it is predominantly achieved through the export of energy resources and of mineral raw materials representing about a half of the export value, and also of the processing of products with low value added content: metals, chemical manufactured products, wood, cellulose, and paper articles. At present, over four-fifth of the value of Russian exports to the West consist of all these goods taken together. At the same time, the share of machinery, equipment and means of transport, in spite of a considerable growth of shipments of armaments, decreased from 18 per cent in 1990 to 6-8 per cent; a decline of 50 per cent, more than twofold of the total value of exports to the far-beyond-the-border countries.

Table 2. Commodity structure of the export of Russia to the far-beyond-the-border-countries
(in per cent of the total value)

Commodity groups	Years						
	1990	1991	1992	1993	1994	1995	1996 (Jan-June)
Mineral products (predominantly the products of the fuel-energy complex)	43	42	52	47	43	40	45
Semi-manufactured goods: products of initial processing (metals, chemical products, wood, cellulose and paper articles)	12	27	26	33	43	44	37
Machinery, equipment and means of transport	18	10	9	7	6	8	8
Others	27	21	13	13	8	8	10
Total: 100	100	100	100	100	100	100	100

References: Data for 1990-1991: Benedicte Vibe Christensen, 'The Russian Federation in Transition: External Developments', *Occasional Paper*, No.111; The International Monetary Fund, Washington, 1994, February, p. 39.
Data for 1992-1996: 'Russia in Figures', *Finances and Statistics*, Moscow, 1966, pp.146-147.

The present structure of Russian foreign trade relations is defined predominantly by the importation of foods and consumer goods, representing half of the domestic market at the expense of the exportation of energy resources and raw materials. This means the spending of not-replenishable resources. Their extraction aggravates the country's ecological situation. The spending of oil-dollars on food, for which the leadership of the USSR was often reproached increasing even more at the present. Such a situation is evidently intolerable, and a radical change of the export structure is an actual and acute problem.

Current account

In connection with the fact that the balance of services of Russia is negative, the surplus on the current account is considerably less than it is on the commodity trade. It is still of an impressive value: 12.3 billion dollars in 1995 and 10.2 billion dollars during the first 9 months of 1996. In principle, inflowing currency resources could become an important contributor of productive accumulation, and could help to overcome the economic crisis. However, under the conditions of the liberalization of the currency machinery the adminintration is incapable of finding instruments which could canalize the flow of these resources in the direction of the productive sphere. As a result, they are predominantly left on foreign currency accounts of commercial banks and are replenishing the dollar cash on hands of the population.

According to the data available in 1996, the net inflow of foreign currencies to commercial banks not only absorbed completely the entire trade surplus with the far-beyond-the-border countries but exceeded it by 21.4 per cent. In their turn, the expenditures of the population for purchasing foreign currency (48.9 billion dollars) proved to be half as much as the net import of currencies by the banks. In the end, this has led to the expenditure of gold and currency reserves.

According to moderate appraisals, the net cash of currencies on hand of the population is approximately 20-22 billion dollars, or 110-120 trillion roubles by the rate of exchange at the end of 1996. This sum exceed even the rouble cash in circulation (103 trillion roubles which was at the end of 1996). There are even higher estimaties of the sum of currencies in cash on hand of the population – up to 70 billion dollars.

The inflow of the foreign currencies into the country favours a growth of an external component of the money base. Therefore, in a long perspective, the sustained balance of payments surplus together with the transformation of the currency accumulation of Russian judicial and physical persons into roubles which will be going on side by side with the intensification of a de-dollarization of the money circulation – could be fraught with the danger of stimulating the inflation process.

Overall balance of payments deficit and foreign financing

While the current account is in a favourable condition, the 'analytical presentation' of the overall balance of payments exposes an enormous deficit. Here the demarcation line runs between autonomous everyday transactions of participants of foreign economic activity and balancing and compensating state operations. According to official data, this deficit was 11.1 billion dollars in 1995 and 19.3 billion dollars during the first 3 quarters of 1996.

A transformation of the current account surplus into an enormous deficit of the overall balance of payments is mainly explained by payments in accordance with foreign debt servicing schedule, including interest and the repayment of capital. At present, the aggregate foreign debt of Russia – an overwhelming part of it is the debt of the former USSR – exceeds 130 billion dollars, of which the debt to Western creditors is over 90 billion dollars. It constitutes about 36 per cent of the GDP of Russia in 1995 at the then current exchange rate.

External financing serves as the basic source of countervailing the balance of payments deficit. It includes the resources given by the international monetary and financial organizations; first of all by the IMF and the World Bank, bilateral international credits, loans of private commercial banks, resources obtained through a distribution of Eurobonds, and finally, delays and respites of foreign debt servicing payments. The above items absorbed 39 per cent in 1995 and 44 per cent in the first 3 quarters of 1996 out of the total sum of the external financing through new loans by government organizations.

The authorities were forced to external financing, because of balance of payments, and federal budget considerations. There are estimates, according to which about 40 per cent of the full amount of foreign credits, attracted by the state, is employed for budgetary purposes.

The total of resources, which were received from abroad for financing the balance of payments deficit and government expenditures since 1991 up to September 1996, amounted to 25.2 billion US dollars. 15.8 billion dollars, or 62.7 per cent of the total were actually utilized. However, according to official estimates, approximately 60 to 100 billion dollars (or more) left the country during the same period of time illegally, evading currency legislation. The reasons of the capital flight were the economic crisis, political instability and also the inadequacy of foreign exchange controls.

The increase of foreign debt, resulting from raising money abroad, entails, naturally, a problem of servicing this debt. At the present time, this problem does not arouse too much concern, since the scheduled (to say nothing of actual) debt-service ratio has sunk lower than 25 per cent of yearly exports, the level which is considered critical by international standards. The agreements on rescheduling the former USSR foreign debt which have been reached within the frame of the Paris and the London Clubs and which envisage repayment of the debt during 25 years with 5 years grace period, reduce the pressure on the budget connected with debt servicing. However, one should not forget that they place the burden of solving this problem on the shoulders of future generations. It is also appropriate to mention that the foreign debt of Russia itself is continuing to grow.

Proposed measures

At the present time, an apprehension is expanding in Russian society that a full-scale liberalization of external economic activities which had been executed at the beginning of the 1990s was, to a certain extent, hasty and thoughtless. Consequently, a propensity to employing during a definite period, certain defensive measures, is emerging. The survival – not to mention an upsurge – of the national economy is believed to be rather problematic without applying such measures. Certainly, nowadays, when Russia has officially introduced free convertibility of the rouble for current operations and is seeking admission to the World Trade Organization (WTO), a return to the situation of the early 1990s is not possible. The general orientation toward the openness of the national economy is not called in question. There is an understanding that protective measures could be undertaken only within the rules and requirements of the existing international institutions.

In the sphere of foreign trade – though the ultimate aim of reducing custom tariffs for imported goods and services remains, as before, in force – a temporary freezing, in some cases even an increase, of those tariffs as well as the use of certain non-tariff barriers (quotas, an obligatory certification of products, et cetera) would seem to be required under present circumstances. This would be particularly justified in cases of unfair foreign competition. This would be 'fine tuning'. The purpose of using this machinery consists of defending the most vulnerable of national producers from certain foreign competition categories. In connection with this, it is appropriate to note that the rules of the WTO itself allow to resort to such defensive actions, when imports inflict, or even threaten to inflict, serious damage to national production.

In the international monetary domain, first, proposals are put forward, which aim at establishing a more clear-cut distinction between current and capital international transactions, at tightening of foreign exchange controls and the rules governing the exportation of national capital. In this context, a number of quite radical steps are brought forward, such as: an introduction of compulsory sales by exporters of their entire foreign exchange earnings to the central bank, or to market agents, (at present, they are obliged to sell 50 per cent of their earnings); a gradual dismantling of foreign exchange accounts owned by enterprises, which implies a conversion of foreign exchange held on these accounts into national currency; a limitation of sales of foreign currencies to physical persons and an announcement of strictly definite cases that could justify such sales (for example, travels abroad).

Second, there is an aspiration for an introduction of the rouble into international settlements of the Russian participants of foreign economic dealings. This presupposes a removal of restrictions on bringing roubles abroad and also on the non-residents' rights to own them. Some other similar measures are considered, including establishment of a requirement of compulsory payments by foreign customers for imported Russian products with roubles.

Third, some experts favour a substantial (1.5-2 times) devaluation of the rouble vis-a-vis the US dollar. A simultaneous establishment of a stable official exchange rate of the rouble in relation to the dollar for a definite period (for example, for one year) is also suggested. These measures, could, certainly, facilitate a revival of manufacturing industries owing to a possible rise of production for export purposes. However, to all appearances, its main fruits would be still obtained by producers of fuel and raw materials. In any case, such a step could be undertaken only in conjunction with other measures intended to sterilize its potential inflationary effect.

With all the significance of the proposed measures in the fields of foreign trade and monetary arrangements, the fundamental strengthening of the economic security of the country and of assuring of an adequate place for the latter in the system of the world economy remain, mainly, to be the task of *the domestic macroeconomic policy*. The accomplishment of this task requires a radical structural reconstruction of the national economy, a large-scale redistribution of resources which ought to be executed in a rather short time.

While the apprehension of the priority of this task is practically unanimous, as to the way of achieving it, two main approaches confront one another. The adherents of one of them are guided by liberal models and set their hopes on the operation of the notorious 'invisible hand'. The proponents of the other approach share dirigist (or Keynesian) views and advocate a more effective participation of the public institutions in economic activities, including the investment process. It is still uncertain, which of these two approaches will gain the upper hand.

Notes and references

1. Jan Kregel, Egon Matzner, Gernot Grabher, *The Market Shock*. Edited for the AGENDA Group. An AGENDA for the Economic and Social Reconstruction of Central and Eastern Europe, Austrian Academy of Sciences/Research Unit for Socio-Economics, International Institute for Peace, Vienna, 1992, p. 260.
2. Ibid., p. 141.
3. Kaulman, Richard F. and John P. Hardt (eds.), *The Former Soviet Union in Transition.* Joint Economic Committee, Congress of the United States, M.E. Sharpe, Armonk, New York; London, England, 1993, p. 956.
4. *Kommersant*, (daily), No. 82. May 21, 1996, p. 2.

21 Closing the Development Gap between Hungary and the European Union

János Hoós

The basic situation

The Hungarian economy with per capita GDP $4,400 (1996), belongs to the middle income economies, with per capita GDP of $726-8,956. Countries of the European Union – except Greece – belong to the high income economies with a GDP per capita of $8,955 or more.[1] *The 1994 Hungarian per capita $ GDP is about one-fifth of the EU average. The development gap between Hungary and the EU is rather wide. It must be narrowed by economic growth.* The Hungarian economy must grow faster than that of the EU. The closing of the development gap is not a precondition for becoming a full member of the EU, but if this gap would widen, the possibility of joining the EU would be decreased, due to the growing costs of integrating Hungary. At least the low rate of growth can make harder or even impossible to meet the Maastricht convergence criteria.[2] That is why the economic growth has come into the focus of the economic policy debate in Hungary as the issue of joining the Union has become more and more relevant.

There are many growth scenarios inspired by this debate. Among them the World Bank's (1996)[3] and the Hungarian government's (1995)[4] will be presented and evaluated here in order to judge realistically future growth possibilities and the chances of the Hungarian economy.

The scenarios of the World Bank

The World Bank has two scenarios of Hungarian economic growth: a high- and a lower-growth scenario.

The high-growth scenario

The high-growth scenario 'has been elaborated on the assumption that Hungary fully implements its enterprise, bank and fiscal reforms, including reforming the pension system during the next few years. The full implementation of these reforms should eliminate the structural bottlenecks that still affect Hungary's economy, and create the conditions for an increase in the levels and efficiency of fixed investment'.[5] In this scenario the fiscal deficit, would be further reduced. The current account deficit would be reduced to the level of foreign direct investment (FDI) preventing further increases in net external debt. Social programmes would be streamlined. The tax structure would be changed, reducing the tax burden. Through rapid privatization of state-owned enterprises and banks by 2005 Hungary would reduce the size of its public sector to the level of the EU average and would have also improved markedly its relative economic position.

These reforms would enable Hungary

- to sustain fixed investment at a level around 22-23 per cent of the GDP; and
- enjoy a long-run growth of 4-5 per cent a year (the real GDP of more developed EU members grow by an average rate of 2-3 per cent, so Hungary would grow at a higher rate than these countries);
- allowing the country to start catching up with EU member states at the turn of the 21st century.

A scenario of limited adjustment and lower growth

According to the World Bank, the high-growth scenario stands a reasonable chance of realization, given Hungary's will to join the EU. However, the World Bank makes an alternative scenario under which reforms are only partly implemented. It involves less than full implementation of:

- the enterprise and bank reforms, and
- non-implementation of comprehensive fiscal reforms.

Under this scenario, the government would refrain from implementing additional fiscal corrections beyond those achieved by the March 1995 package of the government, no fundamental restructuring of social expenditure would be undertaken, there would be no significant cuts in government consumption beyond those achieved by the March package. These would avoid a significant decline in direct taxes, in particular, payroll contributions would need to remain above 50 per cent of the wage bill by the end of the next five years, implying that the size of the informal sector (black market) would remain large.

This strategy – called 'muddle through' strategy by the World Bank – implies weaker growth performance, not only because the ratio of fixed investment (around 20 per cent of the GDP) is stabilized at a lower level but also because the persistence of loss-making activities by enterprises and banks, the presence of a large state sector and of high inflation, all imply smaller productivity gains relative to the high-growth scenario.

Thus the growth rate would equal the EU average – around 2 per cent a year – and the large income gap between Hungary and the EU would not be closed. The current account deficit would remain higher than the level of FDI, implying further increases in the net external debt and a great vulnerability to balance-of-payments shocks and changes in the perception of foreign creditors.

According to the World Bank, there may be a temptation to pursue a 'muddle through' strategy by the Hungarian government. This option would appear to offer some benefits as the transformation related social tensions would be dampened in the short run, but this strategy would also entail substantial risks and costs: the economy would remain under constant threat of balance-of-payment crises, macroeconomic and political instability might undermine Hungary's likelihood of joining Europe. According to the judgment of the World Bank, all of these can be avoided by selecting the first scenario.

The scenario of the Hungarian government

The Hungarian government's forecast of the economic growth is very similar to the World Bank's high-growth scenario. The basic aim of the government is to facilitate sustainable and dynamic economic growth that can be financed on a long-term basis. The realization of this aim requires:

- stabilizing and freezing the level of net foreign debt, i.e. the deficit of the balance of payments should be equal to FDI;
- fast change in income distribution for the benefit of enterprises in order to increase investment;
- strict control of consumer demand, real wage, and real income;
- decreasing the state's redistributive role and the huge financing demand of general government deficit;
- rational exchange rate policy based upon the promotion of competitiveness and reducing the inflation rate;
- privatization, deregulation, public sector reform;
- complete restructuring of human resources systems (pension, health care, education systems, for example);
- reduction of taxes and rates, first of all, of social security contributions;
- preparation for EU accession.

By implementation of this economic strategy the Hungarian government intends to achieve a 2 to 3 per cent increase in the GDP in 1997. This growth of the economy will gradually accelerate and it will reach levels of 3-5 per cent by 2000. According to this forecast, like in the World Bank's scenario, Hungary will start to close the development gap now existing between Hungary and the EU.

The assumptions of the scenarios of the World Bank and the Hungarian government

These scenarios assume essential conditions to be examined, evaluated, and judged with respect of their implementation. The main assumptions are the following:

a) Dynamic export, at a higher rate than the growth rate of import, can be achieved. This export will be the main driving force behind growth. Hungary will have proper access to foreign markets; there will be resources (capital, investment) for modernizing the economy, for improving its competitiveness. These resources will come mainly from reallocation of income from consumption to saving

from household to business; and that this reallocation can be done with peaceful management keeping social tensions caused by the reform of the welfare system to a minimum, inspite consumption, real wages and incomes remaining at a low level for a relatively long time.
b) Hungary can manage its huge debt problem, pay the debt service and stabilize, even decrease, the level of the debt and, at the very same time, can provide sufficient amount of resources for modernizing its economy and improving its international competitiveness.
c) The reform, especially restructuring of the enterprises and banks, the modernization of the welfare system and of the public sector can be implemented in such a way and with such a speed that it can provide the needed additional resources for economic development and for the opportunity to decrease the tax burden – and at the same time to decrease the deficit of the budget relative to the GDP.

It cannot be excluded that these (a, b, c) assumptions can turn out to be true, but a great deal of well-founded doubts could also arise, especially if one takes into consideration the following:

1. Hungary is not part of any advanced international economic integration which could provide advantages like the EU. Therefore, Hungary has to face a stiff international competition accompanied very often by economic discrimination, especially, since the EU follows a very strict export and import policy towards non-member countries, including Hungary. Consequently access to the international market for Hungary is rather restricted. This hinders the realization of a higher growth rate of export and of the GDP.
2. Due to the heavy indebtedness of the country, the debt service is very high (30-40 per cent of the export, 4-5 per cent of the GDP), which takes a substantial amount of resources out of the country. That decreases resources available for modernization and hinders the improvement of competitiveness.
3. The restriction of home consumption, decreasing or stagnating living standards due to welfare reform and to restrictive wage policy can intensify social tensions creating unstable social conditions, which can delay reforms and have a negative impact on the inflow of foreign capital.

All of these factors, mentioned under points 1, 2 and 3 can create such an economic and political situation in which:

- the economic growth rate can be lower, and/or
- economic equilibrium can be worse than forecast in the scenarios of the World Bank and the Hungarian government.

Therefore, a 'stop-go' economic policy scenario could be developed.

The scenario of a 'stop-go' economic policy

The rationale of this scenario can be summarized as follows:

- the already mentioned obstacles to export growth, and to economic modernization (absence of efficient international economic integration, inadequate access to foreign markets, heavy indebtedness of the country); the huge and time consuming task of necessary reforms (especially pension and health reform, the reform of the public sector) and its negative impacts on the interests of different social groups, with more or less political influence;
- constitutional parliamentary democracy and pluralistic political system of Hungary with regular elections in every four year, would generate 'election cycles';
- accelerating economic growth and deteriorating economic equilibrium, especially before and during the election year due to the relaxation of strict and restrictive economic, mainly financial, policy and due to the slowing down of the reform process, which has a negative political impact on the voters;
- slowing down of economic growth, speeding up the reform process, and improving macroeconomic equilibria after the elections due to the necessary corrective measures introduced by the previous government.

Having taken into consideration all of these, one can realistically expect the following growth path for Hungary during the next years:

> about 2-3 per cent growth rate of the GDP in 1998, 1-2 per cent growth rate in 1999-2000 and 3-4 per cent growth rate in 2001 and 2002 as the next election is approaching. It means that the Hungar-

ian economic growth probably will be cyclical and the average growth rate will be slower than forecasted by the World Bank and the Hungarian government. So, the catching up process of the Hungarian economy will be less successful and slower than predicted by the World Bank and the government. This process, of course, could be speeded up but, in fact it depends on mainly external factors and not on Hungary's own capabilities.

Two factors need to be mentioned here:

- the possibility of easing the international debt burden of the country; and
- better access of the country to the international market.

However, thinking in a realistic way, there is no great chance for these to be realized in the foreseable future.

As for the debt problem, in Hungary there is no urgent political and economic need to provide the country with such relief as it have been given to Poland and Russia; these countries had and still have such a reason. Such a relief could make an economic miracle in the Hungarian case, but the desire for this miracle is not a sufficient reason for creditors.

Regarding the question of international market access, it could be a major breakthrough in this respect if Hungary became a full member of the EU in the next two or three years, but the reality of this is very small too.

Putting all of these factors together, *the final conclusion could be that Hungary needs to prepare for a relatively low rate of economic growth with cyclical characteristics in the next ten years or so. The development gap between Hungary and the EU could be closed, even taking an optimistic view, only after more than a decade's time.* Becoming a full member of the EU at the earliest time possible (and getting debt-relief) could shorten the time needed to close this gap, but it would probably cost more for the EU (and for the creditors of Hungary too). It is subject to political judgment whether the EU will pay this cost. However, the possible outcome of this political evaluation and decision can be forecasted with much less certainty than economic growth.

Notes and references

1. The real GDP of more developed EU members grew by an average rate of 2.3 per cent a year during the period 1980-90, whereas the real GDP of the middle income countries in the Union (Ireland, Portugal, and Spain) grew by an average rate of 3.3 per cent a year during the same period. Hungary would have to grow at higher rates than these countries as it attempts to approach the EU average from a lower base.
2. The 1991-1992 period was characterized by an extreme decline of the economy, with a 12 per cent and 4 per cent drop of the GDP, respectively. It was after election time accompanied by strict economic restrictions. Due to this restriction, the foreign trade balance and the financial balance developed favourably. It declined strongly in the 1992-1994 period – 1994 was election year – accompanied by economic growth (in 1994, the GDP increased by 2.9 per cent). The financial balance improved considerably in 1995 again due to the March package introduced by the government elected in mid-1994. The intention of this programme was to implement reforms aimed at the elimination of macroeconomic disequilibria and the removing of Hungary's longstanding structural problems. The growth of the GDP slowed down, in 1995 it was 1.5 per cent and 0.5 per cent in 1996. The forecast of growth of the GDP is 2.0 per cent for 1997 and 3.1 per cent for 1998 (an election year). This growth is also accompanied by the tendency of declining foreign trade and financial balances.
3. *From Plan to Market*. World Development Report,. Published for the World Bank, Oxford University Press, 1996.
4. *Hungary, Structural Reforms for Sustainable Growth*, June 12, 1995. Document of the World Bank.
5. *Medium-term Economic Strategy of the Hungarian Government.* Budapest, September, 1995.

22 The Banking System in Slovakia – Actual Problems

Otto Sobek

Up to 1989, the banking system of former Czechoslovakia (Slovakia was a part of it in this time) showed all characteristic features of a communist banking system. There was a big Czechoslovak State Bank (ŠBÈS) concentrating the functions of a central bank and a universal commercial bank as well, a savings bank, and some special banks (for foreign trade etc.). All banks were state-owned. The management of the banks did not follow commercial principles, the managers were directed by the state and had to fulfil all tasks given to them by the state authorities.

Since then significant structural changes have taken place in Slovak banking. In 1990, the former ŠBČS was divided into a Western type real central bank and some big commercial banks. At the same time, the establishment of new commercial banks was liberalized. A number of new banks were etablished in Slovakia and the number of branches and employees in the banking system increased significantly.

Today's Slovak banking system consists of the National Bank of Slovakia, Slovakia's central bank, 30 universal commercial banks and 5 banks with special functions. The market, however, is dominated by three big banks arisen from the former ŠBČS. The three biggest commercial banks are Všeobecná úverová banka (VÚB – General Credit Bank), Slovenská sporitel'na (SSB – Slovak Savings Bank), and Investičná a rozvojová banka (IRB – Investment and Development Bank). SSB existed already under the communist regime, VÚB and IRB were separated from the former ŠBČS in 1990 as its general successors in the field of commercial banking. All these three banks are still totally or to a very high extent state-owned.

VÚB is the largest Slovak bank with a total balance sheet volume of 174 billion Sk (all figures refer to June 30, 1996); 48 per cent of its equity capital were privatized by means of voucher privatization and are now owned by small individual owners, 52 per cent are owned by the National Property Fund (FNM – Fond národného majetku), a state-owned institution.

SSB has a balance sheet volume of 169 billion Sk. Up to now, it is totally owned by the National Property Fund.

IRB has a balance sheet volume of 53 billion Sk. 65 per cent of its equity capital were privatized by means of the voucher privatization and 35 per cent are owned by the National Property Fund. 29 per cent of the equity capital are now dominated by Východoslovenské zeleziarne (VSŽ – Eastern Slovakia Steal Works), Slovakia's largest company.

All the other commercial banks in Slovakia were established after 1990 under the conditions of the new Bank Act as private companies. The largest of them are Poľnobanka (Agricultural Bank) with a balance sheet volume of 24 billion Sk, which is partially owned by foreign investors (e.g. EBRD) and Tatra banka owned by Austrian investors with a balance sheet volume of 21 billion Sk. The balance sheet volume of all the other commercial banks is considerably smaller.

The most important foreign bank's branch in Slovakia is Československá obchodná banka (CSOB – Czechoslovak Commercial Bank) with a balance sheet volume of 37 billion Sk. ČSOB existed already under the communist regime and was specialized in foreign trade operations. After the division of Czechoslovakia, the bank remained unchanged and today it is partially owned by the National Bank of Slovakia. Other important branches of foreign banks are the ING Bank with a balance sheet volume of 10 billion Sk and two Czech commercial banks: Agrobanka and Banka Haná with a balance sheet volume of about 5 billions Sk each. (The branch of Agrobanka is going to be sold to Slovak companies in the near future.)

Banks with special functions are Konsolidačná banka (KB – Consolidation Bank) and Slovenská záručná banka (SZB – Slovak Guarantee Bank). Both are state-owned banks. The first of them was established with a balance sheet volume of 35 billion Sk and took over some large loans which were granted under the communist regime by the Czechoslovak State Bank and didn't respond to commercial principles. The aim of the KB is the gradual liquidation of these loans.

SZB is a state-owned bank established with the aim of giving guarantees for loans granted by other commercial banks.

To the banks with special functions further belong two real funds savings banks and a newly established state-owned Export-Import Bank (Exim banka). Up to now, Slovakia has no special mortgage bank, although mortgage loans are regulated by the new Bank Act.

The existing structure of the Slovak banking sector is influenced by the structure inherited from the communist regime. Prior to 1989, bank operations clearly differed between the ŠBČS and Slovenská sporiteľňa. Saving deposits of private individuals were concentrated exclusively in the SSB. This bank, however, provided only customer loans to private individuals and the rest of the resources were deposited in the ŠBČS where they were used as a source for credits to the business sphere.

Today, all banks are legally universal ('all-purpose') banks, the former division of labour, however, in practice continues. The basic mass of primary resources (49 per cent) is still concentrated in the Slovenská sporitelna (the share of deposits of private persons is even 76 per cent) which, however, grants only 21.4 per cent of the total loans to clients. The difference, secondary deposits, are deposited in other commercial banks. This situation makes numerous transfers necessary between banks and leads in the end to an increase in the price of credits. In VÚB, for example, deposits of private individuals account for only 17.8 per cent of liabilities, while the accounts of other banks contribute 23.8 per cent. This bank grants to the business sphere 35 per cent of all loans.

Another very serious problem of the Slovak commercial banks (mainly the four largest ones) is the existence of 'bad debts'. The majority of these debts were inherited by the present large banks from the former ŠBČS, which when granting loans often preferred political criteria to commercial ones. The existence of non-performing loans reduces the liquidity of banks and negatively affects their economic results. Solving the bad debt problem is thus an important precondition for restructuring commercial banking. (This problem was in more detail discussed in Sobek 1995/c.)

The necessity of restructuring the existing banking structure is the key problem of today's Slovak banking sector. Theoretical literature deals rather intensively with this question. Some of its conclusions can be quoted here.

Recommended instruments for bank restructuring are: sale, merger, closure and liquidation, twinning arrangements and privatization of state-owned banks (Dziobek 1995).

Sale is the most convenient method if it is possible to find a private buyer willing to buy the whole bank with its complete portfolio. If the portfolio is bad, such a solution is realistic only if the state as former proprietor respects the bad quality of the loans portfolio when negotiating selling conditions. Total sale is an adequate solution in the case of small banks in which the government has no specific interest, and which in the past didn't grant loans to subjects of large economic or political importance.

Mergers can take place either between two weak banks (in order to establish a stronger bank) or between a weak and an economically stronger bank. A merger between a strong and a weak bank can lead to a weakening of the stronger bank. Generally, mergers are a suitable instrument of bank restructuring only in exceptional cases.

Such a case in Slovakia could be a merger between a bank very strong in deposits with a bank very strong in credit activities, e. g. between VÚB and SSB. Such a merger would substantially improve the structure of assets and liabilities of the newly established bank and further make it possible to establish a bank able to compete at least under Central European conditions.

Closure and liquidation are suitable instruments of restructuring in the case of small banks in which the government is not interested and can, therefore, go to some distance in agreeing to the process. Such a solution is not realistic in the case of large banks.

Some countries tried to solve restructuring by 'twinning arrangements' between domestic and foreign banks in order to receive know-how and technical aid from foreign banks. The experience with this arrangement, however, is not very favourable, as foreign banks are interested in such a solution only in the case where they have the intention to take part in the bank's equity.

All specialists stress the necessity of an active participation of the government in the restructuring process. This is necessary mainly in order to avoid negative social and political consequences which could be caused by restructuring. Vital are also coordinated activities of all central organs involved in this process (parliament, government, and central bank). What is necessary is an agreement as to the total volume of state support, the role of foreign capital, the necessity of preserving a certain equity share in the largest banks in the hands of the government and the speed of privatization. In order to avoid restructuring to become a political problem it is useful to co-ordinate all decisions with representatives of the opposition. Public disputes on these questions can be very harmful for the banks' credibility. Restructuring strategy should be based on an unanimous agreement of all involved institutions.

The majority of the restructuring costs should be covered by the banks themselves. Governmental authorities should limit their interventions to the activities in favour of large companies where restructuring is complicated or where social and political implications are too important; and leave the rest to commercial banks. A complete cleaning of the banks' portfolio is not always the best solution because it weakens the pressure on bank management to improve their activities.

All governmental decisions (and even their absence) influence the long-run structure and efficiency of the banking system. Therefore, it is necessary to have a clear conception as to the future structure of the banking system. This conception must be the starting point for solving the problems of individual banks. At the same time, it is necessary to consider the influence of the realized activities on other banks not involved into the restructuring process.

In solving the problem of individual banks, it is necessary to consider their function in the whole of the banking system and the effect of the restructuring on their profit and liquidity. If the bank is not able to survive and is of no strategic importance, the cheapest solution is its liquidation, eventually the integration of its healthy parts into another bank.

The discussion of banks' restructuring problems leads us now to the privatization problem. Everybody in Slovakia agrees that commercial banks should be privatized but there are many unfinished discussions how to realize this task.

As already mentioned, large Slovak state-owned banks were partially privatized already in 1992 in connection with the voucher privatization. Due to the fact that the state remained the decisive proprietor and was able to influence management decisions from a political point of view, this partial privatization did not lead to an improvement in bank management.

So the problem of big banks' privatization remains one of the most important problems of the Slovak banking sector.

Bank privatization is much more complicated and difficult than the privatization of any other company. Banks work with money entrusted to them by their depositors which enables the privatizer to obtain, with a relatively small investment of his own resources, the right to manage a very large amount of money.

Bank privatization, therefore, has to be realized after careful preparation and a profound consideration of all possible consequences. Two questions are of special importance: whether the government wants to retain some share in the largest banks and how big this share should be, and further: whether and to what extent foreign capital should be involved in the privatization.

It is clear that bank privatization is not an aim in itself. It is reasonable only if it helps to improve significantly the performance of the banking system. And this is possible only if commercial banks' activities are free from political interventions.

The best method of privatization evidently would be the sale to a foreign partner. Such a solution probably would be the best in order to improve the management and performance of Slovak banks. This solution, however, is not unanimously accepted. Sale to foreign partners is not acceptable to some 'nationalist' economists who would prefer a 'Slovak solution', i.e. sale to some Slovak economic subject. The problem, however, is that there are only few Slovak subjects who are able to buy. These would be mainly the largest Slovak companies. And these companies, at the same time, are the largest borrowers of commercial banks. A sale of the state-owned banks to these companies would lead to the paradoxical phenomenon of lenders owned by their borrowers. And just such a solution is proposed by certain representatives of Slovak politics. On the other hand, most serious economists strongly oppose such a solution. In this, they are supported by the World Bank.

Another important problem is that bank privatization in Slovakia has become an object of fervent political discussions in which politicians of different parties represent the interests of different influential pressure groups. The present Slovak governmental coalition, composed from three political parties – the centrist party of Meciar, a right-wing nationalist party, and a left-wing workers' party – started in 1996 an attempt to privatize the three state-owned banks by big Slovak companies. Internal disputes within the coalition prevented this solution and the coalition itself survived only by postponing bank privatization.

A law was adopted which postponed the privatization of state-owned banks up to March 1997. In 1997, the question of bank privatization again became actual. The opposition supported by the workers' party succeeded in carrying through a law forbidding the privatization of state-owned banks, up to 2003. This law is at the moment an object of fervent political discussion. It will be discussed in parliament once again and Meciar even wants to offer his abdication if it would be accepted.

The National Bank of Slovakia which is independent from the government and in the past has preserved a very strong position against political pressures has published a statement in which it refuses a complete privatization of the three big banks at the moment. The statement analyses in detail the conditions and the recommended procedure in each of the three big banks. It expresses the opinion that a partial privatization of the banks is possible, but only with the participation of foreign investors. The NBS recommends to the government to retain an adequate equity share in the VÚB and SSB (as well as in the biggest insurance company – Slovenská poist'ovna) as long as the reconstruction process is not yet finished and as long as their dominant position in the banking sector prevails.

The statement accents the fact that bank privatization is useful only if it leads to the stabilization and financial strengthening of the banks. The NBS strictly refuses a privatization of the biggest Slovak banks by their borrowers. If borrowers became owners of the banks, it would be necessary to deduct loans granted to the proprietors from the adequate equity of the banks, which would considerably weaken their economic position.

The NBS insists that each company interested in privatizatizing some banks has to declare the source of the money used for this purpose. It is by no means acceptable to allow a privatization financed by a loan granted from another bank.

As to the different banks which should be privatized, the position of the NBS is the following.

In deciding about the privatization of SSB, it is necessary to consider the dominating position of this company on the interbank market. The new proprietor would be able to influence practically the whole banking sector and also the interest rate on the interbank market, the investment possibilities of the banks into the government's development programmes and the restructuring of the economy. All this leads NBS to the conclusion that the privatization of SSB should not exceed 33-49 per cent of its equity. The decisive share of its equity should remain by the FNM in order to protect the public interest. This situation should be maintained for the whole time of restructuring the SSB and the existence of its dominant position on the bank market. Up to 10 per cent of the SSB's equity could be privatized by foreign partners.

As to VÚB, the National Bank of Slovakia recommends to the government to retain not less than 34 per cent of its equity and to preserve in it decisive competences up to the end of restructuring. The rest of the present state-owned share (16.8 per cent) could be sold to domestic or foreign investors willing to respect the general principles of privatizing the banking sector.

As to IRB, NBS recommends its complete privatization by domestic and foreign investors, the privatization should be realized by increasing IRB's equity capital.

Another problem being discussed remains the question whether state-owned banks should be privatized before restructuring. The experience from other countries (e. g. Hungary) shows that privatization before or after their restructuring leads in many cases to new government activities which can be characterized as renationalization.

Bibliography

Berggren, A. (1995), 'Government-led Bank Restructuring', *Workshop on Systemic Bank Restructuring in Central and Eastern Europe*, Warsaw, September.

Borish, M., M. F. Long, M. Noël, (1995), 'Restructuring Banks and Enterprises', *World Bank Discussion Papers*, Washington.

Dziobek, C. (1995), 'Policy Instruments for Systemic Bank Restructuring', *Workshop on Systemic Bank Restructuring in Central and Eastern Europe*, Warsaw, September.

Nyberg, P. (1995), 'Authorities' Roles and Organizational Issues in Systemic Bank Restructuring', *Workshop on Systemic Bank Restructuring in Central and Eastern Europe*, Warsaw, September.

Nyberg, P. (1995a), 'Macroeconomic Aspects of Systemic Bank Restructuring', *Workshop on Systemic Bank Restructuring in Central and Eastern Europe*, Warsaw, September.

Sobek, O., (1995a), 'Present-day Slovak Banking', *Slovak Financial Revue, 2*.

Sobek, O. (1995b), 'Risk Management in Transformation Countries: The Case of Slovakia', paper prepared for the colloquium 'Risk Management in Volatile Financial Markets', Thun, October.

Sobek, O. (1995c), 'The Banking System in Slovakia', paper prepared for the conference 'The Role of the Banking System in the Economic Transformation of Central European Countries', Warsaw, May.

23 The 'Principal-Agent' Conflict in the Period of Post-communist Transformation in Central and Eastern Europe

Márton Tardos

Marx's idea of overcoming the capitalist market economy failed as early as in the 1920s, directly after the so-called socialist revolution. The Stalinist dictatorship created a new structure of economic control for the operation of coercively nationalized capital: the socialist model of central planning. Neither did this control system lead towards the Marxist ideals – the disappearance of the state and the evolution of genuine social ownership – nor was it able to surpass the general efficiency of market economies. Yet, the system was operational for decades with the help of continuous transformations and reforms. Moreover, it proved to be suitable for achieving not insubstantial results. The so-called socialist countries reached growth faster than many a capitalist country, but under conditions of the wasteful use of the factors of production, forced accumulation, the low level satisfaction of consumer demand and the vigorous restraining of consumer sovereignty. At the same time, the Soviet Union managed to keep up the pace with the United States also in the arms race.

Nevertheless, the regime collapsed in 1989-1990. This was primarily a consequence of the fact that the leading elite of the socialist countries not only realized but also acknowledged that they were unable to approach their goals formulated in terms of communism and also perceived their inability to simultaneously cope with the demands of their own social base and the requirements arising from the superpower position of the Soviet Union.

The happy fact that the communist regime collapsed in 1989-1990 confronted the nations released from dictatorship with specific tasks. Their countries or rather the economies of their countries had to be suddenly transformed in three aspects:

- After the elimination of the Iron Curtain, the former production structure, protected from competition and established under the highly specific conditions of CMEA co-operation, had to be transformed in adjustment to the requirements of world market competition, simultaneously trying to limit the extent of the not insignificant economic decline, which took place as a result of the change in regimes. Budgetary income centralization and redistribution possible under the dictatorship had to be eliminated, taking into account as much as possible the opposite interests of the public and, within it those of the economic agents.
- Assets earlier held by the state and by the co-operatives, which could be regarded as near-state, had to be privatized all of a sudden; this was inevitable, as an efficient market economy cannot operate without the predominance of private ownership.
- The rapid transformation of ownership structures was also inevitable because the ownership operations of the weak state evolving after the dictatorship and lacking continuous traditions, was expected to be even worse than before.

In the course of solving these three very difficult tasks regulating the transformation, four other objectives had to be reached:

- Privatization had to handle the rightful claims of those injured as a result of earlier nationalization processes (compensation).
- The feelings of citizens had to be considered. Declining incomes due to the general economic decline, and sentiments against privatization, which was concomitant with increasing income and wealth-polarization, has generated considerable discontent.
- The proceeds of privatization was intended to assist the transformation of the structure of production, and also the management of the debt burden inherited from the previous era.
- Finally, the assets privatized should be put in the hands of competent owners, able to enforce their interest in profits and capital gain with adequate strength.

The new Hungarian government and the resolutions of the democratic parliament – taking the experiences of British privatization as the point of departure – gave priority to sales against cash, while they allotted a relatively modest role to compensation and employee and management buyouts. The concept of the Hungarian privatization started out from the assumption that the owners putting their own investments at stake would well meet the requirements set against a 'principal'. The established practice of privatization in Hungary was, therefore, basically characterized by an avoidance of fragmented ownership, of voucher or coupon privatization. According to some, the established Hungarian ownership structure is characterized by intertwining, irrespective of the intentions of the authors of the idea.

Even though I admit that its full clarification requires additional analysis, I believe that, as a result of Hungarian privatization, three new important groups of owners evolved:

- the dominant ownership by foreign multinational companies,
- employee ownership under the predominance of former managers continuing their operation,
- bank ownership in the hands of banks which swapped the debts of companies accumulated earlier against equity.

In the second and third case, at present, we have to admit that till now even after the partial privatization, the state has remained an important owner of assets.

The question now is whether and how the three types of ownership stand up to the test from the viewpoint of the enforcement of ownership interests. Of course, an adequate reply to this question would require a more detailed analysis:

- It seems that, from the viewpoint of enforcing ownership interests, the multinational group passed the test best. They aim at making a return on their substantial investments. They also ensure that their agent, the manager, subordinates himself to the will of the owner. The only cause for complaint in this respect is that the new owner is in some cases satisfied with a long-term return on his capital, and a rapid result is not important for him, in contrast to the national economic interest.

- The workers and the managers as owners – beside their occasional carelessness – are frequently concerned, with objective difficulties. They have obvious difficulties on capital and credit markets due to the weakness of the collateral they can offer. It is, also probable that the above group of owners and managers having ownership rights are not sufficiently aggressive with respect to production restructuring. They might fear that the inevitable conflicts within the company, arising in the course of radical changes in the production structure, might bring unacceptable consequences to them. They hesitate to violate the interests of individual colleagues in the course of radical restructuring; who, in response, might question the legitimacy of their acquisitions in the course of privatization, and that the 'damaged' parties might take legal action against them.
- Unfortunately, the majority of the banks are unable to bring about an improvement in the income generating capacity of their holdings and to control managers with sufficient thoroughness. Experience shows that their many other preoccupations, including the management of their transitory liquidity problem, prevents them to do so.

One of the most important issues of the Hungarian economy after the de facto completion of privatization is to provide statutory regulations for companies – such that would facilitate a favourable evolution in the principal/agent conflict from the viewpoint of national economic efficiency.

References

Bodó, Péter, (1996), 'Az ügynökprobléma néhány aspektusa az átmeneti gazdaságban' [A Few Aspects of the Agent Problem in an Economy in Transition], *Közgazdasági Szemle*, No. 4.

Bruszt, László-Stark, David, (1996), 'Vállalatközi tulajdonhálózatok a kelet-európai kapitalizmusban' [Interenterprise Networks of Ownership in East European Capitalism], *Közgazdasági Szemle*, No. 4.

Major, Iván, (1992), *Privatization in Eastern Europe*, Institute of Economics, Budapest.

Mihályi, Péter, (1996), 'Privatization in Hungary, Communist Economics and Economic Transformation', *Közgazdasági Szemle*, No. 8.

Stark, David, (1994), 'Új módon összekapcsolt rendszerelemek' [System Elements Linked in a New Way], *Közgazdasági Szemle*, No. 11-12.

24 Financing Social Projects in Support of Convergence

Martin Murtfeld

Introductory remarks

It is a great honour and pleasure for me to present a brief statement at this joint conference of RTSF and SUERF. May I congratulate both organizers of the conference for having chosen particularly challenging subjects which require careful research and forward looking solutions. Budapest is an excellent venue at which to discuss the interrelated topics of ascertaining what are the best practices in the financing business and of assuring that global and regional convergence evolves prudently. Hungary has taught us exemplary lessons. You will forgive an observer of German nationality recalling Hungary's decisive role in gradually transforming towards decentralization the practice under which COMECON member countries were centrally planned and managed; and – on the political front line – in getting the Berlin wall down. As a banker, I feel entitled to praise the determination and discipline of the Hungarian authorities in fulfilling their international debt service obligations at difficult times, when other countries in the region choose to confront their foreign creditors with far-reaching schemes of rescheduling and even partial forgiveness of debt. It took years of painful negotiations for those countries to reach 'Brady type' or other solutions for a new order to their debt; agreements on the former Soviet debt are about to be signed only now. Hungary, by comparison, has been able to reap the fruits of its impeccable performance in terms of credit standing on the international financial markets without interruption.

Apparently, my paper is the only one on the agenda dealing with 'social' issues. I am grateful, indeed, to be able to present briefly the institution to which I now belong, the Council of Europe Social Development Fund. This institution is active on financial markets on a worldwide basis. Analysing and evaluating the behaviour and efficiency of private, public, and supranational participants in the markets is the basic work required in order to obtain the best results in terms of interest rates, currencies and long-term maturities for the funding of loans for social purposes.

Corporate governance is an increasingly important subject for supranational lending organizations themselves, but also, of course, for judging clients and business partners in general. Although the issues of corporate governance are relevant predominantly for corporations owned by stockholders and for the business in the securities markets, the subject concerns managers and supervisory boards responsible for development finance institutions as well. The EBRD and the Asian Development Bank have put corporate governance on the agendas of their annual meetings this year. The task of financing social projects through loans, therefore, fits into the general themes of this conference. Adequate solutions need to be found by interaction: applying good rules in public administration when investing in sound social projects in support of conversion.

Self-reliance, market economy, and human rights as determinants for social action

The dimension of social problems is huge: unemployment, misery, institutional and administrative deficiencies, individual misbehaviour; a list of concerns virtually without end. Many of us in Western Europe, increasingly confronted with new challenges for action on social policies at home, find it difficult to perceive the much bigger problems and to assess the usefulness of outside contributions as we go East. Serious social problems have always emerged after periods of historical disaster – such as World War II or communist dictatorship. Is it an illusion to search for an adequate 'ideological superstructure' and a basic set of principles for action against which we can check decisions on financial measures and investments in the social fields? Certainly not.

One important guideline is *self-determination* and the willingness to achieve change by one's own initiatives. We gratefully remember in these days the 50th anniversary of George Marshall's speech at Harvard in early June 1947, and the launching of the vast support programme for 18 European countries during the post-World War II period. The 'grand design' of the US Foreign Assistance Act of April 3, 1948 was to enable the revitalization of European countries through their own initiatives; 'piecemeal' help for specific transitory needs would not have brought about restructuring and growth on a broad basis. Monetary reforms, measures to restore international creditworthiness and institution-building for channelling long-term funds into priority sectors were corollary policies, which, if introduced, ensured a long lasting impact of the Plan on national macroeconomics as well as on the gradual improvement of the income and savings potential of individuals.

We should recall that in 1989 much thought was given to the question of whether a Marshall Plan-type of multilateral support was needed to achieve East-West convergence. (One of the prominent proponents at that time was Alfred Herrhausen, the speaker of the Board of Deutsche Bank AG, who was later murdered.) As we all know, the decision was instead to reinforce the existing organizations such as the Bretton Woods and the EC-based institutions, and to create the EBRD, in view of the new historic challenge. My institution, the Council of Europe Social Development Fund, also received a capital increase in view of the imminent East-West convergence. A wide, although not necessarily transparent, range of resources for advice, investment capital, loans and – to a lesser extent – grants, is available for countries in transition. In the absence of a comprehensive and uniform approach, integrated use of the different multilateral, bilateral and market sources is of utmost importance, and the self-reliance of countries in transition all the more decisive. Admittedly, these tasks and the fulfilment of conditions attached are specifically difficult to be tackled by the poorer countries of Eastern Europe.

Individual self-determination is made possible in line with the freedoms offered by the 'market economy', the catch phrase connected with transition. I do not agree with those who discard the theoretical foundations of the principles of 'social market economy' by Eucken, Röpke, Rüstow and others as being outmoded. It is true that this typically German model of thinking encountered later difficulties in its transmission to politics. It was distorted in recent history both:

- in the West (to a regrettable extent in Germany), since costly social insurance systems, subsidies and rigidities in the labour markets were admitted in the short-sighted aim of pleasing large sectors of the population, and
- in some transition countries, through a dangerous misinterpretation of 'market economy' as 'free market economy' and capitalism.

Ideally, the 'social' I would add, and environment-friendly market economy presupposes a strong state involvement in order to protect individual freedoms against unfair competition and dominance of all sorts. Besides prime political and economic tasks, the government must in particular play a convincing role in protecting individuals in their efforts to accumulate wealth by saving and investing (supervision of financial institutions and markets). An indirect and sometimes even direct role of the state is necessary to counterbalance competitive disadvantages of certain sectors or regions of the economy through market-oriented financial offers. Social protection and public investment in social projects is not incompatible with the well understood principles of a 'social market economy'; on the contrary, they cross-fertilize each other!

It is interesting to note that researchers (and political practitioners), such as Müller-Armack wanted the principles of social market economy to be embedded in a set of values. He 'suggested investing in human capital, demanded protection of the environment, regional and municipal planning, and wanted to give more people the chance of self-reliance in the spirit of true subsidiarity' (quoted from *Frankfurter Allgemeine Zeitung*, April 26, 1997).

Social values have been meticulously identified by the Council of Europe. This institution, now comprising 40 member states (Hungary since 1990), has played a pivotal role since its inception in 1949, and especially after 1989, in securing democratic values, political pluralism, rules of law and respect for *human rights*. The corner-stones are the European Convention on Human Rights of September 3, 1953, special programmes and ample practical advice in political, legal, environmental and social matters. Mechanisms of monitoring the compliance by member countries with commitments accepted have been set up. The European Social Charter (1961) covers a wide range of social rights in the spirit of human freedom:

- strengthening social cohesion;
- aiming at an adequate level of social security;
- promotion of employment and vocational training;
- providing protection for the most vulnerable groups of society;
- combating exclusion and discrimination; and
- consolidating European co-operation on migration.

Martin Murtfeld

The Council of Europe Social Development Fund

In 1956, eight member countries of the Council of Europe created the Council of Europe Resettlement Fund in order to finance social projects through loans. The first loans were channelled into housing and education projects, partly related to migration, in Germany, Greece, Italy, and Turkey. Some of the loans were extended to well-established public banking institutions, others to the member governments themselves. The name of the institution – which in comparison to the European Investment Bank, the EBRD, and the Nordic Investment Bank is now the oldest of the 'peer group' of pan-European long-term finance institutions – was changed in 1989 to 'Council of Europe Social Development Fund' (CEF). The CEF has presently twenty-five members, four of which are Central and Eastern European countries (Bulgaria, Lithuania, Romania, and Slovenia). Given its range of members, the CEF represents in a unique manner the 'wide' concept of European cooperation and solidarity.

Although operating within the general goals and rules of the Council of Europe, the CEF has a distinct legal identity and is financially independent. Four additional member states of the Council of Europe – Hungary, Croatia, Estonia, and Macedonia – have recently submitted their official request to join the CEF. Conditions of adhesion have been communicated and remain valid for one year during which internal procedures like ratification etc. may be completed.

The CEF is, to my knowledge, the only supranational institution which provides long-term finance exclusively for social projects. (It should be noted that among the regional IFIs, the Inter-American Development Bank and also the Asian Development Bank have recently refocused their activities towards social strategies.) The mandate is complex: the CEF has to fulfil the role of a bank as well as the role of a social development agency.

The funds of the CEF stem from worldwide borrowing on the international and some national bond markets, where the institution operates in competition with other first rate issuers. Proceeds from bond issues are regularly swapped into those interest rates (variable or fixed) and currencies which the clients wish to accept. One example is our 1 billion Czech koruna issue of January 1997 which was swapped into DM. The annual borrowing volume (around 1.5 to 2 billion ECU) and total outstanding issues (as of Dec. 31, 1996: 8.0 billion ECU) are in line with a subscribed capital of 1.3 billion ECU and net assets of about 900 million ECU, accumulated over the years essentially through retained earnings. The CEF has therefore to meet all the prerequisites of a banking institution with international lending, funding, and derivatives activities. Although not profit-oriented by mandate, the CEF has to achieve good financial results in order to maintain its standing on the markets as well as – in the absence of any regular budgetary contributions except capital from new member states – to fulfil its social function (net profits 1996: 85.9 million ECU). The CEF enjoys preferred creditor status and has – throughout its 40-year history – not participated in any country debt rescheduling or suffered from any repayment default (with the exception of a loan to ex-Yugoslavia which was seized by the UN embargo and is now recovered). The CEF has the intention to pursue this policy in the future.

Member countries present projects for financing are within the following priority areas:

- projects in favour of refugees or migrants (either to help solve problems of migration flows into member countries or to assist in the voluntary return of migrants through loans or guarantees);
- in the event of natural disasters, such as earthquake or floods, the CEF is entitled to disburse very rapidly for dwelling and infrastructure rehabilitation upon request of a member country;
- job creation through investments in small and medium-sized enterprises;
- housing for low income groups;
- education (basically all sectors are eligible);
- health (hospitals);
- social infrastructure, improvement of the environment through water supply and sanitation projects, irrigation and rural modernization projects; and
- social infrastructures designed to improve living conditions in disadvantaged urban areas.

The CEF finances up to 40 per cent, in special cases up to 50 per cent (natural disasters, up to 100 per cent) of project cost. Project documentation – and, upon commitment, loan documentation – follow international standards. Major emphasis is on the socio-economic justification of the projects (in each case the Secretary General of the Council of Europe has to issue an opinion); the technical preparation and the soundness of the financing proposals (standing of the borrower, necessary guarantees, organizational and financial execution of the project). As far as advanced member countries are concerned, 'global loans' may be envisaged to first rate financial institutions which have a proven track record of long-term financing in CEF eligible areas; in these cases, the precise nature of the individual projects to be financed under such programmes as well as the financing conditions for the end users are determined well in advance.

While the CEF actively pursues the initiation and conclusion of loan programmes of substantial size in its highly rated member countries, the institution now welcomes after much preparatory work the beginning of a thorough co-operation within Central and Eastern Europe.

The linking of the social perspective with the need for economic growth, which is behind the scale of eligibility criteria for CEF financing, will enhance the attractiveness of the institution as a genuine partner in conversion. Socially oriented projects are forthcoming to adapt existing systems – in health, education and social insurance – to the requirements of more efficiency. Improved education, and health will result in greater economic productivity. Human capital must be maintained, with due respect to the motivation of the elite and of the younger generation, and should be adapted to the manifold needs of public administration and the market. Increased labour productivity depends on workers' knowledge, skills and health. Investments are needed in technology (also to improve social delivery systems), the environment, and in the relief of extreme poverty.

On the other side, we have to anticipate projects intended to mitigate poverty which results from corrective measures embarked upon transition: elimination of public support and of subsidies; decline in social protection; privatization with subsequent laying off of labour; and bankruptcies. There are winners in this process, e.g. in the sectors of communication, financing services and energy. The loosers are staff in public services, education, and health as well as workers in agriculture. Transition particularly affects unskilled people, women, and young people. A vast reallocation of labour has therefore to be envisaged. Regional disparities should be mitigated since cities and industrial areas are being favoured. Social housing programmes are needed to correct a deficient housing market and to enable labour to be mobile. The financing of the small and medium-sized enterprises is important for job creation.

Examples of projects for which the CEF has approved loans are described in the enclosure for illustration. These are projects in education, health and social housing. Loans to development banks for small and medium-sized enterprises and, possibly, to municipal programmes are expected in the future.

It should be noted that the CEF has established from the net profits in 1995 and 1996, a 'selective trust account' of ECU 25 million in order to grant interest subsidies for priority projects of exceptionally high social value in the poorer countries of Central and Eastern Europe. Part of this money is earmarked as indicated in the enclosure.

The CEF is interested in co-operating closely with all its member countries as well as with major international and national development institutions in fostering convergence. The new tasks ahead are certainly not only of a financial dimension. Advise, experience, obeyance of values and the will for action, based on mutual understanding, will be decisive.

Examples of the CEF's participation in Central and Eastern Europe

Slovenia

Project approved in 1996 on the financing of **an Education programme aimed at meeting European educational standards and at preparing students to the challenges of the new market mechanisms.** The total cost of the project amounts to ECU 131.1 million and the CEF's loan to ECU 48.7 million. The main components of the project are the construction and rehabilitation of education buildings of universities, secondary schools (grammar schools, professional and vocational education), and centres for school and extramural activities. The reforms in the education sector in Slovenia aim at improving the quality of education by widening the scope of primary, secondary, and university curricula in order to cope with the economic transition and to assist the country in the ongoing European integration.

Lithuania

Project approved in 1996 on the financing of the **Returning Deportees Programme favouring socio economic reinsertion.**

This project, as part of the programme on Provision of Housing to Returning Deportees launched by the government of Lithuania in 1992, is in line with the social objectives of the CEF in that it aims at providing housing for about 1,600 political prisoners, ex-deportees and their families. Besides the financing of the housing programme, the CEF provides social assistance in the logistics of the resettlement operations.

The total cost of the project amounts to ECU 26.4 million and the CEF's loan to ECU 9.8 million.

Bulgaria

Project approved in 1995 on the financing of a **Health project co-financed by the World Bank and the European Union (PHARE programme).** The total cost of the project amounts to US$ 29.7 million and the CEF's loan to US$ 6.8 million. The project's objective is to assist in the improvement of efficacy in health services through the provision of the necessary infrastructures for primary health care in 132 local clinics, emergency medical services in 66 hospitals and in 6 blood transfusion centres.

Programme of construction of social housing for low-income population of the city of Radnevo (region of Haskovo, in Southeast Bulgaria).

The cost of the project amounts to USD 1.5 million and consists of the construction of 62 individual dwellings in order to provide housing for about half of the gipsy population of the city of Radnevo, in the same neighbourhood where they are presently living under insalubrious conditions (cob constructions, lack of running water and sewage, etc.). About 410 persons are expected to benefit from the construction of these social dwellings which should also contribute to better integration into Bulgarian social and economic activity. The loan approved by the Fund amounts to USD 574,000, or 38 per cent of the total cost.

Romania

Baltesti Rural Hospital, providing hospital services to a low-income population in seven villages in the county of Prahova

The total cost of the project amounts to USD 788,000 and entails civil works and equipment for the reconstruction of the hospital which was destroyed almost totally (80-90 per cent) by a storm in late June 1996.

The Baltesti Rural Hospital serves a total of 20,000 inhabitants in an area of 100 km^2 which includes seven villages, six of which are described as having difficult access conditions.

The loan approved by the Fund amounts to USD 219,765, or 27.8 per cent of the total cost, and shall be used to cover the purchase of medical equipment for the central and pediatric units of the hospital, the construction work being covered by local resources.

A loan of about USD 16.9 million is requested for a project aiming at providing 1,300 dwellings to low income households: the project is currently being evaluated from the technical and financial viewpoints.

The CEF is also in the process of negotiating the co-financing with the World Bank of an education project aiming at rehabilitating about a thousand of severly damaged schools, which have been found to be in imminent danger of collapse. Its implementation would safeguard the school occupants and maintain the educational process.

Bosnia-Herzegovina

Although this country is not a member of the CEF, the following loans have been approved as part of the international support programmes in favour of Bosnia-Herzegovina.

Refugee and War Victim Rehabilitation Programme providing emergency medical aid for the victims of war in Bosnia-Herzegovina.

The total cost of the project amounts to USD 30 million and seeks to reduce the enormous burden of disease and disability due to physical and psycho-social trauma on the most at risk segments of the population, namely the direct victims of the war, as well as women and children.

The project is being co-financed by the Fund and by the World Bank, as well as other donors. The Fund's loan amounts to USD 5 million, or 17 per cent of total cost. The World Bank's participation is 33 per cent.

Drinking Water Supply Project for the refugees and local population of Tuzla

The project entails the repair of war damaged water treatment units and the addition of water improvement facilities. The objective is to assist the local population and the refugees who are in a desperate situation and to provide a supplementary 400 to 500 litres per second of drinking water to an overcrowded city. In the long term, the project could also contribute to environmental protection by preventing the pollution of rivers and preserving the water resources of the city of Tuzla.

The Fund has approved a loan of USD 1.5 million. The project is currently in the process of being finalized as regards the planned works, work schedule and financing plan.

25 The Hungarian Banking System and the Development of Capital Markets

Katalin Botos

I. The status and prospects of the Hungarian banking system

1. The Hungarian banking system in the 1990s[1]

The Hungarian banking system, similarly to those of other East European countries, is the offspring of the transition from a centrally planned (CPE) to a market economy.

The transition to a two-tier banking system in Hungary did not begin with the change of the regime. Recognition of the failure of the traditional mechanism of CPE and the demand of institutions for capital allocation has intensified in the early and mid-1980s. Thus, the establishment of the two-tier banking system and the separation of commercial banks from the National Bank of Hungary (NBH) took place already in the second half of the 1980s. The Budapest Stock Exchange and the Commodities Exchange have been set up in the early 1990s.

However, the most important transitional step has been taken with the change of the regime, which have recognized that a **market economy** can be based only on **private ownership**. It is impossible to find a proper mechanism for the allocation of capital without 'cutting the process of financing into pieces'. The stock of means for financial investments should be developed, channelled and directed by managing institutions towards **real investors**, who need capital with shorter or longer maturity.

This seems obvious in the western part of the world. It is still an open question, however, whether the continental, Japanese or Anglo-Saxon types of financial intermediation will be more dominant in the world. For Eastern European countries, social passivity and the absence of necessary expertise, both being the results of the centrally planned system, which has prevailed for over 40 years, had to be overcome before a stable banking system could be established even in the most developed CPEs of Eastern Europe. Although the technical bases of transition to market economy have been established by the mechanisms of self-interest, profit, and interest rates, and Hungary was among the first to do this – the society's whole mentality had to be changed to erect the building of a stable and effective economy on these foundations.

Just as in every planned economy, the most characteristic feature of the Hungarian banking system before 1990 was that in the one-tier system the central bank (national bank) financed companies, eventually complemented by a few functionally specialized banks, like a foreign trade bank, an investment bank, or a state bank for development.

The savings of the population were collected by savings banks, which operated in co-operative or state forms. Then these savings were 'channelled' and directed to the central (national) banks to meet the requirements of central financing.

The centre of collecting deposits in Hungary was the National Savings Bank (OTP), which granted credits to people, mainly loans to support housing from the population's own resources. This function was important not only from the perspective of meeting the population's needs, but also from that of macroeconomic policy. The building of homes financed from central funds was almost exclusively replaced by the latter way of financing. The role of the 'housing industry' is an important indicator of the economic cycle in both market and centrally planned economies.

The two-tier banking system came into being with **inborn defects:**

- the banks were undercapitalized;
- they represented **sectoral risks, as** their clients were concentrated in the individual fields of the economy, like heavy industry, agriculture, infrastructure, etc.;
- they were heavily dependent on the **interbank market,** or, first and foremost, on the refinancing of the central bank, as they had very meagre retail banking activities or none; at the beginning only the central bank – or, to a lesser degree, the foreign trade bank – might have thought of getting access to f foreign funds, as it was difficult to be accepted abroad; structural disproportion was typical of the

banking system due to the one-sided corporate financing of deposit-taking institutions;
- the expertise of bankers was based on the one-tier system generating banking plan directives. This knowledge was adjusted by rapid and dynamic change. In practice, fairly good economists, specialized in finance, foreign trade and industry have joined banks. Bank managers and employees acquired on-the-job technical knowledge of actual banking.

The change of the regime in Hungary could rely on significant legislation. The Banking Act **(Act on Financial Institutions)**, passed in 1991, outlined **the main trends of the development** of the banking system.

- The fundamental norms of **international banking regulation** should be met over a relatively short, i.e., three years' period of adjustment.
- The existing banks should be transformed into **universal banks** with broker firms, dealing in securities according to German and British patterns. The possibility of establishing new banks was made rather easy, and was regulated by legal norms. Foreigners may open subsidiaries subject to government permission, excluding branches. During the past four years this rule has not been strictly complied with when banks were established.
- The law provided for **privatization** by the stipulation of reducing state ownership within a given time.

The Act was tested in 1992; 1993 may be considered as the year **of attempts for correction.** The experiment began in 1992, and it did not end in 1993.

1.1 Consolidation is required (1*)

The data measured on the basis of the Banking Act made the banks – primarily state-owned – realize that neither the sector nor the individual banks were able to meet the legal, or the privatization requirements of the government. The position of the economy, reflected in the portfolio of banks, made it clear that it cannot be covered with their income, and sometimes even with their capital. The loss of capital due to the provisioning requirements did not result in **illiquidity** (technical insolvency). Larger banks were covered by the relative excess liquidity, which continued even in 1993, as savings were put into banks and directed to interbank markets. However, liquidity is not income or capital, and banking losses may not be **'swallowed'** at its expense. It is hardly possible to privatize banks which include uncovered losses amounting, in some cases even up to 20 per cent of the portfolio, unless somebody **'pays the buyer'**.

In 1993, the government still faced a situation that, in addition to the **significant** efforts of 1992, the banks **still had to be consolidated**. In 1993, there was a **will** for that: however, there were lengthy discussions about the methods. Finally, in 1993, a decision was made that capital increase should go together with an increase in the **ownership share of the state**, since if the bill of consolidation had to be paid by the government (and the **tax payers, in the end**), control should **also be taken over** from the often accidental corporate owners who were in most cases **not ideal owners in the full sense of the term. Consequently,** by increasing ownership shares compared to the management and other owners, **the state itself**, as a direct owner, began to control the privatization process as well.

This decision involving the appearance of a new owner, **the Ministry of Finance**, and other governmental institutions in the background has created an almost incomprehensible system of **ownership rights**. The State Privatization Authority – SPA; SPA, SHCo, MoF and NCTD – all acted as **state owners**. Co-ordination between the state owners was not complete and the principles of **asset management** were not entirely clear.

At the end it was decided that consolidation should be controlled by the Ministry of Finance. **Since the legal framework for this control was missing, it was based on contracts**. In this contract the Ministry of Finance, an institution of the government, has entered into a contract with the banks where **the Ministry of Finance** was in most cases the main owner. In fact **one of the departments of the Ministry of Finance entered into a contract with another department of the Ministry of Finance.**

1.2 Surveillance and governance

On the basis of this arrangement the Ministry of Finance, the main state owner, made an attempt to establish an ownership structure for itself approximating the responsibilities of the Boards of Directors. In some sense, this could result in a similar centralization to the single-tier banking and planning system. This would not be desirable. Instead, the responsibilities of the Board of Directors for controlling the management in both state-owned and privately-owned banks should be increased.

The responsibility of the Board of Directors is based on the Company Act. It should be independent from government influence. Should it be a state-owned or a privately-owned **bank, the Board of Directors is responsible** for the bank, and also for the depositors' money.

At this point, it is worth referring to the views of the American Banking Supervision on this issue:

> The Board of Directors must expect and require certain things from the Management. The team of the Chairman and Chief Executive must control the everyday activities of the bank with the help of the internal controls of the system, on the basis of the business strategy of the Board of Directors and in compliance with the laws and regulations. The Management must supply the directors the necessary information and must answer the questions of the Board of Directors quickly and thoroughly. In addition, the management should use their skills to come up with new and innovative ideas and submit their proposals to the Board of Directors for decision. The Board of Directors and the Management must mutually support each other but both must fulfil their own roles and implement their own tasks. While the Board of Directors may leave the everyday work to the Management, it must maintain overall control. The bank does not benefit if the Management dictates to the Board of Directors and the Board cannot fulfil its own tasks.[2]

There are very good reasons for quoting the views of the American Banking supervision. Mistakes and misunderstandings have occurred often in the Hungarian banking sector concerning the tasks of various institutions. We think that **the owner's control cannot be exercised** directly by a public administration institution, but only by **a Board of Directors** representing the relevant skills and involving members with undoubted honesty. The members of this Board of Directors are not *eo ipso* public servants but **banking experts trusted by the owner state,** entrusted with the control of the bank, exercised **in accordance with the Company Act, on behalf of the state.** The quotation indirectly refers to the decrease of the controlling role of the **Board of Directors** if there is a **personal union** between **the Chairman and the Managing Director.**

Among the characteristic features of the Hungarian situation this latter configuration was generally the case since the number of available experts was very limited and – since the banks were state-owned – loyalty also counted. If someone made a good chief executive, he also seemed suitable as a chairman. This is why the first signs of dividing the positions of chairman and chief executive occurred first only in 1993. **The first line of protection of** depositors' money is **a good Board of Directors**. There is no escape if the board plays together with the operative leadership of the bank, giving misleading signals to the supervising authorities. This was the case in 1992, when three banks with private majority ownership displayed an imprudent behaviour. The State Banking Supervision (SBS) discovered the insolvency situation through a cross-ownership manipulation when one of the three banks got near to a liquidity crisis and asked for a bridging loan from the National Bank. The authorities closed this bank, where the owners were not ready to cover the missing assets by capital injections.

This lesson came too early; the Hungarian population, depositors and other clients, and the authorities as well, were not ready to evaluate crisis signals like too high, nonmarket-conform interest rates, which could indicate the liquidity problem in the bank and make potential depositors cautious.

After these events the law has been changed; but both private and **public organs had to pay the** 'learning fee' for the bankruptcies. It became urgent to create some fund to protect the depositors. Incidentally, this happened almost simultaneously with the BCCI case in a more advanced and sophisticated society, where the financial culture was higher than in a post-communist country.

1.3 Banking supervision and deposit insurance

Compared to the previous year, in 1993 the Banking Supervision received less **criticism for not protecting** the depositors' money from any potential failures, but the issue remained alive. In 1993, a number of savings co-operatives had to be closed.

While in 1992 the bankruptcy and liquidation of small banks and savings co-operatives caught the financial government unprepared, by 1993 Hungary had an up-to-date Banking Act and developed a deposit insurance system which are considered good even by international comparison and were followed as an example by many East European countries.

In 1993, the **National Deposit Insurance Fund (NDIF), established with the help of the intellectual, technical and financial assistance of the Banking Supervision, began to operate.** The Act which was passed in 1993 had been prepared by the Banking Supervision in 1992, benefiting from the generous support of the government by providing the appropriate international experts as consultants.

When Heves County and Vicinity Savings Co-operative went bankrupt and SBS had to initiate liquidation, the NDIF fulfilled its task but, could only partially compensate large depositors. This is why all efforts still must be made to prevent any possible problems in the banking sector.

However, the role of the Banking Supervision cannot ever be mistaken for that of a deposit insurance institution. Let us refer to a foreign example again. The exact definition of **the aims** of banking supervisory activities are important both for the banking sector and for the public at large. The banking supervision of South Africa stated its philosophical views as follows in the Introduction to its *Annual Report 1993*:

> Protection of the interests of depositors is not the Banking Supervision's task, and it cannot be so, either. It can only be the task of the Board of Directors and the management itself. Yet, we believe that the banking supervisory activity will definitly contribute to a healthier and more stable banking sector in which depositors are given more protection.[3]

These ideas match very well those which were said about the responsibilities of the Board of Directors and also put into the right place the functions and significance of the banking supervisory activities. The aim and function of the latter is not to take over the responsibility but to assist effective risk management in the banking **sector by providing adequate regulatory environment.**

1.4 1993 – a year of big changes

In 1993, the Banking Supervision focused on putting the banking sector in order, making it stable and consolidate it. SBS can only fulfill its **preventive function** if the provisions of the law can be generally complied with. It is difficult to apply laws **if exceptions are the rules**.

Estimating the risks included in the investment portfolio and off-balance sheet items of the banks (e.g., guarantee), and bringing forward the regulatory amendments entering into force at the end of the year, the government assessed the capital requirements, of banks on the basis of model calculations. A decision was made to cover external liabilities in all the banks to be consolidated in the first step, i.e., to cover the depositors' funds, because capitalization at 0 capital adequacy means that.

The second phase of consolidation took place at the general meetings in May, when the registered capital was raised to 4 per cent of capital adequacy. In the coming years more and more injections arrived to the banking sector in forms of capital raises, credits and guarantees. By the beginning of 1996 nearly all of the banks had a good capital adequacy ratio.

1993 was definitely a year of great changes. Of course, the major and most important government decision was the one on consolidation, but **spontaneous market processes** also took place.

1993 was the **year of a rising number of joint venture and foreign banks. Six** new banks were established. While in 1992 joint venture banks (banks owned by foreigners) increased their balance sheet total only very slightly, in 1993 their balance sheet total rose by almost two-thirds. This was partly due to the fact that the 1993 figures contained CIB data, not included in the reporting system of the SBS before. The placement policy of joint venture banks is very prudent: they pay great attention to collateral and guarantees. If those exist, their customers have a good chance. The former high adequacy ratio, which exceeded the required level 3-4 times, decreased in 1993 from 30 per cent to 24 per cent, which also indicated that foreign banks established in the last one or two years have begun their business expansion. Their profit after tax increased as compared to their equity capital, and they paid very high dividends, sometimes using even the profit reserve from the previous year.

The other obvious sign of development in the banking sector is that joint venture banks and large banks began **retail banking.** It is a special feature of the Hungarian banking sector that the banks collecting households-deposits are also authorized to act as universal banks, like the NBH successor banks and some other banks founded since then. While joint venture banks can obtain relatively cheap funds through foreign depositors (parent bank deposits), smaller banks heavily depend on NBH refinancing and repo deals, as well as the interbank market. Naturally, the large Hungarian-owned banks operate with strong NBH dependence. Following consolidation this dependence even strengthened. Since a stricter monetary policy could be foreseen, the larger banks turned towards private individuals even more intensively. This attempt involving the sale of banking securities and aiming at the collection of funds was not new, but it became stronger in 1993.

The fact that OTP's monopoly is now threatened by the increasing number of competitors cannot be considered as a negative sign on its own, and hopefully competition will serve the interest of customers. However, it would be erroneous to expect that the liquidity position of large banks can be stabilized quickly this way since attracting deposits will take a long time. Establishing the institutional and human requirements of a universal bank needs capital and takes time, and those who are mostly affected are short of both. **The government had to develop a comprehensive concept to settle the issues of the banking structure, bank privatization, and consolidation.** During the development of this concept further necessary legal amendments must be decided on, in addition to those recommended by the Banking Supervision itself on the basis of practical experience and only part of which was reflected in the amendments of 1992.

1.5. 1993 – the year of integration of savings co-operatives

The establishment of OTIVA (National Savings Co-operatives' Institutions Protection Fund), the top organization of the savings co-operatives, was an important event in 1993. Dealing with savings co-operatives represented and still represents a huge part of the activities of the Banking Supervision. While the proportion of savings co-operatives is 5 per cent of the balance sheet of all banks; more than three-fourth of the number of banks are savings co-operatives. Although savings co-operatives are tiny financial institutions regarding their licence, **they are just the same as any other bank.** Outdated skills and technical equipment as well as their co-operative features generate even more problems than the ones observed in our commercial banks during the supervisory activities. The government had to decide what to do with the co-operative bank groups; to **terminate their existence** or to provide assistance **for the development of an integrated co-operative network.** This decision was inevitable, since SBS **reports indicated loss of capital, and** audits performed according to several criteria revealed too high risks. In several cases risks exceeded all capital.

On the basis of Central European examples (Raiffeisen bank group) the Banking Supervision suggested that they should clarify, voluntarily, their relations to their top bank – mutual 'subsidiary bank: Takarékbank[4] – individually, and with the help of the government they should create a protective fund which in given cases supports the co-operatives under **definite conditions.**

This is why the establishment of OTIVA, represented a considerable progress in the area of co-operative thinking and problem-prevention. On the other hand, from the point of Banking Supervision, it **does not reduce the**

institutional and legal responsibility of SBS for the prudent operation of these members of the banking sector. This is why, supervision of this sector and co-operation with the NBH, as well as the Ministry of Finance which has a veto in these cases, concerning the use of budgetary funds in OTIVA will be very important to ensure that in the future less banking supervisory measures should be necessary.

2. 1994 – privatization starts

While the previous two years were characterized by the integration of savings co-operatives, by the amendment of the banking law as the result of bankruptcies, and by the implementation of the consolidation because of the lack of capital, 1994 might be characterized as the year of starting privatization and as the ending of the significant chapter of consolidation.

In this year, one of the most important Hungarian banks the Hungarian Commercial Bank had been privatized. The bank was in a more or less 'sellable' state, since its balance sheet was audited for some years not only according to Hungarian but also according to international standards. The **risks of the bank were** covered and the company was profitable. The consolidation of the bank was carried out in 1994 by raising its capital. The process of consolidation continued in the following years. Practically the whole banking sector of Hungary was in privatizable status by the end of 1994. Since the Hungarian capital market was not developed, and the number of domestic investors was relatively low, most of the investors were foreigners. Therefore, the ratio of foreign owners in the Hungarian banking sector became higher than the European average.

The complex revision and renewal of the Banking Act started in 1994 and have been completed in 1996. Since Hungary intends to join the EU, the Act was modified according to the directives of the EU. It is an important novelty that the Act makes a step toward universality and allows the banks to function on the stock exchange concerning government securities and close-end issuances. Another considerable novelty of the Hungarian regulation is that it creates a uniform supervision of the money and capital markets by founding the Hungarian money and capital supervision. This means that the Hungarian market is becoming more complex.

We should have a look at the analyses of the Banking Supervision and the NBH for the year 1995 for a better view on the Hungarian banking sector.

3. The banking system in 1995[5]

3.1 Number of financial institutions

At the end of 1995, 42 financial institutions were in operation in Hungary. **The number of newly incorporated financial institutions fell as compared to previous years.**[6] Several applications for a banking license were submitted in 1995. These are in the process of evaluation. New financial institutions in foreign ownership are likely to start operating in 1996.

A longer-term view of the changes in the number of banks shows a significant increase in the number of new participants in the financial sector in the 1990s. The transitional rise in the number of banks with majority of state-ownership in 1993 came as a result of the government programme of bank consolidation, which increased the stake held by the government. **The market started to settle and become more concentrated as a result of mergers, liquidations and acquisitions in 1995.**

3.2 The structure of the banking system

There has been a significant shift in the distribution of banks by size and controlling majority in recent years:

The ownership structure of the banking system changed radically in 1995. In contrast with **previous years, privatization accelerated in the banking system** with the sale of the majority stake in the Hungarian Foreign Trade Bank in late 1994, and the partial privatization of the two additional large banks, OTP and Budapest Bank in 1995. The owner, acting on behalf of the state (ÁPV Rt.), retained 25 per cent + 1 vote in OTP and sold the remaining shares to foreign institutional investors (23 per cent), Social Security authorities (20 per cent), employees (5 per cent) and other investors. Foreign (strategic) investors acquired 64 per cent of the shares of Budapest Bank. There was a significant capital increase in Postabank.

Table 1. Number of financial institutions

	1989	1990	1991	1992	1993	1994	1995
Commercial banks	22	28	29	30	34	35	34
Specialized financial institutions	4	4	6	5	5	7	7
Investment banks	-	-	-	-	1	1	1
Banks, total	26	32	35	35	40	43	42
Savings co-operatives	260	260	260	257	255	254	243
Credit co-operatives	-	-	-	-	-	4	4
Savings institutions, total	260	260	260	257	255	258	247

Table 2. Number of banks according to size and major owner

	1989	1990	1991	1992	1993	1994	1995
1. **Large banks**	5	5	6	6	7	7	7
2. State banks	5	5	5	5	5	4	2
3. Private banks	0	0	1	1	2	3	5
4. **Medium-sized banks**	4	5	9	8	8	11	12
5. State banks	-	-	-	-	3	3	5
6. Private banks	4	5	9	8	5	8	7
7. **Small banks**	17	22	20	21	25	25	23
8. State banks	3	4	5	5	9	11	9
9. Private banks	14	18	15	16	16	14	14
Total banks (1+4+7)	26	32	35	35	40	43	42
State banks	8	9	10	10	17	18	16
Private banks	18	23	25	25	23	25	26

Besides the moves to privatize and increase capital, the reduction of registered capital in most of the banks participating in the consolidation programme also contributed to **lowering direct state ownership below 40 per cent by the end of 1995 and to increasing the ratio of foreign ownership above 25 per cent**, which is unusually high in comparison to the level in other countries.

Using shareholders equity rather than registered capital as a basis for comparing the business potential of the different groups of banks adds another dimension. The ratio of shareholders' equity in state-owned banks came to some 25 per cent at the end of 1995.

Table 3. Ownership structure of banks[7]

	1994		1995	
	Ft bns	%	Ft bns	%
1. Direct state ownership	193.3	65.95	86.7	39.44
2. Social secunty funds	2.6	0.89	8.3	3.78
3. State ownership, total (lines 1+2)	195.9	66.84	95.0	43.22
4. Local authorities	0.6	0.20	2.0	0.91
5. Other domestic ownership	52.3	17.84	44.6	20.29
6. Domestic ownership, total (lines 3, 4, 5)	248.8	84.88	141.6	64.42
7. Foreign ownership	44.3	15.12	78.2	35.58
8. Registered capital, total (lines 6+7)	293.1	100.00	219.8	100.00

The structural changes seen in previous years continued in 1995. Large banks with majority state ownership lost additional market share, while the market share of the small and medium-sized state-controlled banks remained essentially unchanged. Small and medium-sized banks not owned by the state increased their share. Large private banks increased their market share slightly. The share of savings co-operatives within the banking system is close to what it was in 1994.

Medium-sized and large banks in foreign ownership applied more and more pressure to increase competition in the domestic market. This process gained new momentum in 1995, when corporations showed preference for foreign borrowing. This allowed the market participants with comparative advantages in foreign currency financing to expand their business activities substantially.

3.3 The general position of financial institutions

The position of the banking system continued to stabilize in 1995 after the consolidation measures taken between 1992 and 1994. Although capital adequacy and profitability of the banking system as a whole and of the majority of market participants improved, and the liquidity position of the system as a whole and of certain participants strengthened, there still existed a strong tendency of differentiation. Writing off the negative provisions for results against registered capital was a major challenge banks faced in 1995, as a consequence of the consolidation process and crisis management. Banks increased the speed of writing off and selling bad loans and non-profitable investments against existing reserves. Consolidated state-owned banks embarked on **internal rationalization projects** required by efficient banking operations and several of these also began to reduce staff levels. However, no actual reduction in cost could be expected from a significant part of the moves targeted at cost savings, as some of these rationalization measures themselves incurred extra initial expenses.

Table 4. Balance sheet total of banks according to size and controlling majority

	Balance sheet total Ft bns			Distribution %	
	1994	1995	Index	1994	1995
Large banks of which:	2,234.7	2,518.7	112.7	71.5	67.3
private banks	1,494.7	1,805.4	120.8	47.8	48.2
state banks	740.0	713.3	96.4	23.7	19.1
Medium-sized banks of which:	494.3	695.2	140.6	15.8	18.6
private banks	284.6	436.6	153.4	9.1	11.7
state banks	209.7	258.6	123.3	6.7	6.9
Small banks of which:	241.1	343.7	142.6	7.7	9.2
private banks	145.8	228.8	156.9	4.7	6.1
state banks	95.3	114.9	120.6	3.0	3.1
Banking system, total	2,970.1	3,557.6	119.8	95.0	95.1
Co-operative financial institutions	156.0	182.4	116.9	5.0	4.9
Financial system, total	3,126.1	3,740.0	119.6	100.0	100.0

3.4 The business policy of financial institutions

Due to the changes in liabilities, financial institutions focused more heavily on high quality service in the retail business and in the management of accounts in 1995. Some of the joint venture banks continued to expand their regional branch networks. In order to offer improved banking access to large corporate customers with a strong capital base, several banks, including joint ventures and large banks, installed computer terminals for direct electronic banking. Typically, banks would heavily select among clients in the asset side activities, in supplying credit, whereas on the liabilities side, in collecting deposits they would widen their customer base and open up to households. In respect of the latter, joint venture banks also followed suit by offering a variety of transactions to a variety of retail customers and by giving priority to services tailored to high income groups. These banks only accepted large deposits from private individuals. Seeking to diversify their liabilities, most of the banks increased heavily the issuance of bank securities offered to retail customers. Borrowing from foreign sources was another important factor in the expansion of bank liabilities in 1995.

3.5 Main indicators of financial institutions' activities

3.5.1 Fundamental balance sheet data and indicators

The consolidated balance sheet total of financial institutions increased by 19.6 per cent in 1995. **Thus, the increase in banking sector operations fell short of both nominal GDP growth and the growth rate of annual inflation.** This tendency has continued since 1991 and may be **fundamentally attributed** to modified corporate borrowing strategies developing as privatization progressed. More funds are raised directly from parent companies and **foreign** entities, tighter financial discipline is applied as a result of the wave of bankruptcies and liquidation procedures, savings outside the banking system and government securities issued to finance the budget directly have gained ground. **In 1995, a few new factors complemented these longer term developments, including the stronger role** of self-financing due to improved corporate earnings positions, the steps taken to restructure balance **sheets in order** to complete the consolidation process, e.g., portfolio cleansing, buying out or **down-scaling the** portfolio of government securities.

3.5.2. Liabilities of the banking system

Banking system liabilities maturing over a year increased by 3 per cent only, which was much lower than the expansion of 22.2 per cent recorded for shorter term liabilities. Hence the proportion of liabilities maturing over a year to total liabilities of the banking system dropped when compared to the year before.

At 33.4 per cent, the rise in the own funds of the banking system was substantially higher than the average increase in liabilities. The growth of HUF 30 billion and HUF 18.7 billion in balance sheet profit and subordinated capital, respectively, is responsible for most of the increase. The consolidated registered capital of the banking system decreased by 15.3 per cent, which – however – coupled with reducing the negative provisions for results to a quarter, indicating that several banks increased registered capital while those included in the consolidation programme reduced it.

Table 5. Assets and liabilities of the banking sector, 1994-95
(Per cent)

Assets	1994	1995	Liabilities	1994	1995
			Own funds	8.6	10.0
Long-term assets	53.8	46.8	long-term liabilities	22.4	19.4
Of which:			Of which:		
central budget	20.2	17.6	central budget	0.4	0.2
enterprises	11.8	10.5	enterprises	0.2	0.3
households	8.2	6.3	households	4.8	4.0
non-residents	1.6	1.3	non-residents	3.8	5.3
central bank	7.5	6.8	central bank	11.5	7.9
interbank	0.5	0.5	interbank	0.4	0.7
non-credit	4.0	3.8	securities	1.3	1.0
Short-term assets	42.8	47.1	Short-term liabilities	63.0	65.0
Of which:			Of which:		
central budget	2.5	3.7	central budget	4.7	4.0
enterprises	17.5	16.0	enterprises	17.1	17.1
households	0.6	0.5	households	25.4	27.1
non-residents	1.4	1.5	non-residents	4.5	5.6
central bank	10.1	14.1	central bank	1.4	0.3
interbank	3.1	2.8	interbank	3.9	4.2
non-credit	0.7	0.6	securities	6.0	6.7
other assets	6.9	8.0			
Other assets	3.4	6.0	Other liabilities	6.0	5.6
Total	100.0	100.0	Total	100.0	100.0

Within external funds, the household sector remained the most important source. Households as ultimate savers continued to increase their share in financing the banking system. Retail deposits maturing over a year remained practically unchanged, while the volume of deposits fixed for less than a year grew by HUF 218 billion or 27 per cent. In this category, most of the rise came from the high growth rate (49 per cent) of the stock of foreign currency deposits, which surpassed the rate of devaluation (29.86 per cent). Banks with foreign ownership (or minority interest) increased competition for retail deposits, and although the volumes achieved were insignificant, the rate of growth was dynamic.

The major element of growth within **corporate deposits** was the stock of foreign currency deposits. HUF 76 billion of the total liability expansion of around HUF 100 billion. 1 billion came from the increase of foreign currency deposits. Representing a minor amount, corporate deposits maturing over a year increased by 45 per cent (HUF 10.9 billion), while deposits fixed for less than a year grew by 17.9 per cent during the year.

At HUF 144 billion, **foreign funds** showed the most dynamic growth among the liabilities of the banking system. The high increase was motivated by both foreign funds being less expensive than domestic and the foreign exchange risk becoming easier to calculate. Foreign liabilities maturing over a year grew by 66 per cent, representing 36.4 per cent adjusted for devaluation, while those maturing within a year increased by 44.6 per cent or 15.0 per cent adjusted for devaluation.

Due to improved liquidity positions, banks were able to reduce the stock of short-term refinancing credit on their balance sheets from HUF 45 billion to 9.4 billion. Although the balances of these loans fluctuated widely, the trend is clear. In accordance with the intentions of the **central bank,** the stock of long-term refinancing credit continued to fall in 1995, which in the major part came as a consequence of the central bank cancelling the foreign currency deposit swap facility. Thus the stock of refinancing credit maturing over a year fell by 18 per cent or HUF 66 billion.

3.5.3 Assets of the banking system

In 1995 the lending developments of financial institutions were similar to that of their liabilities developments. Funds allocated for under a year increased at a substantially slower rate of 3.8. per cent (HUF 65 billion) than did total assets, while short-term lending showed dynamic growth at 30.6 per cent (HUF 413 billion).

Increased participation in the short-term financing of the central budget in 1995 represented the most marked change in the asset side activities of banks, reflected by a rise of HUF 55 billion or 65.7 per cent. The explanation for the phenomenon lies first of all in PSBR generating a high level of interest rates in the government securities market. In contrast, the increase in long-term loans extended to the government sector was marginal, reaching about 3.5 per cent or HUF 21.9 billion.

The moderate growth resulted from the composite effect of the two opposite forces. Depending on the business decision by banks, increasing long-term finance for the budget drove the balance up, while central bank purchases or swaps of part of the consolidation bonds held in bank portfolios decreased the stock of long-term loans.

Another important change on the assets side of the balance sheet of the banking system was the increase of deposits held at the **central bank** for less than a year. These grew by 66 per cent (HUF 209 billion) in 1995, including foreign currency deposits as the major growth factor (HUF 160 billion, 51.6 per cent). The long-term assets held at the central bank increased at a much slower rate of 8.5 per cent. Repeated increases in reserve requirements and the expansion of liabilities are responsible for around HUF 70 billion worth of expansion in the settlement accounts of banks.

Bank lending to households continued to decrease following the tendency seen in previous years. Insignificant in absolute terms, the loans extended to the retail sector for less than a year fell by 4.3 per cent to HUF 17.1 billion, while there was a larger decline of 7.6 Per cent (HUF 19.5 billion) in the loans maturing over a year. The closing balance of these loans stood at HUF 236 billion at year end.

Bank lending to the corporate sector also grew at a substantially slower rate of around 8-9 per cent than average lending. This includes a decrease of around 5 per cent in loans denominated in forints and a rise in foreign currency loans by two and a half times. These movements reflect the **changes in** the structure of bank liabilities. The impact of portfolio cleansing focused mainly on loans extended in forints during the year was of similar significance.

As foreign exchange risk became easier to calculate, enterprises enjoyed more favourable terms in foreign exchange borrowing. Actual corporate sector borrowing was higher in 1995 because enterprises borrowed more funds directly from foreign entities.

3.5.4 The portfolio of the banking system

Total lending by the banking system (claims as well as off-balance sheet contingent and future liabilities) stood at HUF 2,554 billion on December 31, 1995 representing an increase of 7.4 per cent (HUF 175 billion) on the closing balance of 1994.

The stock of qualified loans in the banking system dropped from HUF 524 billion at the end of 1994 to HUF 424 billion. The reduction in the ratio of qualified loans to total lending from 26.3 per cent in 1993 to 16.6 per cent represents a definite portfolio improvement over the last three years.

Substandard, doubtful and bad loans (including underqualified loans) decreased by more than 40 per cent or HUF 184.5 billion over the last two years, while the loans needing special attention increased by HUF 60.1 billion (47.7. per cent). Portfolio cleansing was the main factor responsible for the decrease in the stock of qualified loans which led to the selling of HUF 93 billion worth of principal and interest claims in 1995, and to the write-off of HUF 41 billion worth of principal and interest claims. The majority of claims was sold to subsidiaries. Considering also the portfolio cleansing measures in 1994, a total of about HUF 250 billion worth of principal and interest claims has been removed from the assets of financial institutions over the last two years.

The ratio of provisions to total qualified loans decreased from 43.7 per cent to 37.5 per cent. Banks accumulated provisions to cover the loans grouped in the various categories of qualified lending in line with provisions by the Banking Supervision, which specify a band for the rate of provisions for each category (0-10 per cent for those needing special attention, 11-30 per cent for substandard, 31-70 per cent for doubtful, 71-100 per cent for bad loans).

3.6 The profit and loss of financial institutions

Profit after tax in the banking system stood at HUF 36.9 billion at the end of 1995, **showing slow improvement after the low** in 1993.

In contrast with 1994 when 13 financial institutions reported a year end loss, there were 'only' 8 loss-making banks last year. However, 1995 losses were more than double of those in 1994.

In contrast with previous years, the profits of the banking system **were increased** by:

- higher interest income;
- reduced need to generate reserves;
- while the factors reducing profits included:
- lower earnings from other banking' operations (commissions, trading in securities and foreign currency, etc.);
- higher increase in operating costs than in gross operating profits; and

- deterioration in the balance of other income and expenses, which was primarily due to higher lending losses incurred by selling claims and writing off bad loans.

Table 6. Qualified loans of the banking system

Classification	Dec. 31, 1994		Dec. 31, 1995	
	Ft bns	%	Ft bns	%
1. Problem-free	1,854.5	78.0	2,129.7	83.4
2. Qualified				
a) needing special attention	185.5	7.8	186.0	7.3
b) substandard	50.9	2.1	43.5	1.7
c) doubtful	84.8	3.6	61.6	2.4
d) bad	202.9	8.5	133.1	5.2
Qualified (a + b + c + d)	524.1	22.0	424.2	16.6
Total (1 + 2)	2,378.6	100.0	2,553.9	100.0
Qualified/total loans	-	22.0	-	16.6
(Doubtful + bad)/total (c + d)	-	12.1	-	7.6
Provisions for loans	229.1	-		159.6

Table 7. Changes in banks' profits
(In billions of forints)

	1993	1994	1995	Per cent '95/'94
1. Interest revenues	346.5	444.2	590.1	132.8
2. Interest expenses	235.2	297.1	407.5	137.2
3. Interest income	111.3	147.1	182.5	124.1
4. Other revenues of which:	43.2	52.1	50.8	97.5
5. commission on financial services	23.4	26.5	28.4	107.3
6. revenues	36.0	43.3	49.1	113.5
7. costs	12.5	16.8	20.7	123.4
8. Gross operating profit (3+4)	154.5	199.2	233.3	117.1
9. Operating expenses	77.3	96.7	122.0	126.1
10. Trading profit (8+9)	77.2	102.5	111.3	108.6
11. Other revenues	27.1	165.0	179.3	177.4
12. Other expenditures	38.9	102.4	181.7	-3.8
13. Profit or loss on other revenues and expenditures (11-12)	-11.7	62.6	-2.4	66.0
14. Net operating profit (10-13)	65.5	165.1	109.0	56.2
15. Provisions	214.3	107.7	60.5	84.3
16. Ordinary profit (15-14)	-148.9	57.5	48.5	2.8
17. Extraordinary profit	-2.0	-35.7	-1.0	217.9
18. Profit before taxation (16+17)	-150.8	21.8	47.5	110.4
19. Taxation	3.2	9.5	10.5	301.4
20. Profit after tax (18, 19)	-154.0	12.3	36.9	
Balance sheet profit	-156.1	-6.8	27.6	-

The increase of interest income by 24.1 per cent originates in the expansion of business activities by about 20 per cent in the banking system and in the widening of the interest margin.

1995 brought a turning point in respect of the ration of interest income to the balance sheet total of the different groups of banks. In 1994, state-owned banks recorded a higher ratio, **private banks could** claim the same in 1995.

The extremely high proportion of reserve accumulation required by poor portfolios reduced the profitability of the banking system in previous years. Last year, however, (continuing the favourable trend started in 1994) **reserve** accumulation fell to 1.7 per cent of the balance sheet total. (The same ratio was about 8 per cent in 1993.)

Expressed in terms of their proportion to the balance sheet total, the income from commissions and the trade of securities and foreign currency – as part of core business – declined. Net **commission income grew by a mere 7.3 per cent, a rate** that falls short of both the rate of inflation and the increase of cash flow. Some banks suffered significant exchange rate losses due to certain costs incurred by raising funds, and as a **result securities trading** turned **loss making across the whole banking system.**

The operating costs of the banking system **increased at a slightly lower rate** (26.1 per cent) **than inflation.** Despite the on-going favourable developments, the increase in operating costs was higher than the rise in the profit of core operations, which led to **a slight deterioration of cost efficiency in the banking system.**

The banking system continued to cleanse its portfolio, a development which has began in 1994. In contrast with the positive effect in 1994, these **measures had an adverse effect on the results in 1995.** Financial institutions released and used a smaller proportion of their reserves than in 1994 and the amount of lending losses charged to the accounts increased.

II. The development of capital markets and exchanges[8]

In 1995, the financial markets had a lively year, and the development was dynamic in some areas. However, the weight of Hungarian exchanges – the Budapest Stock Exchange and the Budapest Commodity Exchange – in the national economy, as compared to the ones in developed countries, is still light.

1. The Budapest Stock Exchange (BSE)

The BSE reopened in 1990, and it exclusively traded shares until 1991. After introducing government bonds and treasury bills in 1992, corporate stocks lost their supremacy. They became the most popular securities again only in 1995, representing 34 per cent of the total traded volume (1994: 27 per cent; 1993: 10 per cent). The increase in the traded volume of shares was partly due to the privatization of some large companies by public offering on the exchange, and partly due to foreign interest which strengthened in the second half of the year.

Table 8. Situation and composition of the turnover on the Budapest Stock Exchange between June 1990 and December 1995

	1990	1991	1992	1993	1994	1995
Turnover in billion forints (twice)	6.12	10.11	33.67	185.69	211.23	253.18
out of which:						
shares	6.12	10.11	6.01	18.26	57.11	87.27
government bonds	-	0.3	12.36	73.38	53.89	77.16
corporate bonds	-	-	-	-	0.01	0.05
treasury bills	-	-	15.06	85.00	81.22	81.11
investment bonds	-	-	0.03	0.1	0.06	3.43
compensation coupons	-	-	0.21	8.95	18.74	4.16
Number of transactions	4,962	14,509	8,565	23,749	73,784	71.240
Average daily no of transactions	27	58	34	94	293	286
Average daily turnover (millions of forints)	33.8	40.1	133.6	736.9	838.2	1,016.8
Turnover per transaction (millions of forints)	1.2	0.7	3.9	7.8	3.1	3.6
Number of business days	181	252	259	252	252	249

Spot trading of securities on the Budapest Stock Exchange (counting both sides of each transaction) increased from HUF 211 billion of the previous year to HUF 253 billion in 1995. This close to 20 per cent increase – still under the 28 per cent inflation rate of the previous year – was primarily the result of the changes in the traded volume of shares and government bonds, while the turnover of treasury bills stagnated, and the one of compensation coupons (after reaching an all-time high in 1994) fall back to a quarter. Both the average daily turnover and the average size of transaction increased.

Despite the above-mentioned facts, the weight of BSE in the national economy did not increase significantly. The market value of securities listed on the exchange was only about 22 per cent of the GDP (5.6 per cent for shares, 8.2 per cent for government bonds, 6.8 per cent for treasury bills), representing a slight increase over the previous year (20.3 per cent). At present, the BSE does not play a dominating role in the effect of monetary policy on the real economy (i.e. the transmission mechanism), or in corporate finance.

Table 9. Market value of listed securities on the Budapest Stock Exchange (1990-1995)
(In billions of forints)

	June	Dec.	1991	1992	1993	1994	1995
Market value	0.1	16.4	53.6	201.9	457.0	883.8	1,221.0
Of which:							
Shares	0.1	16.4	38.2	47.2	81.7	181.5	327.5
Government bonds			15.3	82.3	241.7	392.9	454.0
Corporate debentures			0.1	0.1	0.3	1.8	1.7
Treasury bills				54.4	74.0	239.6	376.3
Fund certificates				1.9	5.5	19.3	42.8
Compensation coupons				16.0	53.8	48.7	18.7

1.1 Equity

In 1995, five newly introduced shares and five capitalizations increased the number of securities and their total value on the BSE. The nominal value of the newly introduced shares increased 2.7 times. The share prices on the stock market – from HUF 189 billion at the end of 1994 to HUF 328 billion in a year – only increased 1.8 times, lagging behind the increase calculated in nominal value.

The sales revenue of companies introduced on the stock exchange – based on quick preliminary and not complete reports – increased by 31 per cent, and the profit before taxation with 41 per cent. Although, in case of most companies, the behaviour of share prices does not perfectly reflect the improvement in profitability of companies: even the ones that produce profit in the long-term do not show real exchange gain.

The changes in the official stock index (BUX) – already amended a few times – were not only influenced by corporate performance, stock exchange privatization, and the macroeconomic environment, but also by international trends. The spectacular rise starting with the third quarter of the year coincided with the global decrease in interest rates, with the US taking the initiative. As a result, investors including international investors – similarly to the events at the turn of 1993-1994 – took similar market actions.

The Prague, Warsaw and Budapest stock exchanges have agreed upon forming a joint stock index in order to generate and strengthen the investors' interest in the region. The initial value of this index, named CESI, was 1,000 points on 30 June 1995. From the 27 shares introduced on the three stock exchanges 13 were Polish, 6 Czech and 8 Hungarian. These shares represented 67 per cent of the overall stock capitalizations at the introduction of the index. The basket is being reviewed twice a year. Throughout 1995, the BUX and the CESI moved closely together.

The strong correlation is especially important as the three economies chose rather different ways of transition, privatization techniques, and their external and domestic equilibrium fairly differed from each other. The changes in the indices suggest that in the eye of foreign investors the three countries mean one region, and their decisions have a greater impact on the share prices on these stock exchanges than domestic economic developments or the decisions of domestic investors. (Note: such strong correlation could also be observed among indices of such remote stock exchanges as the Mexican and some of the South East Asian exchanges.) This result is not surprising: it shows the weakness of the capital power of resident investors as compared to foreign ones, the low liquidity of the stock exchange, and the not too relevant weight of institutional investors, on the one hand. On the other hand, it **indicates that the** investors of developed countries, when the yield on their own capital markets is decreasing do seek investments on emerging markets, not being in close correlation with developed ones. Within these limits, they invest in a diversifying manner, and eventually not the previous market performance of the given country has the primary importance to them but the fact that at the moment, these stock exchanges have a low level of integration into developed markets – this being expressed by the lack or weakness of correlation.

In **transition countries** the changes in the ratios expressing the valuation of the securities of companies listed on the stock exchange, the indices of price per book-value (P/BV), or the expected dividend (Div. Y), and the price/ earnings (p/e), refer to the fact that the performance of the securities of these companies keep fluctuating, therefore, investment in shares is risky.

The p/e ratios did not show signs of overpricing even during the upswing at the beginning of the year. The aggregate indicator moving around 10, was close to the value measurable at the established markets of developed countries.

1.2 Debt securities

Although in 1995, of all the securities, the turnover of shares represented the majority of the overall turnover, the total value of **government bonds and treasury bills** is still significant at the BSE. The volume of government securities traded **at the stock market decreased in proportion.** While the volume of government securities traded outside the stock exchange in 1994 represented five times more than the one at the stock exchange, this trade meant ten times more in 1995. The Hungarian National Bank also contributed to this, since it was a seller at the government securities market, and was very active mainly in the OTC market.

The secondary market of government securities followed more or less the same tendencies as the primary market. In the first two months of the year the demand for government securities was low because of the low liquidity at the forint market, the investors were speculating on devaluation. Following the large one time devaluation in March and the introduction of the crawling peg, the confidence in the forint and government securities strengthened gradually. The development of the DWIX index (Daiwa Index), representing the weighted yield for government securities, shows perfectly that the growing yield tendencies in 1994 turned into a 34 per cent decline in the summer of 1995.

After the large devaluation at the interbank foreign currency market in March, prices dropped to the bottom of the intervention band, and practically stayed there for the rest of the year. The Hungarian National Bank was unilaterally a foreign currency buyer on the interbank foreign currency market. As a result of the high forint availability, the turnover of government securities jumped from the HUF 4 billion in August – duplicated value – to HUF 24 billion in September and HUF 40 billion in October. Unusually, within this turnover, government **bonds represented** up to 60-65 per cent and treasury bonds only 30-35 per cent in the traded volume. This shows that – because of the relatively high liquidity – interest in longer-term securities increased.

It is interesting to note the **relationship between yields on government securities and shares.** The yield on government securities was higher **all through 1995 than the one** on shares. Although, by the end of the year, thanks to the abundance in the forint market, the DWIX representing the yield on government securities, started to decline, mainly as a result of foreign demand, the share price index started to rise in a steady manner. As a result, already in the first weeks of 1996, the yield on stocks were higher than on government securities.

The differing movement of the share and bond-indices cannot be interpreted as the manifestation of the optimizing strategy of the same investment circles, according to which, as a reaction to the changes in the relative yields, they would change the composition of their portfolios. The **two markets are still segmented:** foreign funds investing in shares rearranged their international portfolios, and purchased Hungarian shares within this framework. In spite of the fact that, the DWIX representing the yield on government securities reacts to the liquidity situation and lending opportunities of commercial banks, is closely linked to foreign currency market processes. Thus, it is impossible to interpret the changes of the BUX and DWIX in the same usual way as on integrated markets.

Throughout 1995, besides government securities, the three corporate bonds and one bond issued by the EBRD presented a negligible turnover. New corporate debentures were not introduced to the stock market in the previous year.

1.3 Investment funds

The number of investment fund certificates quoted on the stock market increased by 16 in 1995 to 36, their related aggregate face value from almost HUF 24 billion to HUF 43 billion, and their price value from HUF 19 billion to HUF 43 billion. This latter means 3.5 per cent of the total stock market capitalization, which is still low, yet more promising than the previous year's 2.2 per cent. 22 government securities, 9 shares and 5 investment notes of funds were transacted on the BSE. These meant 43 per cent, 8 per cent, and 49 per cent respectively of the HUF 3.43 billion (duplicated) turnover of the year.

Until 1995, yields on and popularity of investment funds was mainly **due to the tax breaks given** in case of at least three years of holding certificates. This tax regulation was favourable **for starting closed-end investment funds,** which had to be listed on the stock exchange according to the law.

Beginning with 1 January 1995, **a new type of tax break is in** force for investments in open end funds, which is actually not a definite tax break but a 'tax credit'. This can be made use of up to 30 per cent increase in the volume of publicly traded shares and investment notes after opening the respective capital account as long as the volume does not decrease. As its effect, **open-end funds have started** throughout 1995, which ensured liquidity almost as the one of bank deposits, since the investments could be cashed not only on the stock market or on the OTC market, but also by the fund manager on a price corresponding to the proportion of the net asset value at any given point in time of the investment bill to be cashed.

In 1995, the yields of investment funds – for the first time in their history – **topped the interests on bank deposits.** The funds mainly investing in government securities – based on the data on net asset values – could reach a yield up to 33-36 per cent. A role in this process, besides the high yield on government securities, had the consequence that some fund managers, as a reaction to the increasing competition, completely or partly assumed the costs from the investors, thus being able to ensure higher net asset values and yields.

1.4 Compensation coupons

During most of 1995 the price of these securities fluctuated around their historically lowest levels. The value of transactions was gradually declining as well. The annual (duplicated) **turnover** reached almost HUF 33 billion.

1.5 The BSE futures market

One of the most significant outcome in 1995 on the BSE was the opening of the futures section. This market was opened in April with two foreign currencies, the USD and the DEM, as well as the BUX index and the three-month treasury bills; and in November a new product, the ECU was added. Although, **the BSE represented a smaller portion of the trade on the futures market:** the previous year a HUF 10.2 billion turnover was registered, out of which HUF 7 billion in the last two months. The Budapest Commodity Exchange, with its HUF 162 billion foreign currency market, **maintained its advantage, owing to an early start** and other membership conditions. On a long-term basis, the BSE counts on the fact that if foreigners investing in shares can cover the exchange rate risks locally, this would compensate the above advantages of the BCE.

2. The Budapest Commodity Exchange futures market (BCE)

The BCE established its foreign exchange section in March 1993 offering USD and DEM transactions. In 1994, the money market was expanded by introducing the 90-day interbank deposit interest futures, as well as JPY transactions. By November 1995 the ECU was available on the BCE as well. The ECU has been very popular ever since its introduction (in January 1996 it became the leading product in both futures markets). The reason was that the European 'currency' makes up 70 per cent of the official basket of foreign currencies to which the forint is pegged, while the USD's share is 30 per cent. Those interested in hedging the exchange rate risks will reproduce the forint basket's composition in the future. Before the ECU transactions were offered on the exchange markets, there was a roundabout way to do the same thing through a substitute currency. Generally, the DEM, representing the largest weight in the ECU, lends itself to such exchange rate coverage transactions since the two currencies (DEM and ECU) mostly move together. With the introduction of the ECU this substitution is theoretically not necessary.

Last year, however, the ECU and the DEM moved frequently in opposite directions, thus the DEM became a more suitable currency vehicle. The HUF 1.5 billion turnover of the first year rose to HUF 26 billion in 1994. In 1995, the HUF 162 billion total turnover of foreign currency futures market made it the section with the highest turnover on the BCE. (The turnover of the foreign currency market came to around 2.9 per cent of the GDP).

The increase in the turnover of foreign exchange contracts was mainly due to the forint's yield advantages. In addition, more and more of the business organizations make use of the opportunities offered by the foreign exchange futures market. The changes in the interbank forint and foreign exchange market liquidity situations after March influenced the turnover and prices on both exchange. The relative benefit of the yield on forints against foreign currencies, coupled with the foreseeable devaluation, led to the increase of the forint conversion against foreign currencies. The confidence in the crawling peg and in monetary policy took some time to develop. The signs of confidence were shown in mid-summer, and it strengthened in the second half of the year, as reflected by the turnover of open positions and the prices at the futures exchange.

Banks responded reasonably and **fairly rapidly to the new exchange rate regime** enforced in March. Under the former regime, it was worth speculating against the forint. Both corporations and individuals did so. Exporters held on to the foreign currency income from goods shipped to delay conversion into forints as long as possible because the rate of devaluation was frequently larger than the interest rate on forint investments. A large number of households took efforts to convert forint savings into foreign exchange for identical reasons. Banks engaged in the forward sale and spot purchase of foreign exchange. This way they made gains because the implicit interest rate involved in the futures sale price was higher than the actual interest rate. On the other hand, such transactions proved profit making for the customers of banks (speculators and importers) because forward purchase prices were lower than the (actual) market rate increased with devaluation. As banks ran practically no risk with such transactions, they acted as arbitrageurs. An arbitrageur always assumes two positions to eliminate risk. Banks would turn the exchange rate losses made on futures positions into gains by lending foreign currency on the spot market and such loans will be repaid in foreign currency at a certain rate of interest. Market anomalies may evolve due to the lack of full integration between the two markets. Risk free arbitrage presents itself as an option to **market** participants with access to both markets due to a unique position. As liberalization progresses, **integration** will become more complete and market access will not be granted to **banks** exclusively.

Speculation may tempt importers too, although speculative opportunities are not too clear-cut because of the strong relationship with foreign trade transactions. **Speculators will normally take one way** or uncovered positions and thereby expose themselves to high risks. The risk for them is that the rate of devaluation of the forint might be below the level of the HUF interest rates. The appreciation of the forint was not a real threat. Since any entity could claim their foreign exchange allowances at spot rates in commercial banks under the effective regulations, the value of forints received by the NBH later on against foreign exchange was less, due to repeated devaluation thereafter. Losses were first incurred by the NBH and were eventually assumed by the **budget**: the NBH would either pay less to the budget or – if the central bank turned loss-making – the amount of budgetary support would grow. Speculation against the forint was the reason why liquidity on the interbank forint market remained mostly poor before March.

Once the crawling peg was introduced, the situation changed gradually. Clearly, market participants **adopted wait and see** attitudes between March and June. This is reflected by a near match between futures assets and liabilities of banks. The increase in foreign exchange futures assets against liabilities is a sign of developing confidence in the forint. After the introduction of the crawling peg, market **participants traded places but** not roles.

Under the new exchange rate regime, speculators in favour of the forint take selling positions on the BCE. Such speculators include exporters and other entities with foreign currency income or foreign savings. Buying positions are not worth opening for importers under the new circumstances because they would need to finance such positions from funds with higher domestic interest rates (be these actual in the accounting sense or opportunity cost due to giving up higher domestic rates). Hence, it is mostly commercial banks that assume buying positions. They find it worthwhile because speculators want to sell at present. Banks, on the other hand, are in the position to lend forints (to customers and the budget) and they are those who manage conversion. They do not even need to stand idle waiting for clients with foreign currency, as they may borrow abroad in foreign currency to be returned in the same currency upon maturity and will invest the funds into high yielding government securities or on-lend to customers at high rates. Although at present enterprises may also borrow foreign currency abroad, which they may invest into government securities, they are not in the same position as banks (they do not convert currency into forints) and therefore arbitrage in the form outlined above is not available to them.

Banks would purchase foreign exchange futures, convert the currency into forints and lend it at high interest rates to customers or to the budget, by purchasing high yielding government securities. The role of government securities as the instruments of sterilization diminished in the first quarter of 1996 and were replaced by increasing the stock of reverse repos at the NBH. Eventually, this will also allow banks to pocket the difference (yield benefit of the forint) between domestic and foreign interest rates corrected for the change of the exchange rate without exposure to risk (interest rate arbitrage).

Speculators that sell foreign exchange to commercial banks at future dates are still needed. They will open uncovered positions as before, but by forward selling foreign currency with the crawling peg in effect, they assume **two types of risks:** either because the authorities come under pressure to devalue at a higher rate than announced due to some extraordinary reason or because the exchange rate of the forint may move away from the bottom of the NBH intervention band, i.e. the forint depreciates, without offcial and extraordinary devaluation. Yet the degree of the risk, a maximum of 4.5 per cent (2.25 per cent), is clearly determined by the limits of the intervention band applied under the regime. Market participants will evaluate the likelihood of that occurring when making decisions on a futures position.

The size of the amounts used solely for taking advantage of the yield benefit of the forint may only be calculated by inference. The size of the net forward buying positions of banks is **likely to be the top limit** in this type of transaction as speculators may only sell such a net amount forward to banks. The very nature of their circumstances allows banks to act as counterparts to futures transactions. It is difficult to estimate the size of speculation because – as seen above exporters and foreign currency earners and holders will turn into speculators even if their only or overriding intention was not to take advantage of the yield benefit of the forint. For prudential reasons, they will speculate in favour of the forint when deciding on holding or converting before March, reason obviously dictated that they should speculate against the forint.

Interest rate differences that motivate speculation will decrease with capital inflows because once the money is converted into forints, **domestic liquidity** and the supply of forints will grow. The NBH relieves the supply side downward pressure on interest rates by open market operations, such as selling government securities and by setting appropriate repo rates. The reason for this is to prevent losing the confidence placed in the forint suddenly, which would reverse these flows, the forint would be converted into foreign currency again, which would in turn boost the demand for foreign currency and the government securities needed to finance the budget could only be sold at much higher interest rates. Without sterilizing, converted capital inflows could temporarily reduce interest rates through increase in forint *supply,* but the related increase in aggregate demand would then result in a combination of higher inflationary pressure and poorer balance of payments and in an erosion of the trust placed in being able to maintain the exchange rate regime. Should such a situation develop, the central bank **would need to raise interest** rates or devalue the forint radically or apply a combination of these two measures, which would – in effect – undermine the confidence placed in the forint and run down the exchange rate regime. Hence, lowering interest rates without a corresponding **reduction in budget** deficit could be dangerous, because financing the budget would depend too much on the propensity of foreigners to lend. One must also take into account that the performance of the Hungarian economy is not the single factor that influences the investment decisions of foreign investors. There are others, such as the events in developed countries and other emerging markets. A sudden end or reversal of the present cycle of interest rates declining in the developed part of the world would reorient funds invested in Hungary into developed countries, without regard to the developments of the economy here.

Influencing the demand for forint is another means of reducing the **difference between domestic and foreign interest** rates. Arriving at an **interest**

rate sustainable both in internal and external terms can primarily rely on eliminating the pressure PSBR places on money markets. The resulting reduction in interest rates is desirable as it goes without the above-mentioned dangers. The fiscal adjustment initiated during the previous year and the record-breaking privatization proceeds collected at the end of the year relieved financial pressures and thereby contributed substantially to strengthening the credibility of monetary policy.

Contract sizes are larger on the BSE: lot sizes are ten thousand for all three currencies, while the **BCE trades all** currencies in lot sizes of one thousand, except or JPY, where the size is one hundred thousand. Open positions started to grow on both futures exchanges at roughly the same time around the middle of 1995. Speculation also existed in the previous exchange rate regime and surged especially when devaluation was clearly predictable. It also burdened the authorities and the taxpayers with costs. Both exchange rate regimes lend themselves to speculation by reason of the lack of general macroeconomic equilibrium. If no such equilibrium exists, speculation will not disappear, it will only change form.

The central bank does not underestimate the **potential threat** represented by purely speculative inflows motivated by the interest rate differential. The NBH was clearly aware of the advantages and disadvantages of the crawling peg before enforcing it. It also took international experiences into account. A comparison of the disadvantages and the advantages created by greater stability indicated that it was worth suffering the former for the sake of the latter. Threats may transform into real trouble if macroeconomic discipline becomes loose and market participants lose confidence in the credibility of monetary policy. To achieve and maintain credibility, co-ordination between monetary and fiscal policies, managed successfully last year, is needed.

Consequently, the NBH intends to develop a level of interest rates that is high enough to generate domestic savings at a level that can cover the majority of domestic borrowing required and is, at the same, time low enough to discourage exaggerated foreign currency conversion targeted only at taking advantage of interest rate differentials.

3. The OTC market and the clearing house

The NBH transferred its function to clear government securities accounts of banks to the **Central Clearing House and Depository** (KELER Rt.) in September 1994. Since then KELER Rt. has acted as the organizer of OTC markets. KELER also clears the spot futures transactions realized of both exchanges and also offers custodian and risk management services. Hence, compared internationally, **KELER has multiple responsibilities as most** countries distribute these functions across several institutions.

OTC markets are open to spot, repo, Giro repo, and Giro repo freezing transactions in government paper. The connection between KELER and the Interbank Giro System (IGS) allows the Clearing House to effect settlement of repo transactions of commercial banks. KELER settled 13,102 contracts at a total (single accounting) value of HUF 6,298 billion, including HUF 889 billion in spot deals and HUF 5,409 billion in repo and repo freezing transactions. The large and growing proportion of OTC trade is mostly due to more and more government securities being traded in the interbank market.

3.1 Government securities

Government securities represented 90 per cent of the OTC trading, of which treasury bills made up 60 per cent. (The share of government securities in stock trading was 57 per cent.) As turnover of government securities – mainly treasury bills – traded, OTC picked up speed in April, already before growth started on the stock exchange. September brought a turning point as the demand for government bonds topped that for treasury bills both in the OTC market and on the stock exchange.

3.2 Compensation coupons

Brokerage firms can offer OTC transactions to a significant portion of retail investors. They publish daily OTC ask and bid prices in the press. The spread between the two prices clearly reflects the risks and liquidity of some of the securities traded.

4. Institutional investors on capital markets

Liquidity growth on domestic capital markets depends on the increased participation of institutional investors. Social security funds that represent the greatest potential as institutional investors are still part of the general government in Hungary. Yet, the development of the regulatory and supervisory environment of the other institutional investors has started, and some investors are already operational, such as:

- investment funds,
- 14 Hungarian insurance companies focusing 55 per cent of their investments on government securities,
- pension funds, as newcomers to domestic capital markets. As the government intends to assign important functions to these pension funds in the reform of the public sector, it supports the contributions to such funds by employers and employees with significant concessions. Pension funds may be organized on a regional, sectoral or corporate basis.

The share of institutional investors in capital market investments was HUF 210 billion (or 3.8 per cent of GDP). More time and major institutional reforms are needed to increase this amount to a level that ensures a safer environment for the economic and financial integration of Hungary internationally and allows improved protection for domestic capital markets against the impact of international capital flows.

5. Primary issuance of government securities

Although the new system of trading government securities was to be enforced in 1996 only, the majority of preparations had been made in 1995 under the auspices of the newly established National Debt Management Agency. A tender has been invited to select primary dealers (market makers) that will have to comply with specific requirements, will regularly participate in the issuing of government securities and will quote ask and bid prices to investors.

It is expected that the introduction of the system of primary dealers will allow the budget to base the terms at which government securities are issued on sound planning and to even out the calendar of issues due to the information reported and the minimum market-making obligations agreed to by primary dealers. An additional advantage comes from the obligation of primary dealers to quote two-way (ask and bid) prices, which creates a liquid secondary market for a definite number of government securities maturing at specified dates. (A maximum of 25 securities from those scheduled for issuance after January 3, 1996 have been assigned to each primary trader.)

Primary dealers are responsible for:

- offering government bonds for sale (subscription) to investors;
- accepting orders for purchasing discount treasury bills at auctions;
- keeping record of subscriptions;
- acting as a site of disbursements, a back office, and a custodian;
- accepting orders on the stock exchange.

Primary dealers are classified in two groups:

- those selling to institutional or wholesale investors;
- those trading in small lots via a network of branches.

Both groups earn proper commissions between 0.04 per cent and 0.8 per cent on the quantities sold or underwritten, with the size of the commission depending on both maturity and lot size.

Notes and references

1. This chapter partly relies on the *Annual Report, 1993* of the State Banking Supervision of Hungary.
2. The text is from the following publication: *Comptroller of the Currency*, The Director's Book – the Role of a National Bank Director, Washington D.C. Office of the Comptroller of the Currency, 1987, pp. 15-16.
3. Source: *Annual Report 1993*, Pretoria, South African Reserve Bank, Bank Supervision Department, 1992, p. 2.
4. Hungarian Savings Co-operative Bank plc.
5. This chapter is based on the *Annual Report 1995* of the National Bank of Hungary.
6. Four smaller financial institutions (a savings co-operative, two credit co-operatives and a savings bank limited by shares) were incorporated in 1995 and are to start operating in 1996.

7. 1994 registered capital shows the actual opening balance on January 1, when none of the banks participating in the consolidation programme had reduced their registered capital to offset losses in negative retained earnings. Due to the reports submitted by banks, different figures are used in tables below.
8. Part II is based on the *Annual Report 1995* of the National Bank of Hungary.

Part IV

Global Convergences

26 Agenda for a New Monetary Reform

Otto Hieronymi

To the memory of the late Hungarian Prime Minister József ANTALL

1. Has the pendulum gone too far?

The period since the 1970s has witnessed an unprecedented pace of change in both domestic and international monetary order. One of the most striking developments has been the globalization of financial markets, and the simultaneous loss of power of domestic and international official institutions. Parallel with the globalization of financial flows, there have been attempts both at regionalization and at uniformization (deregulated) of financial institutions operating in what are today still very different economic environments.

Many of the features of this new world are positive and should be recognized as such. Nevertheless, politicians and the general public are increasingly concerned about the domestic and international monetary system(s) and about reforms that continue to strengthen markets at the expense of national and international monetary authorities' responsibilities.

Increasingly it is felt that the *pendulum may have swung too far* and that once more the time has come for a fundamental rethinking of our assumptions about the role of money in the economy and about the appropriate monetary and financial policies and institutions in the 'good society' – at the national level and in the world at large.

The need is particularly great to redefine fundamental objectives and the respective roles of governmental rules and of markets and private interests; and to recreate conditions for effective international co-operation and for a true international monetary order.

2. Why is there a need for a new approach to monetary and financial reform?

The main arguments in favour of a new, fresh approach to domestic and international monetary and financial theories and policies can be summed up under three headings.

2.1 The increasingly dogmatic character of dominant monetary and financial theories and policies

The first set of arguments has to do with the increasingly dogmatic character of today's dominant monetary and financial theories and the policies and institutional reforms that they inspire. This approach includes: the blind belief in the unlimited efficiency of markets with respect both to prices and exchange rates; the excessive emphasis on short-term financial objectives at the expense of other economic and social variables, and the implicit or explicit transposition of the 'stock-market approach' to the analysis of all economic structures and problems. One of the most questionable manifestations of the current intellectual and policy environment with respect to money and finance is the branding of the search for balanced institutional and policy approaches as heresy, the betrayal of economic liberalism, and of the principles of the market economy.

2.2 We are in uncharted waters: the world has changed profoundly in the last 15 years

The second group of reasons for a thorough, open debate about domestic and international monetary reform is linked to the *extraordinary changes that have occurred in the world during the last 10 to 15 years*. These changes include the collapse of communism, the spreading of the principles of democracy, of the market economy and free trade, the realization of world-wide currency convertibility, the easing of inflation, the impending creation of the European Monetary Union, the reduction of the economic weight of the state, and the freeing of private initiative in most countries around the world.

In addition to political, economic and social changes, the world is witnessing a technological revolution that helps intensify competition between rich and poor countries and may provide in the long run a major impetus to growth throughout the world economy. Beside its global economic consequences, the information and telecommunications revolutions are also having a direct impact on the monetary and financial system itself. It may be argued that the impact of the information revolution on the monetary system could be as important as, for example, the passage from metallic to paper money.

Some of the changes in the world in the last 10 to 15 years have been closely linked to the liberal revolution. The role of money, of monetary policy, of financial markets and institutions have been at the heart of these changes. What became today's dominant theories were part of a necessary and welcome reaction to the rigidities and inefficiencies prevalent in economies increasingly dominated by direct or indirect bureaucratic controls.

Yet, time has come to take stock again and to raise the question whether the pendulum has possibly gone too far. Some of the theories and policies that replaced the old orthodoxy in the 1970s and 1980s also had their shortcomings or did not tell the full story. Some of the negative consequences were obvious from the start, others became evident in the light of the emerging situation that the new policies helped to bring about.

In fact, today we are in uncharted waters as far as the monetary and financial system is concerned. The current orthodoxy has played a crucial role in bringing about this new world we live in, but (and this is the central thesis of this article) it does not provide a complete and reliable blueprint for an efficient and equitable management of the new monetary and financial order.

2.3 Deflationary bias and the danger of a protectionist-interventionist backlash

In addition to the increasingly rigid character of mainstream monetary and financial theory and policies, and to the fact that this conventional wisdom does not deal with many of the entirely new (and unexpected) features and problems of the current situation, there is a third group of reasons for calling for a new look at monetary reform and ultimately for a new consensus. These can be summed up under the heading of the *legitimate fears of a major backlash* against liberalization, deregulation and globalization in the financial sector and in the 'real economy'.

There are several scenarios that could lead to a sharp reversal of the current liberal policies. These include the potential ripple effect of regional financial crises, the growing impression that current policies aggravate rather than alleviate structural problems, such as unemployment, and the flight from a major currency (e.g., the US dollar). Last but not least, there could be a backlash as a result of the concern about the real or alleged deflationary bias and excessive social costs of current theories and policies.

Such a return to full-scale economic nationalism, regionalism and government intervention, would obviously have devastating economic and social consequences in rich and poor countries alike. The real danger of a potential backlash is systemic. It is not due exclusively to the short-sightedness of politicians or of the public at large, but rather to the unbalanced nature of past and current monetary and economic reforms and to the rigidity of the experts, defending them.

The objective of the monetary reform agenda is not to reverse the liberal revolution and the trend towards more freedom throughout the world. Rather it is to consolidate its positive results through a more balanced approach to the division of labour between government institutions and private decision makers, between market winners and losers and domestic and international solidarity.

3. Items on the agenda

The items on the proposed agenda for monetary reform are summed up under eight sub-headings. They include both monetary issues as well as questions related more to financial markets and the banking sector. Some questions are more technical, others more political or even philosophical. It is not the objective of this article to give a complete list of all the aspects of current monetary and financial theory and policy that need serious rethinking. The principal aim here is to raise questions rather than to give answers.

As noted above, it would be as wrong to throw out current theory and policies altogether (the danger of backlash) as it is to adhere too rigidly to the dominant doctrine. A global review should allow both to *confirm* and to *complement and replace*: in this spirit it is better to re-examine old truths and to have a new confirmation than to take the truth for all dominant doctrines for granted.

3.1 Rules versus markets?

The history of the last 15 to 20 years has been marked by a movement from widespread 'over-regulation' (and of over-regulated markets) to a systematic (and even excessive) deregulation. In fact, what had started out as a legitimate reaction to excessive and often misguided regulation and government intervention (and to the frequent breakdown of rules and regulations due to changed circumstances) gradually led to a veritable crusade against all forms of rules and to an almost blind belief in the perfect functioning and self-regulation of markets. This trend has been the most pronounced in the monetary and financial field.

Thus, the first and central set of issues, in the domestic and the international context, has to do with the basically false dichotomy 'rules vs. markets', or 'rules or markets' that is part of today's conventional wisdom. In fact, by now it should be clear to all that the wholesale rejection of all rules (in favour of the pure self-regulation of markets) is as much of a dead-end street as the model of central planning used to be.[1]

The modern market economy, and this is true for money and finance, is and has to be a rule-based economy: thus, the question is not 'markets or rules', but rather 'what kind of rules (and what kind of freedom), for what types of markets?'

3.2 The need for a return to a true international monetary order

No doubt one of the most urgent political and theoretical tasks is the creation of the rules and institutions of a new universal international monetary order.

The first, and for many people the most difficult, step will have to be the revision or the outright abolition of the Jamaica Agreement of the mid-1970s, and exorcising the spirit which had inspired it. It was, in fact, the 'Jamaica reform' of the Articles of Agreement of the International Monetary Fund that put the final *de jure* seal on the earlier *de facto* refusal of the major monetary powers in the world to abide by a common set of rules in their international monetary relations.

Incidentally, abolishing the rules and objectives of the initial postwar international monetary order, also deprived the IMF of its original *raison d'être*. It was the combination of the search for a new mission for the Fund together with the emerging new monetarist orthodoxy, that transformed the IMF, both at the level of ideas and of operations from a guardian of the international monetary order, into a taskmaster of the developing and later also of the former communist economies.[2]

As a consequence during the last 20 years, the IMF, and the 'IMF vision of the world', instead of helping to recreate a true international monetary order, have been among the principal factors of blocking not only reform, but even a thorough and free discussion of such a reform. There is no doubt that the IMF has become *the* major international organization where intellectual '*Gleichschaltung*' has gone the furthest since the 1970s.

Yet, the negative consequences of international monetary instability have been recognized (or rather re-discovered) for some time even by the die-hard monetarists of the German Bundesbank – although only at the European, regional level.

It is, in fact one of the most bizarre intellectual paradoxes of our time that those who are the most ardent advocates (in academic, official or business circles) of monetary and financial globalization are also the most hostile to a return to a universal rule-based international monetary order.

Today, the United States and American economists are still the most strongly committed to the system of floating exchange rates.[3] At the same time, European economists and officials are also responsible for a major sin of omission in this context: they continue to fail to realise that a return to a global international monetary order is as important in the long run for the success of the European Monetary Union as the fulfilment to the last decimal of the Maastricht criteria.

Similarly, the Japanese, the largest savers in the world and the most faithful creditors of the American government and economy, can blame only themselves for the systematic criticism and humiliation and direct and indirect attacks they have been suffering from foreign experts and speculators. For a long time now Japan should have been in the forefront (together with the Europeans) in insisting on the return to a rule-based international monetary system, with rules binding for all the major governments.[4]

3.3 Politics, globalization, and the role of central banks

The intellectual and practical problems encountered at the level of the international monetary order are closely linked to the confusion concerning the *domestic and international responsibilities of central banks*. The task of restoring the global responsibility of central banks for sound monetary conditions has to be placed very high on the agenda of monetary reform.

Despite the lip-service paid to the objective of global monetary stability, the holders of the current dominant theory are basically suspicious of central banks (this goes back at least partly to Milton Friedman's interpretation of the Fed's performance in the 1920s and 1930s) and they assign a very narrow role to central banks and central bankers. This restrictive theoretical vision does not correspond to the actual real-life practice of even the most conservative central banks, be it the Bundesbank or the Swiss National Bank.

Three aspects of the role of central banks ought to be the subject of a careful scrutiny and debate, if central banks are to fulfil their functions. This applies also to the new European Central Bank.

In the first place, not only the feasibility, but also the desirability of a purely technocratic approach to central banking has to be questioned. The premise of 'no political considerations in the pursuit of monetary policies' is not only the expression of a narrow and even condescending interpretation of the term 'political', but it is also often a smoke-screen for a hidden political agenda.

The second issue has to do with the definition of the geographic scope of monetary policy. In a world of globalized financial markets, and increasingly also of markets for goods and other services, an exclusively national or even continental approach to monetary policy has become anachronistic. This has little to do with 'party politics' since both socialists and conservatives have amply demonstrated that they can have an equally narrow, national and continental view of money. Fortunately, already today, intelligent central bankers do not conduct monetary policy as if political and monetary frontiers coincided and in fact the world stopped at the national or the European borders. If this is the case, then why not recognize it explicitly, and build a true network of joint responsibility and co-operation (and possibly using a reformed IMF as one of the instruments), instead of the current approach of relying on *ad hoc* last minute rescue operations?

Finally, the third question is to what extent is it desirable and realistic to restrict the role of central bankers to watching a single variable on their screens, i.e. the 'domestic price index'? All budding economists ought to be warned of any theories that turn around a single variable, however, important it may be. Declaring 'inflation' as virtually the only legitimate matter of concern for central bankers (and providing rules to deal only with this issue) is a dangerous oversimplification of economic reality. Does not this give an air of abstraction and irrealism (similar to the selection of die-hard technocrats, who may lack an understanding of politics, to run monetary policy) for what is an extremely complex practical job? Are we not pre-programming, in case of even minor emergencies, let alone in big ones, exactly the kind of improvization that we are trying to rule out?

3.4 Finance-driven globalization: money, instability, and the real economy

What is the difference between the traditional concepts of free trade and international economic integration, on the one hand, and the current phenomenon of 'globalization', on the other hand? Without getting into a semantic discussion, for the purposes of the present article a few selected differences may be considered.

During the 19th century and the first three decades of the post-World War II period, international integration was driven primarily by the following factors: the liberalization and growth of trade in goods and services (and of related payments), the growth of foreign direct investments (which also turned out to be one of the principal vehicles of technology diffusion); and finally, to a more limited extent, by cross-border labour movements. This integration led to increased competition, but also provided a stable framework for medium- and long-term decisions and the basis for unprecedented long-term growth (cf. the differences between the performance of the Western market economies and of the autarchic centrally planned economies).

Today, globalization also implies trade liberalization and foreign direct investments. Increasingly, however, globalization means a short-term finance-driven form of world-wide integration. This trend started with the famous 'recycling of petrodollars', orchestrated by the IMF and the leading OECD treasuries and international banks, and led to the crash of the debt crisis of the 1980s. Since then it has gained further momentum, as if the debt crisis had never happened.

Under this system the herd instinct of short-term money managers tends to overemphasize both the virtues and the sins of individual national markets (or of individual companies). The higher the praise of the virtues of a market (be it Brazil, Argentina or Mexico, or more recently Mexico, Thailand, Korea or Japan), the bigger the potential or actual fall. The financial markets giveth, and the financial markets taketh away (in the case of Mexico it happened twice within a short time span, despite the vigilance of the IMF and of all the experts of Wall Street, the City, and the Harvard Business School combined).

This is not a plea for a reintroduction of exchange control on short-term capital movements. Nevertheless, we must not refuse to recognize the systemic problems we have to deal with, as many economists 'are wont' to do. Within the short time span of only a few weeks they praise the financial and economic dynamics of a given region and blame its irresponsibility when the crush comes. They never admit that the systemic shortcomings of the international market institutions are also to be blamed and have played a role in creating the original causes of the financial crisis in East Asia. Today the inherent instability and short-termism of international financial markets under the present system are no longer a distant but an imminent threat to the long-term integration of the world economy and to general prosperity.

If we want to avoid a major backlash, the revival of protectionism and the reversal of international economic integration, we cannot hide behind the assumption that 'money does not matter for the real economy' or that at least 'international money does not matter'. It is precisely because money *does* matter for the real economy, that a primarily short-term finance driven speculative approach to 'globalization' represents a mortal danger for free trade, competition, long-term investment decisions and economic growth. As a footnote one should perhaps also remember that the last time economic integration on a world scale was primarily driven by the management of financial liquidity (in those days gold and silver) by Spain's colonial empire in America.

3.5 'Inflation' versus the impact of 'other' price instability

One should never underestimate the seriousness of the problem of distorted prices, of price volatility, the problem of inflation and deflation. The world has paid enough for the consequences of inflationary policies, of necessary (and unnecessary) anti-inflationary (deflationary) policies, and of price controls and of authoritarian systems that tried to ban real prices altogether.

If the issue of 'inflation' is to be put on the short list of the monetary reform debate, it is not in order to minimize its consequences or to try to reduce to the vigilance to fight inflation.

Inflation is a major issue on the agenda of the necessary rethinking of monetary theory and practice because of the prevalent partial vision of the holders of monetary orthodoxy when it comes to price instability or volatility. There is, in fact, a dangerous paradox that has to be explored: the more one is supposed to be concerned about the slightest changes in the domestic price index (which is mainly made up of prices of tangible goods), the less one is allowed to be concerned about major and even sudden changes in other important prices affecting competitiveness and economic activity, such as exchange rates or the prices of stocks and bonds.

Today, a central bank governor who does not consider an increase in the domestic price index from 1 per cent to 2 per cent p.a. as a major economic crisis (and who might even refer to the margin of error and unreliability of economic indicators in the 1 per cent range), would be considered dangerously adventurous even by a Socialist government. At the same time, if the same central bank governor were to see in an annual increase in the stock market index of 30 per cent or more a source of (inflationary) concern (which could lead to a downward adjustment), he would be viewed as 'anti-business' and one who does not trust the wisdom of the markets. This curious logic applies also to those, be they central bank governors, finance ministers or simple observers, who would have the temerity to argue that a 10 per cent, 15 per cent or more percentage erratic movements in the exchange rate, are as much of an economic calamity in an open economy as an 0.5 per cent, 1 per cent or 1.5 per cent change in the domestic price index.

3.6 Whose risk is it? Financial institutions, (im)prudent management and the lenders of last resort

The incredible volume of short-term domestic and cross-border financial transactions has one single aim: to minimize risk. Of course, minimizing risk in today's sophisticated terminology also means avoiding the risk of not earning the theoretical maximum in dividends, interests or through changes in asset prices (including currency prices).

The implicit admission underlying the claims for the necessity for 24-hour trading around the globe, and for all the other forms of financial wizardry unhampered not only by any kind of government regulations, but even by a minimum of technical understanding by uninitiated outsiders, is that short-term risks lurk all over the horizon. According to the same legend (or is it the reality?), it is only the power of computers, of incredibly sophisticated software, of modern telecommunications and the split-second decision-making of young but nevertheless seasoned traders, that prevents every minute of the 24-hour day these huge potential short-term risks from being translated into real losses.

Has the world really become so unstable, are the major economic trends so unpredictable, is our information about the world's major countries, markets, companies and currencies so incomplete and superficial that decisions involving billions and billions of dollars can be made and have to be made in an environment that resembles most closely that of a Japanese *pachinko* or video-game parlour, on the basis of bits of news items and information that are of the type announced on the loudspeaker, or furtively exchanged between the *habitués* before placing their bets, at the horse races? Is this a caricature? Or is it an image of reality, through the distorted projection of the financial markets? By now there can be no doubt that the current functioning of financial markets exaggerates rather than minimizes the perception of short-term risk and thereby increases rather than reduces potential risk.

But if there is not only 'normal' economic risk, but also artificially created financial market risk, who bears the costs of the ultimate 'real' risk of the simultaneous search of the maximum financial gain and of maximum security? Isn't the international financial community the free rider?

According to the textbooks, money and the various financial instruments do not have a 'utility' of their own. They are there to fulfil various simple or sophisticated *intermediate functions* (medium of exchange, measure and store of value, etc.).

The modern financial system is made up of a 'holy trinity': (a) those who save and lend, (b) those who borrow, invest or spend, and (c) those who 'intermediate' or the banks or money managers. Who makes the decisions, with whose money and who bears the risks for whose decisions?

According to current orthodox theory each member of the 'holy trinity' does and should bear the risk of their decisions. According to this assumption not only are risks (and the costs and gains related to the risks) equitably distributed, but the overall result for the system as a whole is also the most advantageous.

Actual developments during the last 20 years, however, lead to a somewhat different conclusion. This may be partly due to the fact that, for better or worse, this part of the orthodox theory has not been fully implemented and thus not been put to a real test.

In virtually all the instances of major market excesses (which were at least partly due to the current structure and functioning of the system) and of cumulative market errors, the costs of the risk and the costs of the faulty judgements were unevenly distributed *ex-post* between, on the one hand, the lenders and the money managers, and, on the other hand, the borrowers and the community at large.

Sovereign borrowers were not allowed to go bankrupt in the 1980s nor in the 1990s. The reason for this was not to save their honour or credit rating, but to save the creditor banks and their depositors. None of the major international banks, or its depositors, have had to pay the full price yet for the consequences of erroneous decisions, provided these 'errors' were due to general market excesses. One does not have to be a Third World leader to see that a disproportionate share of the real costs of the over-lending in the 1970s was paid by the borrowers in the 1980s. In the same way an unjustly high share of the costs of the speculation and over-lending in the 1980s and 1990s is being borne or will be borne not by 'savers and lenders' or their money managers, but by the borrowers (i.e., the investors and spenders). The over $50 billion package to 'help' Korea, to name only one major example, was not primarily meant to help the country's 'real economy' (which will pay the full price, and over, of its excesses), but to shore up the international financial system.

In fact, in the financial markets the *domino theory* still has an unshakeable hold on the minds of decision makers: savers, money managers (bankers) and the lenders and payers of last resort (i.e., central banks and governments, and their agent, the IMF).

To their credit, some of the purists of the current conventional wisdom denounce this 'moral hazard'. Is this due to their belief in pure theory and rejection of the lessons of historic precedent such as the fading memory of the ripple effect of the *krach* of the Austrian Creditanstalt in the early 1930s?

Whatever the theoretical arguments, as a result of the implicit safety net for lenders and money managers (and of the perhaps legitimate fear of a major domino effect) the speculative excesses of one group of decision makers are not fully tempered by their fear of consequences. Yet, the costs of these excesses *are* real. Thus, it is both economically reasonable and morally just, that we should give serious thought to defining rules that would help reduce the artificial creation of risks and the unequal distribution of the resulting losses.

3.7 Return on capital versus other income: the need for a new redistribution

The principal justification for the systematic liberalization and deregulation of the financial sector has been the goal of increased efficiency. Since the financial sector, as mentioned above, fulfils the function of an intermediary only, this increased efficiency is in principle meant to benefit the rest of the economy, rather than the financial sector itself.

Two striking developments should be mentioned in this context. In the first place, at least until very recently, the very growth of the financial sector itself (in terms of both income and employment) could not be seen as a logical by-product of the increased efficiency of an intermediating sector of the economy.

Of course, the expansion of the staff and of the incomes of the financial sector could be interpreted as the economically justifiable corollary of the increase in the real earnings on financial capital since the early 1980s (through higher dividends, real interest rates and wind-fall capital gains) – which is the second, and more important development that should be stressed here.

The main issue is not what the banks and speculators are earning, although it is also an important one not only from a political or social point of view, but also from an economic one. In fact the excess earnings of the speculators are both a result of the malfunctioning of the system (including the instability and the safety net) and, through their contribution to excessive risk-taking and risk-creation, also a cause of it.

The key issues on the agenda are to determine what are the economic factors responsible for the increased earnings of holders of financial capital and what is the long-term economic rational for this new pattern of income distribution.

The oft-quoted economic and political argument that higher earnings on financial capital are necessary to stimulate savings and to reward the virtuous middle-class is not very convincing especially if one looks at either the American (one of the lowest savings rates) or the Japanese, (one of the highest savings rates) examples. The idea of a systematic conservative plot 'to reward the bourgeoisie and to exploit the workers' holds even less water. In fact, no left-wing government has succeeded, under the prevailing system, to reduce the real rate of return on financial capital, and there is no conservative government that would not like to do it if it could. This would be obviously the least painful way to reduce government spending and government deficits.

While all major developments, such as the increase in real financial earnings, are the result of multiple factors and complex developments, two important elements, that directly or indirectly are linked to the same causes should be mentioned here.

The first one is a certain 'competitive deflationary bias' in national monetary policies. The second one is the rise in real or apparent uncertainty and market risk. Both factors are closely related both to the current international monetary and financial system and to the constant restructuring and downsizing of companies to satisfy short-term financial criteria.

Under the present system of floating exchange rates many countries adopt a margin of security of restrictiveness in their monetary policy. Also, paradoxically, the more stable domestic conditions in some of the 'emerging markets' have led financial investors to expect a narrowing of earning differentials – through higher earnings even in markets like Switzerland. More generally, however, the system of floating exchange rates increases the risks and costs of financial transactions.

The pressure on jobs, wages, on government income transfers and social security payments are all phenomena that increase the general income insecurity of the population. Thus, there is a greater reliance on income from financial investments (be it directly or through pension funds, etc.) and a stronger expectation of higher earnings and implicit willingness of greater speculation and risk-taking. At the same time people expect the safety net to function, and believe that they should not bear the cost of higher risks and of economically unnecessary uncertainty and speculation.

By now there is a broad consensus, at least within the European Union, that this uncertainty and higher risk, at least as far as the exchange rates among the members are concerned, are neither inevitable nor economically useful and the redistribution of income patterns away from financial income towards other forms of income will be beneficial both from an economic and social point of view. In fact, this is one of the principal benefits that both Socialist and Conservative governments expect from the introduction of the euro.

8. Technology or monetary order: are finance and banking really just like any other business?

Today, the modern banking and financial sector is the combined product of the liberalized regulatory environment, on the one hand, and of the technological information revolution on the other.

During the last 25 years, finance and banking have undergone a profound metamorphosis. The changes have been especially striking in the international field. From a traditional and mature sector, in terms of scope, regulation and technology, banking and finance have become a dynamic, high-tech sector, and one of the major forces of change in the world economy.

During the initial period of postwar economic growth, world-wide and regional liberalization and integration of the 1950s, 1960s and part of the 1970s, the banking and financial sector was lagging behind the real economy. International banks were basically following trade and international direct investments. The banks were following their clients rather than leading them.

All this has changed since the 1970s. There were domestic as well as international factors responsible for these developments. These included the monetary disturbances of the 1970s, the impact of the oil crisis on the real economy and on international financial flows (cf. the recycling of petrodollars mentioned above). A decisive factor, however, has been the progressive change in financial and banking regulation (deregulation, liberalization, globalization, etc.) *This has led to a profound change in the perception of what is and what should be considered an acceptable monetary order and what should be its corollary rules with respect to a prudent way of dealing with other people's money.*

As also noted above, the last 20 years have also witnessed extraordinary *technological changes,* in particular in the field of telecommunications and information technologies. The banking and finance sector has been one of the most eager customers of these new technologies. In fact, the information revolution has greatly helped this sector to catch up with manufacturing in terms of productivity and modern management techniques and has allowed to leap-frog it in many respects.

In all businesses, and in fact in all areas of modern society and the modern economy, the information revolution has led to: greater flexibility, greater freedom, and simultaneously (although this may sound paradoxical) to both greater decentralization and greater powers of concentration and centralization.

Having said all this, it is a fallacy to believe that banking and finance are just like any other business. This is, in fact one of the most questionable features of current monetary philosophy. It is erroneous to believe that the objectives and the framework of domestic and international order(s) can or should be determined primarily by technology. The goal is not to slow down or reverse technological progress. Modern information and telecommunications technologies are tools that can and should to be mastered in order to create the appropriate regulatory framework of monetary order(s), at the national and the international level. Understanding this issue has to be one of the principal items on the agenda of monetary reform.

4. The legacy of the Marshall plan: the need for a common effort and for a new consensus on monetary order for the free society

The benefits of the Marshall Plan, fifty years after those bleak postwar years, are still with us – not at the material level, but through its political and moral legacy.

Money, monetary order are fundamental elements not only of the economy but in the broadest sense of the term also of the political order. History has taught us, time and time again that monetary disorders have destroyed the existing political order. Monetary disorder can be a mortal threat to democracy within domestic borders and in the world at large. Without international monetary order we could not enjoy the benefits of an open international political order based on peace, freedom and co-operation. This was the message of the Marshall Plan.

The thrust of this article is that what we need is a common effort to reach a new consensus. The *Agenda for Monetary Reform* does not mean that we need a monetary revolution. What we need is to work together to reach a new consensus that will help secure a lasting monetary order worthy of a free society.[5]

In working together for a lasting monetary order, we can find our inspiration in the work and the commitment of all those who have contributed to the building of the postwar world, the world of today from which we continue to benefit so much: Keynes and Erhard, Acheson, Marshall or Schuman, Röpke or Triffin, Friedman, Hayek or Monnet, without naming the countless others.

The 20th century has provided striking lessons proving that ultimately *values and ideas*, rather than a narrow interpretation of national interests, are the principal determinants of the pattern of international relations.

Our generation is facing a unique challenge: *to create the conditions for global growth and prosperity, peace, freedom and democracy.* These are big words, but these have been the fundamental ideas that provided the driving force for building a broad community of free nations during the last 50 years. In North America, in Europe, in Asia: today the borders of this community are potentially open to all nations, small and large throughout the world. *This is the meaning of the end of the totalitarian threat, this is the opportunity offered by the peaceful success of the Western model of society.* We have the intellectual, moral, political and material resources to meet this challenge, to seize this opportunity.

Agenda for a New Monetary Reform

Notes

1. On the international monetary order and the need for common rules, cf. Hayek's conclusions in his classic 1937 Geneva lectures: 'Since there is no means, short of complete anarchy, of protecting a country against the folly or perversity of the monetary policy of other countries, the only hope of avoiding serious distrubances is to submit to some common rules.' F.A. Hayek: *Monetary Nationalism and International Stability*. Augustus M. Kelley, New York, 1964, Reprints of Economic Classics, p. 94.
2. On the challenge of transition from communism to the market economy cf. Otto Hieronymi: 'The International Financial Institutions and the Challenge of Transition and Reconstruction in the Former Communist Countries of Central and Eastern Europe', in Miklós Szabó-Pelsőczi (ed): *Fifty Years After Bretton Woods*. Avebury, in Association with the Robert Triffin – Szirák Foundation, Aldershot, 1996. On the social market economy and the relevance of the postwar European model for the 'transition economies.' cf. Otto Hieronymi: *Economic Policies for the New Hungary: Proposals for a Coherent Approach*, Battelle, Columbus, Ohio, 1990, pp. 10-18.
3. On the impact of floating cf. Otto Hieronymi: 'In Search for a New Economics for the 1980s: the Need for a Return to Fixed Exchange Rates', in Otto Hieronymi (ed): *International Order: A View From Geneva*, IUHEI, Geneva, 1983, pp. 107-126.
4. Cf. Otto Hieronymi: 'The Case for an 'Extended EMS': A New International Order to be Built by Europe, Japan and the United States', in: Miklós Szabó-Pelsőczi (ed): *The Global Monetary System After the Fall of the Soviet Empire*. Avebury in Association with the Robert Triffin – Szirák Foundation, Aldershot, 1995.
5. On the Marshall Plan and monetary order cf. Otto Hieronymi: *Economic Discrimination Against the United States in Western Europe (1945-1958)*, Librairie Droz, Geneva, 1973.

27 Privatization and Corporate Governance: Some Lessons from the Experience of Transitional Economies*

Tito Boeri and Giancarlo Perasso

1. Introduction

All former planned economies have started privatization programmes. Certain Central and Eastern European Countries are more advanced in transferring property from the state to individuals. Others, mostly former Soviet Republics other than Russia, are just starting. Different methods of privatization have been implemented, ranging from mass privatization through voucher schemes to direct sales of enterprises (often to foreigners), and from spontaneous privatization to well-organized transfers of property rights to employees. These different methods have brought about different models, or structures, of corporate governance that affect the way enterprises are responding to market signals, and, more broadly, to the stimuli of the emerging market environment.

This paper will review evidence from two countries that have followed very different routes and methods in privatizing their productive assets: the Czech Republic and Poland. In the Czech Republic, voucher privatization accounted for the transfer of property rights of a fairly large share of the country's assets; in Poland, insider privatization – ranging from management

---

* Paper prepared for the 20th Colloquium of the Société Universitaire Européenne de Recherches Financières (SUERF) and the 7th Conference of the Foundation Robert Triffin-Szirák, Budapest 15-17 May 1997. The authors would like to thank Rauf Gonenc and Silvana Malle for valuable comments on an initial draft. The views expressed in the paper are those of the authors and cannot be attributed to their respective institutions.

and employee (mostly leveraged) buyouts to the so-called privatization through 'liquidation' – has been the dominant privatization method. Both countries are currently enjoying high rates of economic growth, with a decisive contribution from the private sector. Yet, the different nature of the privatization process has resulted in a much different structure of ownership and control, which, by affecting firms' investment decisions, may increase asymmetries in the performance of private enterprises in the two countries in the years to come.

The plan of the paper is as follows. First, main privatization methods followed in Central and Eastern Europe and Russia are outlined and assessed in the light of commonly accepted normative criteria. Second, evidence on the performance of privatized enterprises in the two countries is reviewed by highlighting the effects of corporate governance on the behaviour of firms. The final section draws some tentative conclusions.

2. Privatization methods

Three main routes have been used to privatize former large and medium-sized state enterprises in Central and Eastern Europe and Russia. The first privatization mechanism is *capital privatization*, i.e., the sale of enterprise assets to strategic investors via tenders, public auctions, and public offerings (usually, but not always, involving only minority stakes) and debt-equity swaps. The second privatization method is the so-called *mass privatization*, i.e., the free (or at a symbolic price) distribution of certificates to the population, which are generally freely marketable. Such vouchers can be either sold or converted into company shares and/or participation in mutual funds set up at the start of the process. Finally, the third privatization route is *insider privatization*, i.e., the creation of a holding through equity issues subscribed mainly by managers and workers. This scheme usually involves the concession of preferential credits, if not the free distribution of shares to workers. Insider privatization can be an alternative to the liquidation of state enterprises, but can also be achieved *de facto* via the liquidation of firms in poor financial condition, and the sale or lease of their assets to managers and (less frequently) to workers.

There is an extensive literature weighing the pros and the cons of the above privatization methods. Such an assessment is usually carried out merely on the basis of theoretical considerations concerning the design features of the various schemes, the incentives they have on managers' and workers' performance, their social acceptability, etc. Six to seven years after the start of privatization processes in Central and Eastern Europe, it is possible to complement these subjective (and rather speculative) evaluations with preliminary evidence on the outcomes of the different privatization methods. Table 1 summarises available information on the privatization strategies followed in the Czech Republic, Hungary, Poland, and Russia – the four countries in the region for which most detailed information on privatization methods and performance is nowadays available – and on their outcomes. In particular, three performance indicators are used, namely the *speed* of privatization, i.e., the proportion of former state enterprises which has changed ownership within the first four years of the privatization process, the relevance of *outside ownership* (percentage of privatized enterprises with dominant outside ownership) in the resulting ownership structure of firms, and finally, the degree of *control* exerted over managerial decisions by the owners of the firm. The latter indicator is proxied by the involvement in privatization of foreign and domestic companies, which are better equipped than investment funds – usually lacking skilled staff and having to manage a vast array of shareholdings – to exert effective supervision over the management of firms.

As shown by the first three columns of the Table 1, the four countries have so far followed quite different privatization strategies: in the Czech Republic ownership changes were mainly achieved via a mass privatization scheme, while in Hungary capital privatization was the dominant route, and in Poland and Russia a strong involvement of insiders was pursued. Given such wide differences in privatization strategies, the four countries' experience offers a natural comparison of the various privatization methods. In Table 1 we use the cross-country variation not only to obtain a ranking of the various countries and overall privatization strategies, but also to provide a rating of the various ownership change mechanisms. As can be grasped by reading horizontally the Table, the privatization strategy followed by the Czech Republic was extremely rapid (with over 99 per cent of state enterprise assets slated for privatization being transferred within a very short timeframe), achieved a significant degree of outside ownership, but has resulted so far in a rather weak control structure. Hungary's strategy was somewhat less rapid, but achieved better results in terms of both relevance of outside ownership and control. Poland was slow to privatize (as discussed in Section 3 below, mass privatization was started only in 1995), achieved a rather low degree of outside ownership, but it resulted in a good control structure within the set of firms dominated by outsiders. Finally, Russia is another success story in terms of the speed of privatization, but this performance has been achieved at high costs in terms of the resulting ownership and control structure insofar as mostly insiders have been the key players in the privatization process.

Overall, each method involves a trade-off between different objectives. By assigning the same weight to the different criteria listed in Table 1, one reaches the conclusion that capital privatization is the most successful method. However, there may be cases where some criteria are more important than others, and, in the early stages of transition, common wisdom deemed speed the most important. The key issue is: How closely do the three criteria listed in Table 1 correspond to the performance of firms? This question will be addressed in the next two sections which cover the rather extreme experiences of the Czech Republic and Poland, respectively.

3. The case of the Czech Republic

A fairly common misconception is that the Czech economy was fully and rapidly privatized, thanks to the use of vouchers. A speedy transfer of property rights was indeed the rationale for implementing the voucher scheme, and great success was achieved in this effort.[2] About half of state holdings slated for privatization in the non-financial corporate sector were privatized via voucher privatization very rapidly, both in terms of employment or output,[3] but – as Table 2 shows – state shareholdings in privatized enterprises, which are all practically vested in the National Property Fund (NPF), remain substantial.[4] These holdings can be divided into two groups: 'residual' holdings, i.e., what could not be sold so far and which the NPF is trying to sell, and 'strategic' companies,[5] that will also be privatized 'in the future'. The NPF may not hold a majority shareholding in these enterprises – hence some of them are correctly, from a purely statistical point of view, classified as 'private enterprises' – however, it exerts control over the enterprises since the other shareholders are either small investors or are investment privatization funds (IPFs), which acquired vouchers from individual holders. The largest IPFs are controlled by banks, especially by the big four banks, whose main shareholder, but not majority except in one case, is the state via the NPF.[6]

This state influence in the Czech enterprise sector – which cannot be revealed by looking at official statistics – may manifest itself in many forms: as a direct shareholder, as a shareholder in banks, as a tax collector, and, in some cases, as a regulator. This happens in other countries as well, but the important point is whether the involvement of the state brings about managerial – and public policy – decisions that are different from those that would be taken in a fully privatized enterprise. Although in the Czech Republic there seems to be rather little direct state intervention in the economy, some indirect influence may be likely through some 'concerted action' or 'cooperation' between the state and/or its agencies and the management of the companies.

A very important case of this 'moral suasion' exerted by the state on enterprises is the Banking Council. Members of the Banking Council are the Governor of the Central Bank, the Minister of Finance, the Chairman of the National Property Fund and, occasionally, the chairmen of the four largest banks. Although there is no indication of government intervention in determining the allocation of credit, the potential for state 'suggestions' concerning banks' strategic options is very high.[7]

It is important to stress that the ownership structure of banks and enterprises is far from being settled. The NPF is still actively trying to sell its residual holdings, and recent indications show that it is ready to dispose of its holding in one of the major banks.

Ultimately, what is important is that the right set of incentives is present for the development of a genuinely market-oriented economy. The lower limit on the level of efficiency in an enterprise is given by the credible threat of bankruptcy. Some bankruptcies have taken place in the Czech Republic but banks, via their IPFs, appear to be reluctant to take large enterprises to court. It follows that the discipline provided by the hard budget constraint is not yet fully and extensively enforced in the Czech Republic.[8]

A semi-hard budget constraint may well be the by-product of voucher privatization. Bank-owned IPFs play a large role in the exertion of corporate governance and, at this stage of the transition, are more concerned to 'preserve the life' of the enterprise that has borrowed from the parent bank than to liquidate it.[9] If this is the case, as it appears to be quite frequently, the question is whether the right incentives for enterprise restructuring are, and will be, present.

Looking at macroeconomic data, there appears to have been, so far, little incentives to restructure enterprises. Despite double-digit investment growth rates in recent years, productivity has increased only slightly; exports are not growing as rapidly as in the past, while imports are booming. Finally, the Czech Republic is the only country in the region currently experiencing an increase in unemployment (although from one of the lowest levels in the OECD area.[10])At the microeconomic level, a survey conducted by Coopers & Lybrand, quoted in OECD (1996), indicated that the managing boards of only 1 in 6 enterprises surveyed had their salary linked to enterprise performance; in almost as many cases (1 in 8) the supervisory board's reward was linked to performance. There was no case of reward linked to the share price. Among managing directors, only half felt that profit maximization was a 'very important' goal (less than half of board members shared this view). Supervising assets and supervising management were the two other important goals identified by board members.

The picture presented so far is that of a system of incentives geared to achieving restructuring gradually and avoiding sharp shocks to the enterprises, most notably hostile takeovers and/or changes in management. The issue is whether this process is being undertaken at too slow a pace.[11] Time will tell, although the deteriorating trade performance does not bode well[12] and may even be an indication of the slowness of restructuring due to the present structure of corporate governance.

Corporate governance in the Czech Republic is evolving neither along the lines of the 'bank-based' model, nor according to the 'stock exchange-based' model.[13] Directly, or via their IPFs, banks are the predominant players, but their strategy of nurturing enterprise growth, and hence of not concentrating on (short-term) profit maximization, could endanger the stability of the financial system, if it is not carefully followed. The return on average assets of Czech banks is lower than those of Hungarian and Polish banks, and the share of their non-performing loans in total loans is twice that of Hungarian banks and much higher than that of Polish banks.[14] There have been cases of closure of small banks, but this process is strengthening the position of the big NPF-controlled banks which, as we saw earlier, are reluctant to take enterprises to court. Such a 'relaxed' attitude concerning the enforcement of the hard budget constraint on the part of banks could, however, cause more damage than good to the Czech economy.

4. The Polish experience

The privatization process in Poland has been much slower than in the Czech lands. By June 1996, privatization had been completed in 2,624 enterprises[15] out of the 8,853 state enterprises having existed in 1990, when the process was started. As in the case of the Czech Republic, these numbers should be interpreted with caution, as the state has in some cases retained substantial participation in privatized units, remaining *de facto*, the controlling shareholder (OECD, 1996b). The size of the residual state sector may provide a better measure of the extent of privatization than the number of privatized units per se: the total book value of the state shares in the business sector was estimated in November 1995 to amount to about 140 billion zlotys. This compares with a book value of about 8 billion zlotys for all firms quoted on the Warsaw Stock Exchange and revenues from the sale of state assets of the order of 2.6 billion in 1996.

Large and medium-sized state enterprises scheduled for privatization in Poland have first to be transformed into a joint stock company under the jurisdiction of the Treasury. Although this so-called 'commercialization' stage does not alter the ownership of firms, it modifies their control structure by phasing out the Workers' Councils and establishing a Board of Directors composed of up to 7 top managers and 2 representatives of workers. This transformation is supposed to break the so-called 'Bermuda triangle' (Belka et al., 1995) control structure of former Polish state enterprises, which apparently involved paralysing negotiations among the Directors, the trade unions, and the Workers' Council. Furthermore, the dismantling of the Workers' Council significantly reduces the power of workers in affecting firms' strategies. Far from being a consultative body (like the German Workers' Councils), the Polish Workers' Council has, in principle, most of the powers typically held by governing bodies in a corporation, including the possibility to appoint and to lay off the managers of the firm. The commercialized unit is therefore still a self-governed state firm dominated by insiders – as most Polish state enterprises are, at least since the 1980s – but one where workers have lost most of their power vis-a-vis the management.

Within two years after being 'commercialized', procedures for the actual sale of the enterprise should start along one of the possible routes envisaged by the 1990 Privatization Law.[16] As shown in Table 1, the dominant privatization track for large and medium-sized enterprises in Poland has been so far the so-called 'liquidation' route. This method involves the sale or lease of state enterprise assets to other private firms or – as in most cases – to the insiders.[17] The sale or lease can either involve the enterprise as a whole or parts of its assets, as in the case of enterprises in poor financial condition.[18] Several concessions have been granted to the insiders, including the lowering of interest rates used to compute the repayments and the postponement of the capital contributions. While these concessions have accelerated the privatization process, they have nonetheless reduced even further the resources of the firm undergoing privatization as well as its capacity to raise loans.

While capital privatization has involved only about 7 per cent of former state enterprises (first column of Table 1), it has been the main source of revenues from privatization: for instance, in the first six months of 1996, revenues from capital privatization accounted for almost 80 per cent of the total funds raised from privatization. Capital privatization typically involves the largest state enterprises and is achieved mainly via tenders and the search for strategic investors, who are, for the most part, foreign or foreign/domestic partnerships. The main problem is the slow pace of this process, which has been further reduced by increasingly complex deals concerning the fate and wages of the enterprise employees as well as investment commitments by the new owner. While these commitments are requested to seek support for privatization, they may make the search for strategic investors more difficult, leaving the commercialized unit in limbo – just when it would require strategic decisions and deeper restructuring.

Although plans for mass privatization date back to late 1990, concrete arrangements to start the process were only made at the end of 1994. An important characteristic of the Polish mass privatization scheme – and one that makes it quite different from the Czech vouchers scheme – is that it ensures that each firm has a strategic investor. Shares of the firms included in the programme are allocated to the 15 National Investment Funds (NIFs) set up in 1995 in such a way that each NIF has shares in all firms, but also a strategic 33 per cent stake in some (randomly selected) units. This design feature of the Polish scheme should result in a better governance structure than that currently prevailing in the Czech Republic. However, the late start of the process and the fact that some of the best performing state enterprises targeted for privatization have displayed some reluctance in being involved in this scheme (because they feared losing potential foreign investors) seem to have negatively affected the quality of the firms involved in the scheme. This will certainly make the task of the NIF managers more difficult, as they are called to supervise a relatively large number of former state enterprises requiring significant restructuring. Moreover, the state retains a significant minority stake (25 per cent) in firms being privatized and another 15 per cent is allotted, free of charge, to the workers. This does not fully rule out the possibility that political pressures may result in supervisory boards postponing the needed deep restructuring of the firms rather than pushing it through. Indeed, there have been a few cases where important conflicts have arisen between the NIF management and the supervisory board of the firm in which the investment fund had a strategic stake. Given the very recent start of the scheme, it is premature to draw any definite conclusion about its effectiveness. History will tell whether or not the present difficulties and tensions between NIFs and the supervisory boards of some firms undergoing privatization are just a by-product of a psychological learning process which ultimately generates an effective supervision of firms.

Pending the evaluation of the outcome of the mass privatization process, the Polish experience offers a good case study on the pros and cons of the insiders versus the outsiders privatization route. Comparisons of the performance of commercialized units, firms being privatized via management/employee buyouts and capital privatization are problematic due to substantial differences in the composition of the various privatization pools prior to the actual sale and on the timing of restructuring (e.g., enterprises sold to outsiders have generally undergone considerable preprivatization restructuring). The fact that governing bodies of commercialized units can opt among the various privatization methods makes such comparisons even more difficult because self-selection is likely to increase even further the asymmetries among the various privatization pools.

Bearing the above caveats in mind, Table 3 offers some information on the control structure and performance of firms of different ownership type. In particular, the first four rows of the Table report findings from a survey of about 200 Polish firms carried out at the end of 1993 (Belka et al.). This suggests that the decision structure of insider-dominated firms is characterized by a very strong position of managers vis-a-vis the other organs, notably the Supervisory Board and the shareholders meetings. In particular, in less than 50 per cent of insider dominated firms, the Board of Directors can appoint or fire managers and decide upon their compensation. The dominance of managers is reinforced by the limited role assigned to workers in the Board of Directors of firms in the commercialization stage (see above).

The next five rows of the Table display results from an enterprise survey carried out by the World Bank in 1993 (World Bank, 1996; Pinto et al., 1994). As argued above, differences in the performance of firms of different ownership type are likely to reflect selection bias. Yet, two facts highlighted by the Table would seem to be particularly important. The first is the much better sales and technology performance of enterprises with foreign owners, within the class of outsider-dominated firms. The latter would seem to have shed more labour than domestic outsiders firms, while granting significant wage increases to the 'surviving' workforce. Another important fact highlighted by the Table is the substantial employment reductions taking place in enterprises that are still in state hands. This confirms the rather bright picture of Polish state enterprises provided by Pinto and van Wijnbergen (1995). Insofar as incentives for managers of state enterprises to pursue profit-maximizing behaviour come from the aspiration of being confirmed and/or rewarded by the new owners, this result suggests that even a slow, but credible, privatization process may produce immediate results on firm performance.

5. Concluding remarks

Governments of Central and Eastern European countries that were/are committed to genuine privatization face a formidable task. The sheer size of the assets to be privatized and the lack of established financial markets and intermediaries presented an incredible challenge to the authorities. Privatization strategies had to be devised which would accomplish three main tasks: first, rapidly increase the size of the private sector; second, prevent a decapitalization of the enterprise in the process and possibly inject fresh capital; third, ensure an effective control structure over management. All this while gaining political support for reforms and developing domestic capital markets.

Many assets still remain to be privatized in Central and Eastern Europe – Hungary being the exception since privatization has gone farther than in any other country, including some Western European countries – and authorities should learn from their, and other countries', past experiences. Privatization strategies actually implemented differed quite substantially across countries. This was due partly to exogenous constraints (e.g., the geographical orientation of foreign direct investments), and partly to political considerations inducing public authorities to give priority to one particular objective over others. In this paper, we have exploited these cross-country differences in privatization methods in an attempt to make some inferences on their effects on corporate governance.

In particular, we have considered the two rather extreme routes taken by the Czech and Polish authorities. In the Czech Republic, a decision was made to go ahead rapidly and give preference to speed in the transfer of property rights. In Poland, a slower and more cautious approach to privatization was taken, giving priority to direct sales of large units and insider privatization of small and medium-sized state enterprises.

The Czech experience shows that speed in transferring property rights may not lead to an effective corporate governance structure if institutional investors controlled by domestic banks take the lead in the privatization process. It also shows that dispersing ownership among citizens without adopting appropriate regulations concerning transparency and minority shareholders' rights brings about a concentration of ownership that is harmful to competition, i.e., it hampers an efficient allocation of resources. The importance of having credible 'rules of the game' that are conducive to an efficient use of resources is highlighted by the Polish experience. When the right set of incentives was finally introduced, it made managers of state-owned enterprises behave efficiently. The experience of Poland also indicates that a prolonged piecemeal approach to privatization may delay the liberalization of markets and not provide adequate information on relative scarcities.

Does this mean that speed should be given less importance than other objectives of privatization? In the end, what is important is that the right set of incentives be in place to guarantee an efficient allocation of resources. In this respect, the enforcement of the hard budget constraint is only a necessary condition – but not a sufficient one – for guaranteeing efficiency. A long-term strategy is also required when restructuring enterprises. This can only be achieved when there is little uncertainty about the evolving corporate governance of the firm.

In a nutshell, speed may be deemed less important than the search for an effective governance structure, but only if there is a well-defined and credible privatization strategy binding the management to immediately adopt practices consistent with profit maximization in the presence of hard budget constraints, while authorities keep pursuing sound macroeconomic policies and creating a regulatory framework that will allow resources to be allocated efficiently.

References

Anderson, R.E., (1994), *Voucher Funds in Transitional Economies, the Czech and Slovak Experience*, World Bank Policy Research Working Papers No. 1324.

Coffee, J.C. Jr. (1996), Institutional Investors in Transitional economies: Lessons from the Czech Experience, in Frydman R., Gray C.W., Rapaczynski A. (Eds), *Corporate Governance in Central Europe and Russia*, Central European University Press.

Deutsche Morgan Grenfell (1997), 'Emerging Markets'. *Focus Eastern Europe*, January 27.

Earle, J. and Estrin, S. (1996), 'Employee Ownership in Transition', in: Frydman R., Gray C.W., Rapaczynski A. (Eds), *Corporate Governance in Central Europe and Russia*, Central European University Press.

EBRD (1995), *Transition Report 1995*, European Bank for Reconstruction and Development, London.

EBRD (1996), *Transition Report 1996*, European Bank for Reconstruction and Development, London.

Johnson, S. and Kroll, H. (1991), 'Managerial Strategies for Spontaneous Privatisation', *Soviet Economy*, 7, pp. 281-316.

Kenway, P. and Klvacova, E. (1995), 'The Web of Cross-ownership among Czech Financial Intermediaries: An Assessment', *Europe-Asia Studies*, 48, No. 5, pp. 797-809.

Kotrba, J. (1995) 'Privatization Process in the Czech Republic: Players and Winners', in Svejnar, J. (Ed.), *The Czech Republic and Economic Transition in Eastern Europe*, Academic Press.

Mejstrik, M. (1994), *Czech Investment Funds as a Part of the Financial Sector and their Role in Privatisation of the Economy*, Reform Round Table Working Paper No.14. Institute of Economic Studies, Charles University.

OECD (1994), *Economic Survey of the Czech and Slovak Republics*, Paris, OECD.

OECD (1995), *Review of the Labour Market in the Czech Republic*, Paris, OECD.

OECD (1996a), *Economic Survey of the Czech Republic*, Paris, OECD.

OECD (1996b), *Economic Survey of Poland*, Paris, OECD.

Pinto, B., Belka, M.. Krajewski, S. (1994), 'Transforming State Enterprises in Poland: Evidence on Adjustment by Manufacturing Firms', Brookings Papers on Economic Activity.

Pistor, K. and Turkewitz, J. (1996), 'Coping with Hydra – State Ownership after Privatisation: A Comparative Study of the Czech Republic, Hungary, and Russia, in: Frydman R., Gray C.W., Rapaczynski A. (Eds), *Corporate Governance in Central Europe and Russia*, Central European University Press.

Shafik, N. (1993*) Making a Market. Mass Privatisation in the Czech and Slovak Republics*, World Bank Policy Research Working Papers No. 1321.

World Bank, *World Development Report*, Washington.

Notes

1. See Johnson and Kroll (1991) for a review of uncontrolled and spontaneous privatization methods.
2. There is, by now, a vast literature on voucher privatization. For the Czech and Slovak experience, see OECD (1994). See also Shafik (1993) and Anderson (1994) for description and analysis of the role of voucher funds in corporate governance.
3. If one considers the book value of these firms, the share of voucher-privatized firms is higher, slightly less than 50 per cent (see Kotrba, 1995). Book value data, though, especially in the first years of the transition could represent an imprecise picture of the enterprise.
4. This is also the finding of a recent study by Pistor and Turkewitz (1996).
5. Strategic companies include electricity distribution companies, coal mines, petrochemical companies, pharmaceutical companies. At the end of 1995, there were 56 strategic enterprises including the country's four largest banks.
6. In this case as well, given the dispersion of other shareholders, the NPF is *de facto* controlling the four largest banks. For example, at the banks' meeting of shareholders in 1996, the NPF 'suggested' a distribution of dividends below what was proposed by the management, and nobody raised any objection.

7. This (in)direct state influence is further reinforced by the web of cross-ownership among banks, see Mejstrik (1994); and financial intermediaries, see Kenway-Klvacova (1996).
8. The case of truckmaker Tatra is a good example of banks' reluctancy to take large enterprises to court. In general, it is difficult to assess whether banks do not enforce their creditor's rights because of the length of the bankruptcy procedures or because they are optimistic about the restructuring effort being undertaken by companies.
9. Furthermore, the staff of bank-owned IPFs was initially, and generally still is, dominated by employees whose careers probably depend on their assesment by the bank hierarchy.
10. See OECD (1995) for a discussion of the factors behind the 'Czech employment miracle'.
11. There are many other issues involved, especially that of transparency, the lack of which is a major shortcoming of the Czech capital markets, see OECD (1996a) for a discussion of this issue.
12. Czech authorities are quick at pointing out that the trade deficit is mainly due to the importation of invesment goods, which account for a large share of imports. Leaving aside the doubts about the criteria used by the authorities for classifying what goods are investment goods, the weak increase in productivity despite the growth in investments remains a cause of concern.
13. See Coffee (1996) for a detailed analysis of the present corporate governance system in the Czech Republic.
14. See Deutsche Morgan Grenfell (1997). Although the criteria for loan classification may differ among countries, differences in the share of non-performing loans in banks' portfolio are as marked as to survive to these definitional problems.
15. See EBRD (1996).
16. Delays in the privatization process have extended the duration of the commercialization phase for a number of enterprises. The new privatization law approved by the Parliament in September 1996 also allows for commercialization without subsequent privatization for enterprises requiring substantial restructuring.
17. According to Earle and Estrin (1996), almost 75 per cent of the firms privatized via liquidation are insider-owned.
18. This is the case of liquidations via article 19 of the 1990 Privatization Law. The possibility offered to 'unbundle' firms in poor financial condition is an innovative characteristic of the Polish privatization route, which has allowed to put idle capacity back into use (OECD, 1996b).

Table 1. Methods of privatization of large and medium-sized enterprises

Country	Privatization method (weights) (a)			Outcomes			
	Capital privatization	Mass privatization	Management/ employee buyout and liquidation	Speed (b)	Outside ownership (c)	Control (d)	Overall country rating (e)
Czech Republic	17.8	74.5	7.7	99.0	58.3	33.0	9
Hungary	93.2	0.0	6.8	66.9	73.9	60.9	10
Poland	6.8	13.9	79.3	25.6	48.4	34.6	6
Russia	0.0	19.5	80.5	81.7	16.3	8.1	5
Method rating (f)	11.3	8.5	10.2				

Notes:
(a) Value of firms privatized with this method (as a % estimated of privatized SOEs)
   Czech Republic: book value; Hungary: transaction value;
   Poland: nr. of firms privatized with this method as % of total nr. of privatized enterprises; Russia: book value.
(b) Number of firms being privatized in the country within the first four years of privatizations (as % of former SOEs).
(c) Percentage of privatized firms with dominant outsider ownership (EBRD).
(d) Percentage of firms with dominant either foreign or domestic outside ownership by companies (EBRD).
(e) Average of the rank of the country (increasing in country's performance) according to the three criteria listed before.
(f) Weighted average (weights are given by the share of privatizations achieved with the method at issue) of the overall country rating.

Table 2. Estimated ownership structure in the non-financial corporate sector
(1994, percentage share)

	Employment	Output
Total	100	100
of which:		
Voucher privatized	27	30
Co-operative (including agriculture)	8	9
Residual state ownership *	5	3
Other private	15	13
'Strategic' holdings of the state	20	21
For privatization but not yet privatized	25	24

* What was left of companies that were split and privatized by segments.
Source: OECD (1996a).

Table 3. Corporate governance and enterprise performance in Poland

Role of the Board of Directors in the following decisions (a)	State	Insiders	Domestic Outsiders	Foreign
Profit allocation			29	10
Hiring/firing managers			43	10
Managerial compensation			48	20
Major investment			57	30
Performance indicators				
Real wages (% changes)	-0.5	0.6	-3.8	14.6
Employment (% change)	-5.5	-0.7	0.8	-5.5
Sales (% change)	5	12.5	10	19.8
Labour productivity (% change)	14.4	28.2		
Firms introducing new technology (%) (b)	51.6	75	71.4	87.5

Source: Belka et al. (1995); EBRD (1995).
Notes:
(a) Percentage of enterprises within the ownership type reporting that the decisions on the subject matter listed below are made by the Board of Directors.
(b) Percentage of firms within the ownership type reporting major investment in new technology in the last two years.

28 Narrow Banks in Today's Financial World: US and International Perspectives

Dimitri B. Papadimitriou

Introduction

As is well-known, banking performs two functions in a modern economy: it provides a safe payments system and it channels funds to borrowers, both individuals and businesses. It has been always assumed that this dual role, *ceteris paribus*, would continue to be played by banks. However, organizations chartered as banks *per se* have seen their role gradually decline with the advent of competition from non-bank financial services firms. These include mutual fund companies offering money market, bond, and equity mutual funds, insurance companies, finance companies, and government affiliated mortgage entities. In the United States, deposits in banks have been growing at a smaller proportion than those in non-bank firms. In addition, more borrowers have turned for their financing needs directly to financial markets rendering the process of intermediation – the bankers' habitat – less and less necessary. These trends, demonstrating the declining significance of banks in terms of their primary role, are expected to continue, thus raising important questions vis-a-vis the conduct and effectiveness of monetary policy.

Furthermore, as banks expand their operations to include non-traditional, yet very profitable activities, i.e., invesment functions and 'off-balance sheet' banking, the central banks that regulate, supervise and examine them, and control the bank money creation, need to evaluate and modify the organizational framework within which they discharge their own regulatory and monitoring responsibilities, by taking into consideration the changing nature and particularity of banks. For banks, like any other profit-making entity, seek to increase market share and revenues from business endeavours that may fall outside the initial scope of their charter. Banks, however, are afforded a financial safety net intended to insure the soundness of the payments system, and as such are special business entities. The developing trends of banking denote the shift of business away from the 'on-balance sheet' toward the 'off-balance sheet' banking. This shift has sparked the ongoing debate regarding the need to reconstitute the financial structure so as to address such questions about the safety net extending to banks' activities not beyond those assumed to need government protection.

In the US, the 1980s S&L crisis, which ultimately cost taxpayers close to half a trillion dollars, gave rise to various proposals including, among others, the institution of 'narrow' banks that would be insulated from market and default risks, thus insuring the safety and soundness of the payments system, and eliminating or substantially reducing the need for deposit insurance. The idea of narrow banks gained substantial currency when it was originally suggested (Litan 1987), and continues to be in the legislative minds not only in the US, but throughout the industrialized and developing worlds. This paper explores the concept of narrow banking within a changing banking environment. First, I briefly review the relevant history of the payments system with reference to narrow banking, then define old problems solved, and new ones created by the narrow banking system. Next, I review the government responses to financial and banking crises abroad. And lastly, I asses the policy implications and feasibility of narrow banking within the perspective of financial modernization in the US and abroad.

Narrow banking in historical perspective

In reviewing the history of the payments system, at least for the US, one finds that from the early beginnings, government debt always served as the stable backing for bank money. Government debt issued in anticipation of forthcoming tax revenues and repaid in commodity money at some future time, was not considered inflationary, because of its fiscal backing (Calomiris 1988). Scholars of American financial history have documented the prevailing usage of government debt to back the means of payment, and in the few instances that other backing was used, the return to government debt obligations was inevitable.

Narrow banking proposals, although they were not known as such, first emerged in the 1930s as alternative schemes to free banking to ameliorate the multifaceted financial crises of the 1930s. The proponents of '100 per cent' reserves – the precursor of narrow banking – were not convinced that deposit insurance instituted for protecting small depositors was the appropriate reform. As Ronnie J. Phillips, my colleague at the Levy Institute, has discovered, there was at least one banker, John M. Nichols, who in 1934 advocated 100 per cent reserves and refused to have his bank become a member of the Federal Deposit Insurance Corporation (FDIC). Instead, he liquidated the bank's non-government securities and loans and substituted his bank's assets almost exclusively with cash and government debt instruments (Phillips 1995, p. 19). The view that banks were to be responsible to their depositors and shareholders was also advocated by a number of economists including Henry Simons, Frank Knight, Lloyd Mints, and Paul Douglas. They 'circulated a proposal that called for the abolition of fractional reserve banking – the separation of the deposit and lending; functions of banks – and the establishment of a federal monetary authority to conduct monetary policy under definite rules established by Congress' (ibid, p. 20). Their proposal was in concert with Article 8 of the US Constitution establishing the right of Congress to issue money and safeguard its value. What was envisaged by the Chicago School economists was that banks could not and should not perform both functions of payment and lending, instead, they are to serve as custodians of deposits, leaving the lending function to mutual savings associations. Allowing banks to perform the dual function risks a *de facto* nationalization of the banking system, which is to be avoided by clearly articulating the respective public and private roles in the payments and lending mechanisms, thus insuring stability in the financial and real sectors of the economy.

A number of narrow-bank style proposals that surfaced in the aftermath of the late 1980s American S&L debacle, and the precarious financial condition of many commercial banks, were directed toward remedying the difficulties facing depository institutions with respect to the payments system. These proposals focused on the creation of financial institutions to be known as 'narrow banks' (Litan 1987) or 'monetary service companies' (Litan 1993; Pierce 1993), which would provide transactions and checkable accounts and have portfolios consisting of only safe assets. Variations of the narrow banking concept include Tobin's 'deposited currency', William Seidman's 'two-window banking', Kareken's '100 per cent reserve' requirements, Spong's 'high liquidity asset', and Haemmerli's 'consumer bank'.

Tobin's deposited currency (1985), and Kareken's (1986) and Spong's (1991) proposals would create transaction accounts banks with the safety of 100 per cent reserves in the form of cash, Federal Reserve balances, and US Treasury liabilities; Seidman's two-window banking (Carns 1994) would establish *insured* and *uninsured* deposits which would be used to finance primarily short-term lending and transaction clearing and a variety of unrestricted business, respectively, since the insured and uninsured windows would be in legally distinct banks. Finally, Haemmerli's consumer bank (1985), would be a separate transactions institution very closely regulated and supervised with 100 per cent deposit insurance. A common thread runs through these proposals, in that their emphasis is on the safety of their portfolio assets, the differences regarding what constitutes a safe asset notwithstanding. The safety restrictions are intended to minimize the exposure to usual risks of banking: credit risk (default), interest rate risk (term), affiliates risk (raids on funds from affiliates or subsidiaries), business risk (bond, foreign exchange trading) and fraud risk (Lawrence and Talley 1988).

There are other proposals with a varying degree of asset safety (Tobin 1987; Burnham 1991; Greenbaum and Boot 1991; Bryan 1991). Clearly, a decrease in safety increases credit risk, and, thus other safety enhancing features would be needed to protect depositors, which may include increased bank capital, interest rate ceilings, and risk-based deposit insurance premiums (Hart 1991). To be sure, a concern arises that narrow-like banks owned by holding companies might have their assets used to make good on losses of a subsidiary of the holding company. Thus, ownership of a narrow bank by a holding company would necessitate a degree of transparency, and specified restrictions that the assets of the narrow bank be kept separate, distinct, and untouchable. The earliest proponent of narrow banking, Robert Litan (1987), envisioned that financial services holding companies would separate their depository and lending functions, while Tobin (1987) would insist that if bank holding companies own investment bank subsidiaries, they be uninsured, and regulated by the Securities and Exchange Commission. Once implemented, this functional approach to banking would firm up the separation of banks into monetary (depository) and finance (lending) companies respectively.

Advocats of narrow banks relentlessly point to the benefits these special institutions would bring, discounting the questions that sceptics raise. These are the issues I turn to next.

Narrow banking: a solution, or a new problem?

Proposals leading to the functional separation of banking address several issues characterizing the present financial structure. These are: safety and soundness of the payments mechanism, improvement of the central bank's ability to control monetary aggregates, lessening of the government's regulation of banks, and eliminating or minimizing the need for deposit insurance.

The central bank would have a good grip of the money supply (currency and transactions deposits), since this would be its monetary base. This can be achieved if the government, through its central bank, monopolizes and monitors the aggregate supply of eligible reserve assets. Even though monetary aggregates may not be useful for targets (Papadimitriou and Wray 1994), the central bank's tools will still affect the monetary base and, via the transmission mechanism, the macroeconomic variables.

Supervision and regulation of banks will also be affected with the institution of narrow banks. There will be more supervision and less regulation. The new financial institutions will require supervision to ascertain if their assets 'marked to market' equal their deposit liabilities. Given the advances in information technology and highly developed securities markets, valuation of assets would be a relatively simple and inexpensive task. Finally, the government regulator can ensure the safe operation of the payments system not with deposit insurance, but with safe collateral against the transactions deposits.

The skeptics of narrow banking have their say as well, and raise a number of issues. Gilbert argues that narrow banks would likely hold deposits from foreign banks, allow overnight overdrafts, and hold foreign exchange, all of which can result in losses and, in some rare cases, perhaps failures. Additional payment systems available in conjunction with narrow banks, i.e., the European giro system or the use of debit cards would reduce this credit risk exposure. Other questions raised include the availability of safe assets of maturities for narrow banks (Litan 1987; Lawrence and Talley 1988). Empirical evidence shows, however, that for the US, the outstanding amount of debt will be adequate to provide the supply of safe assets, especially if alterations to the maturities of government securities were to be made (Spong 1991; Lawrence and Talley 1988). The change would have the added benefit of reducing the cost of government borrowing, since short-term rates are, most of the time, lower.

Another concern relates to the effect narrow banking would have on the availability of funds for small business and low income consumer loans, and loans to residents of unevenly developed regions, that can be accommodated via other types of 'niche' banks (Minsky, Papadimitriou, Phillips, and Wray 1993), or finance companies (Burnham 1991; Bryan 1991). Last, but not least, is the matter of limiting access to the payments system to other than narrow banks. Preventing other financial institutions from gaining access would require 'fire walls', or, as Haemmerli (1985) put it, a quarantine of the bank. But the incentive for non-banks to provide access to the payments system, i.e., mutual funds, would continue to exist, as it does presently, and I expect that attempts to bypass a new system would be made. This will be the new challenge for the banking regulator. On the other hand, some non-banks may convert to narrow banks, to save on clearing costs, or to offer better clearing services.

In a system of narrow banking, foreign banks with transaction accounts in the US will need to comply with the same rules, i.e., either offer uninsured deposits and be globally competitive, as many large money centre banks would do, or set up and operate narrow bank subsidiaries with 'Chinese walls' to protect them.

Are narrow banks politically feasible? Do they make economic and market sense in a modern financial structure? What is the likelihood that such financial institutions are established in the US and abroad? To these issues, I turn next.

Narrow banks and financial reform: an international perspective

Bank failures have not been a uniquely US affair. Their occurance is worldwide, as many other countries, since 1980, have been under the cloud of financial crises, and have had to undertake bank bail-outs of significant proportions. In the developing and transition economies, as Robert Chote recently reported (1996), these costs have approached $250 billion, representing between 10 to 20 per cent of the annual national income for the bank failures in Venezuela, Bulgaria, Mexico, and Hungary. Furthermore, more than two-thirds of the IMF's 181 member countries have suffered banking crises since 1980 (Lindgren, Garcia, and Saal 1996). Resolving the banking crises in Finland, Norway, Spain, and Sweden has been costly in relation to the US, while the extent of similar banking failures in Brazil, Japan, Mexico, and Russia have yet to be fully determined. In a cross-national study of bank insolvencies, Caprio and Klingebiel (1996) find this phenomenon to be widespread, 'with as many as eighty-six episodes in sixty-nine countries' (p. 84). They attribute these episodes to a mixture of 'bad luck, bad policies... and bad banking' (p. 80). It will be noticed that in their compiled information of major bank insolvencies (Table 4), virtually all countries in Africa, Latin America, most transition countries, and a significant number of industrial countries are included. Legislative and regulatory authorities of all nations with financial and banking crises became concerned, and an unusual and heightened level of policy debate followed as to what the new laws and regulatory reforms could and should be. There seems to have been a uniform strategy among most countries in the implementation of legislation enactment and regulatory reform, centering in the dual goal: first, resolving the current and impending problems, and second, avoiding future problems. New standards have been established relating to bank capitalization, risk exposure and pricing of bank products, information disclosure, organizational structure and corporate governance, and restrictions affecting geographic expansion through branching, mergers and acquisitions (Barth, Nolle, and Rice 1997). The reconstitution of each country's financial structure, especially with regard to the organization of supervisory and examination practices and deposit insurance, varied, and reflected two considerations: first, the individual country's economic, political, and social framework and second, the 'general movement toward regional, if not truly international, cooperation and uniformity through the workings of such groups as the Basle Committee on Banking Supervision, established by the central bank governors of the Group of Ten (G-10) countries; under the aegis of the Bank for International Settlements (BIS), and the European Commission, established as the executive and administrative body for the member countries of the European Union (ibid, p. 3). Determining the degree of success of government interventions and financial restructurings in engendering safety, soundness, and confidence in the banking sector is no easy task. How successful is the response to the crisis is dependent on how accurate is the diagnosis of the factors that caused it. To be sure, there is an extensive literature attempting to identify and document the common cause of financial crises. More generally, it has been shown that the root causes can be attributed to both macro- and microeconomic factors.

On the macroeconomic side, Gavin and Hausmann (1996) find in their study of the Latin American crises that excessive credit growth is the dominant factor. Conversely, for economies with negative real rates of credit growth, denoting a credit crunch, as are the cases of African and transition economies, the causes 'may reflect factors such as tight monetary policy, (and) an aversion to lending on the part of banks' (Caprio and Klingebiel 1996, p. 88). There are other possible macrofactors such as those of uncertainty, speculative bubbles, and debt deflation, advanced by Kindleberger (1978) and Minsky (1975, 1982).

On the microeconomic side, the most frequently mentioned factors include financial liberalization, various bank-specific factors such as asset liability mismatches, insufficient diversification, connected lending, and fraud (Caprio and Klingebiel, p. 87).

The factors causing each country's financial system to fail are, for the most part, endogenous to the country's political and social infrastructure. It has been argued, for example, that the transition economies' banking crises were due to the huge debt overhang inherited from bad loans extended to state-owned companies during the pre-transition years (Anderson, Berglöf, and Mizsei 1996), as opposed to the causes relating to moral hazard for the banking failures in market economies. There were also microeconomic factors, such as 'imperfect information' regarding the quality of loans, which took a number of years to produce, as was the situation in Poland, Hungary, and the Czech Republic, and 'bureaucratic distortions of incentives' relating to firms' ownership and financial condition (Anderson, Berglöf, and Mizsei, p. 57).

A scoring scheme, developed by World Bank economists Gerard Caprio and Daniela Klingebiel (1996), has evaluated the responses at restructuring of sixty-four countries, and has shown that the successful cases have been very few; indeed a very significant number of countries, predominantly in Africa, in Central and Eastern Europe, and some in Latin America, scored as unsuccessful or with mixed results (Table 1).

Table 1. Evaluating the restructuring exercises

Successful	Mixed results	Unsuccessful/not yet resolved/insufficient time
Africa		
	Benin (1988-90)	Burkina Faso (late 1980s)
	Côte d'Ivoire (1988-91)	Cameroon (1987)
	Ghana (1982-89)	Central African Republic (1980s and 1991)
	Madagascar (1988)	Chad (1980s and 1990s)
	Mauritania (1983-93)	Congo (1980s and 1991-)
	Senegal (1988-91)	Guinea (1985)
	Zaïre (1991-92)	Kenya (1985-89)
		Mozambique (1987)
		Nigeria (1990s)
		Tanzania (1987, 1995)
		Togo (1993-)
		Uganda (1994)
		Zambia (1995)
Asia		
Malaysia (1985-88)	Bangladesh (late 1980s)	India (1994-)
	Nepal (1998)	Costa Rica (several instances)
	Philippines (1981-87)	Mexico (1994-)
	Singapore (1982)	Paraguay (1995-)
	Sri Lanka (1989-93)	Venezuela (1994-)
	Taiwan, China (1983-84)	
	Thailand (1983-87)	
Latin America		
Chile (1981-83)	Argentina (1980-82	Brazil (1994-)
	Argentina (1989-90)	Costa Rica (several instances)
	Bolivia (1986-87)	Mexico (1994-)
	Colombia (1982-87)	Paraguay (1995-)
	Mexico (1981-91)	Venezuela (1994-)
	Uruguay (1981-84)	
Other		
Australia (1989-90)	Egypt (early 1980s)	Bulgaria (1990s)
Germany (late 1970s)	Finland (1991-93)	Estonia (1992-94)
United Kingdom (1974-76)	New Zealand (1987-90)	France (1994-95)
United States (1984-91)	Norway (1987-89)	Hungary (1991-)
	Romania (1990-93)	Latvia (1995)
	Spain (1977-85)	Lithuania (1995-96)
	Sweden (1991-93)	Poland (1991-)
	Turkey (1982-85)	Russia (1995)
		Slovenia (1990s)

Note: Countries were rated on the basis of four criteria: financial deepening, development of real credit, real deposit rates, and recurrence of problems after banking sector restructuring.
Source: Caprio, Gerard Jr. and Daniela Klingebiel (1996), 'Bank Insolvency: Bad Luck, Bad Policy, or Bad Banking?', *Annual World Bank Conference on Development Economics*, p. 95.

Caprio and Klingebiel used four criteria in their evaluation methodology (pp. 93-4):

- **Financial deepening**: a measure of the ratio of M2 to the GDP is indicative of the banking system's stability after a crisis (a rising ratio denotes stability while a flat or falling one shows that problems remain).
- **Development of real credit**: moderate growth of real credit indicates crisis has passed, while negative real credit growth may denote a credit crunch, and a high growth rate may signify distress borrowing.
- **Real deposit interest rates**: interest rates above 10 per cent are indicative that the banking sector is striving to stay afloat, and negative rates often suggest a credit crunch or government intervention.
- **Recurrent problems in the banking system after restructuring**: a measure of the ratio of non-performing loans to performing loans is indicative of the system's return to stability (a falling ratio denotes stability). Repeated episodes of widespread insolvency is a sign of unsuccessful response to crisis, whereas isolated episodes of single bank failures might mask success.

Even though the authors agree that measuring success and failure is a formidable task, since no single criterion reflects very accurately how a financial system performs its functions, they nevertheless suggest that their evaluation scheme can point to specific areas of reform that need attention, if the attempt at reform is to be successful.

It is apparent, however, that in reviewing the initiatives of financial reform, two observations can be made: first, no single model for reforming the banking sector emerges, and second, no serious attempt that I am aware of appears to have been made to establish a regime of narrow-like banking in any country but instead, considerable effort has been expended in modifying or establishing insurance or guarantee provisions for depositors. In Table 2, that follows, taken from Barth, Nolle, and Rice (1997), the various deposit insurance schemes and extent of coverage are detailed for a sample of nineteen countries, mainly those belonging in the European Union and G-10 countries.

Table 2. Deposit-insurance schemes for commercial banks in the EU and G-10 countries: 1995 (continued)

Country	Name of guarantee/insurance system	Administration of and membership in the system				
		Year first established	Date current system took effect	Administration of system: government or industry	Agency responsible for administering system	Membership: voluntary or compulsory
Japan	Deposit Insurance System	1971	No information	Government/Industry - joint	Deposit Insurance Corporation	Compulsory
Luxembourg	Association pour la Garantie des Depots, Luxembourg (AGDL)	1989	October 1995	Industry	AGDL	Compulsory
Netherlands	Collective Guarantee System	1979	July 1, 1995	Government/Industry - joint	De Netherlandsche Bank N.V.	Compulsory
Portugal	Deposit Guarantee Fund	1992	1994	Government	Deposit Guarantee Fund	Compulsory
Spain	Deposit Guarantee Fund	1977	End of 1995	Government/Industry - joint	Fondo de Garantia de Depositos	Compulsory
Sweden	Swedish Deposit-Guarantee Scheme	1974	January 1, 1996	Government	The Bank Support Authority	Compulsory
Switzerland	Deposit Guarantee Scheme	1982	July 1, 1993	Industry	Swiss Banker's Association	Voluntary
United Kingdom	Deposit Protection Fund	1982	July 1, 1995	Government	Deposit Protection Board	Compulsory
United States	Bank Insurance Fund	1933	January 1, 1996	Government	Federal Deposit Insurance Corporation	Compulsory
European Union (EC Directive on Deposit-Guarantee Schemes)	Determined within each member state	Adopted on May 30, 1994	July 1, 1995	Only directs that each member state shall ensure within its territory one or more deposit guarantee schemes introduced and officially recognized.	Determined within each member state	Compulsory

Table 2. Deposit-insurance schemes for commercial banks in the EU and G-10 countries: 1995 (continued)

Country	Name of guarantee/insurance system	Year first established	Date current system took effect	Administration of system: government or industry	Agency responsible for administering system	Membership: voluntary or compulsory
Japan	Deposit Insurance System	1971	No information	Government/ Industry - joint	Deposit Insurance Corporation	Compulsory
Luxembourg	Association pour la Garantie des Depots, Luxembourg (AGDL)	1989	October 1995	Industry	AGDL	Compulsory
Netherlands	Collective Guarantee System	1979	July 1, 1995	Government/ Industry - joint	De Netherlandsche Bank N.V.	Compulsory
Portugal	Deposit Guarantee Fund	1992	1994	Government	Deposit Guarantee Fund	Compulsory
Spain	Deposit Guarantee Fund	1977	End of 1995	Government/ Industry - joint	Fondo de Garantia de Depositos	Compulsory
Sweden	Swedish Deposit-Guarantee Scheme	1974	January 1, 1996	Government	The Bank Support Authority	Compulsory
Switzerland	Deposit Guarantee Scheme	1982	July 1, 1993	Industry	Swiss Banker's Association	Voluntary
United Kingdom	Deposit Protection Fund	1982	July 1, 1995	Government	Deposit Protection Board	Compulsory
United States	Bank Insurance Fund	1933	January 1, 1996	Government	Federal Deposit Insurance Corporation	Compulsory
European Union (EC Directive on Deposit-Guarantee Schemes)	Determined within each member state	Adopted on May 30, 1994	July 1, 1995	Only directs that each member state shall ensure within its territory one or more deposit guarantee schemes introduced and officially recognized.	Determined within each member state	Compulsory

Table 2.a Coverage of protection

Country	Extent of amount of coverage	Interbank deposits covered	Deposits of foreign branches of domestic banks covered		Deposits of domestic branches of foreign banks covered		Foreign currency denominated deposits covered	Non-resident depositors covered
			Branches located in EU country	Branches located in non-EU country	Branches of EU banks	Branches of non EU banks		
Austria	ATS 260,000 (per physical person-depositor)	No	Yes	Yes	Yes, amount depends on home country	Yes	Yes	Yes
Belgium	15,000 ECU until December 1999; 20,000 ECU thereafter	No	Yes	No	Yes	Yes	Yes, but only deposits expressed in ECU or another EU currency.	Yes
Canada	Can. $60,000 (per depositor)	No	No	No	Yes	Yes	No	Yes
Denmark	300,000 DKK or 42,000 ECU (per depositor)	No	Yes	Yes	Yes	Yes	Yes	Yes
Finland	100 percent (per depositor)	No	Yes	Yes	Yes	Yes	Yes	Yes
France	FF 400.000 (per depositor)	No	Yes	No, except for EEA countries	Yes	Yes	Yes, but only deposits expressed in ECU or another currency.	No information
Germany	100% up to a limit of 30% of the bank's liable capital (per depositor)	No	Yes	Yes	Yes	Yes	Yes	Yes

Table 2.a Coverage of protection (continued)

Country	Extent of amount of coverage	Interbank deposits covered	Deposits of foreign branches of domestic banks covered		Deposits of domestic branches of foreign banks covered		Foreign currency denominated deposits covered	Non-resident depositors covered
			Branches located in EU country	Branches located in non-EU country	Branches of EU banks	Branches of non EU banks		
Greece	20,000 ECU (per depositor)	No	Yes	Yes	Yes	Yes	Yes	Yes
Ireland	90% of deposit - Max. compensation is 15,000 ECU	No	Yes	Yes	No	Yes	Yes	Yes
Italy	100% of first 200 million L It and 75% of next 800 million L It (per deposit.	No	Yes	Yes	Yes	Yes	Yes	Yes
Japan	10 million Yen (per depositor)	No	No	No	No	No	No	Yes
Luxembourg	Lux F 500,000 (per depositor), only natural persons	No	No	No	Yes	Yes	Yes	Yes
Netherlands	20,000 ECU (per depositor), compensation paid in Gulden	No	Yes	No	Yes	Yes	Yes	Yes
Portugal	100% up to 15,000 ECU 75% 15,000 - 30,000 ECU 50% 30,000 - 45,000 ECU (per depositor)	No	Yes	No	Yes	Yes	Yes	Yes
Spain	Ptas 1.5 million (per depositor), to be increased to 20,000 ECU	No	Yes	Yes	Yes	Yes	Yes	Yes
Sweden	SEK 30,000 (per depositor)	No	Yes	No	Yes	Yes	Yes	Yes
Switzerland	SF 30,000 (per depositor)	No	No	No	Yes	Yes	Yes	Yes

Table 2.a Coverage of protection (continued)

Country	Extent of amount of coverage	Interbank deposits covered	Deposits of foreign branches of domestic banks covered			Deposits of domestic branches of foreign banks covered		Foreign currency denominated deposits covered	Non-resident depositors covered
			Branches located in EU country	Branches located in non-EU country	Branches located in non-EU country	Branches of EU banks	Branches of non EU banks		
United Kingdom	90% of protected deposits, with the maximum amount of deposits protected for each depositor being L 20,000 (unless the sterling equivalent of ECU 22,222 is greater). Thus, the most an individual can collect in a bank failure is L 18,000 (per depositor) or ECU 20,000 if greater.	No	Yes, throughout EEA.	No		Yes	Yes	Yes, but only deposits in other EEA currencies and the ECU, as well as sterling.	Yes
United States	100,000 USD (per depositor)	No	No	No		No, unless engaged in retail deposit-taking activities.	No, unless engaged in retail deposit-taking activities	Yes	Yes
European Union	The aggregate deposits of each depositor must be covered up to ECU 20,000. Until December 31, 1999, member states in which deposits are not covered up to ECU 20,000 may retain the maximum amount laid down on their guarantee schemes, provided that this amount is not less than ECU 15,000 (per depositor).	No	If located within the EU, but until December 31, 1999 not to exceed the maximum amount laid down in their guarantee scheme within the territory of the host member state. If the host member state has greater coverage a branch may voluntarily supplement its coverage.	This issue is determined by each member state.		Yes, either by having coverage equivalent to the Directive or by joining the host-country deposit-guarantee scheme if it is more favourable	NA	Yes, if denominated in ECU or currencies of member states of EU.	Yes, determined within each member state.

Source: Barth, James R., Daniel E. Nolle and Tara N. Rice (1997), 'Commercial Banking Structure, Regulation, and Performance: An International Comparison', *Economics Working Paper* 97-6, pp.64-65.

It will be observed that all countries in the sample have deposit insurance systems or have established one. Moreover, deposit insurance funds were instituted in Hungary, Poland, and the Czech Republic, at the onset of transition (Anderson, Berglöf, and Mizsei, p. 69). The specific insurance coverages for each country are shown in Table 3 below.

Table 3. Deposit insurance coverage in selected transition economies

Hungary	1 million forint ($9,000)
Poland	3,000 ECU ($3,500)
Czech Republic	80 per cent of deposits, up to 100,000 korunas ($3,500)

Source: Anderson, Berglöf, and Mizsei.

The common thread of most financial restructurings seems to be the unmitigated reliance on market forces which, in my view, is not the 'indispensable ingredient of a better banking system'.

Narrow banks: a banking structure whose time has (not?) come

Policy proposals, especially those that are not intended for the short term, are not always politically digestible. In the case of financial reform, new proposals must first and foremost be in concert with the evolving nature of the high-tech marketplace, and second, must fit within a regulatory and supervisory framework that fosters two crucial structural objectives: (i) ensure the long-term stability of the financial system, and (ii) promote the financing of the capital development of the economy. These two objectives can be achieved only when linkage and transparency between banks, non-banks and commerce are clearly drawn, the competitive market structures are taken into account, and the safety and soundness of the payments system are ensured (Papadimitriou 1996).

An important issue of financial reform is the organizational structure of government supervision and regulation. If one accepts the 'bad bankers' theory (Minsky 1993), extends it to include other microeconomic factors discussed earlier, and shown in Chart 1 below, and recognizes the ensuing malfunction of the financial system, then the system's supervisory and regulating functions take centre stage in any serious effort of reform (Papadimitriou, p. 5). The 1970s and 1980s phenomena of worldwide bank failures were attributed not only to the inept management and corrupt practices of bankers, but also to the systemic failure of the regulatory and supervisory structure. As the late Hyman Minsky long argued, the financial system is vulnerable to unanticipated monetary surprises and exogenous shocks which can occur even during times of prosperity, and make banks 'fragile', and the entire system unstable (1957, 1971). All these can be seen clearly in Chart 1, which shows that for twenty-nine episodes of banking sector insolvencies over the past fifteen years, the most prominent causes stemmed from deficient management, faulty supervision and regulation, government intervention, or connected and politically induced lending (Caprio and Klingebiel, p. 91).

Chart 1. Factors behind twenty-nine bank insolvencies

Factor	Count
Macroeconomic factors	
Capital flight	2
Dutch disease	4
Asset bubble	7
Recession	16
Terms of trade drop	20
Microeconomic factors	
Weak judiciary	2
Bank runs	2
Fraud	6
Lending to state enterprises	6
Connected lending	9
Political interference	11
Deficient bank management	20
Poor supervision and regulation	26

Note: Shows the number of times each factor was cited in twenty-nine country cases; twenty-nine is the maximum number of citations possible.
Source: Caprio, Gerard Jr. and Daniela Klingebiel (1996), 'Bank Insolvency: Bad Luck, Bad Policy, or Bad Banking?' *Annual World Bank Conference on Development Economics*, p. 91.

Table 4. Major bank insolvencies

Systemic cases
(most or all bank capital exhausted)

Africa
Benin (1988-90)
Burkina Faso (late 1980s)
Cameroon (1987-present)
Central African Republic (1980s and 1994)
Chad (1980s and 1990s)
Congo (1980s and 1991)
Côte d'Ivoire (1988-91)
Eritrea (1993)
Ghana (1982-89)
Guinea (1985, 1993-94)
Kenya (1985-89, 1992, 1993-95)
Madagascar (1988)
Mauritania (1983-93)
Mozambique (1987-present
Nigeria (1990s) Senegal (1998-91)
South Africa (1977)
Tanzania (1987, 1995)
Togo (1993-present)
Uganda (1994)
Zaïre (1991-92)
Zambia (1995

Asia
Bangladesh (late 1980s-present)
India (1994-95)
Nepal (1988)
Philippines (1981-87)
Sri Lanka (1989-93)
Thailand (1983-87)

Latin America
Argentina (1980-82, 1989-90, 1995)
Bolivia (1986-87)
Brazil (1990, 1994-95)
Chile (1976, 1981-83)
Colombia (1982-87)
Costa Rica (several instances)
Ecuador (early 1980s)
Mexico (1981-82, perhaps through 1990-91, 1995)
Paraguay (1995)

Uruguay (1981-84)
Venezuela (1980, 1994-95)

Middle East and North Africa
Egypt (early 1980s, 1990-91)
Israel (1997-83)
Kuwait (1980s)
Morocco (early 1980s)

Europe and Central Asia
Turkey (1982-85)

Transition economies
Bulgaria (1980s)
Estonia (1992-94)
Hungary (1991-95)
Latvia (1995)
Lithuania (1995-96)
Poland (1990s)
Romania (1990-93)
Russia (1995)
Slovenia (1990s)

Industrial countries
Finland (1991-93)
Japan (1990s)
Norway (1987-89)
Spain (1977-85)
Sweden (1991)

Borderline or smaller cases

Asia
Hong Kong (1982-83, 1983-86)
Indonesia (1994)
Malaysia (1985-88)
Singapore (1982)
Taiwan, China (1983-84, 1995)

Industrial countries
Australia (1989-90)
France (1994-95)
Germany (late 1970s)
New Zealand (1987-90)
United Kingdom (1974-76)
United States (1984-91)

Source: Caprio, Gerard Jr. and Daniela Klingebiel (1996), 'Bank Insolvency: Bad Luck, Bad Policy, or Bad Banking?', *Annual World Bank Conference on Development Economics*, p. 85.

One of the most extensively studied approaches to banking involves the functional separation of the depository and lending activities of banks. The policy prescription underlying this approach is the establishment of 'narrow banks', banks maintaining 100 per cent required reserves, banks with 'deposit currency', or 'collateralized money' (Pollock 1992). Narrow banking, the subject matter of this paper, has been widely supported because, as Ronnie Phillips (1993) has suggested, it meets the safety and soundness of the payments system and the goals of banking regulation, it eliminates or reduces the dependence of deposit insurance or guarantees, it enhances stability within the banking system, and it offers an alternative structure that can adjust to market forces and technological innovation. This would seem to be applicable not only for the US, but the developing and transition economies as well. In a list of specific policy recommendations advanced by the Forum Report of the Economic Policy Initiative (Anderson, Berglöf, and Mizsei 1996, p. 78), one reads:

> Savings banks in (Central and Eastern Europe) CEE are special because they tend to have a dominant position in retail deposit taking. Whether or not they are privatized the state will have the important stake in them since they are too important to be allowed to fail. This means, first, that regulatory oversight of these banks should be tighter than for other banks. Supervision should be particularly intensive so as to avoid excessive risk-taking. *One way to do this is to restrict the allowable types of asset holding, possibly by according them a limited banking license.* Second, it should be recognized that these banks should generally be profitable because of their access to low cost funds. Finally, these banks should be exposed to competition (emphasis added).

Is this different from what the narrow banking proposals advocate? I think not. As we look ahead into the future, I am reminded of Hyman Minsky (1994, p. 64) who put the issue most aptly:

> As the 21st century is about to be ushered in, an idea which was on the table during the 1930s discussion of reform can once again be on the table. One virtue of the 100% money scheme is that it separates the two functions that the monetary and banking system perform... By separating these functions it makes us aware that an economy can have too little as well as too much government debt.

References

Anderson, Ronald W., Erik Berglöf and Kalman Mizsei (1996), *Banking Sector Development in Central and Eastern Europe*, Forum Report of the Economic Policy Initiative No. 1, London, Centre for Economic Policy Research.

Barth, James R., Daniel E. Nolle and Tara N. Rice (1997), 'Commercial Banking Structure, Regulation, and Performance: An International Comparison', *Economics Working Paper 97/6*, Office of the Comptroller of the Currency.

Bryan, Lowell (1988), *Breaking Up the Bank*, Homewood, Ill., Business One Irwin.

——, (1991), *Bankrupt: Restoring the Health and Profitability of Our Banking System*, New York, Harper Business.

Burnham, James B. (1991), 'Deposit Insurance: The Case for the Narrow Bank', *Regulation*, 14 (Spring), 2.

Calomiris, Charles (1988), 'Institutional Failure, Monetary Scarcity, and the Depreciation of the Continental', *Journal of Economic History*, 48, pp. 47-68.

Caprio, Gerard Jr. (1992), 'Policy Uncertainty, Information Asymmetries, and Financial Intermediation', *Policy Research Working Paper*, 853, Washington, D.C., World Bank.

Caprio, Gerard Jr. and Daniela Klingebiel (1996), 'Bank Insolvency: Bad Luck, Bad Policy, or Bad Banking?', *Annual World Bank Conference on Development Economics*, Michael Bruno and Boris Pleskovic, (ed.), Washington, D.C., World Bank.

Carns, Frederick S. (1994), 'The Two-Window Proposal for Banking Reform', Federal Deposit Insurance Corporation, unpublished.

Chote, Robert (1996), 'Banking on a Catastrophe', *Financial Times*, October 21.

Gavin, Michael, and Ricardo Hausmann (1996), 'The Roots of Banking Crises: The Macroeconomic Context', *Banking Crises in Latin America*, Ricardo Hausmann and Liliana Rojas-Suarez, (ed.), Baltimore, MD, Johns Hopkins Press.

Greenbaum, Stuart I., and Arnoud W.A. Boot (1991), 'Modified "Narrow Bank" Is Best Reform Plan', *American Banker*, August 23.

Haemmerli, Alice (1985), 'Quarantine: An Approach to the Deposit Insurance Dilemma', *Banking Expansion Reporter*, 4 (September), 7-10.

Hart, Albert G. (1991), 'How to Reform Banks – and How Not To', *Challenge*, March-April, pp. 16-24.

Kareken, John H. (1985), 'Ensuring Financial Stability', in *The Search for Financial Stability: The Past Fifty Years*, San Francisco, Federal Reserve Bank of San Francisco, pp. 53-86.

——, (1986), 'Federal Bank Regulatory Policy: A Description and Some Observations', *Journal of Business*, 59 (January), pp. 3-48.

Kindleberger, Charles Poor (1978), *Manias, Panics, and Crashes: A History of Financial Crises*, New York, Basic Books.

Lawrence, Robert J., and Samuel H. Talley (1985), 'Minimizing Regulation of the Financial Services Industry', *Issues in Bank Regulation*, Summer, pp. 21-31.

——, (1988), 'Implementing a Fail-Proof Banking System', Proceedings of a Conference on Bank Structure and Competition, Federal Reserve Bank of Chicago.

Lindgren, Carl-Johan, Gillian Garcia, and Matthew I. Saal (1996), *Bank Soundness and Macroeconomic Policy*, Washington, D.C., International Monetary Fund.

Litan Robert E. (1987), *What Should Banks Do?*, Washington, D.C., The Brookings Institution.

——, (1993), 'Deposit Insurance, Gas on S&L Fire', *Wall Street Journal*, July 29, A12.

Minsky, Hyman P. (1957) 'Central Banking and Money Market Changes', *Quarterly Journal of Economics*, May, LXXI, 2.

——, (1971), 'Financial Instability Revisited', in *Reappraisal of the Federal Reserve Discount Mechanism*, Washington, D.C., Federal Reserve Board 3, pp. 95-136.

——, (1975), *John Maynard Keynes*, New York, Columbia University Press.

——, (1982), *Can 'It' Happen Again: Essays on Instability and Finance*, Armonk, N.Y., M.E. Sharpe.

——, (1986), *Stabilizing an Unstable Economy*, New Haven, Yale University Press.

——, (1993), 'Introduction', *Public Policy Brief, No. 5*, The Jerome Levy Economics Institute of Bard College.

——, (1994), 'Financial Instability and the Decline (?) of Banking: Public Policy Implications' in *Proceedings: The 30th Annual Conference on Bank Structure and Competition*, Federal Reserve Bank of Chicago (May).

Minsky, Hyman P., Dimitri B. Papadimitriou, Ronnie J. Phillips, and L. Randall Wray (1993), 'A Proposal to Establish a Nationwide System of Community Development Banks', *Community Development Banking, Public Policy Brief, No. 3*, The Jerome Levy Economics Institute of Bard College.

Papadimitriou, Dimitri B. (1996), 'Stability in the US Financial System', in *Stability in the Financial System*, Dimitri B. Papadimitriou, (ed.) London, Macmillan Press.

Papadimitriou, Dimitri B., and L. Randall Wray (1994), 'Flying Blind: The Federal Reserve's Experiment with Unobservables', *Monetary Policy Uncovered, Public Policy Brief, No. 15*, The Jerome Levy Economics Institute of Bard College.

Papadimitriou, Dimitri, B., Ronnie J. Phillips, and L. Randall Wray (1993), 'The Community Reinvestment Act, Lending Discrimination, and the Role of Community Development Banks', *A Path to Community Development, Public Policy Brief, No. 6*, The Jerome Levy Economics Institute of Bard College.

Phillips, Ronnie J. (1993), 'The "Chicago Plan" and New Deal Banking Reform' *Working Paper, No. 5.*, The Jerome Levy Economics Institute of Bard College.

——, (1994), 'Safe Banking During the Great Depression: John M. Nichols, the FDIC and 100% Reserves', *Consumer Finance Law Quarterly Report*, 48, No. 1 (Winter), pp. 15-21.

——, (1994), *The Chicago Plan and New Deal Banking Reform*, Armonk, N.Y., Sharpe.

——, (1995), 'The Functional Approach to Financial Reform', *Narrow Banking Reconsidered, Public Policy Brief no. 17*, The Jerome Levy Economics Institute.

Pierce, James L. (1986), 'Financial Reform in the United States and the Financial System of the Future', in *Financial Innovation and Monetary Policy: Asia and the West, Proceedings of the Second International Conference Held by the Bank of Japan*, Yooshi Suzuki and Hiroshi Yomo (eds.), Tokyo, University of Tokyo Press.

——, (1993), 'The Functional Approach to Deposit Insurance Regulation', paper presented at the symposium 'Safeguarding the Banking System in an Environment of Financial Cycles', Federal Reserve Bank of Boston, November 18.

Pollock, Alex (1992), 'Collateralized Money: An Idea Whose Time Has Come Again', *Challenge*, September/October, pp. 62-64.

Seidman, William L. (1991), 'Testimony on Proposals to Establish a Core or Narrow Bank, Committee on Banking, Finance and Urban Affairs', U.S. House of Representatives, June 18.

Simons, Henry C. (1948), *Economic Policy for a Free Society*, Chicago, The University of Chicago Press.

Spong, Kenneth (1991), 'A Narrow Banking Proposal', Federal Reserve Bank of Kansas City, unpublished.

——, (1996), 'Narrow Banks: An Alternative to Banking Reform', in *Stability in the Financial System*, Dimitri B. Papadimitriou, (ed.) London, Macmillan Press.

Tobin, James (1985), 'Financial Innovation and Deregulation in Perspective', *Bank of Japan Monetary and Economic Studies*, 3, pp. 19-29.

——, (1987), 'The Case for Preserving Regulatory Distinctions', in *Restructuring the Financial System* (Kansas City: Federal Reserve Bank of Kansas City.)

29 Corporate Governance amid Global Monetary and Economic Convergence – Their Appearance and Development in Japan

Yoshiaki Toda

It is a great honour for me to be able to take part in and to speak today at the joint conference of RTSF and SUERF in Budapest. Although I have a long career both in central and commercial banking, I do not have a special background in corporate governance. As a long-time Japanese member of RTSF since 1986 and the only speaker from Japan at this conference, I am responsible to you for explaining the recent development of corporate governance in my country.

1. The appearance of the corporate governance issue in Japan

The term corporate governance (which I will refer to as CG) has only quite recently attracted attention in Japan. Since the Meiji Restoration in 1868, Japan has imported Western European and American culture, particularly their various economic and financial systems, and developed economically. After World War II, in particular, under the influence of the occupation's policies, a democratic market economy was introduced in Japan, leading to a period of high growth often called an economic miracle.

CG can be understood as a field of study that considers the questions: 'For whom do companies exist?' and 'Who should be responsible for controlling management?' The subject of CG was proposed in America in 1932 by Berle and Means in *The Modern Corporation and Private Property*. Since then, research has progressed and especially from the 1960s, CG has been realized in a number of forms such as shareholder democracy, hostile corporate takeovers, and the active intervention by institutional investors in the affairs of management.

In Japan, while CG was discussed by scholars and legislators and had been incorporated in amendments to the Commercial Code (particularly in 1973, 1981 and 1993), it has not really received much attention from the public until the last few years. This was because it did not appear as a problem, at least on the surface, due to the extremely strong economic development enjoyed in Japan after World War II and to Japanese management practices which were the foundation of that development.

For example, from the point of view of the shareholders, the largest stakeholders of a company, they have been able to benefit from constantly rising share prices up until fairly recently. In fact, the price weighted average (the Dow Index) in May 1949 for the 225 listed stocks on the Tokyo Stock Exchange was 176. Forty years later, however, at the end of 1989, it had actually increased 220 times to 38,915. It is clear from this, even though there were exceptions at times and also taking price increases into consideration, that stock prices rose constantly during this period. From the shareholders' point of view, such profits compensated for the low dividends and the fact that their views were not really reflected at shareholders' meetings. On the other hand, the employees, the other important stakeholders, were protected by government policies under the influence of the occupying forces. For example, the creation of labour unions and the ability for employees to strike were mandated. Under this situation and also due to the evergrowing economy, management thought it was natural for workers to benefit from the lifetime employment system and receive regular wage increases. In Japan, in many cases, top management thought the company should exist for the employees rather than for the shareholders and CG did not become an issue to be taken up by the employees.

Moreover, it cannot be denied that large cross-shareholdings in major companies prevented corporate takeovers and intervention by institutional investors in the affairs of management. In addition, the main bank system (where a certain bank is a major shareholder of a company and lends the company large sums of money) peculiar to Japan played an effective role in checking the arbitrary behaviour of management.

You may call this situation a Japanese-style utopia. However, this situation has changed during the past ten years and it seems that the pace of this change has accelerated especially with the bursting of the economic bubble. To be sure, during the US-Japan Structural Impediments Initiatives talks (1989-1991), the American side criticized the existence of *keiretsu* and cross-shareholdings among Japanese companies. Also since 1993, American public pension funds like CalPERS began increasingly to voice strong opinions regarding the management of Japanese companies. These incidents caused the term CG to be established in Japanese business circles. However, the issue was taken up more seriously when there was widespread realization that Japanese-style management would inevitably disintegrate amid the economic downturn that followed the collapse of the bubble economy. In other words, the greatest changes to occur were, from the shareholders' point of view, that investing in stocks was no longer attractive as falling stock prices meant that capital gains could not be expected and, from the employees point of view, that the lifetime employment system, which had up until then been advantageous, was gradually disappearing. Another change worth mentioning was the effect of the revision of the Commercial Code in 1993, which enabled shareholders to sue company directors for failing to fulfil their responsibilities.

2. The current state of corporate governance in Japan and related problems

Earlier I stated that CG attracted increased attention as a result of the revision of the Commercial Code and the bursting of the economic bubble, but the largest impact was from lawsuits shareholders brought against company directors. The number of such suits has increased sharply in the last few years because, at the same time as the collapse of the bubble economy, several well-publicized scandals involving corporate management surfaced. Moreover, following the Commercial Code revision, it became cheap (at yen 8200 per case) for shareholders to sue directors. Even though such lawsuits have only recently become common, there is a tendency for this recourse to be overused, which poses a danger of discouraging active engagement on the part of directors. There is even a view that balance is lacking between the weight of directors' responsibilities and the benefits they receive (in other words, directors receive almost the same level of salary and bonuses as senior employees in the company).

In response to concerns about the excessive weakening of management, the American Business Judgement Rule is being introduced to Japan with a view to protect the appropriate discretionary rights of management. This means that company executives will not be liable under criminal or civil law if they exercise proper care in making themselves aware of facts before making decisions and if the process of doing so is considered reasonable for a company executive. Thus, even if an individual decision by an executive causes the company to incur a financial loss, provided the executive can show that, overall, a proper decision was made based on adequate procedures that fulfilled all the requirements of this rule, then the executive will be able to successfully defend a shareholder lawsuit.

This has significance in Japan where the so-called main bank system until fairly recently often ensured that even a client in financial trouble could receive unsecured loans, if the bank was confident of the company's future.

If we call shareholder lawsuits an 'after-the-fact' check, a 'before-the-fact' check or monitor is the audit system in Japan. As a result of repeated revisions to the Commercial Code after World War II, the power of auditors was greatly strengthened, and since the 1993 revision, large companies have been required to appoint additional Auditors who have had no direct relations to the company. This is a substitute for the outside director system in America and high hopes for its success were expected when it was created. However, we will have to see whether it will prove as effective as hoped.

3. Corporate governance in Japan amid global monetary and economic convergence

It cannot be denied that the unique Japanese-style economic and financial system lies behind the country's dramatic economic development after the war. Of course, every industrialized country has its own historically, socially, and culturally derived system. To reinforce the point, the Japanese system is characterized: i) by the relatively limited reliance on market mechanisms compared with the United States and Europe, ii) by the placing of the highest priority on the interest in both blue and white collar employees rather than on shareholders, and iii) with regard to the financial system, by imposing government regulations along with the protection extended.

Of the above-mentioned points, regulations imposed by the government have come under scrutiny in recent economic and financial discussions between the United States and Japan, and even within Japan, pressure has been increasing to change these regulations. In response, the view that market mechanisms should be relied on has been gaining ground. Moreover, with the growing participation of foreign shareholders in Japanese companies and the efforts of America's powerful pension funds, support is growing for greater shareholder rights.

Finally, what challenges does Japanese management share with management in the various countries of Europe and the United States? The first is to ensure honesty towards shareholders and employees. The second is to work for greater public benefit and to develop a sense of social responsibility. The third is to develop managerial efficiency. Discussion of these challenges in Japan for a long time tended to focus on the first, though since the 1970s (particularly with respect to efforts to overcome pollution problems), the discussion has demonstrated increasing attention to the second. In Europe and America the third point has been given a fair amount of emphasis for some time; however, in Japan it received scant attention at the time of high growth. Since the bubble burst and with corporate profits remaining weak, efficiency of management, or improving companies' business results, has become a crucial concern. This stems partly from the increasing tendency for Japanese business executives to forsake their former entrepreneurship due to fear of shareholder lawsuits and their oversensitivity to their responsibility towards their stakeholders; in other words, towards their shareholders and employees as well as towards their clients and society in general. Recently, the earning power of Japan's major companies has been declining and there is a strong fear that they are losing their competitive edge in the global market.

As such, there is ongoing discussion in Japan of the need to protect directors from excessive shareholder lawsuits while motivating them with performance-based remuneration, such as stock options, as practiced in the United States.

The question of whether to appoint outside directors is also likely to be discussed again in the future. Under Japan's current legal system outside directors may be appointed and actual examples occur in the case of former *zaibatsu*-affiliated companies. However, this is not a common practice and there is no legal obligation to appoint outside directors. The audit system, which places emphasis on checking the performance of management, is one of the important points concerning CG in Japan's Commercial Code. A strengthened auditor system is certainly expected to reinforce the checking function. However, the introduction of outside directors or non-executive directors not just as the representatives of the major shareholders but also intellectuals with a high level of managerial know-how may not only strengthen the checking function, but also increase the ability of the management. In that sense it seems to be essential to this country.

At the same time, there is a shift underway in Japan's financial system from indirect to direct financing, which is changing relationships between companies and banks. As the checking function of the main banks radically diminishes, something will be needed to take its place. The role might perhaps be filled by rating agencies sometime in the future. In Europe and America, rating agencies determine credit ratings for corporate debentures and other financial instruments issued by companies. In Japan, as the importance of credit ratings gradually grows to resemble the situation in Europe and America, credit ratings could become performance indicators for company executives and exert a strong influence over management.

Conclusion

Roughly speaking, there are two types of corporate governance in the industrialized countries: the continental type and the Anglo-American type. The former is represented by the German type which is characterized by 'Aufsichtsrat' (the supervisory board) system. Aufsichtsrat is the control organ of a company, consists of representatives of employees and stock-holders such as bankers and clients, and has the power to elect or to discharge the directors of a company as well as to supervise the execution of the business. The latter is, as already mentioned above, characterized by a system of outside or non-executive directors. From the viewpoint of the market, the latter places more emphasis on the control by the market than direct or internal control by directors.

Before World War II, the Japanese Commercial Code was influenced mainly by continental, and after the war by American laws. In that sense, the Japanese system of CG is a mixture of the continental and the American laws. But it does not resemble its parents very much. As Japan's and other developed countries' economic and financial systems and their management converge, there is no doubt that the problems of CG in Japan will have even more in common with those of the United States and/or countries in Europe. However, because the traditional importance of the relationship between employers and employees will surely remain in Japan, CG may possibly be distinguished from the Western model.

30 Globalization of the World Economy and the Lack of Regulation of the Globalized World

Márton Tardos

Just before the second millennium, the world has to become familiar with new economic phenomena. Boundaries between countries disappear and a globalized world economy is evolving. The change began as early as in the nineteenth century with the reduction in cost- and time-requirement of transportation, which was then followed by the technological change concomitant with the spreading of electronics and the information revolution at the end of the twentieth century. Changes of a technical nature were accompanied by modifications in the regulation of world trade: the substantial reduction in national customs protection which, previously has impeded the development of world trade.

The world economic process of such enormous importance naturally creates its own winners and losers, as well as, its own supporters and opponents.

In relation to these significant world economic changes, there are primarily three issues which preoccupy me as an economist and a Hungarian politician.

- First: what guidance can economic science give for the evaluation and management of the effects of globalization?
- Second: not independently of the first issue, is there a need to modify the new institutional or regulatory order of the world economy as a result of the changes?
- Finally: what are the consequences of the globalization of the world economy for the countries which are simultaneously in between communism and post-communism and a world not yet globalized

and now in the full swing of globalization? And what are these consequences especially for Hungary?

Unfortunately, I have not had the opportunity to bury myself sufficiently deeply in studying and answering these questions with scientific thoroughness. Thus, I do not feel I have sufficient resources to give reassuring answers to these questions. My experiences and impressions obtained in other spheres suggest that human knowledge is sufficient neither for a full understanding of this complicated world society nor for developing an optimal strategy for adjustment to spontaneous processes. In addition, for lack of time, I had not had the possibility of taking enough effort to study the question even within these general limits. Accordingly, the opinion I express here is merely a hypothesis, or even less, the posing of questions, and should be evaluated in this light.

The globalization process of the world-economy

It is an undisputed fact that the world economy of the period between the two world wars was characterized by the separation of national states and a vigorous protection of national interests.

As early as in 1944, the victorious powers of World War II opened the way to a rapid development of international trade through the Bretton Woods agreement and other, no less important institutional changes as early as in 1944. The gradual reduction of customs protection impeding commercial trade and the regulation of currency trade were the two most important systems employed to dismantle the barriers to the development of world trade and the utilization of the advantages arising from comparative costs. The changes were successful. The volume of world trade developed between 1950 and 1980 nearly twice as fast as world GDP. A more efficient enforcement of comparative advantages facilitated not only the development of world trade itself but also increased the incomes generated in the world. More rapid development was also concomitant with the fact that, on average, the gap between the advanced and the developing countries was substantially reduced during this period.

The established order was modified in 1971 with the de facto termination of the Bretton Woods agreement and the subsequent introduction of floating exchange rates. The rapid development of international trade, however, remained the driving engine of growth even in this period, although its growth rate no longer exceeded that of the world GDP as much as before. The maintenance of the positive trend was sustained by the Kennedy Round, the further reduction of customs tariffs; and the gradual dismantling of barriers to international capital transfers. The harmonious, rapid growth of GDP and foreign trade was substantially exceeded by the worldwide growth of direct capital export.

The assured beneficiaries of the changes evolving since 1980 – globalization – were the most important generators of the process, i.e., those who were able to utilize the favourable opportunities, namely, the multinational companies, and those developing countries which were able to attract the most of direct capital investments with their industrious and increasingly well-prepared labour supply offered at low wages.

There are three types of criticism of this process:

- Globalization on the one hand draws off work opportunities in high-income countries from employees who are less well-qualified than the average established there. It is interesting to note that this loss was relatively less felt by the United States (which used to be in a situation less favourable than the West European average from the viewpoint of incomes, and in particular, that of the levelling off of wages which had earlier been regarded as unambiguously positive). The growth in unemployment in the United States was not as significant as in the European countries.
- On the other hand, economic development evolving as a result of globalization launched such destructive environmental processes in certain regions which may lead to the disruption of the world's ecological balance.
- Finally, the criticism was also made that, with the speeding up of the flow of information and the easing of the conditions restricting the international flow of currencies, speculative money movements, including, *inter alia*, money laundering, provides opportunities for income redistributions which lead to major losses in the regions left out of this process and also on the part of not insignificant social strata.

Globalization and economic theory

If general equilibrium theory was to be interpreted as the best developed general economic theory aiming at completeness to the functioning of the capitalist market economy leading to optimal Pareto results, then it would be able to interpret neither globalization nor the problems arising in the real sphere. In actual fact, all we can say about the phenomena created by globalization – similarly to the other tendencies of the functioning capitalist economy – that they are imperfect or flawed. It directly follows then that we cannot expect globalization to have effects that are perfect or optimal. In this respect, the question arises – as concerning all other issues of economics and economic policy – how would it be possible to regulate processes which are basically positive from the viewpoint of business management without violating the market and the vigorous interest enforcement of market agents so as to be able to avoid or reduce unfavourable concomitant phenomena.

It would be expedient to solve this question without confronting the views and endeavours of Hayek and Triffin.[1] Here, however, finding a good solution is made more difficult through the fact that, while the regulation of a national economy is the task of legitimate national parliaments and governments, it is not easy to develop a socially acceptable and controlled institution for regulating international trade and international capital and money movements. Consequently, it is to be feared that we need to calculate with errors and inflexibilities in a worldwide deliberate intervention in respect to globalization even more than what we perceive in relation to the operation of national governments.

Globalization from a Central Eastern European (Hungarian) aspect

The trend of globalization in the world is irreversible. The Central East European countries, *inter alia* Hungary, released from the communist dictatorship and the effects of central planning simultaneously with the unfolding of globalization, can do nothing but adjust to it. The pressure to adjust is irrespective of how the ITO or other international agencies manage to regulate the globalization process. Moreover, it has to be admitted that, by necessity, an unambiguous precondition of the success of post-communist transformation is adjustment.

The main path of adjustment:

- acceptance of the painful and, at the same time, encouraging pressure of the sudden economic opening caused by the dismantling of the Iron Curtain in 1989, and the possibly fastest transformation of the structure of production and its adjustment to market conditions evolving under these circumstances;
- improvement of the skills of the relatively well-trained and at the same time cheap labour force, successful spreading of the skills and knowledge of a computerized world;
- establishing continuous harmony between the price of labour, that is, wages and productivity.

Note

1. Hayek F. von, *The Road to Serfdom*, Routledge, London, 1944, Triffin, Robert, *Europe and the Money Muddle, From Bilateralism to Near-Convertibility, 1947-1956*. New Haven, Yale University Press, 1957.

31 How the World Has Changed Since 1980

Robert Solomon

In a conference dealing with global convergence, it seems appropriate to look back to a period – the end of the 1970s and the beginning of the 1980s – that has some of the appearance of a turning point in economic history. One of the reasons why that period stands out is that a number of important political changes occurred: political changes that had economic consequences.

In May 1979, Margaret Thatcher became the first woman prime minister of the United Kingdom and she was to have an enormous effect on that country's economy. Ronald Reagan was elected President of the United States in November 1980 and had a large impact on American economic developments. Thatcher and Reagan had a lot in common and were often called 'soul mates'. In May 1981, five months after Reagan entered the White House, François Mitterrand was elected President of the French Republic and was to oversee a profound transformation of his country's economy. In October 1982, Helmut Kohl became Chancellor of the Federal Republic of Germany and he too was to preside over historic changes in his country. While he and Mitterrand may not have been 'soul mates', they forged a close relationship with important economic consequences. Elsewhere in the world, Deng Xiaoping became 'paramount leader' of China in the late 1970s and initiated surprising economic reforms in that communist country. In the Soviet Union Leonid Brezhnev died in 1982 and was succeeded briefly by Yuri Andropov who started the process of political and economic reform that was carried on by Mikhail Gorbachev and Boris Yeltsin.

These and other leaders and their successors had an influence on the way the world has changed. Let me not be misunderstood. I am not attributing to political leaders all of the changes we shall take note of. Many of the transformations in the past decade and a half have explanations that have nothing to do with the particular political leaders who happened to be in office.

Major changes in the world economy

With that political background, let me first present a list of ways in which the world economy has altered since about 1980. Then I shall go on to discuss these changes.

1. The so-called Second World – centrally planned economies – are now countries in transition to market economies and most of them are now democracies.
2. OPEC has become a much less powerful force in the world.
3. Much of the so-called Third World – developing countries – is changing rapidly and is less dependent on First World countries.
4. Unemployment has risen sharply in Europe and is a serious political problem.
5. International capital mobility has increased greatly.
6. World trade in goods and services has increased faster than world output and the term 'globalization' is now widely used.
7. Monetary policy has become much more important, and central banks have become much more salient.
8. Current account deficits have lost much of their significance, at least in industrial countries.
9. The member countries of the European Union are in the process of forming an Economic and Monetary Union while also preparing to enlarge to the East.

The world economy in the early 1980s

In 1980, the world – or, at least, that part of it consisting of oil-importing countries – was experiencing the second oil shock. The price of oil, which had quadrupled at the end of 1973, rose by 150 per cent from 1978 to mid-1980. OPEC was a major force in the world economy, racking up a current account surplus of well over $100 billion in 1980. And the oil-price increase had inflationary effects. Consumer prices in the seven largest industrial countries rose by more than 12.5 per cent in 1980. As happened in the mid-1970s, the oil-price rise had both inflationary and depressive effects, acting like an enormous increase in a sales tax. One result was that many industrial countries went into recession in 1982.

A number of developing countries had been heavy borrowers from commercial banks in the 1970s. They too were affected by the oil shocks. And in 1982, Mexico, an oil exporter, was forced to suspend interest payments on its debt. That ushered in the debt crisis of the 1980s as banks cut back their lending to most developing countries. The 1980s became known as the 'lost decade' for many of those countries.

End of the Second World

Who would have dreamed in 1980 that eleven years later Germany would be unified, the Soviet Union would no longer exist, that most communist countries would abandon central planning, and that democracy would take root?

Perhaps a close student of what was happening in the Second World would have predicted it. In the early 1980s, Andropov spoke publicly about the poor quality of many consumer goods and the unwillingness of Soviet citizens to buy them. Gorbachev later complained about economic stagnation. Centrally planned economies, which had fared reasonably well in earlier years, appeared unable to cope with the advances in technology that were occurring in the world economy. For example: while pig iron production decreased in the United States, as well as in France, Germany, and the United Kingdom, from 1970 to 1990, it continued to increase in the USSR.[1] That was the economic background for *glasnost* and *perestroika*, which started the political and economic transformation that Gorbachev was fearful of but which Yeltsin and others, such as Vaclav Klaus in Czechoslovakia, pursued.

China, which is said to have been called a 'sleeping giant' by Napoleon, has awakened. It is a very different case from Russia. China is classified as a developing country by the IMF and as a country in transition by the World Bank. Presumably it is both. In any event, under Deng Xiaoping, it pursued what it called a 'socialist market economy.' As is well known, China has become a much more open economy as an exporter and importer of goods and a recipient of foreign capital. And its growth rate has been impressive.

The status of OPEC

The substantially higher price of oil brought about by the two oil shocks had predictable effects on both supply and demand. The supply of oil from a number of non-OPEC sources responded to the higher price. And the use of oil was economized in many ways – most conspicuously in the design and construction of automobiles and their engines.

These days OPEC is rarely heard about and the meetings of its oil ministers – once the object of close attention – are not even reported in the press in a noticeable way. And oil-exporting countries are in current account deficit.

The Third World

Per capita GDP in Latin America was lower in 1990 than in 1980 – the 'lost decade.' It rose slowly in most developing countries except for those in Asia. In the first six years of the present decade, per capita output rose 2.5 times faster in developing countries than in the industrial world. The developing countries have acted as locomotives for the world economy in recent years instead of being dependent for their economic performance on what was happening in the industrial countries, as was true in the past.

Unemployment in Europe

The rate of unemployment in the European Union (EU) is now more than twice as high as it was in 1980. In 1980, unemployment in the EU was, on average, 5.6 per cent; it was 3.2 per cent in West Germany, 6.2 per cent in France, and 11.5 per cent in Spain. In 1996, unemployment was estimated at 11.4 per cent in the EU; 10.3 per cent in Germany, 12.3 per cent in France, and 22.2 per cent in Spain. A part of the unemployment was, and is, cyclical but most of it is structural, related to high costs of labor, including payroll taxes and the various benefits that employers have to pay along with wages. Probably also playing a role is the revolution in technology that is in progress throughout the world. To say that unemployment is a serious political problem is an understatement.

International capital mobility

The most striking aspect of the increase in capital mobility is the greatly enlarged flow of funds to developing countries. And we shall focus on that. But it is worth noting that international transactions among all countries have risen sharply. The daily average turnover in foreign exchange markets in industrial countries increased from $206 billion in March 1986 to $1570 billion in April 1995. In other words, daily transactions were more than 7.5 times greater in 1995 than in 1986.[2] While American exports rose about 2.5 times from 1980 to 1995, the outflow of portfolio capital was 26 times larger in 1995 than in 1980, despite a decline from a peak in 1993. Direct investment abroad quintupled in the same period.

In the 1980s when many developing countries were burdened by the debt crisis, their capital inflows declined and capital flight increased. As the debtor countries struggled to maintain interest payments on their foreign debt, their economies slowed or declined. The silver lining of this unfortunate situation is that many of the debtor countries, in Latin America and elsewhere, undertook economic reforms, moving toward what has been called the 'Washington consensus'.[3] Those reforms included reducing fiscal deficits, reforming tax systems, privatizing and deregulating, among others.

Conditions changed in the early 1990s. The Brady Plan for debt relief, although it did not involve large reductions in debt service payments, apparently had a catalytic effect, beginning in Mexico, the first country to have a Brady Plan agreement. Mexican flight capital began to come home, foreign portfolio investment increased sharply, as did direct investments.

For Latin America as a whole, the gross inflow of portfolio capital rose from less than $4 billion in 1990 to an estimated $66 billion in 1996, despite the Mexican crisis of 1994-95. Gross portfolio inflows to all developing countries amounted to $134 billion in 1996, compared with $8.5 billion in 1990. Net foreign direct investment in all developing countries increased from $24.5 billion in 1990 to an estimated $109.5 billion in 1996, tripling as a proportion of the GDP of the recipient countries.[4]

Quite apart from the increased magnitude of capital flows to developing countries, there has been a dramatic change in its composition. In 1980 and earlier, those flows consisted to a large degree of bank lending. As noted, portfolio flows became very important in the 1990s. There are a number of explanations for the altered composition of flows. They include deregulation and general reforms in the recipient countries. In the capital exporting countries, the computer and telecommunications revolutions have played an important role. The computer made possible the development of new financial instruments that permit risks to be hedged. Better communications mean that investors can be familiar with the economic, financial, and political conditions anywhere in the world.

World trade and globalization

World trade has increased faster than world output for many years. But the gap has widened in recent years, thanks in part to lower tariffs and other trade restrictions and lower transportation costs. From 1955 to 1980, world trade grew about 1.5 times faster than world output. In the 1990s, world trade grew 2.2 times faster than world output.

The term 'globalization' has come into use. It means more than a growing ratio of trade to output. There has also occurred a dramatic change in the division of labour in the world economy. Developing countries were once regarded as suppliers of food and raw materials to the industrial countries, from which they imported manufactured goods. Now they are producing manufactured goods, often labour-intensive finished goods or components for final goods produced in industrial countries. Some, like Korea, are graduating from low-wage to higher-wage economies producing capital-intensive goods.

From 1980 to 1994, agricultural production declined as a proportion of the GDP in many developing countries while the share of manufacturing and services rose. In some countries, the increase in the share of manufactures in total exports was striking: between 1980 and 1993, the share in Thailand rose from 28 to 73 per cent; in Brazil from 39 to 60 per cent; in Colombia, from 20 to 40 per cent; in Mexico from 12 to 75 per cent.[5]

Monetary policy and the role of central banks

Monetary policy was of course a major instrument of macroeconomic policy before 1980. What has happened since then is that most industrial countries have developed excessive budget deficits. Discretionary fiscal policy has hardly been used as a counter-cyclical device in recent years. That means that monetary policy 'is the only game in town': it is the sole instrument of macroeconomic policy.[6] Another reason for the increased importance of central banks is that anti-inflation policy has assumed greater importance after the inflationary 1970s. Finally, with the deregulation of financial markets, the appearance of new financial instruments, and the globalization of finance, central banks have taken on greater responsibilities for maintaining financial stability and the soundness of financial institutions, especially commercial banks.

There has been a worldwide movement toward granting central banks independence – at least 'instrument independence' if not 'goal independence.' In other words, such central banks decide on the use of their instruments without interference from governments but their goals may be established by parliaments or governments, as in the United States, New Zealand, and many other countries. Even the Bundesbank, regarded as the epitome of an independent central bank, is expected to support the general economic policies of the government.

In these conditions, central banks have become much more salient. Hardly a day goes by when Alan Greenspan is not quoted in the press in the United States. He and Eddie George, Hans Tietmeyer, and Jean-Claude Trichet are much better known to the general public than their pre-1980 predecessors.

Current account balances

In the first 35 years after World War II, current account balances were regarded as major determinants of exchange rates, along with rates of inflation and interest rates. It was only when the United States developed a current account deficit in the late 1960s that the dollar came under severe pressure and the Bretton Woods system was abandoned. As recently as the late 1970s and the early 1980s, the view continued to prevail that the current account balance pointed the direction in which the exchange rate had to move.

With the increased mobility of capital, that is no longer so. At least among industrial countries, little attention is now paid to whether the current account is in surplus or deficit. The dollar has been appreciating recently while the American current account deficit increased.

The explanation appears to be that as long as a current account deficit does not become extraordinarily large, the markets assume that capital will be available to finance it.

European economic and monetary union

In 1980, the European Monetary System (EMS) was in its very early stage, having been established in March 1979. It was designed to be a 'zone of monetary stability' in a world of floating exchange rates. But in its first years, inflation among its members was quite divergent and there were frequent realignments of 'central rates.' After 1987, the system 'hardened' and inflation and interest rates converged. Who would have believed in the early 1980s that France would have an inflation rate and interest rates little different from those in Germany?

Meanwhile the single market was implemented and there was progress toward free movement of goods, services, capital, and people among countries of the European Union. The zone of monetary stability became a D-mark zone. For a number of reasons, both political and economic, the idea of an economic and monetary union – proposed earlier in the Werner Report – was revived. By now, it is widely expected that the new currency, the euro, will be established, along with a 'European System of Central Banks', on January 1, 1999.

At the same time, serious consideration is being given to admission to the European Union of some Central and Eastern European countries.

Both EMU and EU enlargement to the east will be major events in history.

Conclusion

Whether the changes in the world economy in the past 17 years are more profound than in other periods of equal length, I leave to the historians. Certainly in 1967, one could have pointed to enormous transformations from the way the world looked in 1950. Similarly for, say, 1937 as compared with 1920.

The main point is that we live in a very different world today from that of 1980. In many ways, it is a better world, though the unemployed worker in Europe might not agree. What is undeniable is that it is a rapidly changing world.

Notes and references

1. United Nations, *World Economic and Social Survey, 1996*, p. 110.
2. Bank for International Settlements, Central Bank Survey of Foreign Exchange and Derivative Market Activity, 1995.
3. John Williamson, 'What Washington Means by Policy Reform', in John Williamson, ed., Latin American Adjustment, Institute for International Economics, 1990, Ch. 2.
4. World Bank, Global Development Finance, 1997.
5. World Bank, World Development Report, 1996, pp. 216-217.
6. Deane Marjorie and Robert Pringle, The Central Banks, London, Hamish Hamilton, 1994.

Notes on Participants

Akar, László, Secretary of State, Ministry of Finance, Budapest, Hungary

Báger, Gusztáv, Director General, Ministry of Finance, Chairman of the Robert Triffin-Szirák Foundation, Budapest, Hungary

Beck, Hans, Ambassador, EU Commission to Hungary, Budapest

Boeri, Tito, Professor, Universita Bocconi, Milano, Italy

Botos, Katalin, Professor, Pázmány Péter Catholic University, Budapest, Hungary

Brabant, Jozef, M. van, Principal Economic Affairs Officer, United Nations, New York, U.S.A.

Brandner, Peter, Österreichische National Bank, Vienna, Austria

Butorina, Olga, Head of Sector of Economic Integration, Russian Academy of Sciences, Russia, Moscow

Carlier, Michel, Ambassador of Belgium to Hungary, Budapest

Donsimoni, Marie-Paule, Executive Director, Oxford Analytica Ltd., Oxford, UK

Fink, Gerhard, Vienna University of Economics, Institute for European Affairs, Vienna, Austria

Gros, Daniel, Deputy Director, Centre for European Policy Studies, Brussels, Belgium

Haiss, Peter, Vienna University of Economics, Institute for European Affairs, Vienna, Austria

Hieronymi, Otto, Head, Programme of International Relations, Webster University, Geneva, Switzerland

Hochreiter, Eduard, Senior Adviser, Österreichische National Bank, Vienna, Austria

Hoós, János, Professor, Budapest University of Economics, Budapest, Hungary

Notes on Participants

Jones, Erik, Deputy Director, Centre for European Policy Studies, Brussels

Krul, Nicolas, Former Managing Director, Gulf and Occidental, London, UK

Krzak, Maciej, Österreichische National Bank, Vienna, Austria

Lamfalussy, Alexandre, President, European Monetary Institute, Frankfurt-am-Main, Germany

Lankes, Hans Peter, Chief Economist, EBRD, London, UK

Mandy, Paul L., Professor Emeritus, Catholic University of Louvain-la-Neuve, Belgium

Murtfeld, Martin, Vice-Governor, Council of Europe Social Development Fund, Paris, France

Papadimitriou, Dimitri B., Bard College, The Jerome Levy Economics Institute Blithewood, New York, U.S.A.

Raymond, Robert, Director General, European Monetary Institute, Frankfurt-am-Main, Germany

Perasso, Giancarlo, Professor, Universita Bocconi, Milano, Italy

Sakbani, Michael, Director of Economic Cooperation, UNCTAD

Schubert, Aurel, Head of Research Department, Österrichische National Bank, Vienna, Austria

Smyslov, Dmitry, Professor, Institute of World Economy and International Relations, Moscow, Russia

Snoy, Bernard, Director, EBRD, London, UK

Solomon, Robert, The Brookings Institutions, Washington DC, U.S.A.

Sobek, Otto, Professor, University of Economics Bratislava, Slovakia

Stern, Nicholas, Chief Economist, EBRD, London, UK

Surányi, György, Chairman, National Bank of Hungary, Budapest

Szabó-Pelsőczi, Miklós, Chairman Emeritus, Robert Triffin-Szirák Foundation, Budapest, Hungary

Tardos, Márton, Member of Parliament, Budapest, Hungary

Toda, Yoshiaki, Adviser, NCB Systems Co. Ltd, Tokyo, Japan